Contributing Authors

Harold Nathan, Ph.D.
Stephen Fisher, M.A.
Jennifer Harvey, M.S.
William A. Covino, Ph.D.

Consultants

Peter Z. Orton, M.Ed.
Ron Podrasky, M.S.
Carol Binggeli, M.S.
Michael Carr, M.A.
Merritt L. Weisinger, J.D.

By

Jerry
Bobrow,
Ph.D.

You Can Pass the GED

ACKNOWLEDGMENTS

My loving thanks to my wife, Susan, and my children, Jennifer Lynn 10, Adam Michael 7, and Jonathan Matthew 3, for their patience and support in this long project.

My sincere thanks to Michele Spence of Cliffs Notes for final editing and careful attention to the production process.

Jerry Bobrow

I very much appreciate the permissions given by GED Testing Service to reprint here the examination directions, essay writing pages, answer sheets, math formula page, and score requirement information.

In addition, I would like to thank the following authors and companies for permission to reprint their materials:

The Retail Meat Prices *graph, from* Hammond Almanac—*courtesy of Hammond Incorporated*
The World Oil Production *graph by James Francavilla, Copyright 1980, the* Los Angeles Times—*reprinted by permission*
The Distribution of Earned Degrees *graph by Bob Allen, Copyright 1976, the* Los Angeles Times—*reprinted by permission*
The Neutron Nuclear Weapons *cartoon Copyright 1977 by Herblock in the* Washington Post
The Cattle Frontier *map from* America! America! *by L. Joanne Buggey, Gerald A. Danzer, Charles L. Mitsakos, and C. Frederick Risinger, Copyright 1977 by Scott, Foresman and Company—reprinted by permission*
The Anti-Inflation *cartoon by Auth, Copyright 1978, the* Philadelphia Inquirer

PREFACE

We know that passing the GED Examination is important to you! And we can help. As a matter of fact, we have spent the last fourteen years helping test takers successfully prepare for important exams. The techniques and strategies that students and adults have found most effective in our preparation programs at 26 universities and colleges make this book **your key to success on the GED.**

Our *easy-to-use* GED Preparation Guide gives you your key to success by focusing on

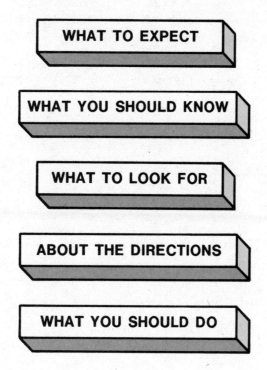

WHAT TO EXPECT

WHAT YOU SHOULD KNOW

WHAT TO LOOK FOR

ABOUT THE DIRECTIONS

WHAT YOU SHOULD DO

We give you lots of strategies and techniques with plenty of practice problems plus directions on how to start reviewing.

If you want to do your best on the GED Examination, follow our Study Plan and step-by-step approach to **success on the GED.**

CONTENTS

1: INTRODUCTION

2: WORKING TOWARD SUCCESS

3: HOW TO START REVIEWING

4: PRACTICE EXAMINATIONS

1

Introduction

GETTING THE MOST OUT OF YOUR STUDY TIME

STUDY PLAN

Check off each step after you complete it.

☐   1.   Read the GED information materials available at your local GED center. Check minimum score, age, and residence requirements.

☐   2.   Look over the Format of the GED Examination (p. 4).

☐   3.   Learn How You Can Do Your Best (p. 5).

☐   4.   Read the Answers to Your Questions About the GED (p. 6).

    5.   Carefully Read Part 2: Working Toward Success and do all the exercises.

         Test 1: Writing Skills (pp. 7–42)

☐   Part I: Multiple Choice (pp. 7–23)

☐   Part II: Essay (pp. 24–42)

☐   Test 2: Social Studies (pp. 45–72)

☐   Test 3: Science (pp. 75–104)

☐   Test 4: Intepreting Literature and the Arts (pp. 107–124)

☐   Test 5: Mathematics (pp. 127–157)

         The Formulas and How to Use Them (pp. 158–173)

☐   Charts, Graphs, Maps, Cartoons, and Diagrams (pp. 177–208)

    6.   Carefully Read Part 3: How to Start Reviewing and do all the exercises.

         Test 1: Writing Skills (pp. 212–250)

☐   Part I: Multiple Choice (pp. 212–225)

☐   Part II: Essay (pp. 225–250)

☐   Test 2: Social Studies (pp. 253–266)

☐   Test 3: Science (pp. 269–282)

☐   Test 4: Interpreting Literature and the Arts (pp. 285–298)

☐   Test 5: Mathematics (pp. 301–305)

☐   7.   Review any basic skills that you need to review.

8. Strictly following time allotments, take Practice Examination 1 (pp. 315–392). **After you take each of the tests** in Practice Examination 1, check your answers on that test and analyze your results using the Answer Key (pp. 394–396), the Scoring Chart (p. 396), the Score Approximators (pp. 397–399), the Explanations (pp. 401–436) and the Reasons for Mistakes chart (p. 400).

☐ Test 1: Writing Skills (pp. 315–330)
☐ Check answers and analyze results

☐ Test 2: Social Studies (pp. 331–346)
☐ Check answers and analyze results

☐ Test 3: Science (pp. 347–362)
☐ Check answers and analyze results

☐ Test 4: Interpreting Literature and the Arts (pp. 363–377)
☐ Check answers and analyze results

☐ Test 5: Mathematics (pp. 379–392)
☐ Check answers and analyze results

9. Strictly following time allotments, take Practice Examination 2 (pp. 443–519). **After you have taken all** of Practice Examination 2 **at one time,** check your answers on the entire examination and analyze your results using the Answer Key (p. 522), the Scoring Chart (p. 524), the Score Approximators (pp. 525–527) the Explanations (pp. 529–566), and the Reasons for Mistakes Chart (p. 528).

☐ Practice Examination 2 (pp. 443–519)
☐ Check answers and analyze results

☐ 10. Review your weak areas in Part 2: Working Toward Success (pp. 11–208) and Part 3: How to Start Reviewing (pp. 212–305).
☐ 11. Carefully read Are You Ready? (p. 567)

FORMAT OF THE GED EXAMINATION

Test 1: Writing Skills
    Part I: Multiple Choice   55 Questions   75 Minutes
    Part II: Essay   1 Essay   45 Minutes

Test 2: Social Studies   64 Questions   85 Minutes

Test 3: Science   66 Questions   95 Minutes

Test 4: Interpreting Literature
         and the Arts   45 Questions   65 Minutes

Test 5: Mathematics   56 Questions   90 Minutes

Since the test is new, times and numbers of questions may be adjusted slightly in later testings.

HOW YOU CAN DO YOUR BEST

A POSITIVE APPROACH

To do your best, use this positive approach:

1. Look for the questions that you can answer and should get right.

2. Skip the ones that give you a lot of trouble. (But take a guess.)

3. Don't get stuck on any one of the questions.

Now let's take a closer look at this system:

1. Answer the easy questions as soon as you see them.

2. When you come to a question that gives you trouble, don't get stuck.

3. Before you go to the next question, see if you can eliminate some of the incorrect choices to that question. Then take a guess from the choices left!

4. If you can't eliminate some choices, take a guess anyway. **Never leave a question unanswered.**

5. Put a check mark on your answer sheet next to the number of a problem for which you did not know the answer and simply guessed.

6. After you answer all of the questions, go back and work on the ones that you checked (the ones that you guessed on the first time through).

Remember, **erase the check marks from your answer sheet before time is called.** If you don't, the marks may be counted by the scoring machine as wrong answers.

Don't ever leave a question without taking a guess. There is no penalty for guessing.

THE ELIMINATION STRATEGY

Sometimes the best way to get the right answer is by eliminating the wrong answers. As you read your answer choices, keep the following in mind:

1. Eliminate poor answer choices right away.

2. On most sections, if you feel you know the right answer, quickly look at the other answers to make sure your selection is best.

3. Try to narrow your choices down to two or three so that you can take a better guess.

Remember, **getting rid of the wrong choices can leave you with the right choice.** Look for the right answer choice and eliminate wrong answer choices.

ANSWERS TO YOUR QUESTIONS
ABOUT THE GED

Q: WHO ADMINISTERS THE GED

A: The GED is administered by the GED Testing Service of the American Council on Education (ACE).

Q: WHEN AND WHERE ARE THE GED EXAMINATIONS GIVEN?

A: The examinations are given continually throughout the nation. You can get administration dates and locations by contacting your local GED Testing Centers, high schools, or adult schools.

Q: MAY I TAKE THE GED EXAMINATIONS MORE THAN ONCE?

A: Yes. But some states may require you to wait a certain amount of time or to complete a course. Contact your local GED Testing Center for specific information. Remember that your plan is to pass on the *first* try.

Q: ARE THERE ANY SPECIAL EDITIONS OF THE GED?

A: Yes. In addition to the U.S. version, there is a Canadian version. The GED is also given in Spanish and French. There are also special large-print, braille, and/or tape-recorded editions for handicapped candidates.

Q: WHAT IS A PASSING SCORE?

A: Each test is scored from 20 to 80, but there are no national standards for the GEDs. Each state has established its own standards for passing the tests. At the end of this book there is a chart which shows you some of the states' requirements. *Be sure to check the current policies in your state.*

Q: HOW MANY DO I NEED TO GET RIGHT TO PASS?

A: This number varies from state to state. Generally, you must answer 50 to 60% right to pass. Remember, no one is expected to answer all the questions correctly.

Q: WHAT GRADE LEVEL ARE THE TESTS?

A: The tests are standardized to reflect the range of knowledge and ability of twelfth-grade students who are certain to graduate. Most current requirements are set so that you must score higher than would 30% of today's high school graduates.

Q: HOW SHOULD I PREPARE?

A: An organized approach is very important. Carefully follow the Study Plan in this book to give you that organized approach. It will show you how to apply techniques and strategies and help focus your review. Also, many states offer preparation programs to help students. Check with your local high school, adult school, occupational center, community college, or GED Testing Center for further information.

Q: SHOULD I GUESS ON THE TESTS?

A: Yes! Since there is no penalty for guessing, *guess* if you have to. If possible, try to eliminate some of the choices to increase your chances of choosing the right answer.

Q: HOW AND WHEN SHOULD I REGISTER AND WHERE CAN I GET MORE INFORMATION?

A: This information is available from your local GED Testing Center, or write to General Educational Development, GED Testing Service, American Council on Education, One Dupont Circle, N.W., Washington, D.C. 20036.

2

Working Toward Success

How to Use This Section

The following section will introduce you to each of the GED tests by carefully pointing out

1. **What to expect**
2. **What you should know**
3. **What to look for: kinds of questions**
4. **About the directions**
5. **What you should do**

This section emphasizes important test-taking techniques and strategies and how to apply them to different question types.

Read this section very **carefully. Underline** or **circle key techniques. Make notes** in the margins to help you understand the strategies and question types.

TEST
1

WRITING SKILLS
PARTS I AND II

TEST 1: WRITING SKILLS

The Writing Skills Test consists of two parts—Part I: The Multiple-Choice Section and Part II: The Essay Section. The scores from these two sections are combined to give the Writing Skills Test Score. The sections are not reported separately.

Part I: Multiple Choice

WHAT TO EXPECT

The Writing Skills Multiple-Choice Section is 1 hour and 15 minutes long and contains 55 questions.

■ Expect a series of paragraphs with each of the sentences numbered.

■ Expect some of the sentences to be correct, but *most contain errors* of structure, usage, or mechanics.

■ Expect to find some obvious errors of spelling, punctuation, capitalization, or grammar.

■ Expect some errors to be more difficult to spot.

■ Expect to find errors that are common to student writing (common mistakes).

WHAT YOU SHOULD KNOW

The Writing Skills Test (Multiple-Choice Section) contains the following areas:

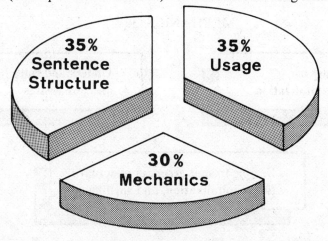

35% Sentence Structure

35% Usage

30% Mechanics

SENTENCE STRUCTURE (35%)

Understand how **sentences** are formed

Understand the **basic parts** of a sentence

Be able to **spot errors** in the **construction** of a **sentence** (sentence fragments, run-on sentences etc.)

USAGE (35%)

Understand how to use the **parts of speech** correctly

Understand how **parts** of a **sentence** fit together

Be able to **spot errors** in **verb tense, agreement, pronoun reference,** etc.

MECHANICS (30%)

Understand the **rules** of **punctuation** and **capitalization**

Understand rules for **contractions** and **possessives**

Be able to **spot errors** in **punctuation, capitalization,** and **spelling**

WHAT TO LOOK FOR: KINDS OF QUESTIONS

APPLICATION QUESTIONS (100%)

The Writing Skills Test, Part I, will ask you to be able to apply the rules of grammar, usage, and mechanics.

Look for three basic types of questions (item types):

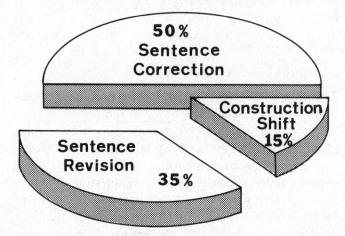

1. **Sentence Correction (50%):** These questions ask you what type of correction should be made to a sentence.

2. **Sentence Revision (35%):** These questions ask you to select possible corrections for the underlined part of a sentence.

3. **Construction Shift (15%):** These questions ask you to select an answer that is an improved "rewrite" of another sentence or sentences. You are selecting a *better* structure.

ABOUT THE DIRECTIONS

Following are the directions you'll find in the Writing Skills Test, multiple-choice section. Become very familiar with these directions *now* so that you will be comfortable with them when you take the actual test. The directions you'll see on the actual test will be wider on the page. Here, though, room has been left for the boxes you see on the right and the left. Read the following directions straight through first, and then carefully read the information in the boxes. It points out and explains important points in the directions.

TEST 1: WRITING SKILLS, PART I

Tests of General Educational Development

Directions

Proper use of English	The Writing Skills Test is intended to measure your ability to use clear and effective English. It is a test of English as it should be written, not as it might be spoken. This test includes both multiple-choice questions and an essay. These directions apply only to the multiple-choice section; a separate set of directions is given for the essay.

Standard written English (no slang)

Separate directions for essay

Two parts: multiple choice and essay

Multiple choice

The multiple-choice section consists of paragraphs with numbered sentences. Some of the sentences contain errors in sentence structure, usage, or mechanics (spelling, punctuation, and capitalization). After reading the numbered sentences, answer the multiple-choice questions that follow. Some questions refer to sentences that are correct as written. The best answer for these questions is the one which leaves the sentence as originally written. The best answer for some questions is the one which produces a sentence that is consistent with the verb tense and point of view used throughout the paragraph.

Fix incorrect **sentences**

Spot correct sentences (no correction needed)

Watch verb tense past, present, future

Who does the sentence refer to *you, us, him,* etc.

Spend no more than 75 minutes on multiple choice (about $1\frac{1}{2}$ minutes per question)

Spend about 45 minutes on the essay

You should spend no more than 75 minutes on the multiple-choice questions and 45 minutes on your essay. Work carefully, but do not spend too much time on any one question. You may begin working on the essay part of this test as soon as you complete the multiple-choice section.

Don't get stuck

Don't stop after multiple-choice Part I (immediately go to Part II and start the essay)

Do not mark in this test booklet. Record your answers on the separate answer sheet provided. Be sure that all requested information is properly recorded on the answer sheet.

To record your answers, mark one numbered space on the answer sheet beside the number that corresponds to the question in the test booklet.

Mark your **answers carefully** on the answer sheet

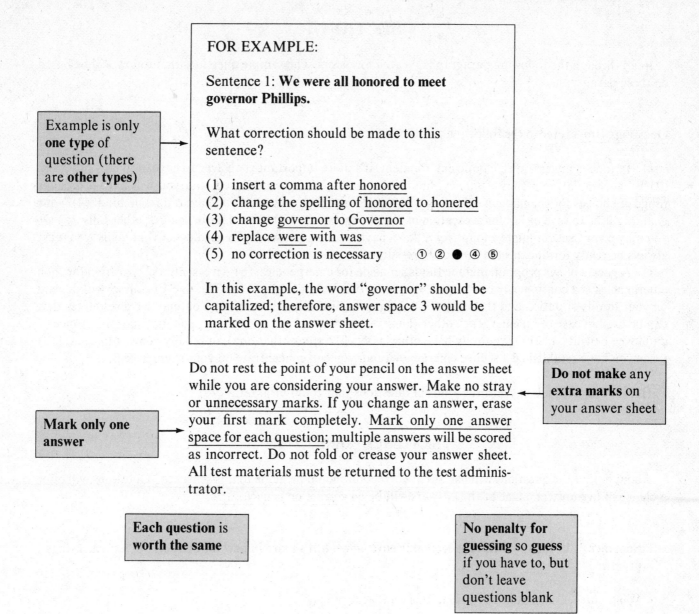

Example is only **one type** of question (there are **other types**)

FOR EXAMPLE:

Sentence 1: **We were all honored to meet governor Phillips.**

What correction should be made to this sentence?

(1) insert a comma after honored
(2) change the spelling of honored to honered
(3) change governor to Governor
(4) replace were with was
(5) no correction is necessary   ① ② ● ④ ⑤

In this example, the word "governor" should be capitalized; therefore, answer space 3 would be marked on the answer sheet.

Do not rest the point of your pencil on the answer sheet while you are considering your answer. Make no stray or unnecessary marks. If you change an answer, erase your first mark completely. Mark only one answer space for each question; multiple answers will be scored as incorrect. Do not fold or crease your answer sheet. All test materials must be returned to the test administrator.

Do not make any **extra marks** on your answer sheet

Mark only one answer

Each question is worth the same

No penalty for **guessing** so guess if you have to, but don't leave questions blank

WHAT YOU SHOULD DO

 First read through the paragraph before beginning to answer the multiple-choice questions. Note any obvious errors of spelling, punctuation, capitalization, or grammar.

 Although there may not be a question on every sentence, you can be sure there will be questions about those sentences in which you have noticed errors.

The following two sections will use examples to carefully explain the **question types,** show you **what to look for,** and point out **what you should do.**

SECTION I

Read through the following paragraphs. Watch for errors. The sample questions that follow will be based on these paragraphs.

<u>Questions 1 to 8</u> refer to the following paragraphs.

(1) In todays uncertain economic environment, it's more important than ever to have a savings program. (2) By accumulating a sum of money, financial security can be established, and you will have a broader range of choices for spending or investing. (3) Your more likely to save if you have a goal in mind. (4) Your goal might be to save either for a vacation or upcoming expenses like taxes, insurance, or other bills. (5) Or you may want to accumulate enough for a down payment on a house. (6) Regardless of your goals, you must always be ready for unexpected financial pressures.

(7) A good savings program include funds set aside for emergencies. (8) An essential preparation for such emergencies is a contingency fund equal to at least two month's salary. (9) The size, of course, will depend on your family situation and the state of your finances, including debts. (10) You may have resources that can be used in case of an emergency other than your savings. (11) For example, you may have insurance or employee benefits. (12) Or you may have other assets like stocks that one can readily convert to cash. (13) Once you have established a secure emergency fund; you can concentrate on your savings goal.

Here is a closer look at the three kinds of questions that could be asked.

SENTENCE CORRECTION

About half of the questions will ask <u>What correction should be made to this sentence?</u> Questions will offer a choice of five answers. One of the answers will be <u>no correction is necessary</u>.

1. Sentence 1: **In todays uncertain economic environment, it's more important than ever to have a savings program.**

   What correction should be made to this sentence?

   (1) change <u>todays</u> to <u>today's</u>
   (2) change the spelling of <u>environment</u> to <u>enviroment</u>
   (3) change <u>it's</u> to <u>its</u>
   (4) change <u>savings</u> to <u>saving's</u>
   (5) no correction is necessary

   The right answer is (1). The apostrophe showing the possessive has been left out. Watch out for incorrect punctuation.

2. Sentence 9: **The size, of course, will depend on your family situation and the state of your finances, including debts.**

What correction should be made to this sentence?

(1) remove the comma after size
(2) remove the comma after course
(3) remove both the comma after size and the comma after course
(4) insert a comma after situation
(5) no correction is necessary

The right answer is (5). This sentence is correct as written.

Keep in mind that some of the sentences will be correct. Don't be afraid to use the *no correction is necessary* answer if the four other answers do not contain a clear error in spelling, punctuation, capitalization, grammar, or usage.

3. Sentence 7: **A good savings program include funds set aside for emergencies.**

What correction should be made to this sentence?

(1) change savings to saving
(2) change savings to saving's
(3) change include to includes
(4) change for to in case of
(5) no correction is necessary

The right answer is (3). The subject of the sentence is the *program,* which is singular. The main verb (*includes*) must also be singular. Watch out for subject/verb agreement errors.

The questions in this form will test your ability to recognize errors in spelling and punctuation. They will also test errors of grammar, especially those mistakes that can be corrected by changing only one word. Errors of agreement (for example, a singular subject with a plural verb: *the boy . . . are*) and errors of verb form (for example, a present tense verb used for a past: *yesterday, I go to the store*) are very common in this type of question.

SENTENCE REVISION

This second kind of question will underline part of one or two sentences. You will asked about the underlined part.

4. Sentence 2: **By accumulating a sum of money, financial security can be established, and you will have a broader range of choices for spending or investing.**

   Which of the following is the best way to write the underlined portion of this sentence? If you think the original is the best way, choose option (1).

   (1) of money, financial security can be established
   (2) of money, financial security will be established
   (3) of money, you can establish financial security
   (4) of money, an establishment of financial security
   (5) of money, financial security can be secured

   The right answer is (3). The sentence begins with the phrase "By accumulating a sum of money." This phrase will *dangle* (will not have a word to refer to correctly) unless a person follows. Someone who can accumulate a sum of money must come right after the phrase. Only in answer (3) is there a person (*you*).

5. Sentence 3: **Your more likely to save if you have a goal in mind.**

   Which of the following is the best way to write the underlined portion of this sentence? If you think the original is the best way, choose option (1).

   (1) Your more likely to save
   (2) Your likely to save more
   (3) You're more likely to save
   (4) You're more than likely to save
   (5) Your more than likely to save more

   The right answer is (3). In this much easier question, the contraction for *you are, you're,* is necessary to give the sentence a subject and a verb.

   The grammar in answer (4) is correct, but this option *changes the meaning* of the sentence. Watch out for answers that change the meaning of the original sentence.

6. Sentence 12: **Or you may have other assets like stocks that one can readily convert to cash.**

   Which of the following is the best way to write the underlined portion of this sentence? If you think the original is the best way, choose option (1).

   (1) that one can readily convert to cash.
   (2) that one might readily convert to cash.
   (3) that is readily convertible to cash.
   (4) that you can readily convert to cash.
   (5) that you can ready convert to cash.

The right answer is (4). Answers (1) and (2) introduce a third person pronoun (*one*) into a sentence that begins by using the second person (*you*). In answer (3), the singular verb *is* does not agree with the plural subject *assets*. In answer (5), the adjective *ready* is used where the adverb *readily* is needed.

Watch out for pronouns that don't match such as *you* and *one*.

CONSTRUCTION SHIFT

This third kind of question will ask you to revise one or two sentences in the paragraph.

7. Sentences 4 and 5: **Your goal might be to save either for a vacation or upcoming expenses like taxes, insurance, or other bills. Or you may want to accumulate enough for a down payment on a house.**

The most effective combination of sentences 4 and 5 would include which of the following groups of words?

(1) insurance, or other bills, or you may
(2) insurance, or other bills; or you may
(3) insurance, or other bills, or for a down payment
(4) insurance, other bills, or a down payment
(5) insurance, other bills; you may also

The right answer is (3). Though answers (1) and (5) are possible, the sentences they produce are wordy. Choice (4) makes little sense since a down payment is not an expense like taxes or insurance. Answer (3) is the shortest and best way to combine the two sentences.

Look for clear, effective, concise answers.

8. Sentence 10: **You may have resources that can be used in case of an emergency other than your savings.**

Which of the following is the best place to put the phrase <u>other than your savings</u>?

(1) at the beginning of the sentence before <u>You</u>
(2) after <u>may</u>
(3) after <u>resources</u>
(4) after <u>used</u>
(5) after <u>emergency</u>

The right answer is (3). Related words should be kept as close together as possible. Here, *other than your savings* refers to *resources*. The most natural place for the phrase is right after *resources*.

Remember to keep related words or phrases as close together as you can.

In a set of eight questions, only one or two will be like these last examples. Two or three questions will be about an underlined part. Most of the questions will ask *what correction should be made*.

SECTION II

Let's take a look at another passage and set of questions.

<u>Items 1 to 11</u> refer to the following paragraphs.

(1) Before you can make up a budget for the year so you can use your money where they're needed most, you have to know just what your yearly income and expenses are going to be. (2) You probably already know some regular expenses, like your rent or monthly car payments, but to complete the list, you'll have to check your records. (3) Like your checkbook, checking account statements, charge card statements, and receipts, such as supermarket register tapes. (4) If you can gather together all of these for a six- or a twelve-month period. (5) You should also determine how much money you spend each year in cash. (6) To do this, you add up the checks you wrote for cash and your withdrawals of cash from automatic teller machines. (7) Don't forget to include all of the expenses, like insurance, that come up only once a year, but include neither contributions or gifts to friends.

(8) You also needed to know your annual net income. (9) The net income being what is left after mandatory deductions like social security and income taxes. (10) Paycheck deductions, that you control, like gifts to charity or payroll savings plans, should not be deducted. (11) You may want to adjust these expenditures when you plan your new budget. (12) If your salary changes from paycheck to paycheck because you work irregularly or work on a commission, one must be sure to estimate your annual income carefully.

1. Sentence 1: **Before you can make up a budget for the year so you can use your <u>money where they're needed most</u>, you have to know just what your yearly income and expenses are going to be.**

   Which of the following is the best way to write the underlined portion of this sentence? If you think the original is the best way, choose option (1).

   (1) money where they're needed most
   (2) money where they're most needed
   (3) money where its needed most
   (4) money where it's needed most
   (5) money, where its needed most

   > The right answer is (4). The error in the sentence is the use of a singular noun (*money*) and a plural pronoun (*they're*). The singular *it's* corrects the error. Since *it's* here is short for *it is,* the apostrophe is necessary.

2. Sentence 2: **You probably already know some regular expenses, like your rent or monthly car payments, but to complete the list, you'll have to check your records.**

   What correction should be made to this sentence?

   (1) change the spelling of <u>regular</u> to <u>reguler</u>
   (2) remove the comma after <u>expenses</u>
   (3) change <u>like</u> to <u>as</u>
   (4) remove the comma after <u>payments</u>
   (5) no correction is necessary

The right answer is (5). The sentence is correct as written.

3. Sentence 3: **Like your checkbook, checking account statements, charge card statements, and receipts, such as supermarket register tapes.**

   What correction should be made to this sentence?

   (1) replace Like with These include
   (2) remove the comma after charge card statements
   (3) change the spelling of receipts to reciepts
   (4) change Like to As
   (5) no correction is necessary

The right answer is (1). As it now stands, the sentence is a fragment; it has no subject and no verb. Only choice (1) gives the needed subject and verb.

4. Sentence 4: **If you can gather together all of these for a six- or a twelve-month period.**

   What correction should be made to this sentence?

   (1) insert a comma after can
   (2) change month to monthly
   (3) change twelve-month to one-year
   (4) change the period at the end of the sentence to a question mark
   (5) no correction is necessary

The right answer is (1). Without a comma after *can,* the sentence seems to have no main verb. The verb *gather* in this case means *you should gather. Gather* must be set off from *can.* The sentence means *if you are able to do so, you should gather.*

5. Sentences 5 and 6: **You should also determine how much money you spend each year in cash. To do this, you add up the checks you wrote for cash and your withdrawals of cash from automatic teller machines.**

   The most effective combination of sentences 5 and 6 would include which of the following groups of words?

   (1) in cash; to do this
   (2) in cash, to do this
   (3) in cash by adding
   (4) in cash, doing so by adding
   (5) in cash, you add

The right answer is (3). The grammar in choices (1), (3), and (4) is correct, but choice (3) is the *most concise* (shortest). Choices (2) and (5) use commas where they should not be used.

6. Sentence 7: **Don't forget to include all of the expenses, like insurance, that come up only once a year, but include <u>neither contributions or gifts to friends.</u>**

   Which of the following is the best way to write the underlined portion of this sentence? If you think the original is the best way, choose option (1).

   (1) neither contributions or gifts to friends.
   (2) neither contributions, or gifts to friends.
   (3) neither contributions nor gifts to friends.
   (4) niether contributions nor gifts to friends.
   (5) neither contributions nor gifts to freinds.

   > The right answer is (3). *Neither* and *nor* go together. *Neither* and *or* do not go together.
   >
   > In choices (4) and (5) *neither* and *friends* are spelled incorrectly.

7. Sentence 8. **You also needed to know your annual net income.**

   What correction should be made to this sentence?

   (1) change <u>You</u> to <u>you</u>
   (2) change <u>needed</u> to <u>need</u>
   (3) change the spelling of <u>annual</u> to <u>anual</u>
   (4) insert a comma after <u>net</u>
   (5) no correction is necessary

   > The right answer is (2). Since the present tense has been used throughout the reading, there is no reason to change to the past tense (*needed*) here.

8. Sentences 8 and 9: **You also needed to know your annual net income. The net income being what is left after mandatory deductions like social security and income taxes.**

   The most effective combination of sentences 8 and 9 would include which of the following groups of words?

   (1) annual net income; the net income being
   (2) annual net income, the net income being
   (3) annual net income, being what
   (4) annual net income, or what
   (5) annual net income, and this is what

   > The right answer is (4). Since the phrase *net income* is used in the first sentence, there is no need to repeat it. Choice (4) is correct and less wordy than any of the other choices.

9. Sentence 10: **Paycheck deductions, that you control, like gifts to charity or payroll savings plans, should not be deducted.**

   What correction should be made to this sentence?

   (1) remove the comma after <u>deductions</u>
   (2) remove the commas after <u>deductions</u> and <u>control</u>
   (3) remove the comma after <u>control</u>
   (4) change the spelling of <u>charity</u> to <u>Charity</u>
   (5) no correction is necessary

   > The right answer is (1). The comma after *deductions* should be removed. The phrase *that you control* is necessary to define a kind of deduction. This is a clause that is needed to show what kind of deductions, and so it should not be set off by commas. The other commas in the sentence are correct.

10. Sentence 11: <u>**You may want to adjust these**</u> **expenditures when you plan your new budget.**

    Which of the following is the best way to write the underlined portion of this sentence? If you think the original is the best way, choose option (1).

    (1) You may want to adjust these
    (2) you may want to adjust these
    (3) You may want to ajust these
    (4) One may want to adjust these
    (5) One might want to adjust these

    > The right answer is (1). The sentence is correct as written.

11. Sentence 12: **If your salary changes from paycheck to paycheck because you work irregularly or work on a commission, one must be sure to estimate your annual income carefully.**

    What correction should be made to this sentence?

    (1) change the spelling of <u>salary</u> to <u>salery</u>
    (2) change the spelling of <u>commission</u> to <u>commision</u>
    (3) remove the comma after <u>commission</u>
    (4) change <u>one</u> to <u>you</u>
    (5) no correction is necessary

    > The right answer is (4). The two paragraphs have used the second person pronoun (*you*). There is no reason to change to the third person (*one*).

Keep in mind that this section of the test is examining your skill in clear and effective written English. The most clear and effective writing is likely to be the most concise. Given a choice between two *correct* versions of the same sentence, choose the *shorter* one.

Part II: Essay

In Part II of the Writing Skills Test, you are asked to write a brief essay. You will have 45 minutes to plan, write, and proofread the essay.

■ Expect an essay topic that will ask you to either give an opinion, state a point of view, or explain something.

■ Expect a topic about an issue or situation of general interest. The topic should be familiar to most adults and high school seniors.

■ Expect scratch paper to be provided for you to use in planning your essay. (Your notes on scratch paper won't be seen by the scorers.)

You should know that your essay will be scored on how well you show (1) an understanding of the topic, (2) a clear purpose, (3) good organization, (4) specific examples and details, and (5) proper grammar, usage, and spelling.

Your essay will be read and scored by two different readers. The scoring scale is 1 to 6, with "1" lowest and "6" highest.

The following scoring guide will give you some indication of how your essay is scored. Remember, the readers are looking for the *overall effectiveness* of your essay.

Score 6

Score 6 for an essay that is well organized and well developed. This essay uses specific supporting examples that are effective. The writing is precise and on the topic. There are very few grammar or usage errors.

Score 5

Score 5 for an essay that is clearly organized and well developed. This essay uses specific examples that are effective. This essay may use fewer examples than the 6 essay and does not flow as smoothly. The 5 essay can have a few minor errors in grammar and usage.

Score 4

Score 4 for an essay that shows organization and a plan. This essay has some supporting examples and shows an ability to write fairly well. The essay may have more than a few writing errors, but they are not serious.

Score 3

Score 3 for an essay that shows some planning and organization. This essay shows poor development with only a limited number of supporting examples. The essay has writing errors that show weaknesses in grammar and usage.

Score 2

Score 2 for an essay that is not organized and uses few examples. This essay is not focused on the topic. This essay contains serious errors in grammar and usage.

Score 1

Score 1 for an essay that shows no plan or organization. This essay is difficult or impossible to understand. There are many serious errors in grammar and usage. This essay shows no control of structure or the writing process.

No score will be given to papers that are written on the wrong topic, are illegible (impossible to read), or are blank.

WHAT TO LOOK FOR: KINDS OF TOPICS

The essay section will ask you to produce your *own* ideas, rather than to understand or analyze others' ideas.

Look for

1. A short descriptive statement followed by a question.

2. Information following the question that will direct your essay.

3. "What the question is asking you to do."

For example:

Many people believe that television has changed the world. For some these changes have been negative, and for others they have been positive.

Write a composition of about 200 words telling about the effects of television on life today. You may write about the positive effects, the negative effects, or both. Use specific examples to support your view.

ABOUT THE DIRECTIONS

Following are the directions you'll find in the Writing Skills Test, essay section. Become very familiar with these directions *now* so that you will be comfortable with them when you take the actual test. The directions you'll see on the actual test will be wider on the page. Here, though, room has been left for the boxes you see on the right and the left. Read the following directions straight through first, and then carefully read the information in the boxes. It points out and explains important points in the directions.

TEST 1: WRITING SKILLS, PART II

Tests of General Educational Development

Directions

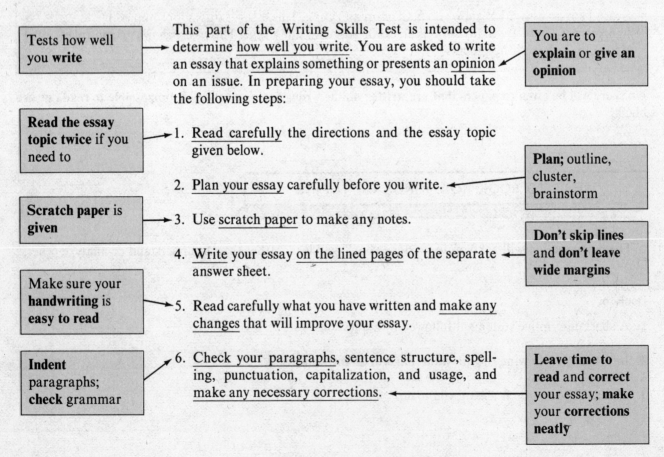

Tests how well you **write**

This part of the Writing Skills Test is intended to determine how well you write. You are asked to write an essay that explains something or presents an opinion on an issue. In preparing your essay, you should take the following steps:

You are to **explain** or **give an opinion**

Read the essay topic twice if you need to

1. Read carefully the directions and the essay topic given below.

2. Plan your essay carefully before you write.

Plan; outline, cluster, brainstorm

Scratch paper is given

3. Use scratch paper to make any notes.

4. Write your essay on the lined pages of the separate answer sheet.

Don't skip lines and **don't leave wide margins**

Make sure your **handwriting is easy to read**

5. Read carefully what you have written and make any changes that will improve your essay.

Indent paragraphs; **check** grammar

6. Check your paragraphs, sentence structure, spelling, punctuation, capitalization, and usage, and make any necessary corrections.

Leave time to read and **correct** your essay; **make your corrections neatly**

Write letter of topic in box at top of page	**Be sure you write the letter of the essay topic (given below) on your answer sheet. Write the letter in the box at the upper right-hand corner of the page where you write your essay.**

45 minutes to write

You will have 45 minutes to write on the topic below. Write legibly and use a ballpoint pen so that the evaluators will be able to read your writing.

Use a **ballpoint pen**

Leave time to organize and proofread

Write your essay on the lined pages of the separate answer sheet. The notes you make on scratch paper will not be scored.

Notes on scratch paper are for your **own use**

Notes will **not** be scored

Your essay will be scored by at least two trained evaluators who will judge it according to its overall effectiveness. They will judge how clearly you make the main point of your composition, how thoroughly you support your ideas, and how clearly and correctly you write throughout the essay.

Your **essay** should be **effective,** be **on the topic,** have lots of **examples,** and use **proper grammar, punctuation,** and **spelling**

TOPIC B

Watch **key words** in topic

In our society today, we use many inventions. Some of these inventions are helpful, and some of them just seem to make life more troublesome.

Identify an invention that is particularly useful or especially troublesome to you. Write a composition of about 200 words explaining why you feel this invention is useful or troublesome. Provide reasons and examples to support your view.

Write on "useful **or** troublesome"; choose one, **not both**

Remember to read the topic carefully

WHAT YOU SHOULD DO

You should follow these basic steps:

 Read the question carefully.

 Spend a few minutes planning your answer using the scratch paper provided.

 Write a clear statement of purpose.

 As you continue writing, keep your purpose clearly in mind.

 Write a conclusion, or ending, that points toward the future.

 Reread your essay, and correct any errors you find.

The following section will use examples to carefully explain the **techniques** in **writing a good essay.**

SECTION I

A SAMPLE ESSAY

SAMPLE TOPIC A

Many people believe that television has changed the world. For some these changes have been negative, and for others they have been positive.

Write a composition of about 200 words telling about the effects of television on life today. You may write about the positive effects, the negative effects, or both. Use specific examples to support your view.

Analysis and Techniques

1. READ THE QUESTION CAREFULLY

As you read the essay question, *note the key words*. Notice that you must discuss "the effects of television on life today" and that you must provide "specific examples." If you do not focus on the effects of television or do not provide specific examples, you will not receive a passing score.

2. SPEND A FEW MINUTES PLANNING YOUR ANSWER

With only a few minutes to plan, you should jot down information quickly and effectively. One technique for doing this is "clustering."

Step One

Jot down the topic you have been asked to discuss, "effects of television," and draw a circle around this phrase.

Step Two

Jot down all of the "specific examples" of the "effects of television" as they occur to you, as illustrated below.

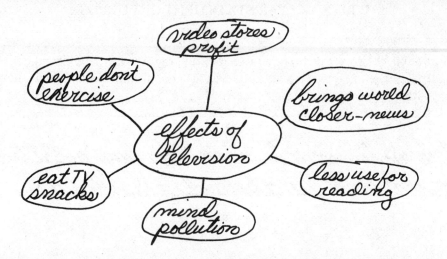

At this point, don't worry about whether your examples are "good" or not; just write down whatever comes to mind.

Step Three

Number the clusters to show which ones you plan to use and in what order.

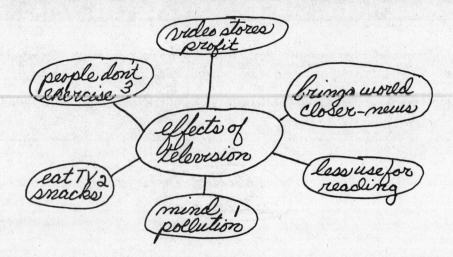

Remember that other ideas will come to you as you write. You might want to include these in your essay.

3. WRITE A CLEAR STATEMENT OF PURPOSE

   Your readers will be looking for a clear theme or position that is supported throughout the essay. To state your purpose, take the topic (effects of television) and give an opinion about the topic that you can support with your examples. For instance,

Watching too much television has polluted our minds and weakened our bodies.

or

Because of television, we are all reading less, but we are learning much more.

or

The positive effects of television far outweigh the negative ones.

or

The negative effects of television far outweigh the positive ones.

or

There are both "positives" and "negatives" about watching television.

> After writing your statement of purpose, add a sentence or two introducing the examples you intend to discuss.

Watching too much television has polluted our minds and weakened our bodies. Most TV shows are written at a low level. They are meant to appeal to a low mentality. People who become addicted to these low level shows spend less time in healthy, outdoor activities. They get out of shape and learn very little.

Watching too much television has polluted our minds and weakened our bodies. Most TV shows are written at a low level. They are meant to appeal to a low mentality. People who become addicted to these low level shows spend less time in healthy, outdoor activities. They get **out of shape** and **learn very little.**

Examples of **negative effects**

Notice that the opening paragraph focuses on two of the *negative effects* of television. The question allows you to focus on "the positive effects, the negative effects, or both." Beginning with a purpose statement that promises to discuss *both positive and negative effects,* you might instead compose an opening paragraph as follows:

> *The positive effects of television far outweigh the negative ones. Although some people may be reading and exercising less because they watch TV too much, many are learning more about the world than ever before.*

Negative effect ⟶ | The positive effects of television far outweigh the negative ones. Although some people may be **reading and exercising less** because they watch TV too much, many are **learning more about the world** than ever before. | ⟵ Positive effect

Since you are given a "choice," either of these opening paragraphs would be appropriate for the topic.

4. AS YOU CONTINUE WRITING, KEEP YOUR PURPOSE CLEARLY IN MIND

Writing the body of the essay means giving specific details that tell more about the examples you have introduced. Make sure that your details are specific and that they support your purpose. For instance, if your purpose is to show that "watching too much television has polluted our minds and weakened our bodies," every detail should be a *particular instance* of how television pollutes minds and weakens bodies. The following example repeats one of the opening paragraphs given above and adds a paragraph of specifics.

> *Watching too much television has polluted our minds and weakened our bodies. Most TV shows are written at a low level. They are meant to appeal to a low mentality. People who become addicted to these low*

level shows spend less time in healthy, outdoor activities. They get out of shape and learn very little.

Consider a family on a typical Thursday night in a typical American home. They begin by watching the evening news, which contains only short, simple overviews of complicated news stories. Then, thinking that they are "informed on the issues of the day," the family switches to game shows and pretends to be smart by watching other smart people answer questions on Wheel of Fortune and Jeopardy. Then, along with millions of others, this family sits and laughs at the same old jokes and the same old plots and the same old characters on The Cosby Show, Family Ties, Cheers, Night Court, and Hill Street Blues. Then one more half-hour of "happy talk" news, weather, and sports, and these TV addicts go off to sleep with laugh tracks and commercial jingles in their heads. Of course, they have been munching TV snacks all this time, rather than enjoying the fresh night air, and maybe exercising.

Watching too much television has polluted our minds and weakened our bodies. Most TV shows are written at a low level. They are meant to appeal to a low mentality. People who become addicted to these low level shows spend less time in healthy, outdoor activities. They get out of shape and learn very little.

Consider a family on a typical Thursday night in a typical American home. They begin by watching the **evening news,** which contains only **short, simple overviews** of complicated news stories. Then, thinking that they are "informed on the issues of the day," the family switches to **game shows** and pretends to be smart by watching **other smart people answer questions** on **Wheel of Fortune** and **Jeopardy**. Then, along with millions of others, this family sits and laughs at the **same old jokes** and the **same old plots** and the **same old characters** on **The Cosby Show, Family Ties, Cheers, Night Court**, and **Hill Street Blues**. Then one more half-hour of **"happy talk" news,** weather, and sports, and these TV addicts go off to sleep with laugh tracks and commercial jingles in their heads. Of course, they have been **munching TV snacks** all this time, **rather than enjoying the fresh night air, and maybe exercising.**

> **Specific examples** of polluting **minds**

> **Specific examples** of weakening **bodies**

So far, this composition is not perfect, but it is strong in its specific examples and its control of purpose.

5. WRITE A CONCLUSION THAT POINTS TOWARD THE FUTURE

Rather than writing a conclusion that just repeats what you have already said, you should use what you have said to make a *final, new point*. To do this, take the information you have discussed and tell how it will probably affect the future. For instance,

If people keep spending more time watching television and less time reading and playing, we will be sorry that TV was ever invented because it will make us a world of out-of-shape illiterates.

Effect on the future →	If people keep spending more time watching television and less time reading and playing, we will be **sorry that TV was ever invented** because it **will make us a world of out-of-shape illiterates.**

With this conclusion, the complete composition about "watching too much television" is about 200 words long, as the directions suggest. However, the length of your essay will probably not affect your score, unless it is so brief that you do not answer the question fully or it contains repeated ideas and points that have nothing to do with the main idea that make it unnecessarily long.

6. REREAD YOUR ESSAY AND CORRECT ANY ERRORS YOU FIND

Always allow a few minutes to proofread your essay for errors in grammar, usage, and spelling. To make sure that you proofread carefully, try this:

With your scratch paper, cover all but the first line of your essay. Read that line carefully. Then uncover and read the second line, and so forth. If you find an error, line it out carefully and write your correction neatly. Keep in mind that your handwriting must be *legible* (easy to read).

A Reminder About Scoring

   Your GED essay will be scored by two readers, on a six-point scale. Scores of 1, 2, and 3 are on the "lower half" of the scale, and scores of 4, 5, and 6 are on the "upper half" of the scale.

Upper-half essays demonstrate a clear purpose, a clear and effective structure, specific and relevant details, and correct use of language.

Lower-half essays demonstrate an unclear purpose, lack of organization, lack of specific details, and incorrect use of language.

   The essay above on "watching too much television" represents an upper-half essay; the essay below, written on the same topic, represents a lower-half essay.

A Lower-Half Essay

The effects of television are both good and bad. I will be writing about some of these effects.

Television has alot of good effects. We can get the news faster than the newspaper, and with more pictures that tell us what is happening. We can relax and laugh when shows are funny. We can also watch TV as a family, doing this with each other for more togetherness.

The bad effects of television are that it is always something to do instead of studying, and that it always does not tell us every-thing. For instance, when the space shuttle blew up, the explotion was on TV over and over, but we didn't really find out why it happened until months later, when it was written in the newspaper. This is just one example of how reading the newspaper and magazines are more informitive than just sitting in front of the TV.

As I have shown, there are goods and bads on television. Especially commershals, which tries to force us to buy everything in site. But if we didn't have the commershal, then *the economy would not have a good way to tell us what is avaleble and we would shop without knowing what to look for.*

In conclusion, knowing the goods and bad effects of television has caused some people to have a better life, but for others it has given us nothing but trouble.

Unclear statement of **purpose** → The effects of television are both good and bad. **I will be writing about some of these effects.**

Television has **alot** of good effects. We can **get the news faster** than the newspaper, and **with more pictures** that tell us what is happening. We can **relax and laugh** when shows are funny. We can also watch TV as a family, doing this with each other for more **togetherness.** ← **Grammar errors**

← **General statements, not specific examples**

Good effects paragraph followed by **bad effects** paragraph; organization **OK** →

The bad effects of television are that it is always **something to do instead of studying,** and that it always **does not tell us everything.** For instance, when the space shuttle blew up, the **explotion** was on TV over and over, but we didn't really find out why it happened until months later, when it was written in the newspaper. This is just one example of how reading the newspaper and magazines **are** more **informitive** than just sitting in front of the TV. ← **Spelling errors**

Grammar errors →

As I have shown, there are goods and bads on television. Especially **commershals,** which **tries** to force us to buy everything in **site.** But if we didn't have the **commershal,** then **the economy would not have a good way to tell us what is avaleble, and we would shop without knowing what to look for.**

Spelling errors →

Information not connected to main point →

Poor organization within paragraphs; no **plan;** sentences **are not tied together**

In conclusion, knowing the goods and bad effects of television has caused some people to have a better life, but for others it has given us nothing but trouble.

Notice that the boxes above point out *some* of the problems in this essay but *not all* of them. See if you can find other problems with spelling, punctuation, usage, and organization.

SECTION II

TWO MORE SAMPLE ESSAYS

Let's take a look at another sample topic.

TOPIC B

Most experts agree that proper nutrition and a healthy diet are essential for a healthy body. Yet, fast-food restaurants are more popular than ever.

With all of the attention today about physical fitness, why are fast-food restaurants doing so well? Write a composition of about 200 words explaining your answer to this question. Give reasons and examples to support your opinion.

Now review the essay that follows to see if you can spot the strong points.

A Topic B Essay

It's hard to explain why humans behave in certain ways. Although people want to be fit, still they eat fast foods which may not be good for them.

People today rush to do everything. They rush to work or play by driving quickly. For example, although the speed limit may be 55 mph, many cars go 60 or even faster. Computers rush us through our work. Almost every business now has one. Kitchens have time-saving devices, like veg-o-matics and microwave ovens which can bake a potato in a minute. What this boils down to is _time_. Many of us simply don't have enough time. So fast-food restaurants save us time "wasted" on eating.

Convenience is another reason fast food is so popular. You don't have to get out of your car to buy it or eat it. You don't have to cook it. All you have to do is unwrap it. It's just plain easy.

But there's a problem. Studies show that a healthy diet is essential for a healthy body and a long life. So the time taken for a good meal is certainly not wasted. Yet, fast-food restaurants continue to be popular. This behavior seems strange. We eat fast foods to save us time, so that we can get to the gym and get in shape. Our placing a high value on time and convenience has in some ways overshadowed the value of having a healthy body.

A Second Look at the Complete Essay

Good, brief introductory paragraph setting up the topic

It's hard to explain why humans behave in certain ways. Although people want to be fit, still they eat fast foods which may not be good for them.

First reason: **time**

People today **rush** to do everything. They rush to work or play by **driving quickly.** For example, although the speed limit may be 55 mph, many cars go **60** or even faster. **Computers** rush us through our work. Almost every business now has one. Kitchens have time-saving devices, like **veg-o-matics** and **microwave ovens** which can bake a potato in a minute. What **this boils down to** is time. Many of us simply don't have enough time. So fast-food restaurants save us time "wasted" on eating.

Well-developed paragraph with lots of **specific examples**

Avoid using **cliches**

Second reason: convenience

Convenience is another reason fast food is so popular. You **don't have to get out of your car** to buy it or eat it. You **don't have to cook** it. All you have to do is **unwrap** it. It's just plain easy.

Good specific examples

But there's a problem. Studies show that a healthy diet is essential for a healthy body and a long life. So the time taken for a good meal is certainly not wasted. Yet, fast-food restaurants continue to be popular. This behavior seems strange. We eat fast foods to save us time so that we can get to the gym and get in shape. Our placing a high value on time and convenience has in some ways overshadowed the value of having a healthy body.

Excellent closing paragraph

A "cluster" for the essay shown above might look like this:

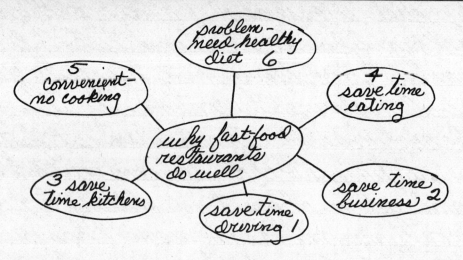

Another Topic B Essay

Let's take a look at another sample essay on the same topic as given before.

TOPIC B

Most experts agree that proper nutrition and a healthy diet are essential for a healthy body. Yet, fast-food restaurants are more popular than ever.

With all of the attention today about physical fitness, why are fast-food restaurants doing so well? Write a composition of about 200 words explaining your answer to this question. Give reasons and examples to support your opinion

---

Now review the essay that follows to see if you can spot the strong points.

Who said fast food isn't good for you? It may not have been years ago, but now its better than most food we eat at home.

Fast-food restaurants let people get their food quickly. And now they provide something new—nutritious food. Now all of the fast-food restaurants have begun to offer healthier types of food. Places that once served only hamburgers now serve fish and chicken as well. Places that once provided only a choice of meat and fish now also serve salads. You can order many different types of salads too—pasta salad, chef's salad, chicken salad, etc. Many fast-food restaurants also offer low-calorie diet food, such as a salad bar with cottage cheese, Jell-o, and many kinds of fresh fruit. So now even the calorie counter can enjoy going to a fast-food restaurant.

Fast-food restaurants remain popular because they have changed with the times. They offer a wide selection of foods for the health nut as well as for the normal person.

A Second Look at the Complete Essay

Opening **question** to **"grab"** the reader's attention

Who said fast food isn't good for you? It may not have been years ago, but now it's better than most food we eat at home.

Good opening paragraph

Fast-food restaurants let people get their food quickly. And now they provide something new—**nutritious food.** Now all of the fast-food restaurants have

Well-developed paragraph → begun to offer healthier types of food. Places that once served only hamburgers now serve **fish** and **chicken** as well. Places that once provided only a choice of meat and fish now also serve **salads.** You can order many different types of salads too—**pasta salad, chef's salad, chicken salad,** etc. Many fast-food restaurants also offer low-calorie diet food, such as a **salad bar with cottage cheese, Jell-O,** and many kinds of **fresh fruit.** So now even the calorie counter can enjoy going to a fast-food restaurant. ← **Lots of specific examples**

Brief concluding paragraph to tie up the essay → Fast-food restaurants remain popular because they have changed with the times. They offer a wide selection of foods for the health nut as well as for the normal person.

A "cluster" for the essay shown above might look like this:

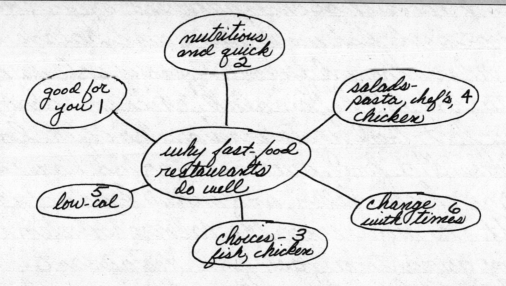

JUDGING YOUR OWN ESSAY

In the How to Start Reviewing section of this book, you'll have a chance to try some of your own practice GED essays. After each practice essay, you'll find a checklist to help you judge how well you've done on your essay. These are the questions you should ask yourself after you've completed each essay.

Did you

1. Focus on the assigned topic?
2. Answer the question?
3. Give a statement of purpose?
4. Flow in an organized manner?
5. Support your view with specific examples?
6. Use correct English?
7. Present the essay well (make it neat, easy to read)?

TEST 2

SOCIAL STUDIES

TEST 2: SOCIAL STUDIES

WHAT TO EXPECT

The Social Studies Test is 1 hour and 25 minutes long and contains 64 multiple-choice questions.

■ Expect questions that ask you to read and reason carefully using social studies materials. You are *not expected to memorize* specific dates or events in politics or history.

■ Expect questions that test how well you understand concepts, ideas, and problems associated with social studies.

■ Expect questions that relate to everyday life—for example, how legislation affects people in the working place or who is qualified to vote in an election.

■ Expect questions that test a high school level understanding of the social sciences. The United States edition of the Social Studies Test emphasizes questions with *a specific U.S. focus.*

■ Expect about two-thirds of the questions to ask you to draw conclusions from information related to the social sciences—especially politics, history, and economics.

■ Expect about one-third of the questions to ask you to draw conclusions from maps, charts, graphs, tables, and political cartoons.

■ Expect about two-thirds of the questions to be in groups, or sets—that is, two to six questions that refer to the same information or chart.

WHAT YOU SHOULD KNOW

The Social Studies Test contains the following areas:

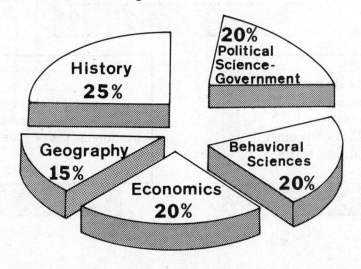

You should be able to answer questions from information given in the following areas:

HISTORY (25%)
(including global issues)

You could be given

> **Information that discusses** how history reflects **social, political, and economic developments**

> **Articles about** how major **events** have **shaped U.S. history**

> **Information that explains** current **U.S. social** and **political problems**

POLITICAL SCIENCE—GOVERNMENT (20%)

You could be given

> **Information that discusses** how **political decisions** have **worldwide impact**

> **Articles, graphs,** or **charts that show** the importance of the **American political system,** political parties, the Constitution, and state and local government

> **Excerpts that explain** current **U.S. political problems** and **foreign policy** issues

BEHAVIORAL SCIENCES (20%)
(psychology—the study of the mind, sociology—the study of modern
society, anthropology—the study of man)

You could be given

Information that discusses how **individuals and groups function** in various societies

Articles that show how **cultures develop,** how people in **groups interact,** and how **values** and **attitudes** are **formed**

Excerpts that explain social changes within modern societies

ECONOMICS (20%)

You could be given

Excerpts that explain how a **free-market system** operates and how the **economy** is **organized**

Information that explains how **capitalism** works and how it differs from **communism** and **socialism**

Articles, charts, graphs, or **maps that explain** economic indicators and the **world economy**

GEOGRAPHY (15%)

You could be given

> **Information that discusses** how **humans** have had a major **impact** on the **natural environment**

> **Maps, charts, graphs,** or **articles** that **show** the major **geographic regions** and the distribution of the **world's population**

> **Excerpts that discuss pollution** and the use of **natural resources**

WHAT TO LOOK FOR: KINDS OF QUESTIONS

The GED Social Studies Test will test higher level thinking skills. The exam will *not* ask you to simply remember facts. For example, you would *not* be expected to know the year that the Monroe Doctrine was signed. However, you *are expected* to understand important social studies principles, concepts, and events.

The social studies questions are grouped as follows:

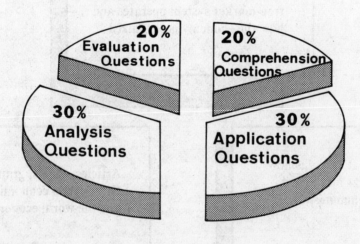

20% Evaluation Questions

20% Comprehension Questions

30% Analysis Questions

30% Application Questions

1. **Comprehension Questions (20 %):** You should be able to understand the meaning of information presented in articles or excerpts, as well as in maps, charts, and graphs. Comprehension questions can be answered simply from the information presented in the reading. Comprehension questions will ask you to understand

   - What is the <u>main</u> point?
   - What is <u>another</u> way of saying this?
   - What is <u>suggested</u> by the information?

2. **Application Questions (30 %):** You should be able to reason one step beyond the comprehension level. You must apply information already stated to solve a problem in a different situation (different context). Application questions will ask you to understand

   - How can you use the <u>suggested information</u> in a <u>new setting</u>?
   - How can you apply <u>general statements</u> to a <u>new situation</u>?

3. **Analysis Questions (30 %):** You should be able to compare information or data. You must be able to explore the relationships of several ideas. Analysis questions will ask

   - Can you find ideas that are <u>not specifically stated</u>?
   - Can you tell the <u>difference</u> between a fact and a hypothesis; can you tell if a hypothesis is <u>based on</u> the passage?
   - Can you tell what <u>makes</u> an event <u>happen</u> and what the <u>results</u> are?

4. **Evaluation Questions (20 %):** You should be able to judge the accuracy of stated or assumed material. Evaluation questions will ask

   - Can you tell if the information given would <u>support</u> a <u>point of view</u>?
   - Can you <u>detect why</u> decisions are made?
   - Can you determine a <u>trend</u> and predict its <u>outcome</u>?
   - Can you find what is <u>not true</u> in an argument?

ABOUT THE DIRECTIONS

Following are the directions you'll find in the Social Studies Test. Become very familiar with these directions *now* so that you will be comfortable with them when you take the actual test. The directions you'll see on the actual test will be wider on the page. Here, though, room has been left for the boxes you see on the right and the left. Read the following directions straight through, and then carefully read the information in the boxes. It points out and explains important points in the directions.

TEST 2: SOCIAL STUDIES

Tests of General Educational Development

Directions

All questions have **five choices**

Look back at the **information** as often as you need to

General concepts; **Don't memorize specific facts**

Information from **short readings** or **diagrams**

The Social Studies Test consists of multiple-choice questions intended to measure general social studies concepts. The questions are based on short readings which often include a graph, chart, or figure. Study the information given and then answer the question(s) following it. Refer to the information as often as necessary in answering the questions.

Spend no more than about **1½ minutes per question**

Don't get stuck on any question; move on

Each question is **worth the same**

You should spend no more than 85 minutes answering the questions in this booklet. Work carefully, but do not spend too much time on any one question. Be sure you answer every question. You will not be penalized for incorrect answers.

No penalty for guessing so **guess** if you have to, but don't leave any questions blank

Do not mark in this test booklet. Record your answers to the questions on the separate answer sheet provided. Be sure all requested information is properly recorded on the answer sheet.

Mark your **answers carefully** on the answer sheet

To record your answers, mark the numbered space on the answer sheet beside the number that corresponds to the question in the test booklet.

Notice that this question **refers to a reading** or **diagram**; almost all questions follow this format

FOR EXAMPLE:

Early colonists of North America looked for settlement sites that had adequate water supplies and were accessible by ship. For this reason, many early towns were built near

(1) mountains
(2) prairies
(3) rivers
(4) glaciers
(5) plateaus   ① ② ● ④ ⑤

The correct answer is "rivers"; therefore, answer space 3 would be marked on the answer sheet.

Do not make any **extra marks** on your answer sheet

Do not rest the point of your pencil on the answer sheet while you are considering your answer. <u>Make no stray or unnecessary marks.</u> If you change an answer, erase your first mark completely. <u>Mark only one answer space for each question</u>; multiple answers will be scored as incorrect. Do not fold or crease your answer sheet. Return all test materials to the test administrator

Mark only one answer

WHAT YOU SHOULD DO

Read the information looking for the following key points:

- What is the <u>main idea</u>?
- Is the author <u>suggesting</u> something?
- Are there <u>conflicting ideas</u>?
- Is the <u>historical time period</u> evident?
- Are <u>causes</u> and <u>results</u> apparent
- What are the specific <u>supporting details</u>?

Refer to the information, chart, graph, or map as often as you need to.

Graphs, charts, maps, and political cartoons often take a second and a third look. Take an extra few moments to make sure you understand how to read the graph, chart, map, or cartoon and what information is being presented.

Make sure you understand <u>what the question is asking</u>, for example—

- According to the passage, which of the following is . . .
- All of the following are possible explanations EXCEPT. . .
- It can be <u>inferred</u> from the chart . . .
- The one <u>factor</u> that <u>contributed to</u> . . .
- Which of the following <u>statements</u> is <u>supported by</u> . . .
- The economy of the South was <u>based</u> on . . .
- Which of the following is an <u>example</u> of . . .

The following four sections will use examples to carefully explain the **question types,** show you **what to look for,** and point out **what you should do.**

SECTION I: SHORT READINGS WITH SINGLE QUESTIONS

In each of the following, short paragraphs or statements will be followed by a question. Read each carefully. Answer the question. Then study the explanation that follows the question.

COMPREHENSION QUESTIONS

You may be given the following type of paragraph:

The belief that all people are created equal is part of the American value system. However, laws, regulations, or statutes do not yet protect all people equally. Legal interpretations of equality are continually being re-evaluated and redefined. Such things as race, religion, or social standing should have no bearing on a person's legal guarantees.

A **political science** question similar to this could follow:

1. Which of the following best summarizes the paragraph's main point?

    (1) In basic rights, minorities are not equal to the rest of society.
    (2) All people are equal in ability.
    (3) All people should have equal protection under the law regardless of their position in society.
    (4) Women are not yet equal to men.
    (5) Rights are not protected by laws and statutes.

The right answer is (3). To answer this question, you must understand the *main idea* of the paragraph. The best answer will be broad enough to include the major points. Watch out for answers that are too specific and focus on only part of the reading, such as choices (1) or (4); they do not state the main idea.

The main idea is that *all* people should have equal rights (3).

In choice (2), the answer has nothing to do with what the reading is saying. Choices (1) and (4) are closer to being right because they mention an *example* of inequalities, but they are not right because they are *examples,* not the *main* idea. Good *wrong* answers, like these, will usually be truths, but not answers to the question on the exam. The main point of the paragraph is not so specific as either (1) or (4). Choice (5) is wrong because the passage mentions "laws" that "do not protect all people equally," so we do know that *some* rights are protected.

You may be given the following type of reading:

In the late nineteenth and early twentieth centuries, the U.S. government followed a policy of laissez-faire (noninterference) which, in effect, allowed business to regulate itself. It was believed that this would not lead to an unfair business advantage, since business would act in the "best interests" of society. In reality, laissez-faire made it possible for businesses to form into giant monopolies—undermining the free-market system.

A **history** question similar to this could follow:

2. According to the reading, the policy of laissez-faire allowed business to

    (1) protect the interests of the people
    (2) control prices and eliminate competition
    (3) control the government
    (4) encourage human rights
    (5) elect political leaders

The right answer is (2). To answer this question, you must be able to *restate* an idea in the passage. The last sentence says that the policy of *laissez-faire* allowed businesses to form monopolies.

If you know that *monopolies* hold exclusive control over a market, choice (2) should be clear. But even if you are not certain about the meaning of *monopolies,* you know the effect was "undermining the free-market system," and this too should point toward choice (2). There is nothing at all in the reading about the "interests of the people" (1), "human rights" (4), or electing "political leaders" (5).

You may be given a chart similar to this:

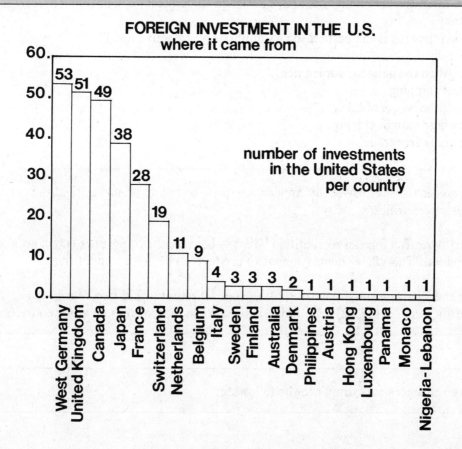

FOREIGN INVESTMENT IN THE U.S.
where it came from

number of investments
in the United States
per country

A **geography/economics** question similar to this could follow:

3. The majority of foreign investments in the United States came from which geographic area?

(1) North America
(2) Eastern Europe
(3) Far East
(4) Western Europe
(5) Canada

The right answer is (4). To answer this question you must be able to recognize that most of the countries listed in the chart with the largest investment (West Germany, United Kingdom, France, Switzerland, Netherlands) are in Western Europe.

The chart at the left shows that eight of the top ten foreign investments in the United States came from Western Europe. This comprehension question requires you to read the chart accurately.

APPLICATION QUESTIONS

You may be given the following type of information and **economics** question:

4. A protective tariff is a tax on imports and is designed to "protect" a country from foreign competition.

Which of the following is the best reason to <u>eliminate</u> a protective tariff?

(1) to strengthen the national government
(2) to protect shipping
(3) to protect the wages of labor
(4) to encourage manufacturing
(5) to encourage free trade

The right answer is (5). To answer this application question you must understand the results of passing a protective tariff.

Protective tariffs restrict foreign competition. *Why?*—because the import tax (tariff) raises the price of foreign products. This allows home (domestic) products to be more competitive.

In answering this question you are looking for the one item that would be a reason to *get rid of* protective tariffs. Choices (1), (2), (3), and (4) could *all* be reasons *to pass* a protective tariff.

You may be given statements similar to the following:

Strip mining is used to recover minerals that lie close to the Earth's surface. Environmental groups have criticized strip mining as shortsighted and dangerous to the environment.

A **geography** question similar to this could follow:

---

5. Which of the following is the most likely environmental argument <u>against</u> strip mining?

    (1) Air pollution increases when factories process mineral products.
    (2) Strip mining is economically efficient and environmentally safe.
    (3) Strip mining destroys the natural state of an area.
    (4) State laws have not been effective in controlling mine companies.
    (5) Minerals should be imported rather than mined in the U.S.

The right answer is (3). To answer this difficult application question, you must understand why environmental groups might believe that strip mining is harmful.

In the first sentence, you are told that minerals are recovered "close to the Earth's surface"; in the second sentence, strip mining is called "dangerous to the environment." How does the second sentence follow from the first? What must be disturbed to make mining possible? Only choice (3) gives an answer to this question.

Choice (1) is wrong because it does not deal directly with strip mining. It deals with mineral products *after* they have been mined, and we do not know if the mining process was strip mining. Choice (4) also does not deal directly with strip mining, but with mining companies.

Choice (2) is an argument *in favor of*, not *against*, strip mining, and choice (5) is an argument *for* something else, not *against* strip mining.

You may be given the following type of statement:

In the twentieth century, the world population rate has been drastically affected by modern medicine and standards of hygiene.

A **behavioral science/sociology** question similar to this could follow:

---

6. Which population controlling factor is probably no longer effective because of modern medicine and standards of hygiene?

    (1) a high death rate from infectious diseases
    (2) a low birth rate
    (3) voluntary birth control
    (4) religious beliefs
    (5) rural settlement patterns

The right answer is (1). To answer this question, you must see a connection between the death rate and population growth. A high death rate limits population growth.

What effect would improved medicine and hygiene standards have on the death rate from infectious diseases? Would it be higher or lower? Improvements in medicine reduce the number of deaths from infectious disease, so a high death rate from infectious disease would no longer be a major factor in controlling population.

You may be given the following types of statements:

"Hawks" and "doves" are terms for people who favor war and people who favor peace. The "hawk" prefers a military solution to international problems.

A **history/political science** question similar to this could follow:

7. Which of the following actions would a dove most likely favor?

    (1) negotiated settlements
    (2) military conflict
    (3) military retaliation
    (4) victory at any cost
    (5) nuclear confrontation

The right answer is (1). Since hawks and doves are *opposites,* and the "hawk prefers a military solution," the dove would favor negotiated settlements—that is, solutions that avoid a war.

Choices (2), (3), (4), and (5) are warlike policies and would be associated with hawks. Choice (1) is the only choice that could be associated with a dove. A negotiated settlement (an agreement) ends hostilities at the bargaining table, not on the battlefield.

ANALYSIS QUESTIONS

You may be given the following type of paragraph:

In the 1970s, the State Department believed that if one country in southeast Asia became Communist, then other countries would, one by one, become Communist. Their analysts pointed to the fact that China was followed by North Viet Nam, by South Viet Nam, and by Laos into the Communist camp.

A **history** question similar to this could follow:

8. Which of the following conclusions can be drawn from the paragraph?

   (1) It is difficult to predict what would happen in southeast Asia if a country fell to communism.
   (2) All of southeast Asia had fallen to communism.
   (3) The State Department did not recognize the threat of communism in southeast Asia.
   (4) A definable pattern was evident in southeast Asia.
   (5) Popular views seldom influence history.

The right answer is (4). Since one country was followed by three others, we can see a definable pattern in the events and draw this conclusion. What has happened in southeast Asia? Several countries have fallen to communism. Because of this, you can eliminate choices (1) and (3).

Choice (2) is a conclusion that is not supported by information in the paragraph. You can eliminate choice (5) because it has nothing to do with what the paragraph is saying.

You may be given the following type of information:

Converting an animal skin into cloth is a laborious task. Uncured skins readily absorb moisture and become stiff when wet. A skin can be cured by rubbing it with fat or smoking it over a fire. But both of these methods produce imperfect results. The most satisfactory results are obtained by soaking a skin in tannic acid. Eskimos successfully cure skins by rubbing them with human urine.

A **behavioral science/anthropology** question similar to this could follow:

9. Which of the following best explains the success of Eskimos' curing procedure?

   (1) Converting raw pelts into cloth is time consuming.
   (2) The process of curing animal skins can be performed in a variety of ways.
   (3) The stronger the curing agent used, the more efficient the curing process.
   (4) Animal skins that are uncured absorb water.
   (5) Human urine contains chemicals like those in tannic acid.

The right answer is (5). To answer this question, you must be able to *infer*, arrive at a fact from, what is *not* definitely stated.

The information says that curing can be accomplished by rubbing the skin with fat, but the results are not perfect. The most effective method involves using tannic acid, and the Eskimos are successful even though they use urine. The fact that the Eskimos are successful suggests that urine contains chemicals like those in tannic acid.

You may be given the following type of paragraph:

Once again our City Council has shown all the firmness of a bowl of oatmeal in deciding to allow the rock concert to be held in Patriot's Hall. It is incredible that the City Council rejected a Planning Commission recommendation that would have prohibited all performances by amplified bands in the concert hall. The last concert in this city resulted in both violence and destruction of property.

A **political science** question similar to this may follow:

10. The phrase "bowl of oatmeal" is used to

    (1) condemn the actions taken by the City Council
    (2) refer to a new rock group
    (3) imply that rock groups eat oatmeal
    (4) praise the City Council for their recent vote
    (5) urge the City Council to overturn the Planning Commission

The right answer is (1). To answer this question, you must understand the speaker's position and the purpose of his or her choice of words. The speaker holds the City Council responsible for allowing the band to perform. A "bowl of oatmeal" has, of course, no "firmness" at all, and by this comparison, the speaker can condemn the council's meekness.

You may be given the following type of statement and **behavioral science/psychology** question:

11. A racist believes that one race is superior to others.

    With which of the following is a racist most likely to agree?

    (1) All races are inherently equal.
    (2) Intelligence is based on race.
    (3) Men are more equal in ability than women are.
    (4) Cultural factors determine intelligence.
    (5) Seventh-grade students are brighter than sixth-grade students.

The right answer is (2). To answer this question, you must look for a statement that agrees with the racist's belief in the superiority of a *race*. Option (1), which says that races are *equal,* contradicts this belief. Options (3), (4), and (5) are concerned with gender, cultural factors, and age, *not* with race. The correct choice (2) says that race determines intelligence. The next step in the racist's argument would be that the race he or she favors has the superior intelligence.

Notice that in answering multiple-choice questions you can often eliminate choices that are clearly wrong. In this question, you can eliminate four of the five, so the remaining one *must* be right. Usually, you can eliminate only two or three, but it is much easier to find the right answer when you choose between only two options rather than among five.

You may be given the following type of paragraph:

The vast changes caused by the industrial revolution in the United States produced particularly unsettling alterations in the lives of American farmers. The farm population, once comprising up to 90 percent of the total population, shrank from 80 percent in 1860 to 60 percent in 1900 on its way to 26 percent in 1980. Yet through the years of the late nineteenth century (as in the twentieth) <u>fewer and fewer people produced more and more</u> foodstuffs and dairy products. The self-sufficient family farms were more and more replaced by large, highly profitable agribusinesses raising cash crops destined for the ever-expanding urban markets and for foreign export as well.

A **history** question similar to this could follow:

12. Which of the following factors is the most likely explanation of the dramatic change in the farm population?

    (1) The farm population increased because there was greater demand for farm products.
    (2) The farm population dropped from 80% in 1860 to 26% in 1980.
    (3) The farm population decreased because industrialization made family farms less profitable than larger businesses.
    (4) Farmers moved to the cities.
    (5) Modern farm machinery increased farm productivity.

The right answer is (3). Why did the farm population decrease dramatically from 1860 to 1980? The first sentence of the passage says the industrial revolution caused vast changes, while the last sentence tells what the changes were.

Although choice (5) is true and it might be argued that because of increased productivity farming attracted businesses, choice (3) is the clearer and more specific answer.

EVALUATION QUESTIONS

You may be given the following type of information:

The following predictions are presented at a business conference.

1. In the next 12 months, the unemployment rate will increase 2% from the last year.
2. In the next 12 months, business profits will decrease 2% from the last year.
3. In the next 12 months, economic growth will decrease 3% from the last year.

An **economics** question similar to this could follow:

13. Based on the information, which of the following is the best conclusion about the future of the economy?

  (1) The country will suffer a mild economic decline followed by rapid growth.
  (2) The country will suffer a severe economic depression.
  (3) The country will suffer a mild economic recession.
  (4) The country will see marked economic gains.
  (5) The country will see no change in its economic outlook.

The right answer is (3). To answer this question, you must understand that the economy is affected negatively by rises in the unemployment rate, and by falls in business profits and growth rates. You must also know the meaning of words like *depression* (an extended period of severe unemployment, falling wages and prices, and low business activity) and *recession* (a temporary falling off of business activity). Finally you would have to decide that because of the small percentages (2 and 3 percent) the falling off is mild. Choice (1) is wrong because the information gives no reason to predict growth after the decline.

You may be given the following sort of paragraph:

A boycott, named after Captain Boycott, an Irish land agent in the 1880s, is a refusal by the public to buy, sell, or use a product or service in order to force the maker or purveyor to take some action. In colonial America, the colonists successfully boycotted British goods to force the repeal of the Stamp Act. In modern times, shoppers in sympathy with farm workers have boycotted lettuce and table grapes.

A **history** question similar to this could follow:

14. Which of the following statements accurately describes the boycott in colonial America?

    (1) It failed to accomplish its purpose.
    (2) It was a boycott before the word "boycott" had been coined.
    (3) It did not distress British merchants or politicians.
    (4) It helped to increase the British export trade to America.
    (5) It was more harmful to the Americans than to the British.

The right answer is (2). To answer this question you must read carefully and notice that the man who gave us the word *boycott* lived in the 1880s. And you must remember that the colonial period in American history was at least 100 years earlier. As choice (2) claims, the word *boycott* had not been invented (coined) when the colonists carried out their boycott.

You can eliminate choices (1), (3), (4), and (5) on the grounds that the paragraph says the boycott was successful and forced the repeal of a tax.

You may be given the following type of paragraph:

In recent history an increasing number of Americans have failed to vote in national elections. Since the presidential election of 1960, when a record 62.8% of voting age Americans went to the polls, voter participation has steadily declined. A political scientist attributed the decline to voter disenchantment with current economic conditions.

A **political science** question similar to this could follow:

15. Which of the following statements, if true, would most <u>weaken</u> the political scientist's conclusion?

    (1) More Americans actually voted in 1960 than were originally reported.
    (2) Voter participation has declined in Communist countries.
    (3) Public information on political issues is limited.
    (4) The standard of living has substantially increased in the past two decades.
    (5) Voting facilities are inadequate.

The right answer is (4). To answer this question, you must be able to see which examples support or do *not* support the author's arguments. In this case, you must look for an answer that shows that the American economy did *not* cause voting to decline.

Choice (2) is simply a fact that has no bearing on the answer. Choice (4) would *weaken* the author's conclusion. If the standard of living substantially improved over the last two decades, discontent with economic conditions would not be the reason for the decline as the author argues.

SECTION II: SHORT READINGS WITH SEVERAL QUESTIONS

Most of the questions on the GED Social Studies Test will consist of short readings followed by two to six questions. These "multiple question" sections will contain many types of questions.

ECONOMICS

You may be given the following type of information:

Items 16 and 17 refer to the following statement.

Inflation is the continued upward trend in the price of goods without a corresponding change in the quality of the goods. A recession is a period of reduced economic growth resulting in a general downturn in the economy.

One of the questions could be similar to this **comprehension/application** question:

16. Which of the following could happen in an "inflationary recession"?

    (1) Prices and buying power both increase.
    (2) Prices go down but unemployment goes up.
    (3) Prices go up at the same time that unemployment increases.
    (4) Unemployment increases but the price of goods and services is unchanged.
    (5) Jobs are created but only for unskilled workers.

The right answer is (3). To answer this difficult question, you must first understand the key terms. The terms *inflation* and *recession* are defined in the statement, but you must also connect the two terms and apply the new definition. During inflation prices go up (upward trend in prices); during recession individuals often lose jobs (reduced economic growth). Choice (3) is the only answer that has a characteristic of inflation (higher prices) *and* a characteristic of recession (unemployment increases).

A second question could be similar to this **application** question:

17. Which of the following groups would be injured <u>most</u> by continued periods of inflation?

    (1) debtors
    (2) people on fixed incomes
    (3) civil service workers
    (4) school teachers
    (5) bankers

The right answer is (2). Remember, you are looking for the group that would be *most* harmed. All people can be affected to some degree by inflation. But people on fixed incomes (such as retired workers) are most affected by continued inflation. Goods and services cost more, but their income level does not increase. Those with jobs (choices 3, 4, and 5) may get salary increases.

Debtors, choice (1), could *benefit* from inflation by paying back loans with "inflated" dollars—the dollars had more purchasing power when the loan was taken out.

HISTORY

You may be given the following type of information:

Items 18 and 19 refer to the following paragraph.

Secretary of State John Adams in a speech in 1821 announced that the two American continents should be closed to any future colonization. Adams believed that U.S. interests would best be served by the expulsion of European imperialists from South America. This policy was directed against Spanish and French activity in Latin America. It was believed that dismantling the Spanish empire in the New World would increase American trade and American military and commercial considerations could be more easily protected.

One of the questions could be similar to this **comprehension** question:

18. Which of the following best explains the purpose of Adams's proposed policy?

    (1) to insure the political stability of Canada
    (2) to prevent Europe from trading in South America
    (3) to prevent the political development of South America
    (4) to gain for America a dominant position in South America
    (5) to prevent free trade in Europe

The right answer is (4). To answer this question you must understand the *central* idea of the paragraph.

The last sentence of the paragraph clearly says that following this policy would directly benefit U.S. military and commercial interests.

A second question could be similar to this **evaluation** question:

19. Which of the following statements, if added to the paragraph, would indicate that America did <u>not</u> intend to become a new colonial power in South America?

    (1) The United States would not interfere with colonies already established in South America.
    (2) The United States would establish military bases in Central America.
    (3) The United States would establish American-backed governments in former Spanish territory.
    (4) The United States would not prevent Europe from establishing colonies in Asia.
    (5) The United States would acquire territory in South America as part of its global right.

The right answer is (1). To answer this question you must apply the *main idea* of the passage (the Americas were closed to European colonization) to a new but related situation. Only choice (1) shows that America did *not* intend to take over European possessions in the New World in order to become a new colonial power itself.

Answers (2), (3), and (5) are wrong because they are all actions that show that America did intend to be a power. Answer (4) is wrong because it has to do with Asia, not South America.

GEOGRAPHY

You may be given the following type of map:

Items <u>20 and 21</u> are based on the following map of the Earth:

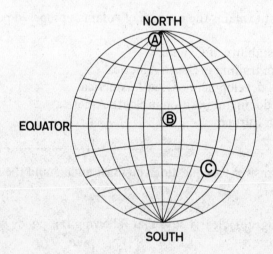

One of the questions could be similar to this **analysis** question:

20. The average daily temperature at point A on the globe is likely to be

(1) higher than at both B and C
(2) higher than at B and lower than at C
(3) lower than at B and higher than at C
(4) lower than at both B and C
(5) about the same as at B and C

The right answer is (4). Point A is very nearly at the north pole and is most likely to be much colder than point B, which is near the equator, or point C, which is a region likely to be temperate.

To answer this question, you do not need any detailed knowledge of geography. But you must be able to recognize the most basic feature of a global map—that the poles are at the top and bottom and that the equator divides the northern and southern hemispheres. You do not need any detailed knowledge of climates, but you must know that temperatures at the poles are cold and temperatures at the equator are usually warm.

A second question could be similar to this **analysis** question:

21. Which of the following circumstances would make it most likely that the average daily temperature at point B is lower than that at point C?

(1) if point B is at sea level and point C is above sea level
(2) if point B is inland and point C is on the sea coast
(3) if point B is at a high altitude and point C is at sea level
(4) if point B is located near a river
(5) if point C is located near a river

The right answer is (3). Again you do not need to know about the climate of any specific place. But you should know that the temperatures at high altitudes (in the mountains, for example) are likely to be lower than temperatures at sea level. So, although point B is at the equator and point C is not, if point B is at a high altitude, it might be cooler than point C.

HISTORY

You may be given information similar to this:

Items 22 and 23 are based on the following information.

Historians, in reconstructing past events, make use of primary and secondary source material. A primary source is an "eyewitness," or firsthand, account of an event.

One of the questions could be similar to this **application** question:

22. Which of the following is the best example of a <u>primary</u> source?

    (1) an encyclopedia definition of taxes
    (2) a movie about the French Revolution
    (3) a biography of Winston Churchill
    (4) an autobiography of Julius Caesar
    (5) a historical novel about the westward movement

The right answer is (4). This is a straightforward application question. A primary source is an *eyewitness* account of an event. An autobiography (4) is the biography of a person written *by him* or *her*. Other examples of primary source materials would be a diary, ship's log, "live" news coverage, and so forth.

Choice (3), a biography, is a written history of a person, but one written by another person who may or may not have known the subject.

A second question could be similar to this **evaluation** question:

23. All of the following accounts of a primary source <u>must</u> be true EXCEPT

    (1) primary sources are more accurate than secondary source material
    (2) primary sources are normally events directly observed
    (3) a diary may be a primary source
    (4) historians rely on both primary and secondary sources
    (5) a letter may be a primary source

The right answer is (1). To answer this question you must decide which of the choices is not always true. It is false to say that a primary source, since it is an *eyewitness* account, *must* be more accurate than a secondary source. Primary sources can often be biased and misleading. For example, a British report on a Revolutionary War battle might differ greatly from an American account of the same battle.

SECTION III: READINGS WITH MORE THAN TWO QUESTIONS

Some of the questions on the GED Social Studies Test are based on longer readings about a single topic. Many types of questions may appear.

Things you should do for passages containing three to five questions:

■ Read some of the questions first. This will give you a preview of what the passage is about.

■ Do *not* read the answer choices when you preread the questions. After reading the questions, read the passage for understanding; then go on to read each question again and each answer choice.

■ Decide on the *main idea* of the passage. What point is the author trying to make?

■ Identify supporting information. What ideas strengthen the arguments?

■ Remember, you can *reread* as often as necessary.

The following examples will help you build confidence in working through sets of multiple questions.

HISTORY

You may be given information similar to this:

Items 24 to 26 are based on the following article.

During the Korean War (1950–1953) the United States was part of a United Nations "peace keeping" force designed to prevent Communist aggression in South Korea. General Douglas MacArthur commanded the United Nations forces. However, fears of the possibility of a world war dominated the political and military climate of the times. Therefore, when General MacArthur requested permission to extend the sphere of battle by striking across the Yalu River and using air strikes over mainland China, President Truman denied his requests.

MacArthur publicly criticized such policies. He felt they undermined the possibility of a military conclusion to the war. MacArthur went so far as to refer to President Truman's foreign policy as "prolonged indecision," and even suggested that the restrictive military policies were, in effect, "appeasement" of communism.

President Truman, on April 11, 1951, recalled MacArthur from Korea and subsequently dismissed him from the service. Truman defended the dismissal by arguing that MacArthur's public criticism increased the risk of a confrontation with Russia.

One of the questions may be similar to this **analysis** question:

24. Which statement best gives the main idea of the article?

    (1) The MacArthur-Truman confrontation demonstrated that the President is Commander-in-Chief.
    (2) The President allowed Korea to fall to communism.
    (3) The United States followed a policy favoring confrontation with the Soviet Union.
    (4) Air strikes over mainland China were not important.
    (5) General MacArthur was a great man.

The right answer is (1). What is the passage about? The first paragraph tells of the roles of Truman and MacArthur. The second paragraph describes MacArthur's criticism, and the third describes Truman's action, which showed his real control as Commander-in-Chief.

None of the other four answers comes close to the main idea. Choice (2) is wrong. The passage does not indicate that Korea fell to communism. Choice (3) is also definitely false—the United States tried to avoid confrontation with Russia. Choice (4) is wrong—if air strikes were not important, MacArthur wouldn't have criticized the President. Choice (5) is not mentioned in the article.

A second question might be similar to this **analysis** question:

25. Which presidential power did President Truman use when he dismissed General MacArthur as commander of the U.N. forces in Korea?

    (1) the power as Commander-in-Chief
    (2) the power to make treaties
    (3) the power to make political speeches
    (4) the power to fire any government official
    (5) the power to veto laws passed by Congress

The right answer is (1). The President, as Commander-in-Chief of the American military, can fire or promote military leaders. See paragraph 3, sentence 1, "President Truman . . . subsequently dismissed him from the service."

A third question of the set could be similar to this **comprehension** question:

26. All of the following statements are supported by evidence in the article EXCEPT

    (1) the Korean War lasted for 3 years
    (2) the U.S. was part of a United Nations peace keeping force
    (3) air strikes over China were permitted after MacArthur was removed from the service
    (4) there were conflicting opinions on how to conduct the war
    (5) politicians were afraid that the Korean conflict could become a world war

The right answer is (3). To answer this question you must look for the one *false* statement.

Through a process of elimination you can quickly arrive at the correct answer. Choice (1) is true. The article says that the Korean War lasted from 1950 to 1953, three years. Choice (2) is true. The second sentence of the article says this is so. We know from the information that President Truman and MacArthur disagreed—they had conflicting opinions, choice (4). And we are told that "fears of the possibility of a world war dominated the political . . . climate of the times," choice (5). So only choice (3) is left as a *false* statement. Air strikes over China were *not* permitted before or after MacArthur's dismissal.

SECTION IV: QUESTIONS BASED ON DEFINITIONS

One type of question gives definitions of five related terms or categories and asks you to determine which of the five applies best to a situation described in each question.

The following questions will give you practice in and examples of this type of question.

Remember,

■ Read each definition carefully. Notice the differences among the categories.

■ Match the situation described in each question to the corresponding category.

■ Refer to the categories as often as you need to.

ECONOMICS

You may be given information and categories similar to this:

Items 27 to 29 refer to the following information.

A business combination consists of a group of firms brought together to increase their profits. Listed below are five types of business combinations frequently used in the twentieth century and brief descriptions of how they operate.

(1) cartel—Active competitors agree to fix prices, divide territories, and pool resources according to a predetermined formula.
(2) trust—Independent firms make arrangements to turn over their stock to a trustee who then exercises full control on behalf of the participating firms.
(3) holding company—A corporation gains control of companies related to the corporation's interests; the corporation holds significant stock control on behalf of the participating firms.
(4) merger—A corporation acquires the assets of a smaller firm or firms which are then dissolved. The resulting corporation controls an increased share of the economic market.
(5) conglomerate—A firm in one industry takes control of a firm in another unrelated industry.

Each of the following statements describes a process that takes place in one of the business combinations described above. Choose the combination in which the process described would most likely occur. The categories may be used more than once in the set of items. No one question has more than one best answer.

An **application** question similar to this may follow:

27. The second largest steel company in the U.S. purchases at market value the eighth largest domestic steel company.

    The type of business combination described is a

    (1) cartel
    (2) trust
    (3) holding company
    (4) merger
    (5) conglomerate

The right answer is (4). This question clearly describes a *merger*. The firms conducted business in the same industry—steel.

An **application** question similar to this might be next:

28. A number of Middle Eastern oil producing countries agree with other oil producing nations in Africa, Asia, and South America to fix the price of oil and limit its production. The group calls itself OPEC.

    The type of business combination described is a

    (1) cartel
    (2) trust
    (3) holding company
    (4) merger
    (5) conglomerate

The correct answer is (1). This question fits the definition of an international *cartel*.

An **application** question similar to this could be next:

29. A group of companies agree to keep their prices the same. They accomplish this by exchanging stock certificates in formerly competing corporations in which certificates entitle them to voting power and dividends. Unlike a holding company, members maintain their own identity.

    The type of business combination described is a

    (1) cartel
    (2) trust
    (3) holding company
    (4) merger
    (5) conglomerate

The right answer is (2). Notice that the information tells you that this combination is *unlike* a holding company, so choice (3) *must* be wrong.

ECONOMICS/POLITICAL SCIENCE

You may be given a set similar to this:

Items 30 and 31 refer to the following information.

Economic systems are classified according to the way wealth is distributed among groups in a society. Like political systems, they can be conservative or ultra-liberal. Listed below are five types of economic systems and brief descriptions of how wealth is distributed.

(1) pure capitalism—Basic economic decisions and activities are made and carried out by individuals and businesses without government interference.
(2) modern capitalism—Private ownership of the means of production and freedom of economic choice are the rule except as modified to a limited extent by government regulations.
(3) democratic socialism—The state is the owner of the major means of production, but political freedom is guaranteed.
(4) communism—All means of producing and distributing wealth are collectively owned and operated by the government; all market factors are controlled by the government.
(5) facism—Private ownership is permitted but subject to complete government control of wages, prices, investments, and profits.

Each of the following statements describes a process that takes place in one of the economic systems described above. Choose the system in which the process would most likely occur. The categories may be used more than once in the set of items. No one question has more than one best answer.

An **application** question similar to this could follow:

30. A group of business investors organizes a corporation to fund and operate a railroad company. The government charters the corporation, but limits the geographic area the company can operate in.

The type of economic system described is

(1) pure capitalism
(2) modern capitalism
(3) democratic socialism
(4) communism
(5) facism

The right answer is (2). This question describes *modern capitalism.* Modern capitalism allows ownership subject to government regulation (government charters the corporation and defines the geographic limit). Under democratic socialism (3), private ownership of railroads would not be permitted.

An **application** question similar to this could be next:

31. A government strictly controls the entire economy; the details of running an industry are rigidly controlled, and government planning is forced upon private industry.

    The type of economic system described is

    (1) pure capitalism
    (2) modern capitalism
    (3) democratic socialism
    (4) communism
    (5) facism

The right answer is (5). This question describes *facism.* The key to answering this question is to understand that the entire economy is controlled but private industry is permitted. (The question says that "planning is forced upon private industry," so you know that private industry is not eliminated.) Communism does not permit private ownership in an industry.

TEST 3

SCIENCE

TEST 3: SCIENCE

WHAT TO EXPECT

The Science Test is 1 hour and 35 minutes long and contains 66 multiple-choice questions.

■ Expect questions that will test how well you understand major concepts, ideas, and principles associated with science.

■ Expect settings that are familiar in everyday life. For example, questions about boiling water in a kitchen or flowers growing in a garden would be set in familiar locations.

■ Expect questions that deal with the natural environment, with people's personal lives, and with explanations of natural phenomena.

■ Expect questions that test a high school level understanding of science.

■ Expect about half of the questions to come from the life sciences (biology) and half from the physical sciences (physics, chemistry, and earth science).

■ Expect about one-third of the questions to ask you to understand information in diagrams, charts, maps, graphs, and tables.

■ Expect most of the questions to be in groups, or sets—that is, two to six questions that refer to the same information, diagram, or chart.

WHAT YOU SHOULD KNOW

The Science Test contains the following areas:

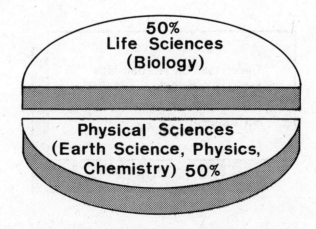

50%
Life Sciences
(Biology)

Physical Sciences
(Earth Science, Physics,
Chemistry) 50%

You should be able to answer questions from information given in the following areas:

LIFE SCIENCES (50%)
(Biology)

Understand information that discusses how **plants** and **animals** are studied by **observation** and **classification**

Understand that the **scientific method** is a way of learning about the physical world

Understand excerpts that explain how **evolution** produced the variety of living things found on Earth

Understand information that deals with how **plants** and **animals grow** and **reproduce**

Understand information that discusses how **DNA** controls the **metabolic processes** of plants and animals

Understand how the **bodies of living things** are **organized** by tissue, organ, and system

Understand the relationships between **living things** and their physical and biological environment

PHYSICAL SCIENCES (50%)
(Earth Science, Physics, Chemistry)

Earth Science

> **Understand** that the **universe** is constantly **changing**

> **Understand** that **erosion, uplift,** and **sedimentation** are always at work on the Earth's crust

> **Understand** that the **Earth's history** can be read in the **fossils** and **changes in** the Earth's **rocks**

Physics

> **Understand** that **energy** is the ability to **move objects**

> **Understand information that explains** Newton's Law of Motion and the relationship between **force** and **motion**

> **Understand information that discusses** how some forms of **energy** can **move** from one place to another by means of **waves**

> **Understand excerpts that discuss** the **difference** between nuclear **fission** and **fusion**

Chemistry

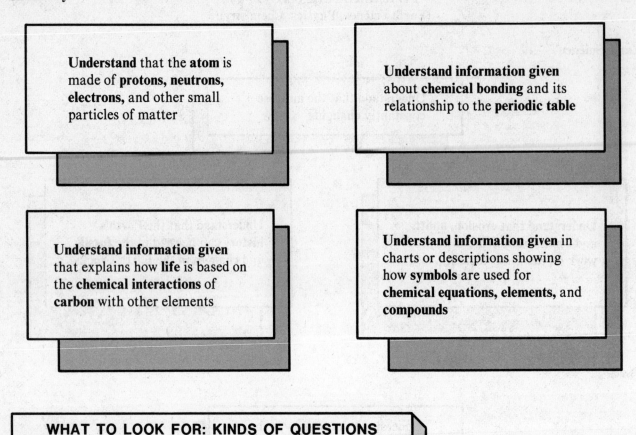

Understand that the atom is made of protons, neutrons, electrons, and other small particles of matter

Understand information given about chemical bonding and its relationship to the periodic table

Understand information given that explains how life is based on the chemical interactions of carbon with other elements

Understand information given in charts or descriptions showing how symbols are used for chemical equations, elements, and compounds

WHAT TO LOOK FOR: KINDS OF QUESTIONS

The GED Science Test will test higher level thinking skills. The exam will *not* ask you to simply remember facts or basic principles of science. For example, you would *not* be expected to know the formula for the acceleration of gravity, or Einstein's Theory of Relativity. However, you *are expected* to understand important concepts and principles in science.

■ Look for questions that ask you to solve a problem.
■ Look for questions that ask you to use your reasoning ability.

The science questions are grouped as follows:

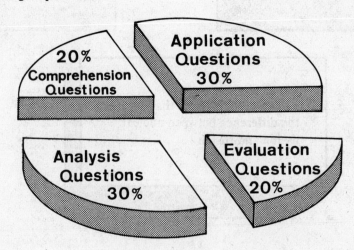

20% Comprehension Questions

Application Questions 30%

Analysis Questions 30%

Evaluation Questions 20%

1. **Comprehension Questions (20%):** You should be able to understand the meaning of information presented in readings as well as in maps, diagrams, charts, and graphs. Comprehension questions can be answered simply from the information presented. Comprehension questions will ask you to understand

   ■ What is the <u>main point</u>?
   ■ What is <u>suggested</u> by the information?

2. **Application Questions (30%):** You should be able to reason one step beyond the comprehension level. You must apply information already stated to solve a problem in a different situation. Application questions will ask you to understand

   ■ How can you use <u>given information</u> in a <u>new setting</u>?
   ■ How can you use <u>suggested information</u> in a <u>new setting</u>?

3. **Analysis Questions (30%):** You should be able to understand the important parts of the information given and the relationships between these parts. You must be able to find the methods used to show how ideas are developed. Analysis questions will ask

   ■ Can you find <u>ideas</u> that are <u>not specifically stated</u>?
   ■ Can you tell what <u>makes an event happen</u> and what are the <u>results</u>?
   ■ Can you tell the <u>difference</u> between a <u>fact</u> and a <u>hypothesis</u>?

4. **Evaluation Questions (20%):** You should be able to judge the accuracy of stated or assumed material and evaluate its importance. Evaluation questions will ask

   ■ Can you tell if the information given would <u>support</u> a <u>point of view</u>?
   ■ Can you detect why <u>events occur</u>?
   ■ Can you find why a <u>hypothesis</u> is <u>not</u> correct?
   ■ Can you <u>predict</u> an <u>outcome</u>?

ABOUT THE DIRECTIONS

Following are the directions you'll find in the Science Test. Become very familiar with these directions *now* so that you will be comfortable with them when you take the actual test. The directions you'll see on the actual test will be wider on the page. Here, though, room has been left for the boxes you see on the right and the left. Read the following directions straight through, and then carefully read the information in the boxes. It points out and explains important points in the directions.

TEST 3: SCIENCE

Tests of General Educational Development

Directions

All questions have **five choices**

The Science Test consists of <u>multiple-choice questions</u> intended to measure the <u>general concepts in science.</u> The questions are based on <u>short readings</u> which often include a graph, chart, or figure. Study the information given and then answer the question(s) following it. <u>Refer to the information</u> as often as necessary in answering the questions.

Information from **short readings or diagrams**

Look back at the **information** as often as you need to

General concepts; **Don't memorize specific facts**

Spend no more than about **1½ minutes per question**

You should spend no more than <u>95 minutes</u> answering the questions in this booklet. Work carefully, but <u>do not spend too much time on any one question. Be sure you answer every question.</u> You <u>will not be penalized for incorrect answers.</u>

Don't get stuck on any question; move on

Each question is **worth** the **same**

No penalty for **guessing** so **guess** if you have to, but don't leave any questions blank

Do not mark in this test booklet. Record your answers to the questions on the separate answer sheet provided. Be sure all requested information is <u>properly recorded</u> on the answer sheet.

Mark your **answers carefully** on the answer sheet

To record your answers, mark the numbered space on the answer sheet beside the number that corresponds to the question in the test booklet.

Unlike this "example," most test questions will **refer to a reading** or **diagram**

FOR EXAMPLE:

Which of the following is the smallest unit in a living thing?

(1) tissue
(2) organ
(3) cell
(4) muscle
(5) capillary   ① ② ● ④ ⑤

The correct answer is "cell"; therefore, answer space 3 would be marked on the answer sheet.

| **Do not make** any **extra marks** on your answer sheet | → | Do not rest the point of your pencil on the answer sheet while you are considering your answer. Make <u>no stray or unnecessary marks</u>. If you change an answer, erase your first mark completely. <u>Mark only one answer</u> space for each question; multiple answers will be scored as incorrect. Do not fold or crease your answer sheet. Return all test materials to the test administrator. | ← | **Mark only one answer** |

WHAT YOU SHOULD DO

Read information looking for the following key points:

- What is the <u>main idea</u>?
- What does the information <u>suggest</u>?
- Can you see <u>causes</u> and <u>results</u>?

Refer to the information, passage, diagram, chart, graph, or map as often as you need to.

Diagrams, charts, graphs, and maps often take a second and a third look. Take an extra few moments to make sure you understand how to read the diagram, chart, graph, or map. Know what information is being presented.

Make sure you understand <u>what the question is asking,</u> for example—

- Which of the following aspects of cats would a veterinarian consider most important?
- All of the following duties are performed by the male ant EXCEPT . . .
- The occurrence of tidal waves in this region indicates . . .
- Which of the following is the <u>best</u> explanation for . . .
- Which of the following behaviors is similar to . . .
- Which of the following has the most value to . . .
- This relationship would best be classified as . . .
- Why is it dangerous to . . .

The following four sections will use examples to explain the **question types**, show you **what to look for**, and point out **what you should do**.

SECTION I: BIOLOGY QUESTIONS

You may be given a **comprehension** question similar to this:

1. During the fertilization of a flower, it is necessary for pollen to reach the central pistil. This fertilization is one mode of sexual reproduction. A male sex cell (pollen) must unite with a female sex cell (ovum within the pistil) to produce a fertile embryo.

   This reproduction requires the contact of two germ cells because

   (1) a chemical reaction initiates the fertilization
   (2) each contains only half the genetic material
   (3) individual cells carry inadequate nutrients
   (4) the wind is too erratic for reliable stimulation
   (5) vegetative reproduction is by the mechanism of budding

The right answer is (2). In this question, you are being asked *why* two germ cells are needed.

The information given explains that this is a form of *sexual* reproduction. "A male sex cell (pollen) must unite with a female sex cell (ovum within the pistil) to produce a fertile embryo." So, each sex cell contains only half the chromosomes (the genetic material) that the plant needs.

You could be given a **comprehension** question similar to this:

2. An amoeba lives in water containing dissolved oxygen, which diffuses, or spreads, from an area of high concentration to an area of low concentration, inward through the cell membrane. The creature's metabolism then produces waste products such as carbon dioxide, which diffuse outward through the cell membrane.

   Which of the following biological processes is most helpful in explaining this life process, or metabolism, of the amoeba?

   (1) hearing
   (2) photosynthesis
   (3) reproduction
   (4) respiration
   (5) secretion

The right answer is (4). You are again asked to understand the information and choose the best explanation for the life process given. Notice the key words, *oxygen* and *carbon dioxide*.

As in other, larger animals, respiration is the central life process during metabolism. Oxygen is taken in to release stored chemical energy, with the production of waste carbon dioxide and water. Remember human respiration: you inhale air rich in oxygen and exhale air rich in carbon dioxide.

You could be given a **comprehension** question similar to this:

3. Milk is pasteurized in order to prevent live disease organisms from being spread to the general public. This heating of the milk for brief periods of time kills any live bacteria but would be useless in the case of chemical contamination.

   Which of the following medical disorders might be <u>prevented</u> by pasteurization?

   (1) halitosis
   (2) lead poisoning
   (3) liver cancer
   (4) tuberculosis
   (5) ulcers

The right answer is (4). To answer this question, you must understand that pasteurization kills "any live bacteria."

Now, which of the answer choices is a medical disorder caused by live bacteria? Tuberculosis could be prevented by pasteurization because it is caused by bacteria.

You could be given an **application** question similar to this:

4. Deer and rabbits are plant-eaters, while eagles and wolves are flesh-eaters.

   Within a single natural community, a rabbit would <u>not</u> interact <u>directly</u> with

   (1) deer
   (2) eagles
   (3) grasses
   (4) shrubs
   (5) wolves

The right answer is (1). Notice that the key word *directly* is underlined. You are looking for what would *not* interact *directly*.

The rabbit would feed on grasses and shrubs. Eagles and wolves would eat the rabbit. But the deer would only *indirectly* compete with the rabbit for the same food.

You could be given an **application** question similar to this:

5. Photosynthesis is the process by which green plants change carbon dioxide and water into sugar and oxygen.

Which of the following should happen to the air in a sealed greenhouse containing many plants?

A. The air becomes poorer in carbon dioxide.
B. The air becomes poorer in oxygen.
C. The air becomes richer in carbon dioxide.

(1) A only
(2) B only
(3) A and B only
(4) B and C only
(5) A, B, and C

The right answer is (1). Because plants use carbon dioxide and water, the air would become *poorer* in those compounds. So A must be true. You can now eliminate answer choices (2) and (4) because they do not contain A.

The plants produce sugar and oxygen, so the air would become *richer* in oxygen. So B must be false. So you can eliminate choices (3) and (5). This leaves only answer choice (1).

You might be given an **analysis** question similar to this:

6. Sickle-cell anemia is a disease you can inherit in which the hemoglobin (an iron-bearing, oxygen transporting) molecule is abnormal. The abnormal molecule has one incorrect amino acid within a chain of over 300 amino acids.

Which of the following best accounts for the origin of this disorder?

(1) carbon monoxide poisoning
(2) infection
(3) mutation
(4) poor nutrition
(5) age

The right answer is (3). To answer this question, you need to carefully analyze the information given.

Notice the important words—*inherit, abnormal molecule, amino acids*. These key words should lead you to the correct answer. Chromosomes carry coded messages (amino acids) with information for the building of the molecules necessary for life. Sometimes the message is slightly altered (abnormal molecule) and that *mutation* would be passed on to succeeding generations (inherited).

Another type of **analysis** question could be similar to this:

7. The Chernobyl nuclear power plant explosion released many radioactive elements, including radioactive iodine. Thyroid glands are known to accumulate iodine, an essential element in its hormone. Soon after the explosion, many Europeans took medical doses of potassium iodide.

Which of the following statements best explains how potassium iodide helped protect them from some radioactivity?

(1) It restored their normal electrolyte balance.
(2) They had filled, or saturated, their glands with nonradioactive iodine.
(3) The potassium was an antidote for radioactive iodine.
(4) They knew the radioactivity would decay rapidly.
(5) The thyroid hormone would stimulate resistance to radioactivity.

The right answer is (2). To answer this question, you must first carefully analyze the information given.

Radioactive iodine was released by the power plant and would probably be absorbed by the thyroid glands of many Europeans. So, by taking harmless iodine in the solution of potassium iodide, these Europeans temporarily saturated their thyroid glands in that element. Their bodies would then not accumulate any radioactive iodine.

You could be given an **evaluation** question similar to this:

8. The tumbleweed almost never grows anywhere but on plowed fields, overgrazed ranges, or along roads.

Which of the following best explains the relationship of the tumbleweed to its environment?

(1) It can't compete with established plants.
(2) It destroys the natural environment.
(3) It interrupts the customary food chain.
(4) It is a delicate, endangered species.
(5) It requires an unusually dry environment.

The right answer is (1). To answer this question you must evaluate the relationship between a tumbleweed and its environment.

The description tells us that the tumbleweed does not grow in normal, undisturbed communities. Evidently it is not able to compete successfully with established plants.

Another type of **evaluation** question might be similar to this:

9. Life may be defined in many ways. Some of the points considered in defining life are metabolism, growth, reproduction, and motion. Viruses are sometimes classified as living organisms and sometimes as chemical compounds.

   Which of the following properties is the <u>best</u> evidence for considering viruses as being alive?

   (1) They are submicroscopic, commonly smaller than bacteria.
   (2) They are found inside animals, plants, and one-celled organisms.
   (3) They may produce diseases in their host organisms.
   (4) They possess nucleic acids to reproduce themselves.
   (5) They possess the ability to become larger in size.

The right answer is (4). To answer this question, you must evaluate the given information and decide which is the *best* evidence.

Metabolism, growth, and motions are all points considered in defining life. But the most important point about life is that living organisms can reproduce. Because viruses have that key ability, they are usually classified as being alive. Choice (5) the ability to become larger in size may be a possibility. But nonliving things can also become larger in size—such as objects becoming larger because of heat. Remember, you are looking for the best evidence.

You could be given an excerpt similar to this followed by two questions:

Items 10 and 11 refer to the following information.

Darwin suggested that natural selection was the method used for the evolution of life forms. Individuals that were able to compete more successfully for food would reproduce more often than less able individuals, and so a species would gradually change toward its more successful variations. Small changes, accumulated over millions of years, could lead to strikingly new forms of life.

An **analysis** question similar to this could follow:

10. In Darwin's theory, the word <u>selection</u> means

    (1) evolution of life
    (2) gradual reproduction
    (3) natural formation
    (4) successful competition
    (5) variation of ability

The right answer is (4). To answer this question you must analyze the information given. The key phrase is "Individuals that were able to compete more successfully . . ."

The individuals that would be selected for reproduction would tend to be those that competed most successfully. Natural selection is often described as "the survival of the fittest."

A second **analysis** question similar to this could be next:

11. For small changes to accumulate eventually into a new life form, each single change or variation in an organism would have to be

    (1) frequent
    (2) inheritable
    (3) mechanical
    (4) probable
    (5) unstable

The right answer is (2). To answer this question you must analyze the information and question carefully. Notice the important phrase "changes to accumulate."

Only changes that could be *inherited* would accumulate (add up). Over many generations, the many small changes would persist and result in a large overall change of the organism.

You could be given information in chart or table form similar to this:

Items 12 to 15 refer to the following table, which shows characteristics of some major groups of animals.

Animal Group	Mobility (ability to move)	Symmetry (evenly proportioned)	Further Description
Arthropods	high	bilateral	organism divided into segments and organism covered with external skeleton
Chordates	high	bilateral	organism has internal skeleton
Coelenterates	none	radial	cavity surrounded by tentacles
Echinoderms	slight	five-fold	organism has heavy protective skeleton
Mollusks	slight	bilateral	organism has one or two hard shells

Note: Bilateral symmetry means that the left side and the right side are mirror images.

An **application** question similar to this could follow:

12. A clam is a muscular animal within a matching pair of protective shells.

    The clam would be best classified in which of the following animal groups?

    (1) arthropods
    (2) chordates
    (3) coelenterates
    (4) echinoderms
    (5) mollusks

The right answer is (5). The clam is a mollusk.

You should notice the phrase "matching pair of protective shells." This is part of the description of a mollusk. The clam has slight mobility on the sea floor, and it lives within two hard shells.

An **analysis** question similar to this might follow:

13. An eagle, a shark, and a squirrel are all vertebrates, characterized by a supportive backbone and advanced nervous system.

    Which of the following animal groups would include all vertebrates?

    (1) arthropods
    (2) chordates
    (3) coelenterates
    (4) echinoderms
    (5) mollusks

The right answer is (2). All vertebrate animals belong in the group of chordates.

The *internal skeletons* of the eagle, shark, and squirrel should point you toward the second answer choice. A human being is also classified as a chordate.

Another **application** question similar to this could follow:

14. The common starfish is not a fish at all. It can flex its stiff body to move along the sea floor by slow crawling.

    The starfish would best be classified in which of the following animal groups?

    (1) arthropods
    (2) chordates
    (3) coelenterates
    (4) echinoderms
    (5) mollusks

The right answer is (4). The starfish is an echinoderm. To answer this question, you need to apply the information given and your knowledge of a starfish.

Since the starfish moves slowly, you can eliminate answer choices (1), (2), and (3). You can eliminate choice (5) because a starfish does *not* have shells. Its body is stiff because of the heavy case which protects it against predators. The starfish has five arms, so its *five-fold symmetry* is another good clue for classification.

The last question could be an **application** question similar to this:

15. Bees, spiders, and lobsters have bodies with many common features.

    Which of the following is the best classification for all three of these animals?

    (1) arthropods
    (2) chordates
    (3) coelenterates
    (4) echinoderms
    (5) mollusks

The right answer is (1). Since all of these animals are very mobile, answer choices (1) and (2) are the only ones possible. The segmented bodies and hard external skeletons are the final clues.

You could be given information in a method similar to this:

Items 16 to 18 refer to the following information and chart.

There are many factors that should be taken into account to find an individual's "ideal" weight. In general, however, fat ordinarily accounts for 10 to 20 percent of the weight of an adult male, and about 25 percent of the weight of an adult female. Any more fat than this is considered unnecessary and unhealthy. The following chart shows acceptable weight in pounds according to height for men and women.

Height ft. in.	Men acceptable weight	Women acceptable weight
4 8		88–113
4 9		90–116
4 10		92–119
4 11		94–122
5 0	106–135	96–125
5 1	109–138	99–128
5 2	112–141	102–131
5 3	115–144	105–134
5 4	118–148	108–138
5 5	121–152	111–142
5 6	124–156	114–146
5 7	128–161	118–150
5 8	132–166	122–154
5 9	136–170	126–158
5 10	140–174	130–163
5 11	144–179	134–168
6 0	148–184	138–173
6 1	152–189	
6 2	156–194	
6 3	160–199	
6 4	164–204	

A **comprehension** question similar to this could follow:

16. The maximum acceptable weight for a 5'9" man is

    (1) 136 lbs.
    (2) 158 lbs.
    (3) 170 lbs.
    (4) 174 lbs.
    (5) 179 lbs.

The right answer is (3). To answer this question you must simply read information next to 5'9" in the men's column (136–170). The maximum (the largest amount) is 170 pounds.

An **analysis** question similar to this could be next:

17. The greatest <u>range</u> of acceptable weight is for a woman who is

    (1) 5' 8"
    (2) 5' 9"
    (3) 5'10"
    (4) 5'11"
    (5) 6' 0"

The right answer is (5). To answer this question you must notice that the *range* (the distance between acceptable weights) increases as the *weight* increases. So it also increases as the *height* increases.

The largest range for a woman is 35 pounds, which is for a woman 6'0" tall (173 − 138 = 35).

Another **analysis** question similar to this could follow:

18. Jack weighs the <u>maximum</u> acceptable weight for a 6'3" man. Gloria weighs the <u>minimum</u> acceptable weight for a 4'8" woman.

    What is the <u>difference</u> between their weights?

    (1)   25 lbs.
    (2)   72 lbs.
    (3)   86 lbs.
    (4) 101 lbs.
    (5) 111 lbs.

The right answer is (5). To answer this question you must read the chart carefully and do one simple calculation.

If Jack is 6'3", his maximum (highest) weight is 199 pounds. Gloria's minimum (lowest) weight for 4'8" is 88 pounds. Now, 199 − 88 = 111 pounds.

You could be given a graph similar to this:

Items 19 to 20 refer to the graph below.

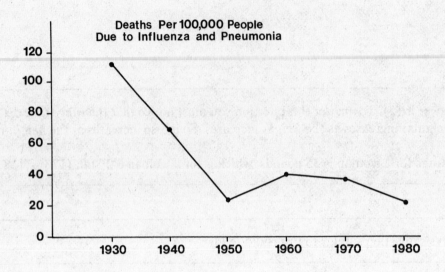

Deaths Per 100,000 People
Due to Influenza and Pneumonia

A **comprehension** question similar to this could follow:

19. Between which of the following years did the deaths per 100,000 people due to influenza and pneumonia <u>increase</u>?

    (1) 1930 and 1940
    (2) 1940 and 1950
    (3) 1950 and 1960
    (4) 1960 and 1970
    (5) 1970 and 1980

The right answer is (3). To answer this question, you must understand how to read the information given in a line graph.

Since the question is asking for the years with an *increase* between them, look for the line that slopes up to the right. The only increase would be between 1950 and 1960.

A **comprehension** question similar to this could be next:

20. All of the following information may be determined from the graph EXCEPT

   (1) the decrease in deaths per 100,000 people due to influenza and pneumonia from 1940 to 1950
   (2) the years that had the fewest deaths per 100,000 people due to influenza and pneumonia
   (3) the years that had the greatest number of deaths per 100,000 people due to influenza and pneumonia
   (4) the decrease in deaths per 100,000 people due to influenza and pneumonia from 1970 to 1980
   (5) the decrease in deaths per 100,000 people due to pneumonia only from 1940 to 1950

The right answer is (5). To answer this question, you must understand what information the graph is giving you.

The graph does *not* separate influenza deaths from pneumonia deaths. So, you cannot determine information regarding pneumonia *alone*.

SECTION II: PHYSICS QUESTIONS

You could be given a **comprehension** question similar to this:

21. If Regina shouts "Hello," her vocal cords vibrate and start the air vibrating. Although individual molecules in the air do not move very far, each moving molecule passes on that motion to the next molecule.

   Which of the following would be the best explanation of the physical process that enables someone to hear her shout?

   (1) A gas expands in all directions to reach you.
   (2) The molecules in the atmosphere are temporarily deformed.
   (3) Movement is generally from high pressure toward low pressure.
   (4) A pattern of vibrations is set up in the air.
   (5) Tiny particles move from her mouth to someone's ear.

The right answer is (4). To answer this question, you must understand the information given.

The paragraph says that "her vocal cords vibrate and start the air vibrating." Another way to say this is "a pattern of vibrations is set up in the air."

Another type of **comprehension** question might be similar to this:

22. <u>Weight</u> is defined as the product of mass and the acceleration of gravity. <u>Weightlessness</u> occurs when the centrifugal force created by orbiting around the Earth precisely counterbalances the gravitational force toward the Earth.

An astronaut in orbit is said to be <u>weightless</u> when

(1) the acceleration due to motion balances that of gravity
(2) the gravitational attraction of the moon balances that of the Earth
(3) gravity vanishes due to high altitude
(4) mass vanishes due to high velocity
(5) mass and acceleration are very nearly equal

The right answer is (1). To answer this question, you must understand the information given. Revolving in orbit around the Earth creates a centrifugal force directed *away* from the Earth. "Weightlessness occurs when that centrifugal force precisely counterbalances the gravitational force toward the Earth."

When this motion pulling *away* from Earth balances the pull of gravity *toward* the Earth, the astronaut becomes weightless. An important word here is *balance*.

You could be given a **comprehension** question similar to this:

23. In Einstein's famous law $\underline{E} = \underline{mc}^2$, the three symbols represent

$\underline{E}$ is energy
$\underline{m}$ is mass
$\underline{c}$ is velocity of light (a constant)

One meaning of that law is that a small amount of matter could be converted into

(1) exactly the same amount of matter
(2) a very low velocity
(3) abundant energy
(4) bright light
(5) a large amount of mass

The right answer is (3). To answer this question, you must understand that the law shows the relationship between mass and energy. The question says "...matter could be converted to..." The mass (of the matter) is on one side of the equation, so the energy is on the other side. That is, the matter could be converted to energy. The equation reads like this: "Energy equals mass times the velocity of light squared (taken times itself)."

Because the velocity of light is very high, the constant *c* is a very large amount. So a small amount of mass could be transformed into a large amount of energy. This explains the high energy released by nuclear fission and fusion.

You may be given an **application** question similar to this:

24. Conservation of energy, the law that says that energy can be neither created nor destroyed, is one of the basic cornerstones of physics.

    Using that principle, which of the following is the best explanation of what has happened to some of the heat energy within a room being cooled by an air conditioner?

    (1) It diminished by reaction with oxygen.
    (2) It has condensed within the air conditioner.
    (3) It is only temporarily extinguished.
    (4) It was lost by expansion of refrigerant gas.
    (5) It was transferred into the outside air.

The right answer is (5). To answer this question, you must apply this law of physics.

Since energy is conserved, the total amount of energy is always the same, or constant. So some of the heat energy in the room must have been pumped to the outside air.

You could be given an **analysis** question similar to this:

25. Imagine that Robert is indoors admiring himself in a mirror by the light of a lamp. The light rays that generate such a good self-image have taken a complicated journey.

    Which of the following is the correct sequence of travel for the light?

    (1) bulb-eye-mirror-face
    (2) face-bulb-mirror-eye
    (3) bulb-face-mirror-eye
    (4) mirror-bulb-face-eye
    (5) bulb-mirror-face-eye

The right answer is (3). To answer this question you must first decide where this journey begins.

The source of the light is the bulb. That light reflects from Robert's face and then is reflected again from the mirror. The light finally enters his eye. If you realize that the light begins at the bulb and ends at his eye, you can eliminate choices (1), (2), and (4).

You could be given an **analysis** question similar to this:

Item 26 refers to the following diagram.

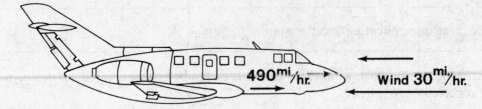

26. A jet airplane is flying against a stiff headwind as pictured above. Inside, a stewardess walks toward the front of the plane. Her walking speed is 2 miles per hour (mi/hr). The jet plane moves through the air at 490 mi/hr. The wind is blowing at 30 mi/hr.

    What is the velocity of the stewardess relative to the ground?

    (1) 458 mi/hr
    (2) 462 mi/hr
    (3) 488 mi/hr
    (4) 518 mi/hr
    (5) 522 mi/hr

The right answer is (2). To find her speed you must combine the three separate velocities.

For this calculation, let's call the plane's forward motion *positive* and the wind's motion against the plane (in the opposite direction) *negative*. The plane's velocity is +490 mi/hr. The wind velocity is −30 mi/hr. The velocity of the stewardess relative to the plane is +2 mi/hr, positive because she walks forward. Combining all three numbers, you get

$$+490 + (-30) + 2 = +460 + 2 = 462 \text{ mi/hr}$$

You might be given an **evaluation** question similar to this:

27. The amount of energy in foods is measured in calories, as are other forms of energy. To lose weight, a person's energy <u>use</u> must be greater than his or her energy <u>consumption</u>. Which of the following activities would allow a person to lose weight?

    A. eat smaller portions of usual foods
    B. eat nutritious foods high in energy
    C. exercise somewhat more than usual

    (1) C only
    (2) A and B only
    (3) A and C only
    (4) B and C only
    (5) A, B, and C

The right answer is (3). Eating smaller portions would *reduce* energy consumption, so you can eliminate answer choices (1) and (4) because they do not contain A. Eating high-energy foods would *increase* the intake of energy, so you can eliminate choices (2) and (5) because they have B in their answers. Energy *use* could be *increased* by exercising more than usual, so C is true. The activities that allow a person to lose weight are A and C.

SECTION III: CHEMISTRY QUESTIONS

<u>Items 28 and 29</u> refer to the following paragraph.

The three active ingredients in baking powder are sodium bicarbonate, sodium aluminum sulfate, and tartaric acid. The sodium bicarbonate can react with either of the other ingredients to yield gas bubbles, which cause dough to swell, or rise.

You could be given a **comprehension** question similar to this:

28. According to the paragraph, which of the following ingredients <u>must</u> be present for gas bubbles to occur?

    A. sodium bicarbonate
    B. sodium aluminum sulfate
    C. tartaric acid

    (1) A only
    (2) B only
    (3) C only
    (4) B and C only
    (5) A, B, and C

The right answer is (1). To answer this question you must understand the information given.

Since the paragraph says that sodium bicarbonate can react with *either* of the other ingredients to yield gas bubbles, the sodium bicarbonate *must* be present. Either sodium aluminum sulfate or tartaric acid *could* be present.

An **application** question similar to this could be next:

29. Considering the information above, why doesn't the chemical reaction occur in the baking powder can rather than in the dough?

    (1) Any reaction needs some time to proceed to completion.
    (2) The can protects the ingredients from contact with the air.
    (3) Gas expands in an open baking dish, not a closed can.
    (4) The ingredients require moisture to initiate the reaction.
    (5) Tartaric acid in the baking powder is the main catalyst for the reaction.

The right answer is (4). To answer this question you must apply some knowledge and reasoning.

The moisture in the dough allows the reaction to begin. The chemicals must be in solution to come into close enough contact to react.

You might be given an **application** question similar to this:

30. One of the ideas of the molecular theory is that molecules are always moving.

    Which of the following would best demonstrate this idea?

    (1) A spoonful of sugar is added to a cup of cocoa and the cocoa becomes sweet in all parts of the cup.
    (2) A small stone is dropped into a glass of water and falls straight to the bottom.
    (3) An ice cube is placed in a cold container and melts very slowly.
    (4) A cup of tea is completely full, yet a tablespoon of sugar can be added and the cup does not overflow.
    (5) A drop of oil is added to a pan of water and the oil stays together and floats on top.

The right answer is (1). To answer this question you must apply this idea to a *different situation*.

If the sugar is added to the cocoa, it is obviously added to one spot. The movement of the molecules helps distribute it to the rest of the cup.

You could be given an **analysis** question similar to this:

31. An electrically neutral atom of neon has 10 protons and 10 neutrons in its nucleus, surrounded by 10 electrons. Each proton has a charge of +1 and each electron has a charge of −1.

   If an electrical current through a lighting fixture changes the number of electrons to create neon atoms with charges of +2, then how many electrons surround each neon nucleus?

   (1) 2
   (2) 8
   (3) 10
   (4) 11
   (5) 12

The right answer is (2). Each neon atom with a charge of +2 must have 10 protons and 8 electrons.

Do the math this way: $10(+1) + 8(-2) = +2$. Since the electrons are on the outside of each atom, the number of electrons can be changed fairly easily.

You may be given an **evaluation** question similar to this:

32. Pure nitrogen is obtained commercially by first liquefying air, which is 78% nitrogen. This liquefying can be accomplished by changing temperature or pressure or both.

   Which of the following would be the best way to condense air to a liquid?

   (1) lowering the temperature very quickly
   (2) lowering the pressure very quickly
   (3) lowering the temperature while raising the pressure
   (4) lowering the pressure while leaving the temperature constant
   (5) raising the temperature

The right answer is (3). Lowering the temperature can change a gas into a liquid. But raising the pressure leads to the same result because it forces the molecules closer together.

The best procedure would be to lower the temperature of the air while you increase the pressure.

You could be given an **evaluation** question similar to this:

33. When air comes in contact with wet iron, the oxygen in the air combines with the iron to form iron oxide, or rust. In trying to stop the rusting process, chemists looked for something to keep the oxygen in the air from touching the iron. But this material could not combine with or damage the iron. Paint is most commonly used to stop rusting, but sometimes using paint is not practical. For example, many tools should not be painted.

   Which of the following materials would be best to stop the rusting of tools?

   (1) baking powder
   (2) oil
   (3) alcohol
   (4) window cleaner
   (5) saltwater

The right answer is (2). Oil acts in much the same way as paint to prevent chemical changes in iron. Wiping tools with an oily rag is a common practice.

You may be given an **evaluation** question similar to this:

34. Some boxes and bottles have labels that read: Keep in a cool, dry place. Do not open near flame. Keep away from excessive heat. Do not expose to light.

   Which of the following is the best explanation for the use of these labels?

   (1) These warnings tell you that undesirable chemical changes may take place if the instructions are not followed.
   (2) These warnings notify you of proper disposal of these materials.
   (3) These labels warn you of the danger of these materials to small children.
   (4) These labels are have little value but are required by law to be placed on certain containers.
   (5) These warnings are included to make sure the user is properly informed of the correct uses of these materials.

The right answer is (1). Excessive heat, dampness, or exposure to light or flame may cause the materials to spoil or react in an undesirable and sometimes dangerous way.

Notice that the labels mentioned do not discuss the *uses* of the materials.

Items 35 and 36 refer to the following diagram.

Circles labeled H and O represent hydrogen and oxygen atoms, bonded into molecules by the straight lines between them. The larger box indicates a greater volume than the smaller box.

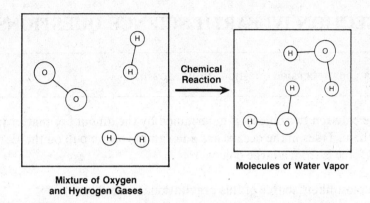

**Mixture of Oxygen
and Hydrogen Gases**

Molecules of Water Vapor

You could be given an **analysis** question similar to this:

35. In the diagram, the relative sizes of the boxes illustrates the rule that the volume of a gas is proportional to the

    (1) number of atoms
    (2) number of chemical elements
    (3) number of molecules
    (4) pressure
    (5) temperature

The right answer is (3). The number of *atoms* and *elements* in each box is the same. But the larger box does have 50% more *molecules* (3 shown) than the smaller box (2 shown).

So the diagram illustrates the rule that gas *volume* is directly proportional to the *number of molecules*. The nature of the molecules does not make any difference in the volume. The diagram gives us no information about pressure or temperature.

You could be given a **comprehension** question similar to this:

36. The diagram shows that molecules of oxygen (O_2) and hydrogen (H_2) can react to yield molecules of water vapor (H_2O).

How would you describe the essence of this chemical reaction?

    (1) a change in the bonding of atoms
    (2) a combination of small molecules into larger atoms
    (3) a splitting of molecules into separate atoms
    (4) a splitting of the atomic nuclei
    (5) a doubling in size of the hydrogen atom

The right answer is (1). The reaction is primarily a change in the bonding of atoms.

The bonds within the molecules on the left side are broken, and new bonds between hydrogen and oxygen atoms appear on the right side.

SECTION IV: EARTH SCIENCE QUESTIONS

You could be given a **comprehension** question similar to this:

37. Gravitational force between two objects is determined by the amount of matter in the objects and the distance between them. Tides in the oceans are an example of the pull on the Earth and its oceans. That gravitational force is from a large object.

    What object is the most likely source of this gravitational force?

    (1) coastal mountain range
    (2) nearest continent
    (3) shallow earthquake
    (4) the moon
    (5) the sun

The right answer is (4). The moon's gravitational attraction produces the tides.

When the Earth is nearest the moon, the ocean surface is pulled upward by several feet. The influence of the larger sun is less important because the sun is so much further away than is the moon.

You might be given an **application** question similar to this:

38. Corrasion is defined as wind erosion. Corrasion would be limited by vegetation (plant cover), snow cover, high rainfall, or lack of wind.

    In which of the following sites would you expect the most corrasion?

    (1) desert basin
    (2) mountain range
    (3) prairie grassland
    (4) sheltered valley
    (5) tropical jungle

The right answer is (1). The desert basin would suffer the most erosion by wind.

The absence of plant cover and abundance of loose material permit much corrasion. Sand-size material that is eroded accumulates downwind as dunes.

You could be given an **application** question similar to this:

39. An <u>igneous rock</u> is produced by the solidification of a melted rock. The molten rock could cool and become solid either deep within the Earth or at the Earth's surface.

Which of the following processes yields an igneous rock?

(1) accumulation of a coral reef
(2) compaction and burial of plant remains
(3) the build-up of deposits along a beach
(4) eruption of a volcano
(5) growth of a stalactite

The right answer is (4). The lava erupted by a volcano is molten rock material at a temperature of about 1200° C. So all volcanic rocks are classified as igneous.

None of the other choices involves melted rock.

<u>Item 40</u> refers to the following diagram of the circulation of water near the Earth's surface.

THE HYDROLOGIC CYCLE

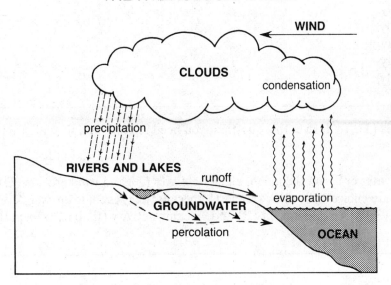

You might be given an **analysis** question similar to this:

40. During the water, or hydrologic, cycle, at which stage would the water be the cleanest, or purest?

(1) cloud
(2) groundwater
(3) lake
(4) ocean
(5) river

The right answer is (1). The purest water is in the clouds.

That water comes from the evaporation of sea water. During evaporation, all dissolved contaminants are left behind in the oceans. The oceans are salty because of evaporation.

You could be given an **evaluation** question similar to this:

41. The moon has no water or air, yet its surface shows rocks and other interesting features.

Which of the following processes would a scientist consider as the most important in forming the moon's surface?

A. glacier activity
B. meteorite impact
C. volcanic activity
D. wind erosion

(1) A and B only
(2) A and C only
(3) B and C only
(4) B and D only
(5) C and D only

The right answer is (3). To answer this question, you need to analyze and evaluate the information given.

Since there is no water or air on the moon, glacier activity (A) and wind erosion (D) are not possible. So you can eliminate choices (1), (2), (4), and (5) because they include answer A or answer D. The only choice left is (3). Meteorite impact (B) and volcanic activity (C) had to form the moon's surface.

TEST 4

INTERPRETING LITERATURE AND THE ARTS

TEST 4: INTERPRETING LITERATURE AND THE ARTS

WHAT TO EXPECT

The Interpreting Literature and the Arts Test is 1 hour and 5 minutes long and contains 45 multiple-choice questions.

■ Expect questions that will test how well you understand selections from different types of literature, such as nonfiction, fiction, poetry, and drama.

■ Expect reading selections to be between 200 and 400 words long.

■ Expect each selection to be followed by two to eight questions.

■ Expect a brief, easy-to-read question (purpose question) before each selection to help you in understanding the reading.

■ Expect to be able to answer the questions based on the reading. (A previous knowledge of literary works is not necessary.)

WHAT YOU SHOULD KNOW

The Interpreting Literature and the Arts Test will use selections from the following areas:

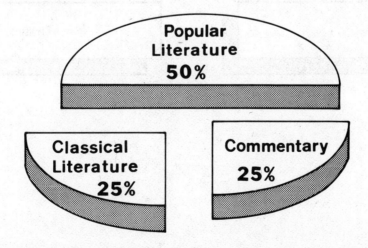

Popular Literature 50%

Classical Literature 25%

Commentary 25%

You should know how to read, understand, and answer questions from the following areas: (Previous knowledge of these types of literature is not necessary.)

POPULAR LITERATURE (50%)

These selections will be written by well-known and respected modern writers.

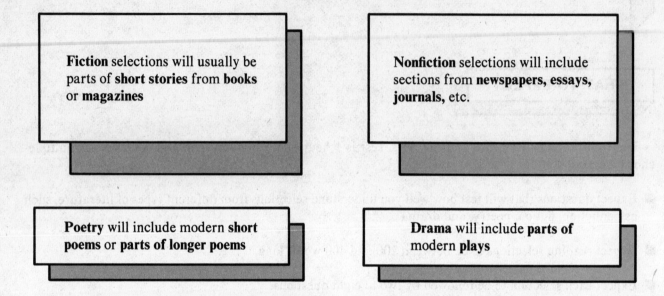

Fiction selections will usually be parts of **short stories** from **books** or **magazines**

Nonfiction selections will include sections from **newspapers, essays, journals,** etc.

Poetry will include modern **short poems** or **parts of longer poems**

Drama will include **parts of** modern **plays**

CLASSICAL LITERATURE (25%)

These selections will be taken from works known as "classics" of the nineteenth and twentieth centuries.

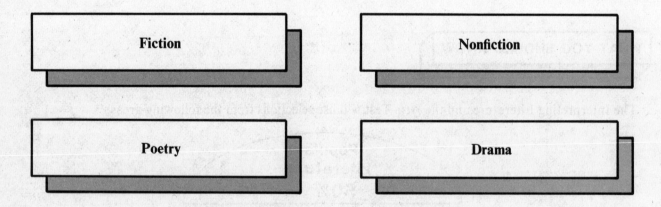

Fiction

Nonfiction

Poetry

Drama

COMMENTARY (25%)

These selections will be *about* literature and arts.

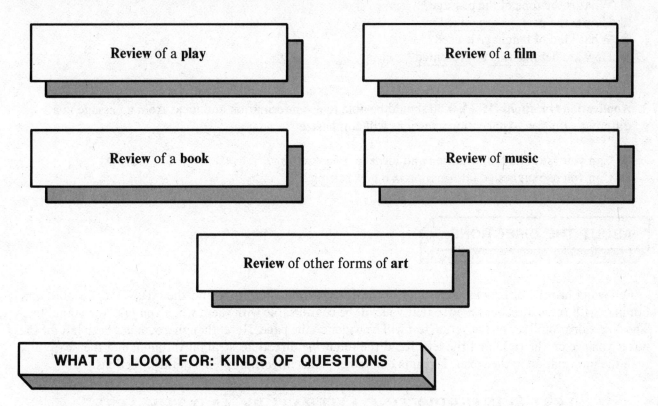

Review of a **play**

Review of a **film**

Review of a **book**

Review of **music**

Review of other forms of **art**

WHAT TO LOOK FOR: KINDS OF QUESTIONS

The GED Interpreting Literature and the Arts Test will test a higher level of thinking skills. You will not be asked to simply repeat or remember information. The exam questions are grouped as follows:

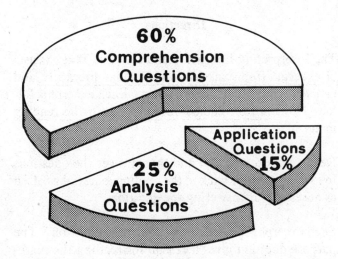

60%
Comprehension
Questions

Application
Questions
15%

25%
Analysis
Questions

1. **Comprehension Questions (60%):** You should be able to understand the meaning and purpose of the reading.

   The comprehension questions emphasize understanding

   ■ What does the reading <u>state</u>?
   ■ What does the reading <u>suggest</u>?

2. **Analysis Questions (25%):** You should be able to examine the style and structure of the passage. Analysis questions will emphasize

- What is the <u>tone</u> of the passage?
- How is the passage <u>organized</u>?
- What kind of <u>language</u> is <u>used</u>?
- How are <u>details used</u> or <u>presented</u>?

3. **Application Questions (15%):** You should be able to use information and ideas from a passage in a different situation. Application questions will emphasize

- Can you use <u>stated information and ideas</u> in a <u>new setting</u>?
- Can you use <u>suggested information</u> in a <u>new setting</u>?

ABOUT THE DIRECTIONS

Following are the directions you'll find in the Interpreting Literature and the Arts Test. Become very familiar with these directions *now* so that you will be comfortable with them when you take the actual test. The directions you'll see on the actual test will be wider on the page. Here, though, room has been left for the boxes you see on the right and the left. Read the following directions straight through, and then carefully read the information in the boxes. It points out and explains important points in the directions.

TEST 4: INTERPRETING LITERATURE AND THE ARTS

Tests of General Educational Development

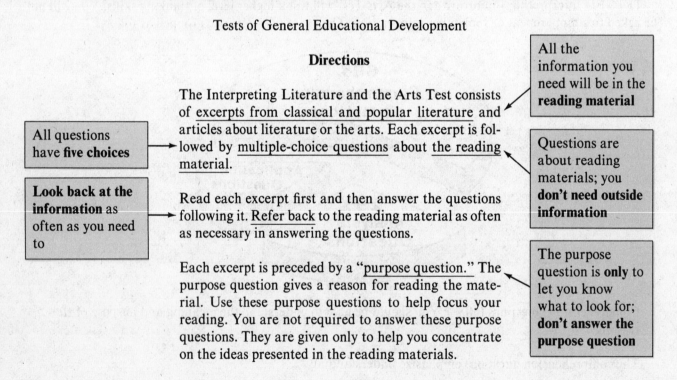

Directions

The Interpreting Literature and the Arts Test consists of excerpts from classical and popular literature and articles about literature or the arts. Each excerpt is followed by <u>multiple-choice questions</u> about <u>the reading material</u>.

Read each excerpt first and then answer the questions following it. <u>Refer back</u> to the reading material as often as necessary in answering the questions.

Each excerpt is preceded by a "<u>purpose question</u>." The purpose question gives a reason for reading the material. Use these purpose questions to help focus your reading. You are not required to answer these purpose questions. They are given only to help you concentrate on the ideas presented in the reading materials.

All the information you need will be in the **reading material**

All questions have **five choices**

Questions are about reading materials; you **don't need outside information**

Look back at the information as often as you need to

The purpose question is **only** to let you know what to look for; **don't answer the purpose question**

Don't get stuck on any question; move on

Each question is **worth** the same

You should spend no more than 65 minutes answering the questions in this booklet. Work carefully, but do not spend too much time on any one question. Be sure you answer every question. you will not be penalized for incorrect answers.

Spend no more than about 1½ minutes per question

No penalty for guessing so **guess** if you have to, but don't leave any questions blank

Mark your **answers carefully** on the answer sheet

Do not mark in the test booklet. Record your answers on the separate answer sheet provided. Be sure all requested information is properly recorded on the answer sheet. To record your answers, mark the numbered space on the answer sheet beside the number that corresponds to the question in the test booklet.

Notice that this question **refers to a reading;** almost all questions follow this format

FOR EXAMPLE:

It was Susan's dream machine. The metallic blue paint gleamed, and the sporty wheels were highly polished. Under the hood, the engine was no less carefully cleaned. Inside, flashy lights illuminated the instruments on the dashboard, and the seats were covered by rich leather upholstery.

The subject ("It") of this excerpt is most likely

(1) an airplane
(2) a stereo system
(3) an automobile
(4) a boat
(5) a motorcycle ① ② ● ④ ⑤

The correct answer is "an automobile"; therefore, answer space 3 would be marked on the answer sheet.

Do not make any **extra marks** on your answer sheet

Do not rest the point of your pencil on the answer sheet while you are considering your answer. Make no stray or unnecessary marks. If you change an answer, erase your first mark completely. Mark only one answer-space for each question; multiple answers will be scored as incorrect. Do not fold or crease your answer sheet. Return all test materials to the test administrator.

Mark only one answer

WHAT YOU SHOULD DO

 Pay special attention to the "purpose" question.

 Sample a few questions before reading each passage.

 Answer each question based only on information in the passage.

 Eliminate answer choices that are not relevant (have nothing to do with the reading).

 Eliminate choices that disagree with something in the passage.

The following sections will use examples to carefully explain the **question types,** show you **what to look for,** and point out **what you should do.**

SECTION I

You could be given the following type of reading:

Items 1 to 8 refer to the following speech.

WHAT IS GOOD ADVICE FOR YOUNG PEOPLE?

Being told I would be expected to talk here, I inquired what sort of talk I ought to make. They said it should be something suitable to youth—something didactic, instructive, or something in the nature of good advice. Very well. I have a few things in my mind which I have often longed to say for the instruction of the young; for it is in one's tender early years that such things will best take root and be
(5) most enduring and most valuable. First, then, I will say to you, my young friends—and I say it beseechingly, urgingly—

Always obey your parents, when they are present. This is the best policy in the long run, because if you don't they will make you. Most parents think they know better than you do, and you can generally make more by humoring that superstition than you can by acting on your own better judgment.
(10) Be respectful to your superiors, if you have any, also to strangers, and sometimes to others. If a person offend you, and you are in doubt as to whether it was intentional or not, do not resort to extreme measures, simply watch your chance and hit him with a brick. That will be sufficient. If you shall find that he had not intended any offense, come out frankly and confess yourself in the wrong

(15) when you struck him; acknowledge it like a man and say you didn't mean to. Yes, always avoid violence in this age of charity and kindliness, the time has gone by for such things. Leave dynamite to the low and unrefined.

(20) Go to bed early, get up early—this is wise. Some authorities say get up with the sun; some others say get up with one thing, some with another. But a lark is really the best thing to get up with. It gives you a splendid reputation with everybody to know that you get up with the lark; and if you get the right kind of a lark, and work at him right, you can easily train him to get up at half past nine, every time—it is no trick at all.

(25) Now as to the matter of lying. You want to be very careful about lying; otherwise you are nearly sure to get caught. Once caught, you can never again be, in the eyes of the good and the pure, what you were before. Many a young person has injured himself permanently through a single clumsy and illfinished lie, the result of carelessness born of incomplete training. Some authorities hold that the young ought not to lie at all. That, of course, is putting it rather stronger than necessary; still, while I cannot go quite so far as that, I do maintain, and I believe I am right, that the young ought to be temperate in the use of this great art until practice and experience shall give them that confidence, elegance, and precision which alone can make the accomplishment graceful and profitable.

Before reading further, **pay attention to the "purpose" question.** This is the question at the beginning of the passage, which is, in this case, "What Is Good Advice For Young People?" Every reading selection will begin with a question of this kind, to give you an idea of what the selection will be about, and to excite your curiosity, so that you will read with interest and attention.

Next, **sample the questions.** Sampling some of the questions lets you know what to look for when you read the passage. Remember, on this GED Test you will see three types of questions:

1. **Comprehension Questions:** These questions ask you to *understand the meaning of information* in the reading. Sometimes the reading states this information in a straightforward, *direct* way, and sometimes the reading only *suggests* the information.

2. **Analysis Questions:** These questions ask you to *understand and analyze how language or ideas are used* in the reading. They may ask about the author's choice of words or the structure of sentences.

3. **Application Questions:** These questions ask you to *apply the information in the reading* to a situation or example *not mentioned* in the reading.

With these question types in mind, we can sample these *questions* based on the passage above:

1. The speaker's audience most likely includes which of the following?

This is an **application** question. This question asks you to *apply information from the reading to the question of audience,* the people being spoken to, even though the audience is not specifically mentioned in the speech. As you read, you should pay attention to any information that helps you determine the speaker's (or writer's) audience.

2. Which of the following conclusions is probably true about the speaker's advice?

> This is an **analysis** question. You are asked to *analyze the speaker's advice* and *draw a conclusion* about it.

3. When the author says "that superstition" (line 9), he is suggesting that

> This is a **comprehension** question. You are asked to *understand the suggested meaning* of a particular part of the reading. As you read, you should pay special attention to the phrase (*that superstition*) mentioned in this question.

4. By "the accomplishment" (line 29), the speaker means

> This is a **comprehension** question. You are asked to *understand the meaning* of "the accomplishment" as used in this passage.

5. When the speaker says that "the time has gone by" for violence (line 15), he suggests that

> This is a **comprehension** question. You are asked to *understand the suggested meaning of the information in line 15.*

6. When the speaker advises youth to "always obey your parents, when they are present," he suggests that

> This is a **comprehension** question. What is the speaker *suggesting*?

7. We cannot take the author's advice in lines 18–21 seriously, because

> This is an **analysis** question. You are asked to *analyze the tone* of the author's advice.

8. Which of the following responses would the speaker probably expect from the audience?

> This is an **application** question. You are asked to *apply information* from the passage to *predict a response* from the audience.

Now that you have sampled some of the questions, **read the passage carefully.** You should notice the parts that are important to remember and understand. These are the parts of the reading that the questions refer to.

After reading the selection, you must **answer questions based only on the information in the passage.** You can eliminate incorrect answers that

■ have nothing to do with the reading or are not mentioned
■ contradict or disagree with the information in the reading

Consider the following questions, answers, and explanations based on the passage above.

You may be given the following type of **application** question:

1. The speaker's audience most likely includes which of the following?

   (1) young people
   (2) parents
   (3) school officials
   (4) law enforcement officers
   (5) families

The right answer is (1). In the first paragraph, the speaker says that his talk should be "something suitable to youth"; so we may assume that the authors's audience includes young people.

None of the other choices is mentioned as necessarily part of the speaker's audience.

An **analysis** question such as this could follow:

2. Which of the following conclusions is probably true about the speaker's advice?

   (1) It is just the sort of advice most parents give to their children.
   (2) It should not be taken seriously.
   (3) It consists of dangerous lies.
   (4) It is the same advice that the speaker followed as a youth.
   (5) It will offend anyone who hears it.

The right answer is (2). Choice (1) is wrong because advice such as "hit him with a brick," most likely does not agree with the "sort of advice most parents give to their children." Choice (3) contradicts the humorous tone of the passage; the speaker does not seem to be a dangerous liar. Choice (4) is not mentioned at all. The author does not tell us whether he followed his own advice or not. The humorous tone of the passage does not agree with the conclusion that it is offensive, choice (5).

Choice (2) is best because many of the speaker's statements seem meant to be taken as jokes.

One of the questions could be similar to this **comprehension** question:

3. When the author says "that superstition" (line 9), he is suggesting that

    (1) parents are always smarter than their children
    (2) parents are superstitious about most things
    (3) superstitious children will be sure to obey their parents
    (4) the belief that parents know better than their children is a false one
    (5) most superstitions are humorous

The right answer is (4). A superstition is a false belief. When the speaker says that "parents think they know better than you do" is a "superstition," he means that it is a false belief.

Each of the other choices has nothing to do with the information in the reading.

You may be given the following type of **comprehension** question:

4. By "the accomplishment" (line 29), the speaker means

    (1) growing up
    (2) becoming one of the "good and pure"
    (3) lying
    (4) taking all of the author's advice
    (5) becoming as wise as he is

The right answer is (3). The speaker disagrees with those who say that "the young ought not to lie at all" (line 26) and goes on to say that they should get "practice and experience" (lines 28–29) to make "the accomplishment [lying] graceful and profitable."

A **comprehension** question similar to this could follow:

5. When the speaker says that "the time has gone by" for violence (line 15), he suggests that

    (1) the past was a more violent time
    (2) the future will be a more violent time
    (3) charity and kindness are things of the past
    (4) using dynamite is a thing of the past
    (5) no one avoids violence anymore

The right answer is (1). If the time has gone by for violence, then the time of violence was in the past.

An **analysis** question similar to this may follow:

6. When the speaker advises youth to "always obey your parents, when they are present," he suggests that

    (1) he never obeyed his own parents
    (2) he is concerned only with the parents of others
    (3) when parents are <u>not</u> present, youth need not obey them
    (4) parents do not expect to be obeyed unless they are present
    (5) the presence of parents is something that annoys young people

The right answer is (3). With this piece of advice, the author suggests that youth should obey their parents *only* when the parents are present.

An **analysis** question similar to this may follow:

7. We cannot take the author's advice in lines 18–21 seriously, because

    (1) training a lark to wake one up at 9:30 is probably not possible
    (2) larks are not available everywhere
    (3) the only ones who get up with the lark are other larks
    (4) there are some mornings when one will not wish to get up at 9:30
    (5) larks are too wise to allow themselves to be trained

The right answer is (1). The idea of training a lark to wake one up is obviously not reasonable.

One question of the set might be similar to this **application** question:

8. Which of the following responses would the speaker probably expect from the audience?

    (1) hostility
    (2) agreement
    (3) boredom
    (4) laughter
    (5) insults

The right answer is (4). Since the speaker's talk consists mainly of humorous statements, he would expect laughter from his audience.

SECTION II

Let's take a look at another reading.

Items 1 to 8 refer to the following excerpt from a novel.

WHAT KIND OF MAN IS MR. PAUL DOMBEY?

    Dombey sat in the corner of the darkened room in the great arm-chair by the bedside and Son lay tucked up warm in a little basket bedstead, carefully disposed on a low settee immediately in front of the fire and close to it, as if his constitution were analogous to that of a muffin, and it was essential to toast him brown while he was very new.

(5)   Dombey was about eight-and-forty years of age. Son about eight-and-forty minutes. Dombey was rather bald, rather red, and though a handsome well-made man, too stern and pompous in appearance to be prepossessing. Son was very bald, and very red, and (of course) an undeniably fine infant.

    Dombey, exulting in the long-looked-for event, jingled and jingled the heavy gold watch-chain that depended from below his trim blue coat, whereof the buttons sparkled phosphorescently in the feeble
(10)   rays of the distant fire.

    "The house will once again, Mrs. Dombey," said Mr. Dombey, "be not only in name but in fact Dombey and Son; Dom-bey and Son!"

    The words had such a softening influence that he appended a term of endearment to Mrs. Dombey's name (though not without some hesitation, being a man little used to that form of address) and
(15)   said, "Mrs. Dombey, my—my dear."

    A transient flush of faint surprise overspread the sick lady's face as she raised her eyes towards him.

    "He will be christened Paul, my—Mrs. Dombey—of course."

    She feebly echoed, "Of course."
(20)   "His father's name, Mrs. Dombey, and his grandfather's!" And again he said "Dom-bey and Son," in exactly the same tone as before.

    Those three words conveyed the one idea of Mr. Dombey's life. The earth was made for Dombey

and Son to trade in, and the sun and moon were made to give them light. Rivers and seas were formed to float their ships; rainbows gave them promise of fair weather; winds blew for or against their enter-
(25) prises; stars and planets circled in their orbits to preserve inviolate a system of which they were the centre.

You may be given the following type of **analysis** question:

---

1. In the first paragraph, the figure of speech used is a

   (1) simile comparing Paul Dombey and his infant son
   (2) metaphor comparing the fire and the dark room
   (3) simile comparing the baby and a muffin
   (4) metaphor comparing warm fire and the warm basket
   (5) simile comparing the new baby and the new fire

The right answer is (3). The figure of speech is a simile, a comparison using *like* or *as*. The simile here compares the baby and a muffin, since both may be placed near a warm fire.

A **comprehension** question similar to this could follow:

---

2. Mrs. Dombey speaks "feebly" (line 19) probably because

   (1) it is late at night
   (2) she has just had a baby
   (3) she is naturally sickly
   (4) she cannot keep warm
   (5) Mr. Dombey has called her "my dear"

The right answer is (2). Mrs. Dombey has just given birth to a baby, less than an hour before this scene takes place. In line 5, the reading says that the baby is about "eight-and-forty minutes" old.

One of the questions could be similar to this **comprehension** question:

---

3. Mr. Dombey's mood is

   (1) excellent
   (2) stoical
   (3) calm
   (4) sympathetic
   (5) depressed

The right answer is (1). We are told that Mr. Dombey is "exalting" (line 8) because of the birth of a son.

You may be given the following type of **comprehension** question:

4. The "long-looked-for event" (line 8) is

   (1) the coming of Christmas
   (2) Mrs. Dombey's death
   (3) the birth of a son
   (4) the success of Dombey's company
   (5) the success of Dombey's son

The right answer is (3). The long awaited event is the son's birth. Mr. Dombey, as we are told, is 48 years old.

A **comprehension** question similar to this could follow:

5. In line 11, "the house" refers to

   (1) Dombey's London residence
   (2) Dombey country estate
   (3) a college
   (4) Mrs. Dombey's residence
   (5) Dombey's company

The right answer is (5). The house is the family company, called Dombey and Son. The last paragraph of the excerpt mentions that "the earth was made for Dombey and Son to trade in," to do business in.

One of the questions may be similar to this **comprehension** question:

6. In line 16, the "flush of faint surprise" is most likely caused by

   (1) Mrs. Dombey's fever
   (2) Mr. Dombey's use of "my dear"
   (3) Mr. Dombey's repetition of "Dombey and Son"
   (4) the heat of the fire
   (5) Mr. Dombey's disappointment

The right answer is (2). Mrs. Dombey is surprised by her husband's use of the term of endearment (*my dear*). We are told he does not usually use that "form of address."

A **comprehension** question similar to this may follow:

7. The most important thing in Mr. Dombey's life is probably his

    (1) firm
    (2) wife
    (3) daughter
    (4) father
    (5) grandparents

The right answer is (1). The last paragraph says that "those three words," Dombey and Son, are "the one idea of Dombey's life."

One question of the set may be similar to this **comprehension** question:

8. The details of the excerpt suggest that Mr. Dombey is probably

    (1) selfish
    (2) an affectionate husband
    (3) impoverished
    (4) generous
    (5) compassionate

The right answer is (1). We can tell from the excerpt that Dombey's real love is for his company, not for his wife or for other people.

We can also tell from details of the excerpt ("the heavy gold watch-chain," for example) that Dombey is not poor (impoverished).

SECTION III

Let's try one more set.

Items 1 to 6 refer to the following poem.

CAN THERE BE SOME GOOD IN DEFEAT?

> Defeat may serve as well as victory
> To shake the soul and let the glory out.
> When the great oak is straining in the wind,
> The boughs drink in new beauty, and the trunk
> (5) Sends down a deeper root on the windward side.
> Only the soul that knows the mighty grief
> Can know the mighty rapture. Sorrows come
> To stretch out spaces in the heart for joy.

You may be given the following type of **comprehension** question:

1. According to the poem, we should expect a person who has experienced great suffering to be

    (1) indifferent to great joy
    (2) indifferent to renewed sorrow
    (3) capable of feeling great joy
    (4) capable of controlling emotions
    (5) especially sympathetic to the sufferings of others

The right answer is (3). The idea of the poem is that great grief expands the soul making it capable of feeling greater joy.

Answers (4) and (5) may be true of life, but there is nothing at all in this poem about these ideas.

An **analysis** question such as this could follow:

2. In lines 3-5, the description of the oak tree

    (1) reminds the reader that people are part of the natural world
    (2) reminds the reader that people and nature are different
    (3) suggests the consolation for grief offered in nature
    (4) suggests a comparison between the soul and the tree
    (5) suggests that defeat is a creation of the mind

The right answer is (4). The point of lines 3-5 is to suggest a comparison between the tree and the soul. The harsh winds are like grief or defeat, but because of them the tree has deeper roots.

One of the questions could be similar to this **comprehension** question:

3. The last sentence of the poem ("Sorrows come to stretch out spaces in the heart for joy.")

    A. echoes the idea of lines 1-2
    B. contradicts the idea of lines 3-5
    C. echoes the idea of lines 6-7

    (1) A only
    (2) B only
    (3) C only
    (4) A and C only
    (5) A, B, and C

The right answer is (4). The poem repeats its central idea four times. Nothing in the poem contradicts the central idea.

You may be given the following type of **comprehension** question:

4. In line 5, the word "windward" means

    (1) leeward
    (2) the direction toward which the wind blows
    (3) the direction from which the wind blows
    (4) easterly
    (5) sheltered

The right answer is (3). The *windward* side is the side from which the wind blows, the unsheltered side. The opposite of *windward* is *leeward,* the side toward which the wind blows, and thus, the sheltered side.

Analysis questions similar to these could follow:

5. All of the following words or phrases in the poem are closely related in meaning EXCEPT

   (1) defeat (line 1)
   (2) straining in the wind (line 3)
   (3) a deeper root (line 5)
   (4) grief (line 6)
   (5) sorrows (line 7)

6. All of the following words or phrases are closely related in meaning EXCEPT

   (1) victory (line 1)
   (2) new beauty (line 4)
   (3) the soul (line 6)
   (4) rapture (line 7)
   (5) joy (line 8)

The right answers to questions 5 and 6 are (3) and (3). The use of repetition in the poem is illustrated in these questions.

Words showing defeat or sorrow and words for victory or joy are used in each of the four sentences. In both questions, the (3) answer is out of place.

Some reminders:

■ Pay special attention to the "purpose" question.
■ Sample a few questions before reading each passage.
■ Answer each question based only on information in the reading.
■ Eliminate answer choices that are not relevant (have nothing to do with the reading).
■ Eliminate choices that disagree with something in the reading.

TEST
5

MATHEMATICS

TEST 5: MATHEMATICS

WHAT TO EXPECT

The Mathematics Test is 1 hour and 30 minutes long and contains 56 multiple-choice questions.

■ Expect questions that will test how well you understand and can apply the basic concepts of arithmetic, algebra, and geometry.

■ Expect settings that are familiar in everyday life. A grocery store, a bank, a theater, and a sporting event would all be familiar settings.

■ Expect about two-thirds of the questions to refer to situations.

■ Expect about one-third of the questions to refer to graphs or charts

■ Expect some of the questions to be in groups, or sets—that is, two to four questions that refer to the same situation, chart, or graph

WHAT YOU SHOULD KNOW

The Mathematics Test contains the following areas:

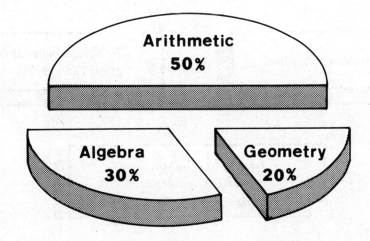

You should be able to answer questions in the following areas:

ARITHMETIC (50%)

Measurement (30%)

Be able to **find length, height, perimeter, area,** and **volume** in simple problems

Be able to **use** basic **rate formulas** to find **distance, time,** and **cost per unit**

Number Relationships (10%)

Be able to **round off, estimate,** and **compare** numbers

Be able to **use exponents, scientific notation,** and **order of operations**

Analyzing Data (10%)

Be able to **find mean** and **median**

Be able to **understand** and **use graphs** and **charts**

Be able to **solve** simple **probability** problems

ALGEBRA (30%)

Be able to **apply** common properties—**associative, commutative**, and **distributive**

Be able to **solve equalities** and **inequalities**

Be able to **solve proportions** and **percent problems**

Be able to **set up** simple **equations**

Understand basic **factoring**

Be able to **evaluate equations** and **relationships**

Be able to **use** algebra **symbols** and **formulas**

GEOMETRY (20%)

Be able to **solve** problems involving the **common triangles** (isosceles, right) and **triangle comparisons** (congruent, similar)

Be able to **solve** problems using **perpendicular** and **parallel lines**

Understand solid figures and their parts

Be able to **use** basic **geometric properties** and **theorems** such as the Pythagorean theorem

Be able to **calculate** the **slope of a line** and the **distance between points on a plane**

WHAT TO LOOK FOR: KINDS OF QUESTIONS

The GED Mathematics Test will test application and problem solving skills. The questions will stress your being able to apply concepts and basic skills.

Look for problems that ask you to

- Visualize

- Set up an expression or equation

- Estimate or approximate

- Do simple calculations

- Work out ratios and proportions

- Apply given formulas

- Use your basic knowledge

- Work from the answers

- Find the reasonable answer

- Decide if you have enough information or need more

ABOUT THE DIRECTIONS

Following are the directions you'll find in the Mathematics Test. Become very familiar with these directions now so that you'll be comfortable with them when you take the actual test. The directions you'll see on the actual test will be wider on the page. Here, though, room has been left for the boxes you see on the right and the left. Read the following directions straight through, and then carefully read the information in the boxes. It points out and explains important points in the directions.

TEST 5: MATHEMATICS

Tests of General Educational Development

Directions

> Review **basic math skills** and practice **problem solving**

> All questions have **five choices**

The Mathematics Test consists of multiple-choice questions intended to measure general mathematics skills and problem-solving ability. The questions are based on short readings which often include a graph, chart, or figure.

> Word problems, graph problems; not **simply computation**

> Spend no more than about 1½ minutes per question

You should spend no more than 90 minutes answering the questions in this booklet. Work carefully, but do not spend too much time on any one question. Be sure you answer every question. You will not be penalized for incorrect answers.

> Each question is worth the same

> Don't get stuck on any question; move on

> No penalty for guessing so guess if you have to, but don't leave any questions blank

> Most formulas you need are given; know how to use them

Formulas you may need are given on page __. Only some of the questions will require you to use a formula. Not all the formulas given will be needed.

Some questions contain more information than you will need to solve the problem. Other questions do not give enough information to solve the problem. If the question does not give enough information to solve the problem, the correct answer choice is "Not enough information is given."

> Know what information is needed to solve a problem; watch for information that is not needed

> Watch for information that is missing and answer choices that say "Not enough information is given"

The use of calculators is not allowed.

> No calculators can be used

Do not mark in this test booklet. The test administrator will give you blank paper for your calculations. Record your answers on the separate answer sheet provided. Be sure all requested information is properly recorded on the answer sheet.

> Scratch paper will be given to you for your work

> Mark your answers carefully on the answer sheet

To record your answers, mark the numbered space on the answer sheet beside the number that corresponds to the question in the test booklet.

Notice that this question requires **basic skills** and some **problem solving** ability

FOR EXAMPLE:

If a grocery bill totaling $15.75 is paid with a $20.00 bill, how much change should be returned?

(1) $5.26
(2) $4.75
(3) $4.25
(4) $3.75
(5) $3.25

 ① ② ● ④ ⑤

The correct answer is "$4.25"; therefore, answer space 3 should be marked on the answer sheet.

Do not make any **extra marks** on your answer sheet

Do not rest the point of your pencil on the answer sheet while you are considering your answer. Make <u>no stray or unnecessary marks</u>. If you change an answer, erase your first mark completely. <u>Mark only one answer</u> space for each question; multiple answers will be scored as incorrect. Do not fold or crease your answer sheet. Return all test materials to the test administrator.

Mark only one answer

WHAT YOU SHOULD DO

 Read the problem carefully.

 Make sure that you understand what information is being given and what the question is asking.

 Before starting any calculations, check the answer choices given.

 Estimating or approximating can be useful.

 Pull out important information.

Use the scratch paper effectively.

 Do your calculations carefully.

The two most common mistakes are misreading the problem and simple calculating errors.

 Refer to graphs, charts, drawings, or geometric figures as often as you need to.

Graphs, charts, drawings, and geometric figures often take a second and a third look. Take an extra few moments to make sure that you understand any visual information given.

The following three sections will use examples to carefully explain the **question types,** show you **what to look for,** and point out **what you should do.**

SECTION I: ARITHMETIC QUESTIONS

You may be given a question similar to this that asks you to set up a **proportion.** You can also work this question using a **common-sense approach**.

1. If eggs sell for $1 per dozen, how much would 96 eggs cost?

   (1) $96
   (2) $84
   (3) $36
   (4) $12
   (5) $ 8

The right answer is (5) $8.

First, pay special attention to the key words in the question: "If eggs sell for *$1 per dozen, how much would 96 eggs cost?* You need to find *how much.* You could set up a proportion as follows:

$$\frac{\text{money}}{\text{eggs}} \qquad \frac{\text{money}}{\text{eggs}}$$

$$\frac{1}{12} \qquad \frac{x}{96}$$

Then cross multiply:

$$\frac{1}{12} \diagdown\!\!\!\!\diagup \frac{x}{96}$$

$$96 = 12x$$

Finally, divide by 12:

$$\frac{96}{12} = \frac{12x}{12}$$

$$8 = x$$

So 96 eggs cost $8.

You could also work the problem this way using a common-sense approach: Ninety-six eggs equal exactly 8 dozen eggs. (Divide 96 by 12, since there are 12 eggs in a dozen.) So, if 1 dozen eggs cost $1, 8 dozen eggs cost $8.

You could be given a question similar to this that can be solved by a **common-sense approach** or by a **proportion**:

2. If Jonathan can mow his entire lawn in ⅔ of an hour, how much of that lawn can he mow in 10 minutes?

(1) $\dfrac{1}{10}$

(2) $\dfrac{1}{5}$

(3) $\dfrac{1}{4}$

(4) $\dfrac{2}{3}$

(5) Not enough information is given.

The right answer is (3) ¼ of the lawn.

First, pay special attention to key words in the question: "*how much* of that lawn can he mow in *10 minutes?*"

Next, to answer this question, you must change hours to minutes. Jonathan can mow his entire lawn in ⅔ of an hour, which is the same as 40 minutes.

$$\frac{2}{3} \times 60 = 40 \text{ minutes}$$

Since 10 minutes is ¼ of 40 ($^{10}/_{40} = $ ¼), he can mow ¼ of his lawn in 10 minutes.

You can also solve this problem by setting up and solving the following proportions:

$$\text{(Entire lawn in 40 minutes) } \frac{1}{40} = \frac{x}{10} \text{ (What part in 10 minutes?)}$$

Multiply by 10:

$$(10) \frac{1}{40} = \frac{x}{10} (10)$$

$$\frac{10}{40} = \frac{10x}{10}$$

$$\frac{1}{4} = x$$

You may be given a **proportion** problem similar to this:

3. Judith drew a drawing of her school, using the scale of

1 centimeter (cm) on the model = 12 feet in real life.

If the length of the main corridor of her school is 180 feet, how long should Judith have drawn the corridor on the scale drawing?

(1) 12 cm
(2) 15 cm
(3) 18 cm
(4) 20 cm
(5) 24 cm

The right answer is (2) 15 cm.

Notice that you must find *"how long"* the corridor should be on the *scale drawing*. To find this *length*, you will need to set up a proportion. Set up the proportion like this:

$$\frac{\text{scale}}{\text{actual}} \qquad \frac{1 \text{ cm}}{12 \text{ ft}} = \frac{x}{180 \text{ ft}}$$

To solve this problem, cross multiply:

$$\frac{1}{12} \times \frac{x}{180}$$

$$180 = 12x$$

Then divide by 12:

$$\frac{180}{12} = \frac{12x}{12}$$

$$15 = x$$

So the corridor on the scale drawing should be 15 cm long.

You may be given a **ratio** question similar to this:

4. There are three times as many girls enrolled in after-school sports as there are boys enrolled in after-school sports. Which of the following could be the number of girls enrolled in after-school sports?

(1) 20
(2) 24
(3) 28
(4) 32
(5) Not enough information is given.

The right answer is (2) 24.

To answer this question, you must use ratios. Notice that you are looking for the *possible number of girls*. Since there are three times as many girls as there are boys enrolled in after-school sports, the ratio is 3 to 1. This ratio could also be given as

$$\underline{\frac{6 \text{ to } 2}{9 \text{ to } 3}}$$
$$\underline{12} \text{ to } 4 \text{ and so on}$$

The girls' total must then be 3 or a multiple of 3 (3, 6, 9, 12, 15, 18, 21, 24 . . .). The *only* answer choice which is a multiple of three is answer (2) 24.

You could be given a question similar to this that asks you to set up a **ratio** and do **simple calculations:**

5. Carol's factory produced 40,000 disks in 1987. In 1986 her factory produced 50,000 disks. What was the percent decrease from 1986 to 1987?

(1) 10%
(2) 20%
(3) 25%
(4) 30%
(5) Not enough information is given.

The right answer is (2) 20%.

First, notice that you are looking for *"percent decrease."* To find percent decrease (set up a ratio) divide the *change* between the two years by the *starting year:*

$$\frac{\text{change}}{\text{starting year}} \qquad \frac{50{,}000 - 40{,}000}{50{,}000} = \frac{10{,}000}{50{,}000}$$

Now change $\dfrac{10{,}000}{50{,}000}$ to a percent.

Reduce $\dfrac{10{,}000}{50{,}000}$ to $\dfrac{1}{5}$

Now divide 5 into 1, which gives .20 or 20%.

You should *memorize* some of the *common fraction to percent conversions.*

$\frac{1}{4} = 25\%$	$\frac{7}{10} = 70\%$	$\frac{4}{10} = \frac{2}{5} = 40\%$
$\frac{1}{10} = 10\%$	$\frac{9}{10} = 90\%$	$\frac{6}{10} = \frac{3}{5} = 60\%$
$\frac{3}{10} = 30\%$	$\frac{3}{4} = 75\%$	$\frac{8}{10} = \frac{4}{5} = 80\%$
$\frac{5}{10} = \frac{1}{2} = 50\%$	$\frac{2}{10} = \frac{1}{5} = 20\%$	

You may be given a problem similar to this that asks you to apply the **averaging formula:**

6. Archie works weekends in a department store stockroom. For the four weekends in February, Archie's checks were $28.30, $32.90, $27.90, and $30.30. What was Archie's <u>average weekly check</u> for February?

   (1) $27.90
   (2) $28.40
   (3) $29.85
   (4) $30.10
   (5) $31.40

The right answer is (3) $29.85.

To get an average, find the *total* and then divide by the *number of items*. In this problem, the items total $119.40.

$$\begin{array}{r} 28.30 \\ 32.90 \\ 27.90 \\ 30.30 \\ \hline 119.40 \end{array}$$

Then divide by 4:

$$\begin{array}{r} 29.85 \\ 4\overline{)119.40} \\ \underline{8} \\ 39 \\ \underline{36} \\ 34 \\ \underline{32} \\ 20 \\ \underline{20} \end{array}$$

$$\$119.40 \div 4 = \$29.85$$

The average is $29.85. Did you notice that answer choices (1), (4), and (5) are not reasonable?

You could be given a problem similar to this that asks you to apply the **distance, rate, time formula:**

7. A train traveling from San Diego to Seattle averages 90 miles per hour for the entire trip. The train's route is direct from San Diego to Seattle with no stops, a distance of 1080 miles. At what time will the train arrive in Seattle if it leaves San Diego at 9 a.m.? (Note: San Diego and Seattle are in the same time zone.)

   (1) 1 p.m.
   (2) 3 p.m.
   (3) 5 p.m.
   (4) 7 p.m.
   (5) 9 p.m.

The right answer is (5) 9 p.m.

To solve this problem, you must first notice that you are looking for "*at what time*." Next, you must understand how to use the *distance, rate, time formula*.

Using the distance equation from the formula page:

$$\text{distance} = \text{rate} \times \text{time}$$
$$1080 = 90 \times t$$

Divide both sides by 90:

$$\frac{1080}{90} = \frac{90t}{90}$$
$$12 = t$$

So it takes the train 12 hours to reach Seattle. The train leaves at 9 a.m.; twelve hours later it will be 9 p.m.

You could be given a problem similar to this that asks you to decide if you have **enough information** to solve the problem:

8. A Zowie battery lasts 60 hours and costs $1.20. A Rayvox battery lasts 75 hours and is sold at $4.99 per package. To determine whether a Zowie battery or a Rayvox battery is the better buy, which additional piece of information is needed?

(1) Zowie batteries cost less than Rayvox batteries.
(2) Rayvox batteries last 25% longer than Zowie batteries.
(3) Rayvox batteries are sold only in packages containing three batteries.
(4) Zowie batteries are sold in packages containing only one battery.
(5) None of the above information is needed.

The right answer is (3).

In order to compare the cost of each battery, you must know *how many* Rayvox batteries are in a package that costs $4.99. Notice that you do *not* have to know which battery is the better buy. You only have to know what information you would need to *determine* which is the better buy.

You may be given a problem similar to this in which you must **work from the answers** and **approximate:**

9. Fred plans to use his savings to equip his new apartment. If Fred has $800 in savings, which of the following combinations of items can Fred purchase <u>without exceeding</u> his savings? (Disregard tax.)

Item	*Cost*
A. Personal computer	$785
B. Microwave oven	$450
C. Stereo system	$555
D. Videotape deck	$285
E. Compact disk player	$395
F. Color television set	$510

(1) A and D
(2) B and E
(3) C and D
(4) D and F
(5) E and C

The right answer is (4) D and F.

To answer this question, you must work from the answers and approximate.
Remember that the total *cannot* be more than $800.

You can easily see by approximating that in choice (1), A (approximately $800) and D (approximately $300) add up to more than $800. By approximating you can also see that in choice (2), B ($450) and E (approximately $400) total more than $800. In choice (3), C (approximately $550) and D (approximately $300) are also larger than $800. Only items D ($285) and F ($510) add up to *less* than $800. (285 + 510 = 795)

Remember, rounding off numbers and estimating, or approximating, can save you time.

You may be given a question similar to this that asks you to use your knowledge of **percents** and do **simple calculations:**

10. Sal purchases a used car for $1200. However, a month later, Sal receives a bill from the motor vehicle bureau for 6% of the purchase price of his car. How much must Sal pay the motor vehicle bureau?

(1) $120
(2) $100
(3) $ 84
(4) $ 72
(5) $ 60

The right answer is (4) $72.

You must find "*How much* must Sal pay the motor vehicle bureau?" To answer this question, you must find 6% of $1200. Six percent of $1200 is the same as .06 times $1200.

$$.06 \times \$1200 = \$72.00$$

Sal must pay $72.00. Does this sound like a reasonable answer? Yes. Ten percent of $1200 is $120, so six percent would be a little more than half of $120.

You may be given a problem similar to this that asks you to use your knowledge of **percents** and do **simple calculations.** You can also make your choice easier by looking for **reasonable answers:**

11. Louisa must pay 10% of her total income to maintain her membership in the union. If Louisa's total income is $9000, how much of her income does Louisa <u>keep</u>? (Disregard taxes.)

    (1) $ 81
    (2) $ 90
    (3) $ 900
    (4) $8010
    (5) $8100

The right answer is (5) $8100.

To determine how much Louisa *keeps,* subtract 10% of her total from her total:

    total − (10% of total) = amount Louisa keeps
           (10% of $9000) = $900
           $9000 − ($900) = $8100

So Louisa keeps $8100.

After working out the answer, make sure it is reasonable. If she loses 10% of the $9000, will she keep most of it? Yes. Notice that choices (1), (2), and (3) are not reasonable. If you don't know how to work a problem, and have to guess, first check the answer choices for a *reasonable* answer.

You could be given a **measurement** question similar to this in which you need to decide if you have **enough information:**

12. A rectangular floor is exactly 20 feet long and 40 feet wide. How many square tiles, each the same size, are able to fit on the floor without overlapping?

(1) 20
(2) 40
(3) 400
(4) 800
(5) Not enough information is given.

The right answer is (5). Not enough information is given.

You are looking for *"how many"* square tiles will fit. To find *how many,* you need the dimensions of the tiles. Since the exact size of the square tiles is not given, you do not have enough information to determine how many tiles can be fitted on the floor.

You may be given the following type of graphs:

Items 13 and 14 refer to the following graphs.

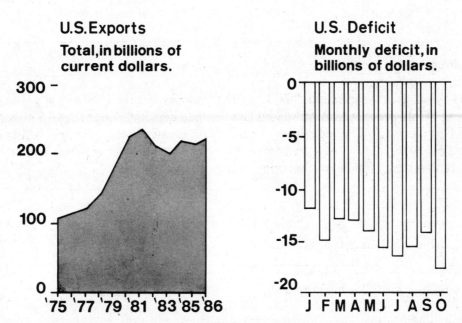

A question similar to this that asks you to **approximate** and do **simple calculations** could follow:

13. According to the graph above, approximately how much greater were U.S. exports in 1981 than in 1975?

(1) 100 billion
(2) 130 billion
(3) 150 billion
(4) 200 billion
(5) 240 billion

The right answer is (2) 130 billion.

Notice that you are trying to find "*how much greater* were U.S. exports in 1981 than in 1975?" In 1981, U.S. exports were about 240 billion. In 1975, U.S. exports were about 110 billion. So, 240 − 110 = 130 billion greater.

A second question similar to this could follow:

14. According to the graph above, for how many months was the U.S. deficit greater than 15 billion dollars?

    (1) 4 months
    (2) 5 months
    (3) 6 months
    (4) 7 months
    (5) 8 months

The right answer is (1) 4 months.

Look for the key words in the question: "*for how many months* was the U.S. deficit *greater than 15 billion dollars?*" Only June, July, August, and October had deficits greater than 15 billion dollars. Note that this graph is drawn "upside down," so a deficit "greater than 15 billion" will have its bottom extend *below* the 15 line. Also, remember to use the edge of your paper as a ruler so you can see more easily which bars fall below that line.

You may be given the following type of pie chart:

Items 15 and 16 refer to the following graph.

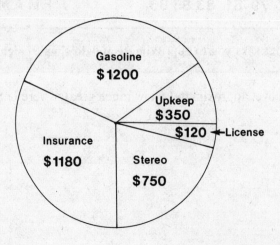

A question similar to this that can be solved by using **proportions** could follow:

15. Approximately what percentage of Tom's automotive expenditures in 1987 was for <u>insurance</u>?

    (1) 12%
    (2) 20%
    (3) 25%
    (4) 33%
    (5) 38%

The right answer is (4) 33%.

First, pay special attention to what the question is asking: "*Approximately what percentage* of Tom's automotive expenditures in 1987 was for *insurance?*" Next, pull out information and try to set up a proportion. To set up a proportion for this percentage problem, use

$$\frac{\text{part}}{\text{whole}} = \frac{x}{100}$$

The *part* representing insurance is $1180, which (since the question says *approximately*) may be rounded to $1200. The *whole* is the total amount of Tom's expenditures, which, added up, equals $3600. So

$$\frac{\$1200}{\$3600} = \frac{x}{100}$$

$$\frac{1}{3} = \frac{x}{100}$$

Cross multiplying: $3x = 100$

                        $x = 33\frac{1}{3}$

A faster technique would be by inspection, noting that the size of the *insurance* slice of the pie is approximately one-third of the entire pie. One-third equals $33\frac{1}{3}$%.

A second question similar to this that asks you to apply the **averaging formula** could be next:

16. What was Tom's <u>average monthly expenditure</u> for his automotive license fees?

    (1) $ 10
    (2) $ 60
    (3) $ 120
    (4) $3600
    (5) Not enough information is given.

The right answer is (1) $10.

First, remember that you are looking for his "*average monthly expenditures* for license fees." To determine Tom's average *monthly* expenditure for license fees, simply divide the yearly total for license fees ($120) by the number of months in a year (12):

$$\frac{\$120}{12} = \$10$$

SECTION II: ALGEBRA QUESTIONS

You could be given a problem similar to this for which you need to do simple calculations with **positive** and **negative numbers:**

17. Susan's home now sits exactly 280 feet above sea level. Geologists estimate that during the Paleozoic age, the site on which Susan's home presently sits was 600 feet lower than it is now. If the geologists are correct, how many feet <u>below sea level</u> was the site during the Paleozoic age?

    (1) 880
    (2) 600
    (3) 420
    (4) 320
    (5) 280

The right answer is (4) 320 feet.

Notice that the question is asking "*how many feet below* sea level was the site?" Presently, Susan's home sits *280 feet above* sea level. If during the Paleozoic age Susan's home was 600 feet lower, then

$$
\begin{array}{cc}
\text{now} & \text{lower} \\
\overbrace{280} - \overbrace{600} = x \\
- 320 = x
\end{array}
$$

The site was 320 feet below sea level. Read the question again after you choose an answer to make sure that your answer is *reasonable*.

You could be given a **number line** similar to the following:

Item <u>18</u> refers to the number line below.

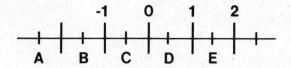

A question similar to this that asks you to use your knowledge of **positive** and **negative numbers** could follow:

18. On the number line above, which letter represents $-\frac{3}{2}$?

   (1) A
   (2) B
   (3) C
   (4) D
   (5) E

The right answer is (2) B.

To answer this question, you must understand *positive* and *negative numbers*. You must also be able to *change fractions to mixed numbers*. Another way of expressing $-\frac{3}{2}$ is as a mixed number: $-1\frac{1}{2}$. To change into a mixed number, simply divide the bottom number into the top number:

$$-3 \div 2 = -1.5 \text{ or } -1\frac{1}{2}$$

B represents $-1\frac{1}{2}$. (E represents $+1\frac{1}{2}$; C represents $-\frac{1}{2}$; A represents $-2\frac{1}{2}$.) You could also answer this question by counting in the negative direction by $\frac{1}{2}$'s: $-\frac{1}{2}, -\frac{2}{2}, -\frac{3}{2}$.

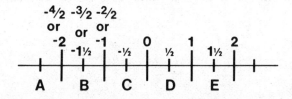

You may be given an **evaluation** problem similar to this that asks you to do **simple calculations**:

19. Evaluate $6x^2 - 4y$ if $x = 3$ and $y = 5$.

   (1) 16
   (2) 34
   (3) 54
   (4) 60
   (5) 74

The right answer is (2) 34.

To evaluate an expression, simply plug in the given numbers or values. These types of problems are usually easy to solve as long as you are *careful in your calculations* and understand the *order of operations*. Plugging in the values given for x and y:

$$6x^2 - 4y =$$
$$6(3)^2 - 4(5) =$$
$$6(9) - 4(5) =$$
$$54 \quad 20 \quad = 34$$

Remember, the order of operations is

> *parentheses*
> *powers*
> *multiplication or division*
> *addition or subtraction*

You could be given a problem similar to this in which you need to solve an **inequality:**

20. For which value of x is the inequality $5x > 5$ true?

(1) -2
(2) -1
(3) 0
(4) 1
(5) 2

The right answer is (5) 2.

To answer this question you must solve the inequality for x. Solve the inequality by dividing both sides by 5:

$$5x > 5$$

$$\frac{5x}{5} > \frac{5}{5}$$

$$x > 1$$

So x is greater than 1. Choices (1), (2), (3), and (4) are all *false* because they are all 1 or less than 1. Answer (5) is true because it is *greater* than 1.

You may be given a problem similar to this in which you must set up and solve an **equation:**

21. Together, Martina and Arline have saved $120. If Martina has saved exactly twice what Arline has saved, how much has <u>Arline</u> saved?

    (1) $20
    (2) $30
    (3) $40
    (4) $60
    (5) $80

The right answer is (3). Arline has saved $40.

To answer this question, you will need to *set up an equation*. Notice that the question asks "*how much* has *Arline* saved?" Set up an equation as follows:

$$\text{let } x = \text{amount Arline saved}$$

Since Martina has saved twice as much as Arline has:

$$2x = \text{amount Martina saved}$$

Together they have $120, so

$$x \text{ (Arline)} + 2x \text{ (Martina)} = \$120$$

Solving: $\qquad\qquad\qquad\qquad 3x = \$120$

Now divide by 3: $\qquad\qquad\qquad \dfrac{3x}{3} = \dfrac{\$120}{3}$

$$x = \$40$$

So Arline has saved $40.

You can also work this problem from the *answer choices*. You could let each answer be how much Arline has saved, then double that amount to find how much Martina has saved. Then, by adding those amounts, you can see if they total $120. Sometimes working from the answers can be very helpful.

You could be given a problem similar to this in which you could set up and solve an **equation.** You could also work from the **answer choices:**

22. Arnold and Karen together scored a total of 25 points for the high school math team. If Karen scored five points more than Arnold did, how many points did <u>Arnold</u> score?

    (1) 5
    (2) 10
    (3) 15
    (4) 20
    (5) Not enough information is given.

The right answer is (2). Arnold scored 10 points.

Notice that you are looking for "*how many points* did *Arnold* score?" You can solve this problem by setting up a simple equation:

$$\text{let } x = \text{Arnold's score}$$

Then
$$x + 5 = \text{Karen's score}$$

$$\text{Arnold's score} + \text{Karen's score} = 25 \text{ points}$$
$$x \qquad + \qquad (x + 5) \qquad = 25 \text{ points}$$

Adding:
$$2x + 5 = 25$$
$$2x \quad = 25 - 5$$
$$2x \quad = 20$$
$$x \quad = 10$$

So Arnold scored 10 points.

You can also solve this problem by *working from the answer choices*. Choice (1) is not correct because if Arnold scored 5 points, then Karen would score 20 points (total of 25 points). And Karen, we know, scored only 5 points more than Arnold did. Choice (2) is correct because if Arnold scored 10 points, then Karen would score 15 points, which *is* 5 points more than Arnold scored.

You may be given a **setup** type problem similar to this that doesn't ask you for an answer, just for the setup:

23. Manuel purchases tickets to an amusement park for his family. If children's tickets cost half price and adult tickets cost full price ($8.00), which of the expressions below represents the total dollars spent for tickets if there are 2 adults and 6 children in Manuel's family?

(1) $2(8) + 3(4)$
(2) $2(4) + 6(6)$
(3) $2(8) + 4(4)$
(4) $2(8) + 6(4)$
(5) Not enough information is given.

The right answer is (4)—$2(8) + 6(4)$.

In this question you are being asked to set up an *expression*. Focus on key words and information given. From the information given you can figure out

the total spent for adult tickets =

$$2 \text{ adults} \times \$8 \text{ for each ticket}$$

the total spent for children's tickets =

$$6 \text{ children} \times \$4 \text{ for each ticket (note: half price of } \$8)$$

So, the total the family spent for tickets was $2(8) + 6(4)$.

You may be given a situation similar to this:

Items 24 and 25 are based on the following information.

At the school football game, Hillary sells programs at 75 cents each and pennants at $1.00 each. At the last football game, she sold 50 programs and 80 pennants.

A question similar to this that asks you to set up an **expression** could follow:

24. Which expression below shows how much more money Hillary collected at that game from selling pennants than she did from selling programs?

    (1) 80($1.00) − 50($.75)
    (2) 80 − 50($.25)
    (3) 30($1.00 − $.75)
    (4) 80 − 50 ($1.00 − $.75)
    (5) Not enough information is given.

The right answer is (1)—80($1.00) − 50($.75).

In this question you are asked *to set up a problem, not to give an answer*. Set the problem up as though you were solving the problem. To find the difference in money collected from selling pennants:

$$80 \text{ pennants at } \$1.00 \text{ each} = 80(\$1.00)$$

Then figure the total money collected from selling programs:

$$50 \text{ programs at } \$.75 \text{ each} = 50(\$.75)$$

Then subtract the total money from programs from the total money from pennants:

$$80(\$1.00) − 50(\$.75)$$

Another question similar to this that asks you to do **simple calculations** could follow:

25. If Hillary gets to keep 20% of the total money she takes in, how much would Hillary keep from the sale of programs and pennants?

    (1) $ 8.00
    (2) $11.75
    (3) $23.50
    (4) $25.00
    (5) Not enough information is given.

The right answer is (3) $23.50.

You need to find *how much Hillary keeps*. First find the total collected:

80 × $1.00 = $80.00
50 × $ .75 = $37.50
$117.50 total collected from pennants and programs

Now multiply by 20%:   (.20)($117.50) = $23.50

SECTION III: GEOMETRY QUESTIONS

You may be given a figure similar to this and a question in which you are asked to **visualize the situation:**

Item 26 refers to the following diagram.

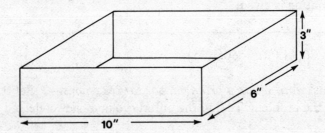

26. The dimensions of an empty box are shown in the diagram above. What is the maximum number of milk containers that can fit into the empty box above if each milk container is 2″ long, 2″ wide, and 3″ high?

    (1)   5
    (2) 10
    (3) 15
    (4) 30
    (5) 60

The right answer is (3) 15 milk containers.

You are looking for the "*maximum number* of milk containers that can fit."

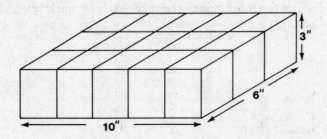

Since each milk container is 2″ wide, 5 milk containers can fit across the length of 10″. Since each container's width is 2″ and the width of the box is 6″, the containers will fit 3 deep (3 rows).

So, 5 containers across times 3 containers deep gives 5 × 3 = 15. (Since the height of the empty box equals the height of the containers, the containers cannot be *stacked* within the box.

You may be given a picture similar to this followed by a question in which you need to apply your knowledge of **ratio** and **proportion:**

Item 27 is based on the following diagram.

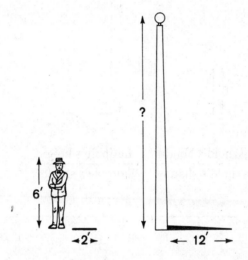

27. A school contest is held that requires contestants to guess how tall the school flagpole is. Arnold, who is 6 feet tall, casts a 2-foot shadow at the same time that the school flagpole casts a 12-foot shadow, as shown in the diagram above. How tall is the flagpole (in feet)?

(1) 30
(2) 36
(3) 42
(4) 48
(5) 60

The right answer is (2) 36 feet.

First, pay special attention to what you are looking for: "*How tall* is the *flagpole*?" You are looking for *height*.

Next, to answer this question, you will need to use similar triangles to set up a proportion. Shadows of objects measured at the same time form triangles which are *similar* and therefore *in proportion*. So a ratio may be expressed:

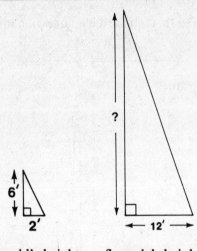

$$\frac{\text{Arnold's height}}{\text{Arnold's shadow}} = \frac{\text{flagpole's height}}{\text{flagpole's shadow}}$$

Now plug in the numbers:

$$\frac{6}{2} = \frac{x}{12}$$

Cross multiply:

$$\frac{6}{2} \diagup \frac{x}{12}$$

$$72 = 2x$$

Finally divide by 2:

$$\frac{72}{2} = \frac{2x}{2}$$

$$36 = x$$

The flagpole is 36 feet tall.

You may be given a diagram similar to this followed by a problem in which you need to use your knowledge of **angles**:

Item 28 is based on the following drawing.

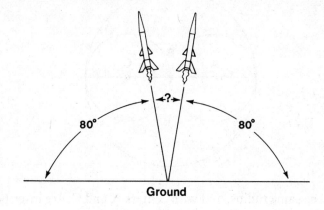

Ground

28. Two model rockets are launched from the same launching pad into the sky, each at an 80 degree angle with the ground, as shown in the diagram above. What angle do the rockets' paths make <u>with each other</u>?

 (1) 10°
 (2) 20°
 (3) 40°
 (4) 100°
 (5) Not enough information is given.

The right answer is (2) 20°.

First, pay special attention to the key words in the question: "*What angle* do the rockets' paths make *with each other*?" Next, use the information given in the diagram and your knowledge of the angle measure of straight lines.

The total number of degrees in a straight line (for instance, the ground) equals 180. So in the diagram,

$$80° + x + 80° = 180°$$

Simplifying the left side gives

$$x + 160 = 180$$

Now subtract 160 from both sides:

$$
\begin{array}{rr}
x + 160 = & 180 \\
- 160 & -160 \\
\hline
x \quad = & 20
\end{array}
$$

So the angle formed is 20 degrees.

You could be given a diagram similar to this followed by a question asking you about **radii** of a **circle:**

Item 29 is based on the following diagram.

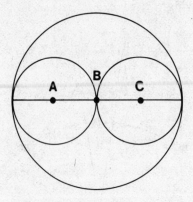

29. Two small circles with the same radius, and with centers A and C, are inscribed in a large circle whose center is at B, as shown in the diagram above. If the distance from A to C is 10 cm, what is the radius of the large circle?

   (1)   5 cm
   (2) 10 cm
   (3) 20 cm
   (4) 25 cm
   (5) Not enough information is given.

The right answer is (2) 10 cm.

Notice that you are looking for the "*radius* of the *large circle*." To solve this problem, you will need to use your knowledge of *radii* and *diameters*.

If AC = 10 cm, then since the small circles have the same radius, AB = 5. So the radius of the circle A is 5 cm. Its diameter is double its radius, or 10 cm, which also happens to be the radius of the large circle. This can be more easily seen in the diagram below:

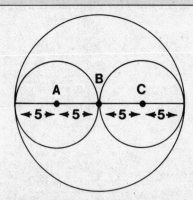

You may be given a diagram similar to this followed by a question in which you have to use a **formula** (in this case, the Pythagorean theorem):

Item 30 is based on the following diagram.

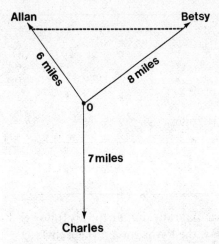

30. Allan, Betsy, and Charles each begin at point 0 and each travel in a straight line away from each other, as shown in the diagram above. Allan walks 6 miles and stops. Betsy walks 8 miles and stops. Charles walks 7 miles and stops. If the angle between Betsy's path and Charles's path is 120 degrees, and the angle between Allan's path and Charles's path is 150 degrees, <u>how far will Allan be from Betsy</u> after they all stop walking?

    (1)   6 miles
    (2)   7 miles
    (3)   8 miles
    (4) 10 miles
    (5) Not enough information is given.

The right answer is (4) 10 miles.

To answer this question, you will need to determine a right triangle and then use the Pythagorean theorem. Notice that the question is asking "*how far*." So you will need to find a distance, or length. Now let's use the information given and do some careful thinking.

Since there are 360 degrees in a circle around any point, the angle between Allan's path and Betsy's path is 90 degrees. So the triangle formed by Allan, Betsy, and point 0 is a right triangle (contains a 90 degree angle). You can now use the Pythagorean theorem to find out the length of the third side of the triangle:

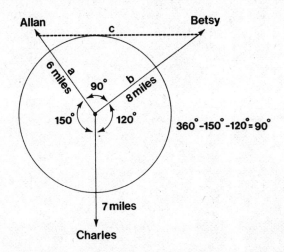

$$a^2 + b^2 = c^2$$
$$(6)^2 + (8)^2 = c^2$$
$$36 + 64 = c^2$$
$$100 = c^2$$
$$10 = c$$

So the distance is 10 miles.

You may be given a diagram similar to this followed by a problem in which you will need to apply a **formula** (in this case, the Pythagorean theorem):

Item 31 refers to the following diagram.

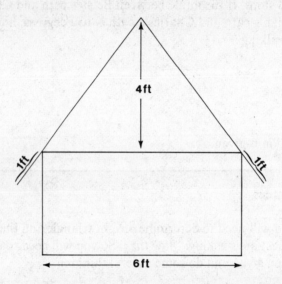

31. An equal-sided roof is to be constructed on top of a rectangular shed, as drawn above. The highest point of the roof is 4 feet above the top of the shed. If the width of the shed is 6 feet, and the roof must overhang the shed by 1 foot on each side, what is the <u>total length</u> along <u>both sides of</u> the roof?

    (1)   5 feet
    (2)   6 feet
    (3) 10 feet
    (4) 11 feet
    (5) 12 feet

The right answer is (5) 12 feet.

First, pay special attention to what you are trying to find—in this case, "the *total length* along *both sides of the roof*." Next, take full advantage of the information given.

Two equal right triangles are formed by the top of the shed and the roof, with sides 3, 4, and *x*. Using the Pythagorean theorem given in the list of formulas, you can solve for *x*:

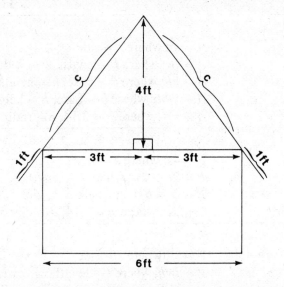

$$a^2 + b^2 = c^2$$
$$3^2 + 4^2 = c^2$$
$$9 + 16 = c^2$$
$$25 = c^2$$
$$5 = c$$

So the total length along the roof is

$$1 + x + x + 1 = 1 + 5 + 5 + 1 = 12 \text{ feet}$$

THE FORMULAS AND HOW TO USE THEM

In the actual GED Mathematics Test, you will be given the following Formulas page to help you. You should understand how to use each formula. The pages that follow the Formulas page in this section explain each of the formulas and show you how they are used.

FORMULAS

Description	Formulas
AREA (A) of a:	
square	$A = s^2$; where s = side
rectangle	$A = lw$; where l = length, w = width
parallelogram	$A = bh$; where b = base, h = height
triangle	$A = \frac{1}{2}bh$; where b = base, h = height
circle	$A = \pi r^2$; where π = 3.14, r = radius
PERIMETER (P) of a:	
square	$P = 4s$; where s = side
rectangle	$P = 2l + 2w$; where l = length, w = width
triangle	$P = a + b + c$; where a, b, and c are the sides
circumference (C) of a circle	$C = \pi d$; where π = 3.14, d = diameter
VOLUME (V) of a:	
cube	$V = s^3$; where s = side
rectangular container	$V = lwh$; where l = length, w = width, h = height
cylinder	$V = \pi r^2 h$; where π = 3.14, r = radius, h = height
Pythagorean relationship	$c^2 = a^2 + b^2$; where c = hypotenuse, a and b are legs of a right triangle
distance (d) between two points in a plane	$d = \sqrt{(x_2 - x_1)^2 + (y_2 - y_1)^2}$; where (x_1, y_1) and (x_2, y_2) are two points in a plane
slope of a line (m)	$m = \dfrac{y_2 - y_1}{x_2 - x_1}$; where (x_1, y_1) and (x_2, y_2) are two points in a plane
mean	$\text{mean} = \dfrac{x_1 + x_2 + \cdots + x_n}{n}$; where the x's are the values for which a mean is desired, and n = number of values in the series
median	median = the point in an ordered set of numbers at which half of the numbers are above and half of the numbers are below this value
simple interest (i)	$i = prt$; where p = principal, r = rate, t = time
distance (d) as function of rate and time	$d = rt$; where r = rate, t = time
total cost (c)	$c = nr$; where n = number of units, r = cost per unit

AREA (A) of a square: $A = s^2$; where s = side

If s stands for the length of a side of a square, then multiply side times side to get the area.

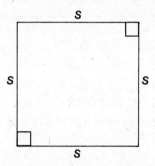

For example:

What is the area of the square below?

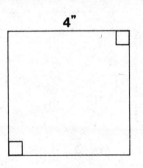

$A = s \times s = 4 \times 4 = 16$ sq in

AREA (A) of a rectangle: $A = lw$; where l = length, w = width

If l stands for the length of a rectangle and w stands for the width, then multiply the length times the width to get the area.

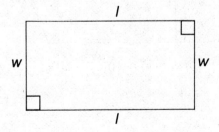

For example:

What is the area of the rectangle below?

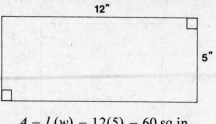

$A = l\,(w) = 12(5) = 60$ sq in

AREA (*A*) of a parallelogram: $A = bh$; where b = base, h = height

To find the area of a parallelogram where b equals the base and h equals the height, multiply the base times the height.

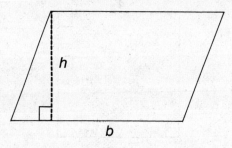

For example:

Find the area of the parallelogram below.

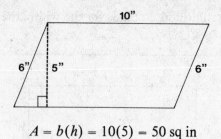

$A = b(h) = 10(5) = 50$ sq in

AREA (*A*) of a triangle: $A = \frac{1}{2}bh$; where *b* = base, *h* = height

To find the area of a triangle where *b* equals the base and *h* equals the height, multiply base times height times ½.

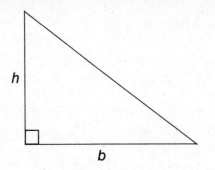 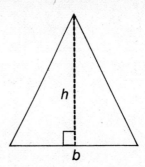

For example:

Find the area of the triangle below.

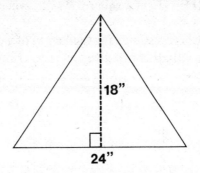

$$A = \tfrac{1}{2}bh = \tfrac{1}{2}(24)(18) = 216 \text{ sq in}$$

AREA (*A*) of a circle: $A = \pi r^2$; where $\pi = 3.14$, *r* = radius

To find the area of a circle where *r* is the radius and $\pi = 3.14$, square the radius and multiply it times 3.14.

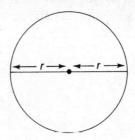

For example:

Find the area of a circle A if the radius is 3".

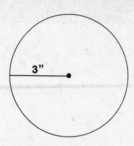

$$A = \pi r^2 = 3.14(3)^2 = 3.14(9) = 28.26 \text{ sq in}$$

PERIMETER means the total distance all the way around the outside of a many-sided figure. This perimeter can be found by adding up the lengths of all of the sides. No special formulas are really needed, but there are a few that you will commonly see.

PERIMETER (*P*) of a square: *P* = 4*s*; where *s* = side

To find the perimeter of a square where *s* stands for the length of a side, multiply the side times four. Since all four sides are the same length, this will give you the perimeter.

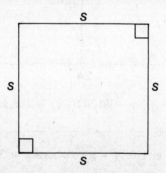

For example:

In the square below, find the perimeter if the length of a side is 2".

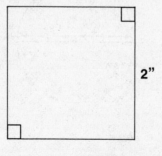

$$P = 4s = 4(2) = 8 \text{ in}$$

PERIMETER (*P*) of a rectangle: *P* = 2*l* + 2*w*; where *l* = length, *w* = width

To find the perimeter of a rectangle where *l* stands for the length and *w* stands for the width, double the length and double the width; then add these two together.

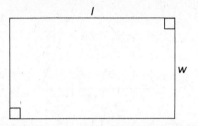

For example:

What is the perimeter of the rectangle below?

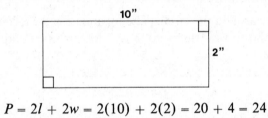

$$P = 2l + 2w = 2(10) + 2(2) = 20 + 4 = 24$$

PERIMETER (*P*) of a triangle: *P* = *a* + *b* + *c*; where *a*, *b*, and *c* are the sides

To find the perimeter of any triangle, add the lengths of each of the three sides together. This total of the three sides is the perimeter. If the sides are labeled *a*, *b*, and *c*, then the perimeter is *a* plus *b* plus *c*.

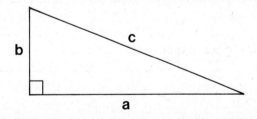

For example:

Find the perimeter of the triangle below.

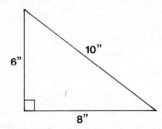

$$P = a + b + c = 8 + 6 + 10 = 24 \text{ in}$$

Another example:

What is the perimeter of the *large* triangle below?

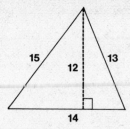

$$P = a + b + c = 14 + 15 + 13 = 42$$

CIRCUMFERENCE (C) of a circle: $C = \pi d$; where $\pi = 3.14$; d = diameter

Circumference is the distance around the circle. The formula for the circumference is $C = \pi d$, where d stands for the diameter of the circle. The formula $C = 2\pi r$, where r stands for the radius, can also be used.

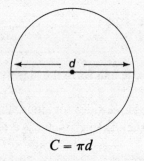

$C = \pi d$

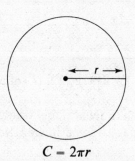

$C = 2\pi r$

For example:

Find the circumference of circle M if the radius is 4″.

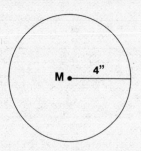

Using the formula $C = 2\pi r$:

$$C = 2\pi r = (2)(3.14)(4) = 6.28(4) = 25.12 \text{ in}$$

In circle M, since the radius is 4″, the diameter (d) is 8″. So using the formula $C = \pi d$:

$$C = \pi d = 3.14(8) = 25.12 \text{ in}$$

VOLUME (V) of a cube: $V = s^3$; where s = side

Since all sides of a cube are the same, to find the volume of a cube, multiply side times side times side. If s stands for the length of a side, then the formula would look like this:

$$V = s \times s \times s$$

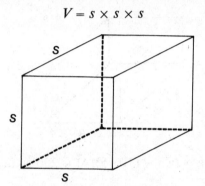

For example:

What is the volume of the cube below?

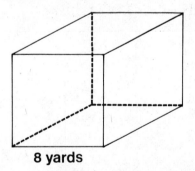

8 yards

$$V = 8 \times 8 \times 8 = 512 \text{ cu yds}$$

VOLUME (*V*) of a rectangular container: *V* = *lwh*; where *l* = length, *w* = width, *h* = height

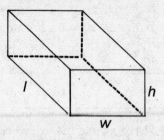

For example:

Find the volume of the rectangular container below.

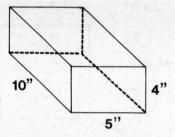

$$V = lwh = (10)(5)(4) = 200 \text{ cu in}$$

VOLUME (*V*) of a cylinder: *V* = $\pi r^2 h$; where π = 3.14, *r* = radius, *h* = height

To find the volume of a cylinder, plug into the formula $V = \pi r^2 h$. You would need to know the radius (*r*) of the bases, the height (*h*), and that π is 3.14.

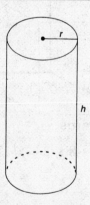

For example:

Find the volume of the following cylinder.

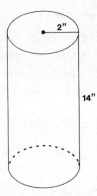

$$V = \pi r^2 h = (3.14)(2)^2 (14) = (3.14)(4)(14) = (3.14)(56) = 175.84 \text{ cu in}$$

PYTHAGOREAN RELATIONSHIP: $c^2 = a^2 + b^2$; **where** c = **hypotenuse,** a **and** b **are legs of a right triangle**

In any right triangle, the relationship between the lengths of the sides is stated by the Pythagorean theorem. The parts of a right triangle are

$\angle C$ is the right angle.

The side opposite the right angle is called the *hypotenuse* (side c). (The hypotenuse will always be the *longest* side.)

The other two sides are called the *legs* (sides a and b)

The three lengths a, b, and c will always be numbers such that $a^2 + b^2 = c^2$.

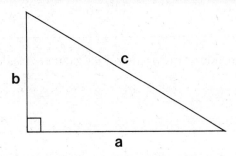

For example:

If $a = 3$, $b = 4$, and $c = 5$.

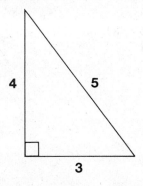

$$a^2 + b^2 = c^2$$
$$3^2 + 4^2 = 5^2$$
$$9 + 16 = 25$$
$$25 = 25$$

So 3-4-5 is called a *Pythagorean triple*. There are other values for *a*, *b*, and *c* that will always work. One is 5-12-13. Any *multiple* of one of these triples will also work. For example, using the 3-4-5: 6-8-10, 9-12-15, and 15-20-25 will also be Pythagorean triples.

Another example:

Find *c* in this right triangle.

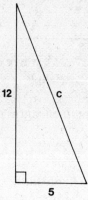

$$a^2 + b^2 = c^2$$
$$5^2 + 12^2 = c^2$$
$$25 + 144 = c^2$$
$$169 = c^2$$
$$13 = c$$

You might be asked to find the *a* side or the *b* side rather than the *c* side.

For example:

Find *b* in this right triangle.

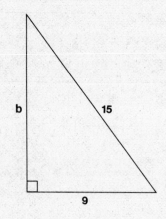

$$a^2 + b^2 = c^2$$
$$9^2 + b^2 = 15^2$$
$$81 + b^2 = 225$$
$$b^2 = 225 - 81$$
$$b^2 = 144$$
$$b = 12$$

DISTANCE (d) between two points in a plane: $d = \sqrt{(x_2 - x_1)^2 + (y_2 - y_1)^2}$; **where (x_1, y_1) and (x_2, y_2) are two points in a plane**

Each point on a plane is located by a unique ordered pair of numbers called the *coordinates*. Some coordinates are shown below.

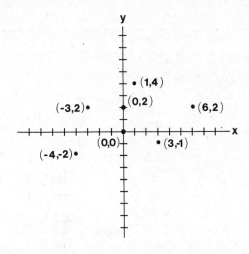

Notice that on the *x*-axis, numbers to the right of 0 are positive and to the left of 0 are negative. On the *y*-axis, numbers above 0 are positive and below 0 are negative. Also, notice that the *first* number in the ordered pair is called the *x-coordinate,* while the *second* number is the *y-coordinate.* The *x*-coordinate shows the right or left direction, and the *y*-coordinate shows the up or down direction.

To find the distance between two points in a plane, plug into the formula
$d = \sqrt{(x_2 - x_1)^2 + (y_2 - y_1)^2}$; where (x_1, y_1) and (x_2, y_2) are two points in a plane.

For example:

Find the distance between the points (9, 7) and (5, 4).

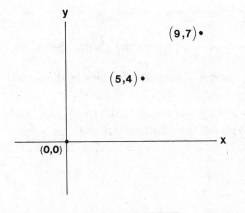

$$d = \sqrt{(9 - 5)^2 + (7 - 4)^2} = \sqrt{(4)^2 + (3)^2} = \sqrt{16 + 9} = \sqrt{25} = 5$$

SLOPE OF A LINE (*m*): $m = \dfrac{y_2 - y_1}{x_2 - x_1}$; where (x_1, y_1) and (x_2, y_2) are two points in a plane

The *slope of a line* is defined as the *rise over the run*—that is, how fast the line goes up as it goes across.

For example:

What is the slope of the line in the following figure?

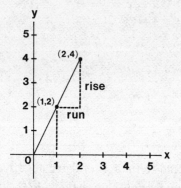

$$\text{rise} = 2$$
$$\text{run} = 1$$

$$\text{slope} = \frac{\text{rise}}{\text{run}} = \frac{2}{1}$$

This slope was easy to determine from the diagram. If we use the formula, it would look like this:

$$m = \frac{y_2 - y_1}{x_2 - x_1} \text{ where } (x_1, y_1) \text{ and } (x_2, y_2) \text{ are two points in a plane}$$

$$(x_1, y_1) = (1, 2)$$
$$(x_2, y_2) = (2, 4)$$

$$m = \frac{(4 - 2)}{(2 - 1)} = \frac{2}{1} = 2$$

MEAN: mean = $\dfrac{x_1 + x_2 + \cdots + x_n}{n}$; where the *x*'s are the values for which a mean is desired,

and *n* = number of values in the series

The mean is usually called the *average*. It is one of the most commonly used measures. To find the mean, add up the items and divide by the number of items.

For example:

What is the mean of 0, 12, 18, 20, 31, and 45?

First add the numbers: $0 + 12 + 18 + 20 + 31 + 45 = 126$

Now divide the total by 6: $126 \div 6 = 21$

The mean is 21.

MEDIAN: median = the point in an ordered set of numbers at which half of the numbers are above and half of the numbers are below this value

The median of a set of numbers is the half-way point, or middle number, when the numbers are in order. To find the median, first put the numbers in order, either from lowest to highest or highest to lowest. Then count in half way. If there is an *odd* number of items, then the median is the *middle item*. If there is an *even* number of items, then the median is the *average of the two middle numbers*.

For example:

Find the median of 7, 5, 3, 4, and 6.

First put the numbers in order: 3, 4, 5, 6, 7

Now find the middle number (the third one in this case): 3, 4, 5, 6, 7

The median is 5.

Another example:

Find the median of 6, 4, 5, and 10.

First put the numbers in order: 4, 5, 6, 10

The two middle numbers are 5 and 6. Now find the average:

$$5 + 6 = 11$$
$$11 \div 2 = 11/2 \text{ or } 5\tfrac{1}{2}$$

The median is $5\tfrac{1}{2}$.

SIMPLE INTEREST (*i*): *i = prt*; where *p* = principal, *r* = rate, *t* = time

To find the simple interest, multiply the principal, rate, and time together. Remember, the time must be in *years* and the rate must be *per year*.

For example:

How much simple interest will an account earn in five years if $500 is invested at 8% per year?

Plug into the formula *i = prt*:

$$i = (500)(.08)(5)$$
$$i = 200$$

The interest will be $200. Notice that you were multiplying the *principal* ($500) times the *rate* (8%, or .08) times the *time* (5 years).

DISTANCE (*d*) as function of rate and time: *d = rt*; where *r* = rate, *t* = time

The formula "distance equals rate times time" (*d = rt*) can be used to find the distance when you know the rate and time.

For example:

How many miles will a speedboat travel going 80 mph for 2½ hours?

First notice that you must find "how many miles." Now, using the information given in the problem, plug into the equation:

$$d = rt$$
$$d = 80(2.5)$$
$$d = 200 \text{ mi}$$

So the speedboat will travel 200 miles.

This same formula can be used to find the time when you know the distance and rate.

For example:

How long will it take a bus traveling 72 km/hr to go 36 km?

First notice that you must find "how long will it take" (time). Now, using the information given in the problem, plug into the equation:

$$d = rt$$
$$36 = 72(t)$$

Divide each side by 72:

$$\frac{36}{72} = \frac{72t}{72}$$

$$\frac{1}{2} = t$$

So it will take one-half hour for the bus to travel 36 km at 72 km/hr.

TOTAL COST (c): $c = nr$; where n = number of units, r = cost per unit

To find the total cost if you know the number of units (n) and the cost per unit (r), plug into the formula $c = nr$.

For example:

Tom bought 20 widgets at $5.00 each. What was the total cost for the 20 widgets? (No tax was charged.)

The formula is c (total cost) = n (20, number of units) $\times$ r ($5.00, cost per unit)

$$c = 20(\$5.00)$$
$$c = \$100.00$$

The total cost is $100.00.

SOCIAL STUDIES
SCIENCE
MATHEMATICS

CHARTS, GRAPHS, MAPS, CARTOONS, AND, DIAGRAMS

CHARTS, GRAPHS, MAPS, CARTOONS, AND DIAGRAMS

WHAT TO EXPECT

The GED Social Studies, Science, and Mathematics Tests will ask some questions about charts, graphs, maps, cartoons, and diagrams.

■ Expect between 20% and 40% of the questions in those tests to refer to visual material—charts, graphs, maps, cartoons, or diagrams.

■ Expect some of this visual material to be part of a paragraph or to include other written information.

Graphs and Charts

WHAT YOU SHOULD KNOW

You should know how to

Read and **understand information** given in the form of a **graph** or **chart**

Analyze and **apply information** given in a **graph** or **chart**

Spot trends and **predict** some **future trends**

177

WHAT TO LOOK FOR

■ A chart or graph is given so that you can **refer** to it. Look for **trends,** or **changing patterns** that might appear.

■ Look for **additional information** given with the chart or graph.

■ Look for **key words** and **headings.**

WHAT YOU SHOULD DO

 Focus on understanding the important information in the graph or chart.

 Don't memorize the information; refer to it when you need to.

 Sometimes skimming the questions first can be helpful. This will tell you what to look for.

 Quickly, but carefully, examine the whole graph and all additional information before you start to work problems. Make sure that you understand the information given.

 Read the questions and possible choices and notice the key words. Decide on your answer from the information given.

 Sometimes the answer to a question is available in extra information given with a graph (headings, scale factors, legends, etc.). Be sure to read and understand this information.

 Look for the obvious large changes, high points, low points, trends, etc. Obvious information often leads to an answer. Unless you are told otherwise, use only the information given in the chart or graph.

By reviewing the following section, you will become familiar with the basic types of charts and graphs.

CHARTS AND TABLES

Charts and tables are often used to give an organized picture of information, or data. Be sure that you understand *what is given*. Column headings and line items give the important information. These titles give the numbers meaning.

You could be given a chart involving **mathematics** similar to the following:

Items 1 to 4 are based on the following chart.

BURGER SALES FOR THE WEEK OF AUGUST 8 TO AUGUST 14

Day	Hamburgers	Cheeseburgers
Sunday	120	92
Monday	85	80
Tuesday	77	70
Wednesday	74	71
Thursday	75	72
Friday	91	88
Saturday	111	112

1. On which day were the most hamburgers sold?

(1) Sunday
(2) Monday
(3) Thursday
(4) Friday
(5) Saturday

The right answer is (1). First pay special attention to what information is given in the chart. This chart shows the number of "Burger Sales for the Week of August 8 to August 14." The days of the week are given along the left side of the chart. The number of *hamburgers* for each day is given in one column and the number of *cheeseburgers* in the other column.

To answer this question, you must simply be able to read the chart. The most hamburgers were sold on Sunday (120).

2. On which day were the most burgers sold (hamburgers and cheeseburgers)?

(1) Sunday
(2) Monday
(3) Thursday
(4) Friday
(5) Saturday

The right answer is (5). To answer this question, you must understand the chart and do some simple computation.

Working from the answers is probably the easiest method.

(1) Sunday   120 + 92 = 212
(2) Monday   85 + 80 = 165
(3) Thursday   75 + 72 = 147
(4) Friday   91 + 88 = 179
(5) Saturday   111 + 112 = 223

Another method is to *approximate* the answers.

3. On how many days were more hamburgers sold than cheeseburgers?

(1) 7
(2) 6
(3) 5
(4) 4
(5) 3

The right answer is (2). To answer this question, you must compare the sales for each day. Hamburgers outsold cheeseburgers every day except Saturday.

4. If the pattern of sales continues,

(1) the weekend days will have the fewest number of burger sales next week
(2) the cheeseburgers will outsell hamburgers next week
(3) generally, when hamburger sales go up, cheeseburger sales will go up
(4) hamburgers will be less expensive than cheeseburgers
(5) there will be no days on which cheeseburgers outsell hamburgers

The right answer is (3). To answer this question, you must notice one of the trends. Most days that hamburger sales go up, cheeseburger sales go up (with the exception of Saturday to Sunday).

Another type of table involving **science** could look like this:

Items 5 and 6 are based on the following chart.

CHARACTERISTICS OF THE BASIC PLANT GROUPS

Plant Group	Chlorophyll	Leaves	Seeds	Flowers
fungi	no	no	no	no
algae	yes	no	no	no
ferns	yes	yes	no	no
gymnosperms	yes	yes	yes	no
angiosperms	yes	yes	yes	yes

5. Which of the following plant groups has chlorophyll and leaves, but <u>no</u> seeds or flowers?

   (1) fungi
   (2) algae
   (3) ferns
   (4) gymnosperms
   (5) angiosperms

The right answer is (3). This table shows what each basic plant group does and doesn't have. Notice that the plant groups are listed along the left and the items (characteristics) are given at the top of each column.

To answer this question, you must be able to read the chart. Ferns have a *yes* in the chlorophyll and leaves columns and a *no* in the seeds and flowers columns. So ferns have chlorophyll and leaves, but no seeds or flowers.

6. Which of the following is the most <u>complex</u> plant group?

   (1) fungi
   (2) algae
   (3) ferns
   (4) gymnosperms
   (5) angiosperms

The right answer is (5). To answer this question, you must understand that on this table, the plant group with the *most characteristics* will be the *most complex*.

Angiosperms (5) have chlorophyll, leaves, seeds, and flowers and would be considered the most complex.

Another **science** or **mathematics** chart could look like this:

<u>Item 7</u> is based on the following chart.

Temperature of Object in Degrees Centigrade	
absolute zero	−273
oxygen freezes	−218
oxygen liquefies	−183
water freezes	0
human body	37
water boils	100
wood fire	830
iron melts	1535
iron boils	3000

7. The <u>difference</u> in temperature between the point at which oxygen freezes and the point at which iron melts is

(1) 1317
(2) 1535
(3) 1718
(4) 1753
(5) 3218

The right answer is (4). To answer this question, you must be able to read the chart and do some simple calculations.

The freezing temperature of oxygen is −218 degrees centigrade. Iron melts at 1535 degrees centigrade. To find the difference between the two you must subtract.

$$1535 - (-218) = 1535 + 218 = 1753$$

A more difficult **social studies** or **mathematics** chart might look like this:

<u>Items 8 and 9</u> are based on the following chart.

AVERAGE EXPENDITURES FOR MONTHLY HOUSING EXPENSES

Metropolitan Area	Mortgage Payment	Property Tax	Hazard Insurance	Utility Cost	Total Monthly Expenses
Large					
Chicago	$291	$ 64	$14	$60	$429
Houston	292	48	26	74	439
Los Angeles	403	99	15	50	567
New York	291	111	25	70	497
San Francisco	445	99	20	50	614
Washington	388	85	14	91	578
All U.S. metropolitan areas with populations of 1.5 million or more	$299	$ 70	$13	$60	$442
All of the United States	$273	$ 54	$13	$60	$400

8. Which city's total monthly expenses were closest to the total monthly expenses for areas with populations of 1.5 million or more?

(1) Chicago
(2) Houston
(3) New York
(4) Los Angeles
(5) Washington

The right answer is (2). First, you must determine the total monthly expenses for all U.S. cities with a population of 1.5 million or more. The last column of the next to last line shows that the number is $442 per month. The column at the left shows the *area,* and the last column shows the *total monthly expenses.*

Second, you must determine which city's total monthly expenses are closest to the $442 monthly figure. The correct answer is Houston, which has a total monthly expense of $439.

9. You could conclude which of the following statements from information presented in the chart?

(1) Los Angeles residents have larger incomes than residents in New York.
(2) The median mortgage payment in Los Angeles is lower than that in Washington.
(3) Housing dollars would stretch further in smaller cities.
(4) Hazard insurance is higher as the total monthly expenses increase.
(5) It costs more for monthly expenses in Washington, San Francisco, and New York than anywhere else in the country.

The right answer is (3). To answer this question you must draw a *conclusion* from information presented in the table.

The information in Choice (1) cannot be determined from the data in the table. (Don't choose as an answer information that is *not presented* in the chart or graph, even if the statement might be based on accepted fact.) You can quickly eliminate choice (2) because the mortgage payment table shows that the Los Angeles average is $403, while the Washington average is $388. You can see that choice (4) is false by looking at the Houston hazard insurance ($26), the highest in the chart, and Houston's total monthly expenses ($439) one of the lowest in the chart. Choice (5) is false because *Los Angeles* has the third highest total monthly expenses ($567).

Notice that the monthly expense column is *not* in rank order—lowest to highest. The correct answer (3) can be supported by data presented in the chart. Notice that all cities with populations of 1.5 million or more have a total monthly expense figure of $442. "All of the United States" (the United States considered as a whole) has a total monthly expense of $400. This means that many small cities reduced the $442 total monthly figure. So you can conclude that housing dollars would stretch further in smaller cities.

GRAPHS

Information may be displayed in many ways. The four basic types of graphs you should know are: *pictographs, bar graphs, line graphs,* and *pie graphs* (or *pie charts*).

Pictographs
Pictographs use *pictures* to help you see information and make comparisons.

You could be given a **mathematics** pictograph similar to this:

Items 10 to 12 refer to the following graph.

During the summer months, Phil works by the beach selling surfboards. Phil decided to chart his sales. Each circle represents $1000 in sales.

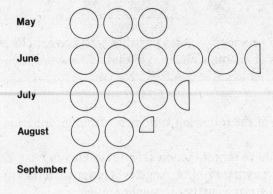

10. About how much money did Phil receive in sales in July?

   (1) $3000
   (2) $3500
   (3) $4000
   (4) $5000
   (5) $5500

The right answer is (2). To answer this question, you must understand how to read this pictograph.

Since each circle stands for $1000, each half circle stands for $500. July has 3½ circles, which equals $3500.

11. In which month did Phil receive the **most** money for his sales?

   (1) May
   (2) June
   (3) July
   (4) August
   (5) September

The right answer is (2). By scanning the graph, you can see that the longest line is the June line and that the most money from sales came in June.

12. About how much more money did Phil receive in his best month than he did in his worst month?

   (1) $1500
   (2) $2500
   (3) $3500
   (4) $4500
   (5) $5000

The right answer is (3). In Phil's best month, June, he had sales of $5500. In his worst month, September, he had sales of $2000. Now, subtracting gives:

$$\$5500 - \$2000 = \$3500$$

Bar Graphs

Bar graphs convert the information in a chart into separate bars or columns. Some graphs list numbers along one edge and places, dates, people, or things (individual categories) along another edge. Always try to determine the *relationship* between the columns in a graph or chart.

You could be given a **social studies** bar graph similar to this:

Item 13 is based on the following bar graph.

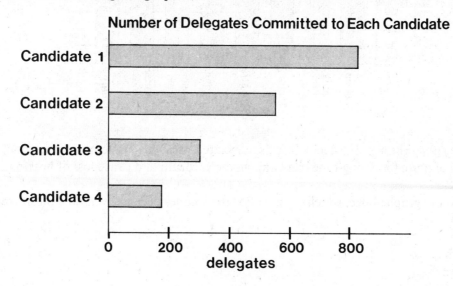

Number of Delegates Committed to Each Candidate

13. Candidate 1 has approximately how many more delegates committed than Candidate 2?

    (1) 150
    (2) 200
    (3) 250
    (4) 400
    (5) 500

The right answer is (3). To understand this question, you must be able to read the bar graph and make comparisons. Notice that the graph shows the "Number of Delegates Committed to Each Candidate," with the numbers given along the bottom of the graph in increases of 200. The names are listed along the left side.

Candidate 1 has approximately 800 delegates (possibly a few more). The bar graph for Candidate 2 stops about three quarters of the way between 400 and 600. Now consider that half way between 400 and 600 would be 500. So Candidate 2 is at about 550. 800 − 550 = 250

A bar graph involving **science** could look like this:

Item 14 is based on the following graph.

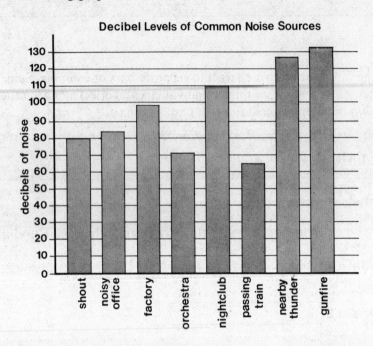

The graph above shows the average decibel levels associated with various common sources of noise. Listening to high levels of noise for a long time can damage the eardrum and cause loss of hearing.

14. According to the graph above, which of the following sources of noise would be <u>most</u> likely to damage the eardrum?

    (1) noisy office
    (2) orchestra
    (3) passing train
    (4) nearby thunder
    (5) gunfire

The right answer is (5). To answer this question, you must be able to read the graph and understand the information included. Notice that the decibels of noise are listed along the left hand side in increases of 10. The common sources of noise are listed along the bottom of the graph.

Since gunfire has the highest decibel rating, it is usually the loudest of the choices. This would cause it to be the most likely to damage the eardrum.

A more difficult bar graph involving **social studies** could look like this:

Items 15 and 16 are based on the following bar graph.

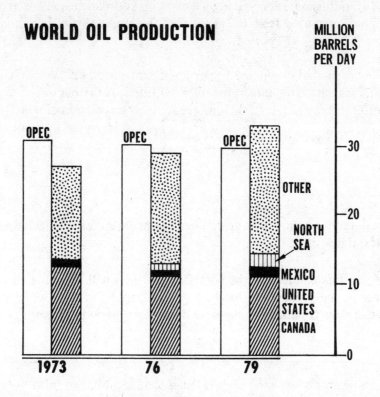

WORLD OIL PRODUCTION

MILLION BARRELS PER DAY

15. Approximately how much oil was produced by the United States and Canada in 1979?

    (1)   8 million barrels per day
    (2) 11 million barrels per day
    (3) 13 million barrels per day
    (4) 20 million barrels per day
    (5) 33 million barrels per day

> The right answer is (2). The bar graph shows the years in study on the horizontal line along the bottom of the graph (1973-1979). The vertical line at the right shows the number of barrels per day stated in millions. Note that the vertical line at the right is spaced in increments of 10 million barrels per day (0 to 10, 10 to 20, etc.).
>
> In 1979 the United States and Canada produced approximately 11 million barrels per day.

16. Since 1973, the rate of United States and Canadian oil production has

    (1) risen sharply
    (2) outpaced OPEC production
    (3) dropped dramatically
    (4) declined gradually
    (5) fluctuated sharply

The right answer is (4). In this question you are asked to make a conclusion based on the facts (data) presented in the graph. You can see from the graph that the production of U.S. and Canadian oil has declined *slightly* over the 1973-1979 period.

The term OPEC refers to the Oil Producing Exporting Countries; Saudi Arabia, the leading producer of world oil, is the most significant member of OPEC. A further question might have asked in what year did OPEC oil production fall behind the total oil production of non-OPEC countries (1979).

Line Graphs

Line graphs convert data into points on a grid. These points are then connected to show a relationship between the items, dates, times, etc.

Notice the slopes of the lines connecting the points. These lines will show increases and decreases. The sharper the slope *upwards,* the greater the *increase.* The sharper the slope *downwards,* the greater the *decrease.* Line graphs can show trends, or changes, in data over a period of time.

You could be given a line graph involving **social studies** that is similar to this:

Items 17 and 18 are based on the following graph.

17. In which of the following years were there about 500,000 American Indians?

(1) 1930
(2) 1940
(3) 1950
(4) 1960
(5) 1970

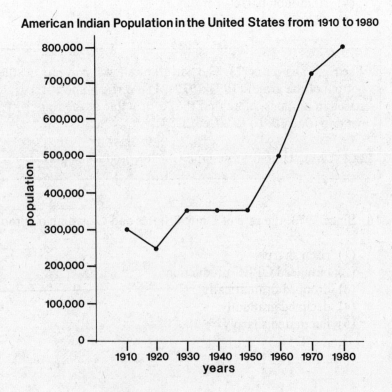

American Indian Population in the United States from 1910 to 1980

The right answer is (4). To answer this question, you must be able to read the graph. The information along the left side of the graph shows the number of Indians in increases of 100,000. The bottom of the graph shows the years from 1910 to 1980.

You will notice that in 1960 there were about 500,000 American Indians in the United States. Using the edge of your answer sheet like a ruler will help you see that the dot in the 1960 column lines up with 500,000 on the left.

18. During which of the following time periods was there a <u>decrease</u> in the American Indian population?

    (1) 1910 to 1920
    (2) 1920 to 1930
    (3) 1930 to 1940
    (4) 1960 to 1970
    (5) 1970 to 1980

The right answer is (1). Since the slope of the line goes *down* from 1910 to 1920, there must have been a decrease. If you read the actual numbers you will notice a decrease from 300,000 to 250,000.

Another line graph involving **science** or **mathematics** might look like this.

<u>Item 19</u> is based on the following graph.

19. The Roadster II accelerated the most between

    (1) 1 and 2 seconds
    (2) 2 and 3 seconds
    (3) 3 and 4 seconds
    (4) 4 and 5 seconds
    (5) 5 and 6 seconds

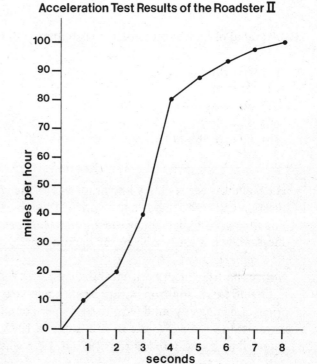

Acceleration Test Results of the Roadster II

The right answer is (3). To answer this question you must understand how the information is presented. The numbers on the left side of the graph show the speed in miles per hour (mph). The information at the bottom of the graph shows the number of seconds.

The movement of the line can give important information and show trends. The *more the line slopes upward*, the *greater the acceleration*. The greatest slope upward is between 3 and 4 seconds. The Roadster II accelerates from about 40 to about 80 mph in that time.

You could be given a more difficult **mathematics** or **social studies** graph similar to the following:

Items 20 to 22 are based on the following line graph.

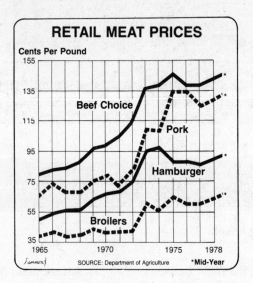

20. A pound of hamburger in 1975 cost approximately how much more than it did in 1970?

    (1) 20 cents
    (2) 25 cents
    (3) 30 cents
    (4) 35 cents
    (5) none of these

The right answer is (1). A line graph shows the relationship between two or more items. This question calls for comparing the price of hamburger in 1975 with the price of hamburger in 1970. You are asked to determine the *approximate price increase during the given period*. To answer the question, you must be able to see the differences among the four items listed on the chart.

Notice that the lower horizontal line indicates the time reference as given in years 1965 to 1978. Each line extending from it represents a one-year increment. The vertical line on the far left gives the price, or cents per pound (35¢ to $1.55 per pound). Each line extending from it represents a 20¢ increment (35¢ to 55¢; 55¢ to 75¢, etc.). In 1975 hamburger sold for slightly more than 85¢ per pound. The price increase from 1970 to 1975 was approximately 20¢ per pound.

21. Which of the following is an accurate statement based on the information provided in the chart?

    (1) The figures for mid-year 1978 indicate a downward trend in retail meat prices.
    (2) Pork prices increased more gradually than broiler prices.
    (3) More hamburger was sold than beef choice.
    (4) The figures for mid-year 1978 indicate a continued increase in retail meat prices.
    (5) The overall price of retail meat declined in the 1970s.

The right answer is (4). To answer this question you must be able to determine the *one* statement that is consistent with the information provided in the graph.

Mid-year 1978 is shown by the continuation of the lines representing meat prices beyond the 1978 line. Notice that all lines represent an *upward* trend.

Choice (1) does not agree with the data in the chart. Choice (2) asks you to compare two items to see which one showed the most consistent price over the entire period of the study. You should notice that pork prices, especially since 1971, increased more dramatically than broiler prices.

Choice (3) cannot be supported by the information given. (*Do not* read information into the chart.) It should be easy to see that statement (5) is wrong. *All* meat items showed an increase in price over the 1970s. The only statement that agrees with the information is (4). All meat prices, as shown by the mid-year 1978 prices, show a continued increase.

22. If a person purchased 20 pounds of beef choice in 1965, how much <u>more</u> money would it cost the person in 1978 to purchase the same amount of beef choice?

    (1) $ 12
    (2) $ 16
    (3) $ 28
    (4) $ 80
    (5) $140

The right answer is (1). You must determine how much *more* money 20 pounds of an item (beef choice) cost over a specific period of time.

In 1965 beef choice cost approximately 80 cents a pound ($.80 × 20 = $16.00); in 1978 beef choice cost approximately $1.40 per pound ($1.40 × 20 = $28.00); the difference is $12.00 ($28.00 − $16.00 = $12.00).

Circle Graphs or Pie Charts

A circle graph, or pie chart, shows the relationship between the whole circle (100%) and the various slices that represent portions of that 100%. The larger the slice, the higher the percentage.

You could be given a circle graph similar to the following that involves **mathematics**:

Items 23 to 25 are based on the following circle graph.

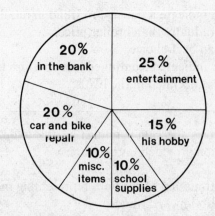

How John Spends His Monthly Paycheck

23. John spends one quarter of his monthly paycheck on

    (1) his hobby
    (2) car and bike repair
    (3) entertainment
    (4) school supplies
    (5) Not enough information is given.

The right answer is (3). To answer this question, you must be able to read the graph and apply some simple math.

Notice how the information is given in the graph. Each item is given along with the percent of money spent on that item. Since one quarter is the same as 25%, entertainment is the one you are looking for.

24. If John receives $100 on this month's paycheck, how much will he put in the bank?

    (1) $ 2
    (2) $20
    (3) $35
    (4) $60
    (5) $80

The right answer is (2). To answer this question, you must again read the graph carefully and apply some simple math.

John puts 20% of his income in the bank. 20% of $100 is $20. So he will put $20 in the bank.

25. The <u>ratio</u> of the amount of money John spends on his hobby to the amount he puts in the bank is

    (1) 1/6
    (2) 1/2
    (3) 5/8
    (4) 2/3
    (5) 3/4

The right answer is (5). To answer this question, you must use the information in the graph to make a ratio.

$$\frac{\text{his hobby}}{\text{in the bank}} = \frac{15\%}{20\%} = \frac{15}{20} = \frac{3}{4}$$

Notice that the ratio of 15%/20% reduces to 3/4.

Another circle graph involving **mathematics** could look similar to this:

Items 26 and 27 refer to the following graph, which shows 1988 expenditures for Pinewood School.

26. The amount of money given to <u>charity</u> in 1988 was approximately what percent of the <u>total</u> amount earned?

    (1) 15%
    (2) 30%
    (3) 40%
    (4) 60%
    (5) Not enough information is given.

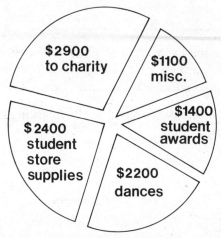

The right answer is (2). Notice how the information is given in the graph. Each item is listed with the amount spent for that item.

By carefully reading the information in the graph, you will find that $2900 was given to charity. The information describing the graph explains that the total earnings were $10,000. Since $2900 is approximately $3000, the approximate *percentage* would be worked out as follows:

$$\frac{3000}{10,000} = \frac{30}{100} = 30\%$$

27. If the Pinewood School spends the same percentage on dances every year, how much will they spend in 1989 if their earnings are $15,000?

(1) $1100
(2) $2200
(3) $2600
(4) $3300
(5) $4300

The right answer is (4). To answer this question, you must first find a percent and then apply this percent to a new total. In 1988 the Pinewood School spent $2200 on dances. This can be calculated to 22% by the following method:

$$\frac{2200}{10,000} = \frac{22}{100} = 22\%$$

Now, multiplying 22% times the *new* total earnings of $15,000 will give the right answer.

$$22\% = .22 \qquad .22 \times 15,000 = 3300 \text{ or } \$3300$$

You could use another common-sense method. If $2200 out of $10,000 is spent for dances, then $1100 out of every $5000 is spent for dances. Since $15,000 is 3 × $5000, 3 × $1100 would be $3300.

Sometimes you could be given more than one circle graph. A more difficult **social studies** or **mathematics** graph problem could look like this:

Items 28 and 29 are based on the following pie charts.

Distribution of Earned Degrees
By Field of Study

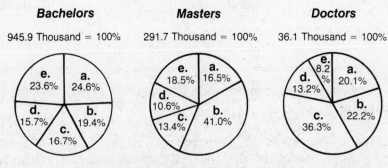

Bachelors	Masters	Doctors
945.9 Thousand = 100%	291.7 Thousand = 100%	36.1 Thousand = 100%

a. social sciences
b. education
c. natural sciences
d. humanities
e. business, accounting, and other

28. Which field of study received the smallest number of earned masters degrees?

    (1) social sciences
    (2) education
    (3) natural sciences
    (4) humanities
    (5) business, accounting, and other

The right answer is (4). Remember that a circle graph, or pie chart, shows the relationship between the whole circle (100%) and the slices or parts of that 100%. The larger the slice, the higher the percentage.

A circle graph makes it easy to see the relationship among the parts that make up the total graph. Two or more circle graphs can be used in the same example to show many relationships.

In this question you must find the field of study that received the *least* number of *masters* degrees. You can see that the humanities, with 10.6% of the total amount, is the correct answer.

Notice that with the data given, you could have calculated the *number* of masters degrees earned in the humanities, although to answer this question you do not need to. 291.7 thousand equals 100% (see the information above the circle graph); therefore 10.6% of 291,700 would be approximately 30,920 earned degrees. This information could be calculated for each segment of the pie chart.

29. In comparing bachelors degrees to doctors degrees, which field of study shows the greatest percentage change?

    (1) social sciences
    (2) education
    (3) natural sciences
    (4) humanities
    (5) business, accounting, and other

The right answer is (3). To answer this question you must compare total *percentage changes*. If the question asked you to find the *negative* percentage change (percentage loss) the correct answer would have been (5). (Business showed a 15% reduction in earned degrees.)

From the chart you can see that choices (3) and (5) show the greatest percentage change. Choice (3) shows approximately a 20% change, while choice (5) shows approximately a 15% change.

Maps

A map can represent all or part of the Earth's surface. Maps are usually classified into four general types:

Political maps: show governments, politics, political parties

Special-purpose maps: show products, vegetation, minerals, population, transportation, etc.

Physical maps: show the Earth's surface, climate, currents

Relief maps: show the shape of the land

WHAT TO LOOK FOR

Geographic factors to be considered in maps:

- Location of the event
- Size of the area involved
- Geographic relationship of the area to other concerned places (How far apart are the places? In what direction?)
- Important water areas
- Means of access to the area (How can we get to the area?)
- Physical factors such as mountains and plains
- Natural resources which play a part
- Soil, climate, and rainfall

Human factors to be considered in maps:

- Industries of the area
- Trade and other relations with the outside world
- Available means of transportation
- Size and location of population
- Large cities concerned in the event
- Racial, religious, and other factors involved
- Developments from history

WHAT YOU SHOULD DO

To understand a map you must first become familiar with the information presented on the map.

For instance, the **title, legend, scale, direction, longitude,** and **latitude** are all important to interpret a map. The legend is particularly important, since it usually explains the **symbols** used on a map.

Notice the main points of the map first, then look at the finer detail.

You could be given a map of the United States that looks similar to this that involves **social studies** or **mathematics:**

Items 30 and 31 are based on the following map.

Percent Change by State
In High-School Graduates 1986-2004

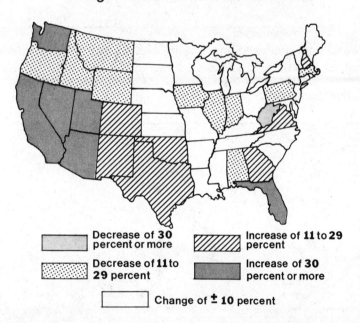

The map above uses different shadings to show how the percentage of high school graduates will increase or decrease in each state in an eighteen-year period.

30. According to the map, which of the following will occur in the <u>most</u> states?

    (1) decrease of 30% or more
    (2) decrease of 11 to 29%
    (3) change of about 10%
    (4) increase of 11 to 29%
    (5) increase of 30% or more

The right answer is (3). To answer this question, you must understand the map and the legend given.

The legend, or key, at the bottom of the map shows what each different type of shading stands for. Read this information carefully. Now simply count the number of states that have the same type of shading. You may have noticed that most of the states had no shading, so most states had a change of about 10%.

31. According to the map, generally the greatest <u>increase</u> is expected in the

    (1) Northeast
    (2) Southeast
    (3) Midwest
    (4) Northwest
    (5) Southwest

The right answer is (5). The dark shading reflects the greatest increase. Most of the dark shading occurs in the lower left-hand corner of the map—the Southwest. If you looking for trends, you might immediately notice that most states with large increases were in the Southwest.

You could be given a world map similar to this that involves **science** or **social studies:**

Item 32 is based on the following map.

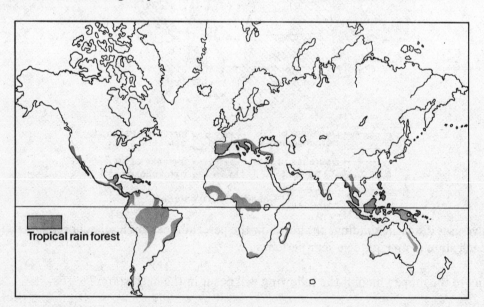

Tropical rain forest

The map above shows the tropical rain forests of the world.

32. Which of the following continents has the largest tropical rain forest area?

    (1) North America
    (2) South America
    (3) Africa
    (4) Europe
    (5) Asia

The right answer is (2). To answer this question, you must understand the legend and know some of the continents. Since the dark shading represents tropical rain forests, notice where most of this dark shading occurs. South America has the greatest amount of dark shading.

A slightly more complex map involving **social studies** could look like this:

Items 33 and 34 are based on the following map.

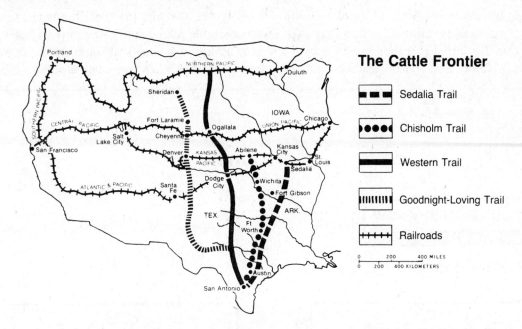

33. Which trail connected the Northern Pacific Railroad with San Antonio?

    (1) Sedalia Trail
    (2) Chisholm Trail
    (3) Goodnight-Loving Trail
    (4) Western Trail
    (5) none of these

The right answer is (4). The Western Trail is the only trail that connects with the Northern Pacific. Notice that the legend and the title "The Cattle Frontier" are clues to the historical importance of this special-purpose map.

You can see that many questions can be made from data included in this map. For instance, what would be the importance of having a western trail cross a major railroad line? Possible answers could include (1) towns would develop around the connecting point or (2) the railroad could be used to bring western cattle to various markets.

34. If you were to leave St. Louis with a final destination of Portland, the most logical route would be to

    (1) go by rail to Chicago; go by rail to Ogallala; go by trail to the Northern Pacific rail connection; proceed by rail to Portland

    (2) go by rail to Santa Fe; connect by rail with the Atlantic & Pacific and Southern Pacific; proceed by rail to Portland

    (3) go by rail to Chicago; go by rail to the Central Pacific and Southern Pacific connection; proceed by rail to Portland

    (4) go by rail to Denver; go by trail to connect with the Central Pacific; proceed by rail to Portland

    (5) go by rail to Sedalia; go by trail to the Atlantic & Pacific connection at Santa Fe; proceed by rail to Portland

The right answer is (3). You can quickly eliminate choices (1), (4), and (5) because they use trails to connect with various railroads. Using a trail with unpredictable road conditions and traveling by wagon would be far slower than traveling by a longer rail route. Choice (3) is the most *direct* rail route to Portland. Look for the shortest route before you eliminate each possible answer.

Cartoons

WHAT YOU SHOULD KNOW

A political cartoon represents

A funny picture of **people**

A funny picture of **places**

A funny picture of **things**

A political cartoon is used to make a special point or to make fun of some subject of popular interest.

WHAT TO LOOK FOR

■ Look for the **current event** used in the cartoon.

■ Look for the **point of view** of the political cartoonist.
What is the cartoonist trying to say? Remember, most good political cartoonists are often critics who comment on the social issues that face the United States and the world.

WHAT YOU SHOULD DO

 Become familiar with the symbols used in political cartoons.

For instance, the "donkey" represents the Democratic Party; the "elephant" is a symbol of the Republican Party; the "dove" is a symbol of peace; the "hawk" is a symbol of war; and "Washington D.C." and "Uncle Sam" are symbols of the United States government.

 Try to understand the meaning of the statement that goes with the political cartoon. This statement is often a clue to the cartoonist's attitude.

You could be given a **social studies** cartoon similar to this:

Item 35 is based on the following political cartoon.

35. How does the cartoonist feel about neutron nuclear weapons?

    (1) The military has been able to develop much larger nuclear weapons.
    (2) Nuclear weapons are necessary if the United States is to maintain the current balance of power with Russia.
    (3) Neutron nuclear weapons are not as deadly as conventional nuclear weapons.
    (4) The military is responsible for developing nuclear weapons.
    (5) Advanced nuclear designs cannot change the deadly nature of nuclear weapons.

The right answer is (5). In this political cartoon a comparison is drawn between neutron nuclear weapons and nonneutron nuclear weapons. The symbols are clues to the cartoonist's point of view.

Notice that the "refined," or technologically advanced, neutron bomb still represents death and destruction. The neutron bomb is dressed in the "cloak of death"; the refined cigarette holder still produces a "mushroom cloud" (a mushroom cloud is a symbol of the destructive nature of the bomb). The question asked by the military—"Notice how much more refined?"—is an indication that the cartoonist considers refinements in nuclear weapons as nothing but more "sophisticated" killing devices.

In other words, in the cartoonist's point of view, a "refined" nuclear weapon is still a nuclear weapon.

Another **social studies** cartoon could look something like this:

Item 36 is based on the following political cartoon.

'AFTER YOU!'... 'NO, AFTER YOU!'... 'NO, AFTER YOU!'... 'NO, AFTER YOU!'... 'NO, AFTER YOU!'... 'NO...

36. The main point of the political cartoon is that

    (1) the business community is a contributor to the inflationary cycle because it encourages the consumption of unnecessary items
    (2) clinics are primarily for the poor and therefore are avoided by the economic policy makers
    (3) weight control clinics are inadequate in determining the basic causes of overweight
    (4) the employer as well as the employee must compromise if inflation is going to be reduced
    (5) people on a fixed income are most affected by inflation

The right answer is (4). The cartoonist indicates that both prices and wages are too high (overweight condition of each item). The weight control clinic suggests that measures that will reduce the rate of inflation (prices rising faster than production) are available. It is clear that in a program of effective weight loss, an individual must be committed to hard work and sacrifice. The cartoonist indicates that economic self-interest is keeping labor (wages) and management (prices) from starting policies that might reduce inflation.

Diagrams

WHAT YOU SHOULD KNOW

Sometimes information will be given in a **simple diagram** or **picture**

Know how to **follow** and **understand** the **information** given in the diagram

WHAT TO LOOK FOR

■ Look for the **main emphasis** of the diagram. (What is the drawing trying to point out?)

■ Look for **key words, markings, directions of arrows, distances,** etc.

■ Look for the **obvious** and the **unusual.**

WHAT YOU SHOULD DO

 You may wish to skim the questions before looking at the diagram.

 Examine the diagram carefully. Make sure you understand the information given.

 Read any additional information given carefully.

Don't try to memorize the diagram.

You could be given a **science** diagram similar to the following:

Item 37 is based on the diagram below.

STRUCTURE OF THE EARTH

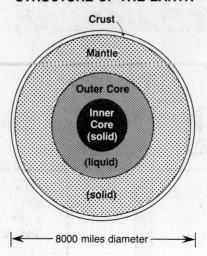

← 8000 miles diameter →

37. According to the diagram, most of the Earth is composed of which of the following?

    (1) crust
    (2) mantle
    (3) outer core
    (4) inner core
    (5) Not enough information is given.

The right answer is (2). By carefully examining the diagram, you will notice that the mantle takes up the largest portion of the Earth's structure.

You could be given a **science** diagram similar to the following:

Item 38 is based on the following diagram.

CROSS SECTION OF THE ATLANTIC OCEAN

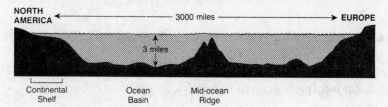

38. According to the diagram, all of the following are true EXCEPT

    (1) Europe does not have a Continental Shelf
    (2) the mid-ocean ridge is about half way between the two continents
    (3) the ocean basin is of fairly consistent depth
    (4) the mid-ocean ridge is less than three miles high
    (5) the ocean basin and the continental shelf are not of the same depth

The right answer is (1). To answer this question, you must understand the information given in the diagram. You must also notice that you are looking for what is *not* true.

Choice (1), "Europe does not have a continental shelf," is *not* true. It *does* have a continental shelf, although it appears smaller than that of North America. Notice also that only the continental shelf of North America is marked in the diagram. You must analyze this diagram to see that this marking is showing *one example*. Notice that the ocean basin is also marked on only one side of the mid-ocean ridge, but there is an ocean basin on the other side. By careful inspection, you will see that all of the other choices are *true,* so you can eliminate them.

A **science** diagram with additional information could look like this:

Items 39 and 40 are based on the following diagram and information.

The diagram below shows how energy is conserved when a baseball is thrown vertically into the air. Its speed upward decreases because gravity is pulling downward. The rising ball loses kinetic energy (slows down) as it gains potential energy (rises higher). At the peak of the ball's flight, before it starts down, the ball has no kinetic energy, but maximum stored potential energy. As the ball falls, the potential energy is transformed into kinetic energy and the ball speeds up. This is illustrated by the following diagram:

39. According to the information, when the ball finally hits the ground, it has

    (1) no potential energy
    (2) maximum potential energy
    (3) no kinetic energy
    (4) decreasing kinetic energy and
        increasing potential energy
    (5) increasing kinetic energy and
        decreasing potential energy

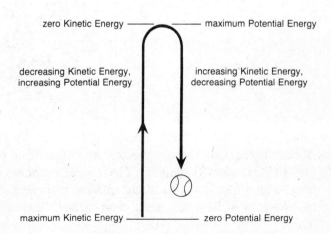

CONSERVATION OF ENERGY

zero Kinetic Energy ——————— maximum Potential Energy

decreasing Kinetic Energy, increasing Potential Energy

increasing Kinetic Energy, decreasing Potential Energy

maximum Kinetic Energy ——————— zero Potential Energy

The right answer is (1). To answer this question, you must simply understand and follow the diagram.

Read the information carefully and follow the direction of the object. Notice that when the ball hits the ground, it has *zero* potential energy.

40. If the ball is thrown perfectly straight up, at the <u>peak</u> of the ball's flight, the ball

   (1) is moving quickly
   (2) is moving slowly
   (3) has minimum potential energy
   (4) has maximum kinetic energy
   (5) is instantly at rest

The right answer is (5). From the diagram, at the peak of the ball's flight it has zero kinetic energy and maximum potential energy. The ball slows down as it reaches its peak, and then comes to a stop before it starts downward. At this point, you should be able to deduce that the ball is instantly at rest.

You could be given a **science** diagram similar to this.

<u>Item 41</u> is based on the following diagram and information.

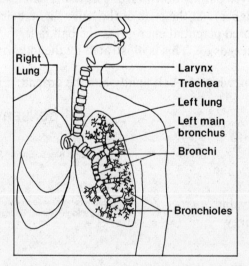

Air enters the body through the nose and mouth and passes into the throat. Next it goes into the larynx and then to the trachea (windpipe). The trachea branches into two main bronchi. Each main bronchus leads to a lung, which also contains many smaller bronchi and bronchioles. Inside these lungs, oxygen enters the bloodstream while at the same time carbon dioxide leaves the blood and enters the lungs to be breathed out.

41. From the information given above, which of the following is the path of <u>carbon dioxide</u> as it is exhaled?

    (1) larynx/trachea/main bronchus/bronchi/bronchioles
    (2) bronchioles/bronchi/main bronchus/trachea/larynx
    (3) trachea/larynx/main bronchus/bronchi/bronchioles
    (4) bronchi/larynx/trachea/main bronchus/bronchioles
    (5) bronchioles/bronchi/main bronchus/larynx/trachea

The correct answer is (2). To answer this question, you must understand not only the diagram, but also the additional information given.

By *reversing* the process of air coming into the lungs, you will get the path *out of* the lungs. Carbon dioxide is exhaled starting from the bronchioles to the bronchi to the main bronchus to the trachea to the larynx.

You could be given a **mathematics** diagram similar to this:

<u>Item 42</u> is based on the following diagram.

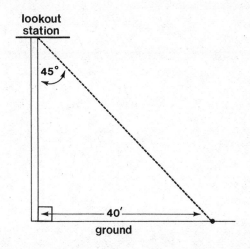

42. As pictured in the diagram above, Felipe has built a lookout station, but does not know the height of the station from the ground. Felipe climbs to the top of the station and spots a coin 40 feet from the base of the station. He accurately marks the angle of his sight as 45 degrees (as shown above). From this information, he correctly determines the height of the lookout station as

    (1) 20 feet
    (2) 30 feet
    (3) 40 feet
    (4) 60 feet
    (5) 80 feet

The right answer is (3). To answer this question, you must understand the diagram and apply some basic geometry.

Since the lookout station is shown to be vertical, or 90 degrees, to the ground, and the angle of sight is 45 degrees, then the third angle must be 45 degrees. This is because there are 180 degrees in a triangle. Now, since two of the angles in a triangle are equal, it is an isosceles triangle and the sides opposite those angles are also equal. So, the sides opposite the 45 degrees are each 40 feet.

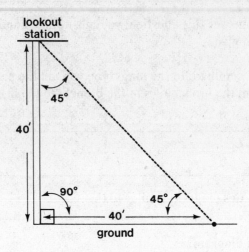

3

How to Start Reviewing

How to Use This Section

The following section will show you **how to review** for each of the GED tests. The section will help you **focus your review** by pointing out basic key questions. Knowing how to focus your review will make your study time much more effective.

TEST
1

WRITING SKILLS
PARTS I AND II

TEST 1: WRITING SKILLS

Part I: Multiple-Choice

In Part I, the multiple-choice section, thirty-five percent of the questions will ask you to recognize errors in *sentence structure*. Another thirty-five percent will test *usage*, and thirty percent will test *mechanics*. The following right hand pages will give you a chance to practice spotting common errors. After you read and answer the questions on each page, turn the page to find answers and explanations. Notice that on these answer pages, you will see the *correct* sentences in **bold type.**

SENTENCE STRUCTURE ERRORS

Sentence Fragments

The most common sentence structure errors are *sentence fragments,* that is, sentences which do *not* have both a subject and a main verb. Can you recognize which of the following examples are fragments and which are complete sentences?

1. Dave forgetting to put his lunch in the car.

2. Leaving his wallet on the table in the kitchen.

3. Dave left his lunch at home.

4. The forgotten lunch on the table in the kitchen.

Comma Splices and Run-On Sentences

Putting together two sentences without using the right punctuation can lead to two other sentence structure errors, the *comma splice* (using a comma instead of a conjunction like "and") and the *run-on sentence* (a sentence with a necessary conjunction left out). Which of the following sentences are incorrect, and what is the error?

5. Dave forgot to put his lunch in the car, he left it on the table.

6. Dave forgot his lunch he left it on the table.

7. Dave forgot his lunch and left it on the table.

8. Dave left his lunch on the table.

Sentence Fragments

1. Dave forgetting to put his lunch in the car. (sentence fragment)

    Dave forgot to put his lunch in the car. (complete sentence)

2. Leaving his wallet on the table in the kitchen. (sentence fragment)

    He left his wallet on the table in the kitchen. (complete sentence)

3. **Dave left his lunch at home.** (complete sentence)

4. The forgotten lunch on the table in the kitchen. (sentence fragment)

    The lunch was forgotten on the table in the kitchen. (complete sentence)

Comma Splices and Run-On Sentences

5. Dave forgot to put his lunch in the car, he left it on the table. (incorrect sentence, comma splice error)

    Dave forgot to put his lunch in the car, and he left it on the table. (correct sentence)

6. Dave forgot his lunch he left it on the table. (incorrect sentence, run-on sentence)

    Dave forgot his lunch, and he left it on the table. (correct sentence)

7. **Dave forgot his lunch and left it on the table.** (correct sentence)

8. **Dave left his lunch on the table.** (correct sentence)

Conjunction Errors

> *Conjunction errors* (errors of faulty coordination) may also be tested. Which of the following sentences is correct?

9. Dave forgot his lunch but left it on the table.

10. Dave forgot his lunch and left it on the table.

Dangling Modifiers and Parallelism Errors

> *Dangling modifiers* and *parallelism errors* are also mistakes of sentence structure. Which of the following are examples of these errors?

11. Having left his wallet at home, Dave would not pay for lunch.

12. Having left his wallet at home, the lunch bill was not paid.

13. Leaving his lunch on the kitchen table and having left his wallet in the bedroom, Dave could not have lunch.

14. Having left his lunch on the kitchen table and his wallet in the bedroom, Dave could not have lunch.

Conjunction Errors

9. Dave forgot his lunch but left it on the table.
(incorrect conjunction—*But* should be replaced by *and* because the meaning of *and* makes sense in this sentence.)

10. **Dave forgot his lunch and left it on the table.** (correct sentence)

Dangling Modifiers and Parallelism Errors

11. **Having left his wallet at home, Dave would not pay for his lunch.** (correct sentence)

12. Having left his wallet at home, the lunch bill was not paid.
(incorrect sentence, dangling modifier—This sentence makes it seem as though the *lunch bill* left the wallet at home.)

    Dave could not pay the lunch bill because he left his wallet at home. (correct sentence)

13. Leaving his lunch on the kitchen table and having left his wallet in the bedroom, Dave could not have lunch.
(parallelism error—To be parallel the two verbs should both be *having left* or one verb should be used for both *lunch* and *wallet*)

14. **Having left his lunch on the kitchen table and his wallet in the bedroom, Dave could not have lunch.**
(correct sentence)

USAGE ERRORS

> The most frequent errors of usage tested are errors of *agreement*, of *verb tense*, and of *pronoun reference*.

Subject/Verb Agreement Errors

> The largest number of agreement errors will be in sentences which use either a singular subject and a plural verb or a plural subject and a singular verb. All but one of the following sentences contain errors of agreement. Which is the *correct* sentence and what are the errors in the other sentences?

15. Dave and Jane is coming to dinner.

16. Vince, like his father and uncle, are more than six feet tall.

17. The author of books on tennis, ping-pong, and squash are speaking this afternoon.

18. There is many choices on the menu.

19. The first to arrive was Dave, Jane, and Vince.

20. Neither Vince nor Wendy is at the party.

21. Neither Jane nor Dave are at the party.

Pronoun Agreement Errors

22. The twins arrived late, and she was the first to leave.

23. Jane loaned Dave the money, and they paid it back this week.

Subject/Verb Agreement Errors

15. Dave and Jane is coming to dinner.
    (incorrect sentence, plural subject *Dave and Jane* with singular verb *is*)

    Dave and Jane are coming to dinner. (correct sentence)

16. Vince, like his father and uncle, are more than six feet tall.
    (incorrect sentence, singular subject *Vince* with plural verb *are*)

    Vince, like his father and uncle, is more than six feet tall.
    (correct sentence)

17. The author of books on tennis, ping-pong, and squash are speaking this afternoon.
    (incorrect sentence, singular subject *author* with plural verb *are*)

    The author of books on tennis, ping-pong, and squash is speaking this afternoon. (correct sentence)

18. There is many choices on the menu.
    (incorrect sentence, plural subject *choices* with singular verb *is*)

    There are many choices on the menu. (correct sentence)

19. The first to arrive was Dave, Jane, and Vince.
    (incorrect sentence, plural verb needed because *first* refers to *Dave, Jane, and Vince*)

    The first to arrive were Dave, Jane, and Vince. (correct sentence)

20. **Neither Vince nor Wendy is at the party.** (correct sentence)

21. Neither Jane nor Dave are at the party.
    (incorrect sentence–After *either/or* or *neither/nor,* the verb should agree with the word following *or* or *nor.*)

    Neither Jane nor Dave is at the party. (correct sentence)

Pronoun Agreement Errors

22. The twins arrived late, and she was the first to leave.
    (incorrect sentence, plural noun *twins* with singular pronoun *she*)

    The twins arrived late, and they were the first to leave. (correct sentence)

23. Jane loaned Dave the money, and they paid it back this week.
    (incorrect sentence—The word *they* doesn't make sense in this sentence.)

    Jane loaned Dave the money, and he paid it back this week.
    (correct sentence)

Verb Tense Errors

Verb tense errors include using a tense that is not the same as other verb tenses in the sentence or the paragraph. A verb tense error can also be caused by using a tense that does not agree with the sense of the information about the time of the action elsewhere in the sentence or the paragraph. Which of the following sentences contain verbs with errors of verb form or verb tense?

24. Yesterday, Jack goes to school.

25. Yesterday, Jack went to school.

26. Jack got up early, ate his breakfast, and leaves for work.

27. Jack got up early, eats his breakfast, and left for work.

28. Jack got up early, ate his breakfast, and leaving for work.

Be sure that the verb tenses are the same throughout the sentence *and* the whole paragraph. At least one question will test verb tense agreement in the whole paragraph.

Other Pronoun Errors

Other pronoun errors tested include using the wrong *relative pronoun* (*which* for *who*, for example) and *pronoun shifts* (using both *one* and *you* to refer to the same person in a single sentence or a single paragraph). Which of the following sentences is correct?

29. The car that I bought is red.

30. My sister which lives in Toledo is a doctor.

31. One should lock your car securely, and you should not leave packages on the back seat.

There will also be sentences with *pronouns* which are either *vague* or which make the person referred to by the pronoun *not clear*. Which of the following sentences have this sort of pronoun error?

32. He argued with his parents and with his in-laws, and so they avoided him.

33. Dave gave Ed his keys.

34. Ed gave Dave his keys.

Verb Tense Errors

24. Yesterday, Jack goes to school.
    (incorrect sentence, *yesterday* (past) with *goes* (present))

25. **Yesterday, Jack went to school.** (correct sentence)

26. Jack got up early, ate his breakfast, and leaves for work.
    (incorrect sentence, *yesterday* (past), *went* (past), *goes* (present))

    Jack got up early, ate his breakfast, and left for work. (correct sentence)

27. Jack got up early, eats his breakfast, and left for work.
    (incorrect sentence, *got up* (past), *eats* (present), *left* (past))

    Jack got up early, ate his breakfast, and left for work. (correct sentence)

28. Jack got up early, ate his breakfast, and leaving for work.
    (incorrect sentence, *got* (past), *ate* (past), *leaving* (present)

    Jack got up early, ate his breakfast, and left for work. (correct sentence)

Other Pronoun Errors

29. **The car that I bought is red.** (correct sentence)

30. My sister which lives in Toledo is a doctor.
    (incorrect sentence, *which* used to refer to a person)

    My sister who lives in Toledo is a doctor. (correct sentence)

31. One should lock your car securely, and you should not leave packages on the back seat.
    (incorrect sentence, both *one* and *you* used to refer to the same person)

    You should lock your car securely, and you should not leave packages on the back seat. (correct sentence)

MECHANICS

> The test questions on mechanics will involve errors of capitalization, punctuation, and spelling.

Capitalization Errors

> The capitalization questions will require that you understand the correct use of *small and capital letters* with dates, places, times, titles, and proper nouns and adjectives. Can you supply all of the correct capital letters in the following sentences?

35. senator Arthur smith of illinois was married to congresswoman martha jones of indiana on april third. They spent the spring in france where mrs. smith continued her french studies. They now live on massachusetts avenue in washington, d.c.

Punctuation Errors

> The punctuation questions focus particularly on the use of the comma. Can you supply all the necessary commas in the following sentences?

36. After eating breakfast Dave wanted to leave but Jane his wife had not finished her packing. When he realized they could not go at once he poured another cup of coffee added sugar and opened the newspaper.

Spelling Errors

> The spelling errors will be chosen from the most often misspelled words. The test will also include the common spelling errors found in words that sound alike and in possessives and in contractions. A list of commonly misspelled words follows this section. Can you find the spelling errors in the following sentences?

37. Its important to pay attenshun to ways to live a happyer life. Weather you are wurking or playing, you're sucess depends on you're state of mind. Most peeple dont unnerstand how to impruve there outlook.

Capitalization Errors

35. senator Arthur smith of illinois was married to congresswoman martha jones of indiana on april third. They spent the spring in france where mrs. smith continued her french studies. They now live on massachusetts avenue in washington, d.c. (incorrect capitalization)

   Senator Arthur Smith of Illinois was married to Congresswoman Martha Jones of Indiana on April third. They spent the spring in France where Mrs. Smith continued her French studies. They now live on Massachusetts Avenue in Washington, D.C. (correct capitalization)

Punctuation Errors

36. After eating breakfast Dave wanted to leave but Jane his wife had not finished her packing. When he realized they could not go at once he poured another cup of coffee added sugar and opened the newspaper. (needed commas missing)

   After eating breakfast, Dave wanted to leave, but his wife had not finished her packing. When he realized they could not go at once, he poured another cup of coffee, added sugar, and opened the newspaper. (correct comma use)

Spelling Errors

37. Its importent to pay attenshun to ways to live a happyer life. Weather you are wurking or playing, you're sucess depends on you're state of mind. Most peeple dont unnerstand how to impruve there outlook. (words misspelled)

   It's important to pay **attention** to ways to live a **happier** life. **Whether** you are **working** or playing, **your success** depends on **your** state of mind. Most **people don't understand** how to **improve their** outlook. (correct spelling)

SPELLING REVIEW

The following list includes words that many people tend to misspell. These words and words *spelled in a similar way* are often found on standardized tests. The parts of the words that most often cause spelling problems are underlined.

A good way to study this list is to have a friend read each word aloud to you. (Have the friend use the word in a sentence if it is one that sounds just the same as another word but has a different spelling, such as *there* and *their*.) Then write the word on your paper and check to see if you've spelled it correctly. If you have **not** spelled it correctly, put a check in the box following the word.

Use the list of checked words as a starting place for more spelling review. Notice the spellings that give *you* the most trouble and look for words that are spelled in a similar way in the reading you do every day. For example, if you have trouble with words that end in *ance* or *ence* or words that sound the same but have different spellings, look for those kinds of words in your reading and pay close attention every time you see them.

a lot ☐	amateur ☐	because ☐	choose ☐
absence ☐	analyze ☐	beginning ☐	chose ☐
abundance ☐	angel ☐	believe ☐	cigarette ☐
accept ☐	angle ☐	benefited ☐	congratulate ☐
accidentally ☐	annual ☐	bicycle ☐	clothes ☐
accommodate ☐	answer ☐	board ☐	coarse ☐
accomplish ☐	anxious ☐	bored ☐	college ☐
accuse ☐	apologize ☐	boundary ☐	column ☐
accustomed ☐	apparatus ☐	brake ☐	comfortable ☐
ache ☐	appetite ☐	breadth ☐	commitment ☐
achieve ☐	appreciate ☐	breath ☐	committee ☐
acknowledge ☐	approximate ☐	breathe ☐	competent ☐
acquainted ☐	arguing ☐	brilliant ☐	competition ☐
acquire ☐	arrange ☐	bulletin ☐	complement ☐
across ☐	article ☐	bureau ☐	compliment ☐
address ☐	artificial ☐	burial ☐	conceit ☐
adequate ☐	ascend ☐	business ☐	conceivable ☐
advantage ☐	assistance ☐		confident ☐
advertise ☐	associate ☐	cafeteria ☐	conquer ☐
advice ☐	athletic ☐	calculator ☐	conscience ☐
advisable ☐	attacked ☐	calendar ☐	conscientious ☐
advise ☐	attendance ☐	campaign ☐	conscious ☐
aerial ☐	attention ☐	capital ☐	consequence ☐
affectionate ☐	audience ☐	capitol ☐	continual ☐
aggravate ☐	author ☐	captain ☐	continuous ☐
aggressive ☐	autumn ☐	careful ☐	controlled ☐
agree ☐	auxiliary ☐	careless ☐	convenience ☐
aisle ☐	available ☐	carriage ☐	convenient ☐
all right ☐	awful ☐	category ☐	corporal ☐
almost ☐	awkward ☐	ceiling ☐	council ☐
already ☐		chaos ☐	counsel ☐
although ☐	bachelor ☐	changeable ☐	counselor ☐
altogether ☐	balloon ☐	characteristic ☐	courageous ☐
always ☐	beautiful ☐	chief ☐	course ☐

courteous ☐
courtesy ☐
criticism ☐
crowd ☐
curiosity ☐

daily ☐
deceive ☐
deception ☐
decision ☐
definite ☐
delicious ☐
descend ☐
descent ☐
desert ☐
desirable ☐
despair ☐
desperate ☐
dessert ☐
development ☐
device ☐
dilemma ☐
dinner ☐
disappear ☐
disappoint ☐
disapproval ☐
disastrous ☐
discipline ☐
doubt ☐

ecstasy ☐
effect ☐
efficiency ☐
eligible ☐
embarrass ☐
emphasize ☐
encouraging ☐
endeavor ☐
enormous ☐
environment ☐
equipped ☐
essential ☐
exaggerate ☐
excellent ☐
exercise ☐
exhausted ☐
exhilaration ☐
experience ☐
explanation ☐

familiar ☐
fascinate ☐

fatigue ☐
financial ☐
flourish ☐
forcibly ☐
forehead ☐
foreign ☐
fourth ☐
fundamental ☐

genius ☐
government ☐
grammar ☐
grateful ☐
grievous ☐
guarantee ☐
guard ☐

handkerchief ☐
happiness ☐
height ☐
heroine ☐
hideous ☐
hoarse ☐
hopeless ☐
hospital ☐
humorous ☐

ignorance ☐
imbecile ☐
imitation ☐
immediately ☐
immigrant ☐
incidental ☐
independence ☐
indispensable ☐
inevitable ☐
influential ☐
initiate ☐
innocence ☐
inoculate ☐
inquiry ☐
intellectual ☐
intercede ☐
interfere ☐
interpreted ☐
interrupt ☐
irrelevant ☐
irresistible ☐
irritable ☐
island ☐
its ☐
it's ☐

jealous ☐
judgment ☐

kindergarten ☐
knew ☐
knock ☐
know ☐
knowledge ☐

laboratory ☐
later ☐
latter ☐
leisure ☐
length ☐
license ☐
lightning ☐
likelihood ☐
literal ☐
literature ☐
loneliness ☐
loose ☐
lose ☐

maintenance ☐
maneuver ☐
marriage ☐
married ☐
mathematics ☐
miniature ☐
miracle ☐
miscellaneous ☐
mischief ☐
mischievous ☐
misspelled ☐
mistake ☐
moral ☐
morale ☐
mortgage ☐
mountain ☐
mysterious ☐

narrative ☐
necessary ☐
negligence ☐
neither ☐
newsstand ☐
niece ☐
noticeable ☐

o'clock ☐
obstacle ☐
occasion ☐

occur ☐
occurred ☐
occurrence ☐
often ☐
omission ☐
omit ☐
opportunity ☐
optimistic ☐
oscillate ☐

panicky ☐
parallel ☐
partner ☐
pastime ☐
patience ☐
peaceable ☐
peculiar ☐
perceive ☐
performance ☐
permanent ☐
perseverance ☐
persistent ☐
personal ☐
personnel ☐
persuade ☐
persuasion ☐
playwright ☐
pleasure ☐
poison ☐
political ☐
positive ☐
possess ☐
prairie ☐
precede ☐
precise ☐
predictable ☐
prefer ☐
preference ☐
preferred ☐
prejudice ☐
presence ☐
prevalent ☐
primitive ☐
principal ☐
principle ☐
privilege ☐
procedure ☐
proceed ☐
professional ☐
professor ☐
profitable ☐
prominent ☐

pronounce □	ridiculous □	stomach □	twelfth □
pronunciation □	role □	strenuous □	tyranny □
propeller □	roll □	striking □	
psychology □	roommate □	studying □	undoubtedly □
		substantial □	university □
quantity □	scarcely □	succeed □	unnecessary □
quarreling □	scene □	successful □	unusual □
quiet □	schedule □	suppress □	usual □
quite □	scissors □	surely □	
	secretary □	surprise □	vacuum □
raise □	seize □	suspense □	variety □
realistic □	sense □	sweat □	vegetable □
rebellion □	separate □	sweet □	vein □
recede □	severely □	syllable □	vengeance □
receipt □	shepherd □	symmetrical □	versatile □
receive □	sheriff □	synonym □	vicinity □
recognize □	shining □		vicious □
recommend □	shriek □		villain □
referred □	siege □	technical □	
reign □	significance □	temperament □	waist □
relevant □	similar □	temperature □	weak □
relieve □	sincerely □	tenant □	weather □
renovate □	soldier □	tenement □	week □
repetition □	solemn □	thorough □	weigh □
requirements □	sophomore □	through □	weird □
resemblance □	source □	tomorrow □	whether □
resource □	souvenir □	toward □	whole □
respectability □	specified □	tragedy □	wholly □
responsibility □	specimen □	transferred □	wretched □
restaurant □	stationary □	tremendous □	
rhythm □	stationery □	truly □	yield □

Part II: The Essay

The best way to review for the essay section of the GED Writing Skills Test is to practice the techniques you learned about in Part 2 of this book. On the following page, you'll find the directions for this part of the exam. Read them through once again. In the pages that follow are seven practice topics very similar to the kinds of topics you'll find on the GED.

To do your best on the test, follow these steps:

1. Write a practice essay every few days.

2. Use the blank space beneath each topic as scratch paper.

3. Use the two lined sheets provided after each essay topic for your writing. This is the amount of space you'll have on the actual test.

4. Use the checklist that follows each set of lined sheets to evaluate your practice essay.

TEST 1: WRITING SKILLS, PART II

Tests of General Educational Development

Directions

This part of the Writing Skills Test is intended to determine how well you write. You are asked to write an essay that explains something or presents an opinion on an issue. In preparing your essay, you should take the following steps.

1. Read carefully the directions and the essay topic given below.

2. Plan your essay carefully before you write.

3. Use scratch paper to make any notes.

4. Write your essay on the lined pages of the separate answer sheet.

5. Read carefully what you have written and make any changes that will improve your essay.

6. Check your paragraphs, sentence structure, spelling, punctuation, capitalization, and usage, and make any necessary corrections.

Be sure you write the letter of the essay topic (given below) on your answer sheet. Write the letter in the box at the upper right-hand corner of the page where you write your essay.

You will have 45 minutes to write on the topic below. Write legibly and use a ballpoint pen so that the evaluators will be able to read your writing.

Write your essay on the lined pages of the separate answer sheet. The notes you make on scratch paper will not be scored.

Your essay will be scored by at least two trained evaluators who will judge it according to its overall effectiveness. They will judge how clearly you make the main point of your composition, how thoroughly you support your ideas, and how clearly and correctly you write throughout the essay.

PRACTICE TOPIC A

It is often said that we should learn from the mistakes of the past. But often, it seems that we do not learn from such mistakes, and we keep making them over and over again.

In a composition of about 200 words, describe one of society's mistakes from the past, and discuss whether the world of today has learned from that mistake. Use specific examples to support your position.

SOCIAL SECURITY NUMBER

Write the letter of your essay topic in the box, then shade the corresponding circle.

TOPIC   Ⓐ Ⓑ Ⓒ Ⓓ Ⓔ Ⓕ Ⓖ Ⓗ Ⓘ Ⓙ Ⓚ Ⓛ Ⓜ Ⓝ Ⓞ Ⓟ Ⓠ Ⓡ Ⓢ Ⓣ Ⓤ Ⓥ Ⓦ Ⓧ Ⓨ Ⓩ

Continue your essay on next page

USE A BALL POINT PEN TO WRITE YOUR ESSAY

PRACTICE TOPIC A CHECKLIST

The following checklist will help you evaluate your Practice Topic A essay. Circle *yes* if you feel you've done well on that task. Circle *no* if you feel that you need considerable improvement on that task. You might want to have a friend who is a good writer or a teacher fill out this checklist for you.

Did you

1. Focus on the assigned topic? **yes no**
2. Answer the question? **yes no**
3. Give a statement of purpose? **yes no**
4. Flow in an organized way? **yes no**
5. Support your view with specific examples? **yes no**
6. Use correct English? **yes no**
7. Present the essay well (make it neat, easy to read)? **yes no**

PRACTICE TOPIC B

None of us thinks that the world is perfect; we all have ideas about improving things.

In a composition of about 200 words, explain how you would improve a particular product or practice. First describe what you wish to improve, and then tell how you would improve it. Give reasons and specific examples to support your opinion.

Write the letter of your essay topic in the box, then shade the corresponding circle.

TOPIC Ⓐ Ⓑ Ⓒ Ⓓ Ⓔ Ⓕ Ⓖ Ⓗ Ⓘ Ⓙ Ⓚ Ⓛ Ⓜ Ⓝ Ⓞ Ⓟ Ⓠ Ⓡ Ⓢ Ⓣ Ⓤ Ⓥ Ⓦ Ⓧ Ⓨ Ⓩ

Continue your essay on next page

USE A BALL POINT PEN TO WRITE YOUR ESSAY

PRACTICE TOPIC B CHECKLIST

The following checklist will help you evaluate your Practice Topic B essay. Circle *yes* if you feel you've done well on that task. Circle *no* if you feel that you need considerable improvement on that task. You might want to have a friend who is a good writer or a teacher fill out this checklist for you.

Did you

1. Focus on the assigned topic? **yes no**
2. Answer the question? **yes no**
3. Give a statement of purpose? **yes no**
4. Flow in an organized way? **yes no**
5. Support your view with specific examples? **yes no**
6. Use correct English? **yes no**
7. Present the essay well (make it neat, easy to read)? **yes no**

PRACTICE TOPIC C

Drug abuse is a widely publicized problem, and although various solutions have been proposed, the problem persists.

In a composition of about 200 words, explain (with examples) how drug abuse is affecting everyday life, and propose a possible solution to the problem of drug abuse. Give reasons and specific examples to support your opinion.

SOCIAL SECURITY NUMBER

Write the letter of your essay topic in the box, then shade the corresponding circle.

TOPIC Ⓐ Ⓑ Ⓒ Ⓓ Ⓔ Ⓕ Ⓖ Ⓗ Ⓘ Ⓙ Ⓚ Ⓛ Ⓜ Ⓝ Ⓞ Ⓟ Ⓠ Ⓡ Ⓢ Ⓣ Ⓤ Ⓥ Ⓦ Ⓧ Ⓨ Ⓩ

Continue your essay on next page

USE A BALL POINT PEN TO WRITE YOUR ESSAY

PRACTICE TOPIC C CHECKLIST

The following checklist will help you evaluate your Practice Topic C essay. Circle *yes* if you feel you've done well on that task. Circle *no* if you feel that you need considerable improvement on that task. You might want to have a friend who is a good writer or a teacher fill out this checklist for you.

Did you

1. Focus on the assigned topic? **yes no**
2. Answer the question? **yes no**
3. Give a statement of purpose? **yes no**
4. Flow in an organized way? **yes no**
5. Support your view with specific examples? **yes no**
6. Use correct English? **yes no**
7. Present the essay well (make it neat, easy to read)? **yes no**

PRACTICE TOPIC D

Many claim that no one can expect to earn a good living without at least a high school diploma. But others argue that what we learn in school is often irrelevant to the demands of the "real world" of work.

In a composition of about 200 words, discuss whether a high school diploma is relevant or irrelevant to success as a worker. You may refer to your own experience, but you should include other relevant information as well. Use specific examples to support your position.

Write the letter of your essay topic in the box, then shade the corresponding circle.

TOPIC (A)(B)(C)(D)(E)(F)(G)(H)(I)(J)(K)(L)(M)(N)(O)(P)(Q)(R)(S)(T)(U)(V)(W)(X)(Y)(Z)

Continue your essay on next page

USE A BALL POINT PEN TO WRITE YOUR ESSAY

_____
_____
_____
_____
_____
_____
_____
_____
_____
_____
_____
_____
_____
_____
_____
_____
_____
_____
_____
_____
_____
_____
_____

PRACTICE TOPIC D CHECKLIST

The following checklist will help you evaluate your Practice Topic D essay. Circle *yes* if you feel you've done well on that task. Circle *no* if you feel that you need considerable improvement on that task. You might want to have a friend who is a good writer or a teacher fill out this checklist for you.

Did you

1. Focus on the assigned topic? **yes no**
2. Answer the question? **yes no**
3. Give a statement of purpose? **yes no**
4. Flow in an organized way? **yes no**
5. Support your view with specific examples? **yes no**
6. Use correct English? **yes no**
7. Present the essay well (make it neat, easy to read)? **yes no**

PRACTICE TOPIC E

It is nearly impossible to get through a day without reading something, even something as brief as the brand name painted on the back of a truck. But what if written language disappeared and none of us read anything?

In a serious composition of about 200 words, describe some of the effects that would take place during a day when written language disappeared. You may discuss positive effects, negative effects, or both. Provide specific examples to support your view.

WRITING SKILLS TEST - PART II

Write the letter of your essay topic in the box, then shade the corresponding circle.

TOPIC Ⓐ Ⓑ Ⓒ Ⓓ Ⓔ Ⓕ Ⓖ Ⓗ Ⓘ Ⓙ Ⓚ Ⓛ Ⓜ Ⓝ Ⓞ Ⓟ Ⓠ Ⓡ Ⓢ Ⓣ Ⓤ Ⓥ Ⓦ Ⓧ Ⓨ Ⓩ

Continue your essay on next page

USE A BALL POINT PEN TO WRITE YOUR ESSAY

PRACTICE TOPIC E CHECKLIST

The following checklist will help you evaluate your Practice Topic E essay. Circle *yes* if you feel you've done well on that task. Circle *no* if you feel that you need considerable improvement on that task. You might want to have a friend who is a good writer or a teacher fill out this checklist for you.

Did you

1. Focus on the assigned topic? **yes no**
2. Answer the question? **yes no**
3. Give a statement of purpose? **yes no**
4. Flow in an organized way? **yes no**
5. Support your view with specific examples? **yes no**
6. Use correct English? **yes no**
7. Present the essay well (make it neat, easy to read)? **yes no**

PRACTICE TOPIC F

Medical knowledge and technology have advanced more quickly in this century than at any other time in the history of humankind. With advances in medicine, life has changed dramatically.

In a composition of about 200 words, describe certain modern advances in medicine and explain how these advances have changed modern life. Use specific examples to support your points.

Write the letter of your essay topic in the box, then shade the corresponding circle.

TOPIC   Ⓐ Ⓑ Ⓒ Ⓓ Ⓔ Ⓕ Ⓖ Ⓗ Ⓘ Ⓙ Ⓚ Ⓛ Ⓜ Ⓝ Ⓞ Ⓟ Ⓠ Ⓡ Ⓢ Ⓣ Ⓤ Ⓥ Ⓦ Ⓧ Ⓨ Ⓩ

Continue your essay on next page

USE A BALL POINT PEN TO WRITE YOUR ESSAY

PRACTICE TOPIC F CHECKLIST

The following checklist will help you evaluate your Practice Topic F essay. Circle *yes* if you feel you've done well on that task. Circle *no* if you feel that you need considerable improvement on that task. You might want to have a friend who is a good writer or a teacher fill out this checklist for you.

Did you

1. Focus on the assigned topic? **yes no**
2. Answer the question? **yes no**
3. Give a statement of purpose? **yes no**
4. Flow in an organized way? **yes no**
5. Support your view with specific examples? **yes no**
6. Use correct English? **yes no**
7. Present the essay well (make it neat, easy to read)? **yes no**

TEST 2

SOCIAL STUDIES

TEST 2: SOCIAL STUDIES

Because the Social Studies Test is very reading oriented, it is important that you learn to focus your reading. Start your review by doing the following exercises. Continue reviewing by applying the techniques to other social studies readings.

The following right-hand pages will show you a variety of social studies readings and will give you a chance to practice answering questions concerning the main point of a reading and some details of a reading. When you've finished each reading and have answered the two questions that follow, turn the page. You'll find the reading and questions repeated there and the answers given. You'll also find arrows that point to the exact spots in the reading where you can find the answers. Notice that these spots are printed in **bold type.**If you study these examples carefully, you'll learn to quickly find the answers you need in the readings you will see in the GED Social Studies Test.

Social Studies Reading 1

Canals are build to connect natural waterways. The most well-known American canals are probably the Panama Canal and the Erie Canal. By making it possible to sail from the Atlantic Ocean to the Pacific without circling all of South America, the Panama Canal saves thousands of miles on a journey from Miami to San Francisco. Completed in 1825, the Erie Canal connects the Hudson River and Lake Erie. The Suez Canal joins the Red Sea and the Mediterranean.

Questions

A. What is the main point in this paragraph?

B. What examples of natural waterways connected by canals are there in the paragraph?

Social Studies Reading 1

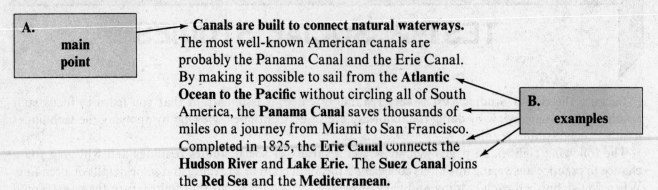

A. main point

Canals are built to connect natural waterways. The most well-known American canals are probably the Panama Canal and the Erie Canal. By making it possible to sail from the **Atlantic Ocean to the Pacific** without circling all of South America, the **Panama Canal** saves thousands of miles on a journey from Miami to San Francisco. Completed in 1825, the **Erie Canal** connects the **Hudson River** and **Lake Erie**. The **Suez Canal** joins the **Red Sea** and the **Mediterranean.**

B. examples

Questions

A. What is the main point in this paragraph?

B. What examples of natural waterways connected by canals are there in the paragraph?

Answers

A. The first sentence, which tells the purpose of canals, is the main point of the paragraph.

B. The paragraph gives three examples: the connecting of the Atlantic and Pacific Oceans by the Panama Canal, of the Hudson River and Lake Erie by the Erie Canal, and of the Red Sea and the Mediterranean by the Suez Canal.

Social Studies Reading 2

What is *Watergate*? It is a large building in Washington, D.C., where the offices of the Democratic National Committee were located. But for most Americans, *Watergate* refers to the political scandal that toppled President Nixon from office. The term *Watergate* became synonymous with the cover-up of illegal activities designed to reelect President Nixon in 1972. Those illegal activities included the use of government agencies to harass political opponents, unlawful wiretaps, campaign financing violations, and burglary. Because of the high-ranking government officials involved in Watergate and the fact that Nixon was forced to resign rather than risk an impeachment trial, many Americans became disillusioned with the federal government.

Questions

A. What is the main point in this paragraph?

B. What kind of a sentence is the first sentence of the paragraph and what does it do?

Social Studies Reading 2

What is *Watergate*? It is a large building in
Washington, D.C., where the offices of the
Democratic National Committee were located.
But for most Americans, *Watergate* **refers to the**
political scandal that toppled President Nixon
from office. The term *Watergate* became
synonymous with the cover-up of illegal activities
designed to reelect President Nixon in 1972.
Those illegal activities included the use of
government agencies to harass political opponents,
unlawful wiretaps, campaign financing violations,
and burglary. Because of the high-ranking
government officials involved in Watergate and
the fact that Nixon was forced to resign rather
than risk an impeachment trial, many Americans
became disillusioned with the federal government.

Questions

A. What is the main point in this paragraph?

B. What kind of a sentence is the first sentence of
   the paragraph and what does it do?

Answers

A. The third sentence of the paragraph makes the
   main point.

B. The first sentence is a question. The answer to
   this question is the subject of the whole
   paragraph.

Social Studies Reading 3

When a candidate or political party wins an overwhelming victory in an election, it is referred to as a landslide victory. The presidential and congressional election in 1936 is a classic example of a landslide victory. In that election Franklin Delano Roosevelt received 420 electoral votes to Alfred M. Landon's 8, and the Democrats controlled both the House (322 to 103) and the Senate (69 to 25). Johnson's victory over Goldwater and Nixon's over McGovern are also often cited as landslides.

Questions

A. What is the main point in this paragraph?

B. What examples of landslide victories does the paragraph give?

Social Studies Reading 3

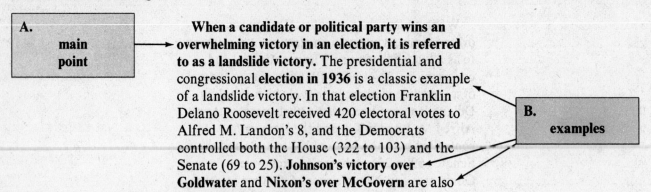

A.

main point

When a candidate or political party wins an overwhelming victory in an election, it is referred to as a landslide victory. The presidential and congressional **election in 1936** is a classic example of a landslide victory. In that election Franklin Delano Roosevelt received 420 electoral votes to Alfred M. Landon's 8, and the Democrats controlled both the House (322 to 103) and the Senate (69 to 25). **Johnson's victory over Goldwater** and **Nixon's over McGovern** are also often cited as landslides.

B.

examples

Questions

A. What is the main point in this paragraph?

B. What examples of landslide victories does the paragraph give?

Answers

A. The first sentence, which tells us what landslide victories are, is the main point of the paragraph.

B. The examples are the election in 1936, Johnson's win over Goldwater, and Nixon's win over McGovern.

Social Studies Reading 4

Boston and New York grew rapidly because they were located on the ocean and closer to Europe than other American cities were. Denver grew when the silver mines were active and the price of silver was high. Los Angeles remained small for as long as its water supply was limited. The natural environment (forests, oceans, mountains, mineral and water resources) is a fundamental influence on the development of an area or region, and the subsequent historical development of a society or culture is basically determined by the availability of natural resources.

Questions

A. What is the main point in this paragraph?

B. Why did Denver grow?

Social Studies Reading 4

Boston and New York grew rapidly because they were located on the ocean and closer to Europe than other American cities were. **Denver grew when the silver mines were active and the price of silver was high.** Los Angeles remained small for as long as its water supply was limited. **The natural environment** (forests, oceans, mountains, mineral and water resources) **is a fundamental influence on the development of an area or region, and the subsequent historical development of a society or culture is basically determined by the availability of natural resources.**

A.
    **main
    point**

B.
    **reason
    Denver grew**

Questions

A. What is the main point in this paragraph?

B. Why did Denver grow?

Answers

A. The last sentence sums up the main point of the paragraph.

B. Denver grew because the price of silver was high and it had silver mines.

Social Studies Reading 5

How does a capitalist democracy differ from a nation that practices democratic socialism? A capitalist society is characterized by private ownership of property in a competitive free-market and free-price system. In a democratic socialist society, the major means of production are controlled and owned by the government (coal, railroads, health care, broadcasting). Many industries are privately owned, and the forces of supply and demand operate in determining prices and production levels. In democratic socialism, the people have a direct voice in the operation of the government and are able to exert economic pressure to protest policies they disagree with. The difference, then, is the government's greater role as owner in a democratic socialist society.

Questions

A. What is the main point in this paragraph?

B. Who controls the major means of production in a democratic socialist society?

Social Studies Reading 5

How does a capitalist democracy differ from a nation that practices democratic socialism? A capitalist society is characterized by private ownership of property in a competitive free-market and free-price system. **In a democratic socialist society, the major means of production are controlled and owned by the government** (coal, railroads, health care, broadcasting). Many industries are privately owned, and the forces of supply and demand operate in determining prices and production levels. In democratic socialism, the people have a direct voice in the operation of the government and are able to exert economic pressure to protest policies they disagree with. **The difference, then, is the government's greater role as owner in a democratic socialist society.**

B. control of production

A. main point

Questions

A. What is the main point in this paragraph?

B. Who controls the major means of production in a democratic socialist society?

Answers

A. The last sentence sums up the paragraph. It answers the question of the first sentence.

B. In a democratic socialist society, the major means of production are controlled by the government.

Social Studies Reading 6

Though the Fourth Amendment limits the right of the government to search and seize people or property, a search may take place if there is "probable cause," that is, a reasonable justification for the search. Before the search can take place, warrants must be obtained describing the place to be searched and the person or thing to be seized. The courts have called searches in which the police have invaded a person's privacy beyond the specific terms of the warrant "unreasonable searches" and have disallowed any evidence obtained in these cases. A legal search and seizure is one in which there is "probable cause" for the search, a warrant for the search, and a careful following of the terms of the warrant.

Questions

A. What is the main point in this paragraph?

B. What do the courts consider "unreasonable searches"?

Social Studies Reading 6

Though the Fourth Amendment limits the right of the government to search and seize people or property, a search may take place if there is "probable cause," that is, a reasonable justification for the search. Before the search can take place, warrants must be obtained describing the place to be searched and the person or thing to be seized. **The courts have called searches in which the police have invaded a person's privacy beyond the specific terms of the warrant "unreasonable searches"** and have disallowed any evidence obtained in these cases. **A legal search and seizure is one in which there is "probable cause" for the search, a warrant for the search, and a careful following of the terms of the warrant.**

A. main point

B. unreasonable searches

Questions

A. What is the main point in this paragraph?

B. What do the courts consider "unreasonable searches"?

Answers

A. The last sentence sums up the statements of the paragraph.

B. The courts have called searches in which the police have invaded a person's privacy beyond the specific terms of a warrant "unreasonable searches."

Social Studies Reading 7

Though both are social movements organized to change societies, a revolutionary movement differs from a reform movement. Both may espouse goals or programs which give them recognition and meaning. But a reform movement tries to achieve its goals by working within the existing system; a revolutionary movement rejects the current system and seeks to replace it with a new social structure. The civil rights movement, especially the nonviolent policies of Dr. Martin Luther King, Jr., is an example of a social movement working within the system.

Questions

A. Which is the summarizing sentence of the paragraph?

B. What is an example of a social movement working within the system?

Social Studies Reading 7

Though both are social movements organized to change societies, a revolutionary movement differs from a reform movement. Both may espouse goals or programs which give them recognition and meaning. **But a reform movement tries to achieve its goals by working within the existing system; a revolutionary movement rejects the current system and seeks to replace it with a new social structure.** The **civil rights movement,** especially the nonviolent policies of **Dr. Martin Luther King, Jr.,** is an example of a social movement working within the system.

A.
main
point

B.
example

Questions

A. Which is the summarizing sentence of the paragraph?

B. What is an example of a social movement working within a system?

Answers

A. The third sentence has the main point of this paragraph.

B. The civil rights movement, especially the nonviolent policies of Dr. Martin Luther King, Jr., is an example of a social movement working within the system.

Now that you have completed these exercises, continue reviewing by applying this focused review to other social studies readings.

TEST 3

SCIENCE

TEST 3: SCIENCE

Because the Science Test is reading oriented, it is important that you learn to focus your reading. This focused reading will also help you gain some general knowledge that will be valuable in answering some questions. Start your review by doing the following exercises. Continue reviewing by applying the techniques to other science readings. Remember, reading additional science articles will help you gain general knowledge in science.

The following right-hand pages will show you a variety of science readings and will give you a chance to practice answering questions concerning the main point of a reading and some details of a reading. When you've finished each reading and have answered the two questions that follow, turn the page. You'll find the reading and questions repeated there and the answers given. You'll also find arrows that point to the exact spots in the reading where you can find the answers. Notice that these spots are printed in **bold type.** If you study these examples carefully, you'll learn to quickly find the answers you need in the readings you will see in the GED Science Test.

Science Reading 1

The retinal lining of the eye is made up of countless light-sensitive cells called rods and cones. Color vision involves three types of cones, each of which responds to one primary color—red, green, or blue. We experience red, green, or blue when the red, green, or blue cones (respectively) are stimulated by the corresponding frequencies of light. Other colors are seen as a result of the more or less intense stimulation of some combination of the cones. The sensation of white appears to result from the equal stimulation of all three types of cones.

Questions

A. What is the main point in this paragraph?

B. In which sentences does the author give examples of the experience of color vision?

Science Reading 1

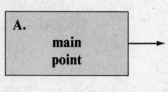

The retinal lining of the eye is made up of countless light-sensitive cells called rods and cones. **Color vision involves three types of cones, each of which responds to one primary color—red, green, or blue. We experience red, green, or blue when the red, green, or blue cones (respectively) are stimulated** by the corresponding frequencies of light. **Other colors** are seen as a **result of** the more or less intense **stimulation of some combination of the cones.** The sensation of **white** appears to result from the **equal stimulation of all three types of cones.**

B.   example

Questions

A. What is the main point in this paragraph?

B. In which sentences does the author give examples of the experience of color vision?

Answers

A. The second sentence describing color vision is the main point of the paragraph.

B. The third, fourth, and last sentences of the paragraph are examples of the vision of primary colors, of other colors, and of white.

Science Reading 2

How can the study of fossils support the argument for the gradual development or evolution of life? Evolution of life is indicated by the fact that fossil organisms in rock strata are different from modern organisms. As we go back in time, searching lower and older strata, the organisms diverge more and more from those living today. Yet the variation in life forms appears to be relatively continuous. For example, 60 million years ago horses were quite small and had four toes on each foot. As time passed, horses evolved through a series of larger sizes and fewer toes to today's large, single-toed creature.

Questions

A. What is the main point of this paragraph?

B. What kind of a sentence is the first sentence in this paragraph and what does it do?

Science Reading 2

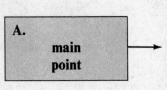

A.

main
point

B.

question
answered by
paragraph

How can the study of fossils support the argument for the gradual development or evolution of life? Evolution of life is indicated by the fact that fossil organisms in rock strata are different from modern organisms. As we go back in time, searching lower and older strata, the organisms diverge more and more from those living today. Yet the variation in life forms appears to be relatively continuous. For example, 60 million years ago horses were quite small and had four toes on each foot. As time passed, horses evolved through a series of larger sizes and fewer toes to today's large, single-toed creature.

Questions

A. What is the main point of this paragraph?

B. What kind of a sentence is the first sentence in this paragraph and what does it do?

Answers

A. The second sentence of the paragraph makes the main point.

B. The first sentence is a question. It asks a question which the rest of the paragraph answers.

Science Reading 3

In any habitat the various organisms compete for food. The ultimate source of food is photosynthetic plant life. Of the three major habitats, the oceans, fresh water, and land, the oceans have the greatest proportion of living things. The upper layers of the oceans contain microscopic plants collectively called phytoplankton. Through photosynthesis, phytoplankton produce food for the marine life of the depths. Because ocean conditions are relatively uniform, most marine species are broadly distributed. But all of the life in the ocean is ultimately dependent on the photosynthetic plants for existence.

Questions

A. What is the main point of the paragraph?

B. Which sentence specifically supports the statement that the ultimate source of food is photosynthetic plant life?

Science Reading 3

A.
main
point

In any habitat the various organisms compete for food. **The ultimate source of food is photosynthetic plant life.** Of the three major habitats, the oceans, fresh water, and land, the oceans have the greatest proportion of living things. The upper layers of the oceans contain microscopic plants collectively called phytoplankton. Through photosynthesis, phytoplankton produce food for the marine life of the depths. Because ocean conditions are relatively uniform, most marine species are broadly distributed. **But all of the life in the ocean is ultimately dependent on the photosynthetic plants for existence.**

B.
supports
main
point

Questions

A. What is the main point of the paragraph?

B. Which sentence specifically supports the statement that the ultimate source of food is photosynthetic plant life?

Answers

A. The main point of the paragraph is made in the second sentence, that the ultimate food source is photosynthetic plant life.

B. The last sentence supports the main idea of the paragraph, giving the ocean habitat as an example.

Science Reading 4

The geological activity of the wind is usually associated with deserts, where sand dunes are created by the wind. Eddies cause it to raise aloft some fine sediment, but most material is transported just above the surface. The lifting of fine material by wind is called deflation. The bouncing of sand along the ground is referred to as saltation. A reduction in energy and the presence of obstacles cause wind to deposit its load of sediment. Wind deposits include volcanic ash and sand dunes.

Questions

A. What is the main point of the paragraph?

B. How many words associated with the wind's activity does the paragraph define?

Science Reading 4

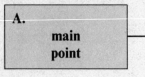

A.
main
point

The geological activity of the wind is usually associated with deserts, where sand dunes are created by the wind. Eddies cause it to raise aloft some fine sediment, but most material is transported just above the surface. **The lifting of fine material by wind is called deflation. The bouncing of sand along the ground is referred to as saltation.** A reduction in energy and the presence of obstacles cause wind to deposit its load of sediment. Wind deposits include volcanic ash and sand dunes.

B.
two words
defined

Questions

A. What is the main point of the paragraph?

B. How many words associated with the wind's activity does the paragraph define?

Answers

A. The first sentence gives the paragraph's main idea.

B. Two words, "deflation" and "saltation," are defined in the passage.

Science Reading 5

What is the temperature of a glass of water with three or four ice cubes in it? What is the temperature of another glass of water that contains crushed ice?

As long as both ice and water are present in thermal equilibrium, they must be at the melting/freezing point, exactly 32 degrees F. The water temperature could not be lower, nor the ice temperature higher. An armchair experiment with a thermometer in a glass of ice and water will convince you that the temperature remains constant until all the ice has melted.

Questions

A. What is the main point in these paragraphs?

B. How are the first two sentences of this reading alike?

Science Reading 5

A.
**main
point**

B.
**two questions
answered by
third sentence**

What is the temperature of a glass of water with
three or four ice cubes in it? What is the
temperature of another glass of water that contains
crushed ice?

As long as both ice and water are present in
thermal equilibrium, they must be at the
melting/freezing point, exactly 32 degrees F. The
water temperature could not be lower, nor the ice
temperature higher. An armchair experiment with
a thermometer in a glass of ice and water will
convince you that the temperature remains
constant until all the ice has melted.

Questions

A. What is the main point in these paragraphs?

B. How are the first two sentences of this reading
alike?

Answers

A. The main point of the paragraphs is stated in
the first sentence of the second paragraph.

B. Both the first and second sentences are
questions. The answer to both questions is
given in the third sentence.

Science Reading 6

A magnet can attract or repel. All of us have had the opportunity to study the interesting properties of permanent magnets, small bars or horseshoes of iron which have aligned internal structures induced by other magnets. The north pole of one magnet attracts the south pole of another, but like poles repel each other. Either pole can attract unmagnetized iron objects. Iron filings spread on a piece of paper above a bar magnet become arranged in a pattern which maps a magnetic field in the space around the magnet. The Earth's magnetic field orients the iron needles of navigational compasses.

Questions

A. What is the main point of this paragraph?

B. How many sentences mention a magnet's power to repel?

Science Reading 6

A.
main point

A magnet can attract or repel. All of us have had the opportunity to study the interesting properties of permanent magnets, small bars or horseshoes of iron which have aligned internal structures induced by other magnets. The north pole of one magnet attracts the south pole of another, but **like poles repel each other.** Either pole can attract unmagnetized iron objects. Iron filings spread on a piece of paper above a bar magnet become arranged in a pattern which maps a magnetic field in the space around the magnet. The Earth's magnetic field orients the iron needles of navigational compasses.

B.
mention of power to repel

Questions

A. What is the main point of this paragraph?

B. How many sentences mention a magnet's power to repel?

Answers

A. The first sentence gives the main point of the paragraph.

B. Two sentences ("A magnet can attract or repel" and ". . . like poles repel each other") mention the magnet's power to repel. Most of the paragraph is about the magnet's ability to attract.

Science Reading 7

To produce sound, there must be present both a vibrating source that initiates a mechanical disturbance (wave) and an elastic medium through which the wave can be transmitted. Consider a simple experiment to demonstrate the need for an elastic substance to carry the sound. If an electric buzzer is hung inside a bell jar so that it does not touch the sides of the jar, the sound of the buzzer can be heard when air is inside the jar, because the air transmits the sound waves. As soon as the bell jar is exhausted by a vacuum pump, the sound can no longer be heard because there is no material through which the disturbance can travel. By tilting the evacuated bell jar so that the buzzer touches the wall of the jar, the sound can once again be heard: therefore a solid (the glass of the jar) can carry the sound wave as well as a gas (the initial air). In a second experiment, you could show that a liquid, too, can transmit sound by ringing a small bell beneath the surface of water in a sink or large pan.

Questions

A. What is the main point of the paragraph?

B. How many experiments to support the explanation of conditions necessary to produce a sound does the paragraph give?

Science Reading 7

A.
main
point

To produce sound, there must be present both a vibrating source that initiates a mechanical disturbance (wave) and an elastic medium through which the wave can be transmitted. Consider a simple experiment to demonstrate the need for an elastic substance to carry the sound. If an electric buzzer is hung inside a bell jar so that it does not touch the sides of the jar, the sound of the buzzer can be heard when air is inside the jar, because the air transmits the sound waves. As soon as the bell jar is exhausted by a vacuum pump, the sound can no longer be heard because there is no material through which the disturbance can travel. By tilting the evacuated bell jar so that the buzzer touches the wall of the jar, the sound can once again be heard; therefore a solid (the glass of the jar) can carry the sound wave as well as a gas (the initial air). In a second experiment, you could show that a liquid, too, can transmit sound by ringing a small bell beneath the surface of water in a sink or large pan.

B.
two
supporting
experiments

Questions

A. What is the main point of the paragraph?

B. How many experiments to support the explanation of conditions necessary to produce a sound does the paragraph give?

Answers

A. The first sentence defining the two conditions necessary to produce a sound gives the main point.

B. The paragraph suggests two supporting experiments: one using a bell jar and a second using water in a sink or large pan.

Now that you have completed these exercises, continue reviewing by applying this focused review to other science readings. Remember, using a focused reading on other science articles will help you gain some of the general knowledge you will need in science.

TEST
4

INTERPRETING LITERATURE AND THE ARTS

TEST 4: INTERPRETING LITERATURE AND THE ARTS

Because the Interpreting Literature and the Arts Test is based completely on your ability to read and understand, it is important that you learn to focus on your reading. Start your review by doing the following exercises. Then continue your review by applying this focused reading to other works of literature and articles about the arts.

The following right-hand pages will show you a variety of readings on literature and the arts and will give you a chance to practice answering questions concerning the main point of a reading and some details of a reading. When you've finished each reading and have answered the two questions that follow, turn the page. You'll find the reading and questions repeated there and the answers given. You'll also find arrows that point to the exact spots in the reading where you can find the answers. Notice that these spots are printed in **bold type.** If you study these examples carefully, you'll learn to quickly find the answers you need in the readings you will see in the GED Interpreting Literature and the Arts Test.

Interpreting Literature and the Arts Reading 1

> Even in a country where "highbrows" and "television" are not mutually exclusive terms, Britain's Channel 4 seemed to be courting disaster. Created in November 1982 as an experimental alternative to the existing networks, its programming caused it to be dubbed "Channel Snore" and "Channel Bore" by early critics. The audience for Channel 4's nightly newscast was tiny. All that has changed. Less than four years later, Channel 4 is British TV's most heartening success story and a growing presence in the U.S. as well.

Questions

A. What is the main point of this paragraph?

B. Of the five sentences in the paragraph, how many refer to the failures of Channel 4?

Interpreting Literature and the Arts Reading 1

Even in a country where "highbrow" and "television" are not mutually exclusive terms, Britain's Channel 4 seemed to be **courting disaster.** Created in November 1982 as an experimental alternative to the existing networks, its programming caused it to be dubbed **"Channel Snore"** and **"Channel Bore"** by early critics. The **audience** for Channel 4's nightly newscast was **tiny.** All that has changed. **Less than four years later, Channel 4 is British TV's most heartening success story and a growing presence in the U.S. as well.**

A. main point

B. failures

Questions

A. What is the main point of this paragraph?

B. Of the five sentences in the paragraph, how many refer to the failures of Channel 4.

Answers

A. The main point of the paragraph is made in the last sentence.

B. The first three sentences point to the failures of the channel. The fourth sentence says that all "has changed," and the last tells of the channel's success.

Interpreting Literature and the Arts Reading 2

She dwelt among the untrodden ways
Beside the springs of Dove.
A maid whom there were none to praise
And very few to love.
She lived unknown, and few could know
When Lucy ceased to be.
But she is in her grave, and oh,
The difference to me.

Questions

A. What is the main point of this poem?

B. The poem contrasts the dead girl and the past
   with the speaker and the present. Which lines
   deal with the speaker?

Interpreting Literature and the Arts Reading 2

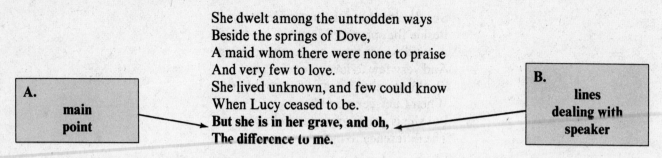

She dwelt among the untrodden ways
Beside the springs of Dove,
A maid whom there were none to praise
And very few to love.
She lived unknown, and few could know
When Lucy ceased to be.
But she is in her grave, and oh,
The difference to me.

A.
    main
    point

B.
    lines
dealing with
    speaker

Questions

A. What is the main point of this poem?

B. The poem contrasts the dead girl and the past with the speaker and the present. Which lines deal with the speaker?

Answers

A. The main point is made in the last two lines in which the speaker tells of his grief.

B. The first six lines of the poem use verbs in the past tense (dwelt, lived, ceased) to describe Lucy. When the speaker talks of his own feelings in the last two lines of the poem, he uses the present tense.

Interpreting Literature and the Arts Reading 3

Wordsworth is an uneven poet. *The Excursion* and *The Prelude* are Wordsworth's longest poems, but they are by no means his best. His best work is in his shorter pieces, and many of these are first-rate. But in the collections of Wordsworth's poetry, pieces of high merit are mingled with very inferior poems. It is surprising that the same poet should have produced both. When one reads Wordsworth, the impression made by one of his fine pieces is too often spoiled by a very inferior piece coming after it.

Questions

A. What is the main idea of the paragraph?

B. What sentence repeats the idea of the first sentence of the paragraph?

Interpreting Literature and the Arts Reading 3

A. main point

Wordsworth is an uneven poet. *The Excursion* and *The Prelude* are Wordsworth's longest poems, but they are by no means his best. His best work is in his shorter pieces, and many of these are first-rate. **But in the collections of Wordsworth's poetry, pieces of high merit are mingled with very inferior poems.** It is surprising that the same poet should have produced both. When one reads Wordsworth, the impression made by one of his fine pieces is too often spoiled by a very inferior piece coming after it.

B. repeats idea of first sentence

Questions

A. What is the main idea of the paragraph?

B. What sentence repeats the idea of the first sentence of the paragraph?

Answers

A. The first sentence states the main idea of the paragraph.

B. The fourth sentence, which begins "But in the collection," restates the point of the first sentence, that Wordsworth wrote both good and bad poems.

Interpreting Literature and the Arts Reading 4

"Had silicon been a gas, I would have been a major general," James Whistler quipped. In 1854, he had been dismissed from West Point for failing chemistry. The following year, he left the United States to study art in Paris. He became one of the most important and certainly one of the most controversial American painters of the last quarter of the nineteenth century. His wit and eccentricities of chess made him a conspicuous figure in London. His painting and his writings on art antagonized the academic painters and England's leading art critic, John Ruskin. Meanwhile Whistler produced paintings, interior designs, and etchings as well as a number of witty works of prose.

Questions

A. What is the main point of the paragraph?

B. What sentences support the main point of the paragraph?

Interpreting Literature and the Arts Reading 4

"Had silicon been a gas, I would have been a major general," James Whistler quipped. In 1854, he had been dismissed from West Point for failing chemistry. The following year, he left the United States to study art in Paris. **He became one of the most important and certainly one of the most controversial American painters of the last quarter of the nineteenth century.** His **wit and eccentricities of chess** made him a conspicuous figure in London. His **painting and his writings on art antagonized** the academic painters and England's leading art critic, John Ruskin. Meanwhile Whistler **produced paintings, interior designs, and etchings as well as a number of witty works of prose.**

A.   main point

B.   support main point

Questions

A. What is the main point of the paragraph?

B. What sentences support the main point of the paragraph?

Answers

A. The main point is the fourth sentence of the paragraph beginning "He became."

B. The last three sentences of the paragraph give evidence of Whistler's achievements and controversial nature.

Interpreting Literature and the Arts Reading 5

My mistress' eyes are nothing like the sun;
Coral is far more red than her lips red;
If snow be white, why then her breasts are dun;
If hairs be wires, black wires grow on her head.
And yet, by heaven, I think my love as rare
As any she belied with false compare.

Questions

A. What is the main point of the poem?

B. Poems in praise of a lady's beauty are likely to
claim that her eyes are as bright as stars, her
lips as red as coral, and her skin as white as
snow. In what lines does the poet describe his
mistress and how does he describe her?

Interpreting Literature and the Arts Reading 5

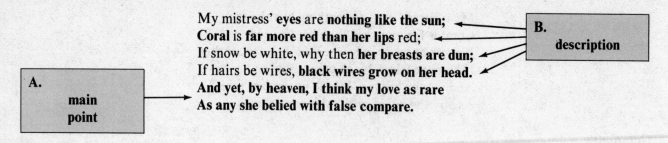

My mistress' **eyes** are **nothing like the sun;**
Coral is **far more red than her lips** red;
If snow be white, why then **her breasts are dun;**
If hairs be wires, **black wires grow on her head.**
And yet, by heaven, I think my love as rare
As any she belied with false compare.

A. **main point**

B. **description**

Questions

A. What is the main point of the poem?

B. Poems in praise of a lady's beauty are likely to claim that her eyes are as bright as stars, her lips as red as coral, and her skin as white as snow. In what lines does the poet describe his mistress and how does he describe her?

Answers

A. The main point is made in the last two lines in which the speaker says his love is as rare as any woman, even those who are lied about by other lovers.

B. Lines 1-4 describe the lady, but do so realistically. Her eyes are not like stars or like the sun; her skin is dun colored, not white as snow; and her hair is black, not golden.

Interpreting Literature and the Arts Reading 6

When a filmmaker refers to "cuts," what does he mean? Cuts are transitions in a film, the moving from one scene to another. A "straight cut" is created by splicing two strips of film together. This appears on the screen as an immediate shift from one scene to another. Older films were more likely to use more complex cuts such as the "dissolve," where a scene disappears slowly while a new scene emerges or the "wipe," where what appears to be a windshield wiper crosses the screen erasing the first scene and revealing the one to follow.

Questions

A. What is the main point of the paragraph?

B. How many examples of kinds of cuts does the paragraph present?

Interpreting Literature and the Arts Reading 6

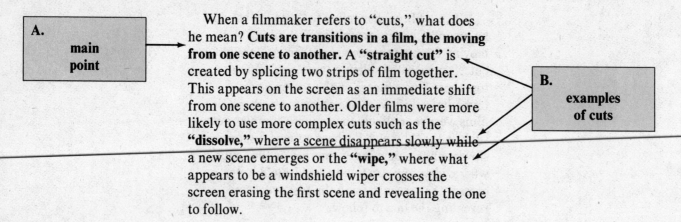

A. main point

When a filmmaker refers to "cuts," what does he mean? **Cuts are transitions in a film, the moving from one scene to another.** A "straight cut" is created by splicing two strips of film together. This appears on the screen as an immediate shift from one scene to another. Older films were more likely to use more complex cuts such as the **"dissolve,"** where a scene disappears slowly while a new scene emerges or the **"wipe,"** where what appears to be a windshield wiper crosses the screen erasing the first scene and revealing the one to follow.

B. examples of cuts

Questions

A. What is the main point of the paragraph?

B. How many examples of kinds of cuts does the paragraph present?

Answers

A. The second sentence makes the main point of the paragraph.

B. The paragraph presents three kinds of cuts, the straight cut, the dissolve, and the wipe.

Interpreting Literature and the Arts Reading 7

The Tanner family of NBC's sitcom *ALF* has an unusual pet—an E.T.-like visitor from outer space—but in most other respects the Tanners are the very picture of TV normalcy. When Dad comes home from work and gets fawned over by his teenage daughter, he instantly guesses, as TV fathers have done for decades, that she wants to borrow the car. And as they have also done for decades, he puts his foot down: no driving on a school night. "If we don't respect the rules we make, we're never going to respect each other," he says at the dinner table. "I mean, have we learned nothing from watching the *Cosby Show*?"

Questions

A. What sentence states the main point of the paragraph?

B. What examples does the paragraph give of TV normalcy?

Interpreting Literature and the Arts Reading 7

A. main point

The Tanner family of NBC's sitcom *ALF* has an unusual pet—an E.T.-like visitor from outer space—but in most other respects the Tanners are the very picture of TV normalcy. When Dad comes home from work and **gets fawned over by his teenage daughter,** he instantly **guesses,** as TV fathers have done for decades, **that she wants to borrow the car.** And as they have also done for decades, **he puts his foot down: no driving on a school night.** "If we don't respect the rules we make, we're never going to respect each other," he says at the dinner table. "I mean, have we learned nothing from watching the *Cosby Show*?"

B. examples of normalcy

Questions

A. What sentence states the main point of the paragraph?

B. What examples does the paragraph give of TV normalcy?

Answers

A. The main point is made in the first sentence.

B. Both the second sentence and the third give examples of predictable TV behavior.

Now that you have completed these exercises, continue reviewing by applying this focused reading to other works of literature and articles about the arts.

TEST
5

MATHEMATICS

TEST 5: MATHEMATICS

Because the Mathematics Test asks you to apply many basic skills in arithmetic, algebra, and geometry, it is important that you first review these basic skills. The following section will help you focus your review.

Start your review by taking the following Review Test. As you check your answers, notice your strengths and weaknesses. Check the box following each answer for any question for which you had the wrong answer. Continue your review of basics by focusing on these weak areas.

REVIEW TEST

ARITHMETIC

1. What is the perimeter of a square if one of its sides has a length of 2"?

2. What is the area of a rectangle with length 8′ and width 3′?

3. If the length of the edge of a cube is 3″, what is the volume of the cube?

4. If a car travels at 50 mph, how long will it take to travel 400 miles?

5. What is the cost of 1 bar of soap if the package reads 3 for $2.07?

6. What is 30% of 20?

7. $3 + 2(6 + 4) =$

8. Which of the following is the greatest? $\frac{1}{5}$, $\frac{1}{3}$, $\frac{2}{7}$, $\frac{1}{4}$, $\frac{3}{10}$

9. What does .0043 equal in scientific notation?

10. $3^3 \times 3^4 =$

11. Round 324,170 to the nearest thousand.

12. Find the mean and median of the following numbers: 9, 8, 4, 7, 8, 6, 9

<u>Item 13</u> refers to the following graph.

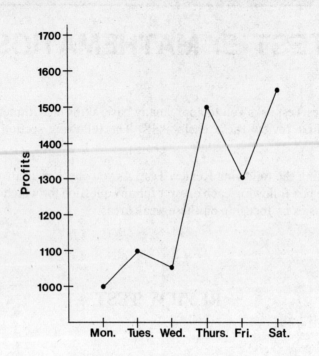

13. In the graph above, the greatest one-day increase in profits was from

14. Tom pours 15 red marbles, 6 blue marbles, and 9 green marbles into a jar. What are the odds of pulling a <u>green</u> marble from the jar on the first try?

ALGEBRA

15. Solve for x: $3x + 6 = 2x + 9$

16. "Three less than x" can be written in symbols as

17. Solve for x: $6x < 12$

18. Evaluate the expression $7x + 2y^2$ if $x = 2$ and $y = 3$.

19. $2x(3x - 4) =$

20. Factor completely: $5x^2 + 10x$

21. Bill's starting salary was $16,000 a year. His salary for the next year increased to $20,000. What was his <u>percentage increase</u> in salary?

22. Solve for x: $\dfrac{x}{21} = \dfrac{3}{7}$

GEOMETRY

Item 23 is based on the following drawing.

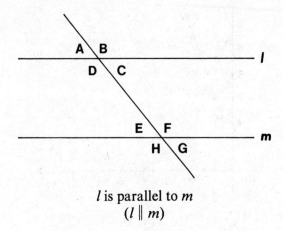

l is parallel to *m*
(*l* ∥ *m*)

23. In the diagram above, if angle A measures 50°, what is the measure of angle F?

Item 24 is based on the following drawing.

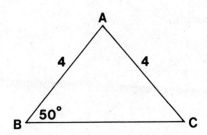

24. In the isosceles triangle above, what is the measure of angle A?

Item 25 is based on the following drawing.

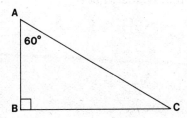

25. In the right triangle above, what is the measure of angle C?

26. If the area of a circle is 9π sq in, what is the length of its radius?

27. How many diagonals are in a regular pentagon?

Items 28, 29, and 30 refer to the following coordinate graph.

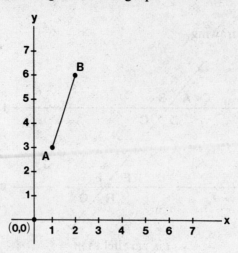

28. Point A has the coordinates (,)

29. The slope of line AB is

30. The distance between points A and B is

Item 31 is based on the following drawing.

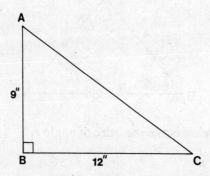

31. Find the length of side AC in the right triangle above.

REVIEW TEST ANSWERS

ARITHMETIC

1. 8 square inches ☐
2. 24 square feet ☐
3. 27 cubic inches ☐
4. 8 hours ☐
5. 69 cents ☐
6. 6 ☐
7. 23 ☐
8. ⅓ ☐
9. 4.3×10^{-3} ☐
10. 3^7 or 2187 ☐
11. 324,000 ☐
12. mean = 7²⁄₇ ☐
    median = 8 ☐
13. Wednesday to Thursday ☐
14. ⁹⁄₃₀ or ³⁄₁₀ ☐

ALGEBRA

15. $x = 3$ ☐
16. $x - 3$ ☐
17. $x < 2$ ☐
18. 32 ☐
19. $6x^2 - 8x$ ☐
20. $5x(x + 2)$ ☐
21. 25% ☐
22. $x = 9$ ☐

GEOMETRY

23. 130° ☐
24. 80° ☐
25. 30° ☐
26. radius = 3 inches ☐
27. 5 ☐
28. (1, 3) ☐
29. 3 ☐
30. $\sqrt{30}$ ☐
31. 15 inches ☐

Now that you have completed and corrected your Review Test, continue your review by focusing on a "brush up" of your weak areas.

4

Practice Examinations

How to Use This Section

This section contains two full-length simulation GED examinations. These examinations are followed by answers and complete explanations. The Score Approximators and analysis charts that follow the Answer Keys are valuable tools that will help you pinpoint your weaknesses and give you a very general score range.

The format, levels of difficulty, question structure, and number of questions are similar to those of the actual GED examination. The actual GED examination is copyrighted and may not be duplicated. These questions are not taken from the actual tests.

When you take these tests, try to duplicate the test conditions by using only the time allowed. You'll find the time allotments listed in this book immediately before each of the practice examinations.

GED

PRACTICE
EXAMINATION 1

When you take Practice Examination 1, try to duplicate the test conditions by using only the time allowed.

TEST 1: WRITING SKILLS		
Part I: Multiple-Choice	55 questions	75 minutes
Part II: Essay	1 essay	45 minutes

TEST 2: SOCIAL STUDIES	64 questions	85 minutes

TEST 3: SCIENCE	66 questions	95 minutes

TEST 4: INTERPRETING LITERATURE AND THE ARTS	45 questions	65 minutes

TEST 5: MATHEMATICS	56 questions	90 minutes

Since this test is new, times and numbers of questions may be adjusted slightly in later testings.

Before you take Practice Examination 1, cut out the answer sheets and the lined essay sheets that you'll find following and use them to mark your answers. Use a single sheet of your own paper for scratch paper for your essay. On the actual test, scratch paper will be given to you along with the answer sheets.

Be sure to mark the answers for the test you are taking in the correct section of the answer sheet. For each test, find the "form" on your test booklet cover, and mark the circle corresponding to the form in the box labelled Test Form.

TEST 1: WRITING SKILLS - PART 1

TEST FORM

AA AB AC AD AE AF AG AH AI AJ AK AL AM AN AO AP AQ AR AS AT AU AV AW AX AY AZ

1 ① ② ③ ④ ⑤	12 ① ② ③ ④ ⑤	23 ① ② ③ ④ ⑤	34 ① ② ③ ④ ⑤	45 ① ② ③ ④ ⑤
2 ① ② ③ ④ ⑤	13 ① ② ③ ④ ⑤	24 ① ② ③ ④ ⑤	35 ① ② ③ ④ ⑤	46 ① ② ③ ④ ⑤
3 ① ② ③ ④ ⑤	14 ① ② ③ ④ ⑤	25 ① ② ③ ④ ⑤	36 ① ② ③ ④ ⑤	47 ① ② ③ ④ ⑤
4 ① ② ③ ④ ⑤	15 ① ② ③ ④ ⑤	26 ① ② ③ ④ ⑤	37 ① ② ③ ④ ⑤	48 ① ② ③ ④ ⑤
5 ① ② ③ ④ ⑤	16 ① ② ③ ④ ⑤	27 ① ② ③ ④ ⑤	38 ① ② ③ ④ ⑤	49 ① ② ③ ④ ⑤
6 ① ② ③ ④ ⑤	17 ① ② ③ ④ ⑤	28 ① ② ③ ④ ⑤	39 ① ② ③ ④ ⑤	50 ① ② ③ ④ ⑤
7 ① ② ③ ④ ⑤	18 ① ② ③ ④ ⑤	29 ① ② ③ ④ ⑤	40 ① ② ③ ④ ⑤	51 ① ② ③ ④ ⑤
8 ① ② ③ ④ ⑤	19 ① ② ③ ④ ⑤	30 ① ② ③ ④ ⑤	41 ① ② ③ ④ ⑤	52 ① ② ③ ④ ⑤
9 ① ② ③ ④ ⑤	20 ① ② ③ ④ ⑤	31 ① ② ③ ④ ⑤	42 ① ② ③ ④ ⑤	53 ① ② ③ ④ ⑤
10 ① ② ③ ④ ⑤	21 ① ② ③ ④ ⑤	32 ① ② ③ ④ ⑤	43 ① ② ③ ④ ⑤	54 ① ② ③ ④ ⑤
11 ① ② ③ ④ ⑤	22 ① ② ③ ④ ⑤	33 ① ② ③ ④ ⑤	44 ① ② ③ ④ ⑤	55 ① ② ③ ④ ⑤

TEST CODE

Enter the test code from your test booklet. Then mark the circles below each box.

⓪ ⓪ ⓪
① ① ①
② ② ②
③ ③ ③
④ ④ ④
⑤ ⑤ ⑤
⑥ ⑥ ⑥
⑦ ⑦ ⑦
⑧ ⑧ ⑧
⑨ ⑨ ⑨

GO ON TO WRITING SKILLS - PART II

TEST 2: SOCIAL STUDIES

TEST FORM

AA AB AC AD AE AF AG AH AI AJ AK AL AM AN AO AP AQ AR AS AT AU AV AW AX AY AZ

1 ① ② ③ ④ ⑤	14 ① ② ③ ④ ⑤	27 ① ② ③ ④ ⑤	40 ① ② ③ ④ ⑤	53 ① ② ③ ④ ⑤
2 ① ② ③ ④ ⑤	15 ① ② ③ ④ ⑤	28 ① ② ③ ④ ⑤	41 ① ② ③ ④ ⑤	54 ① ② ③ ④ ⑤
3 ① ② ③ ④ ⑤	16 ① ② ③ ④ ⑤	29 ① ② ③ ④ ⑤	42 ① ② ③ ④ ⑤	55 ① ② ③ ④ ⑤
4 ① ② ③ ④ ⑤	17 ① ② ③ ④ ⑤	30 ① ② ③ ④ ⑤	43 ① ② ③ ④ ⑤	56 ① ② ③ ④ ⑤
5 ① ② ③ ④ ⑤	18 ① ② ③ ④ ⑤	31 ① ② ③ ④ ⑤	44 ① ② ③ ④ ⑤	57 ① ② ③ ④ ⑤
6 ① ② ③ ④ ⑤	19 ① ② ③ ④ ⑤	32 ① ② ③ ④ ⑤	45 ① ② ③ ④ ⑤	58 ① ② ③ ④ ⑤
7 ① ② ③ ④ ⑤	20 ① ② ③ ④ ⑤	33 ① ② ③ ④ ⑤	46 ① ② ③ ④ ⑤	59 ① ② ③ ④ ⑤
8 ① ② ③ ④ ⑤	21 ① ② ③ ④ ⑤	34 ① ② ③ ④ ⑤	47 ① ② ③ ④ ⑤	60 ① ② ③ ④ ⑤
9 ① ② ③ ④ ⑤	22 ① ② ③ ④ ⑤	35 ① ② ③ ④ ⑤	48 ① ② ③ ④ ⑤	61 ① ② ③ ④ ⑤
10 ① ② ③ ④ ⑤	23 ① ② ③ ④ ⑤	36 ① ② ③ ④ ⑤	49 ① ② ③ ④ ⑤	62 ① ② ③ ④ ⑤
11 ① ② ③ ④ ⑤	24 ① ② ③ ④ ⑤	37 ① ② ③ ④ ⑤	50 ① ② ③ ④ ⑤	63 ① ② ③ ④ ⑤
12 ① ② ③ ④ ⑤	25 ① ② ③ ④ ⑤	38 ① ② ③ ④ ⑤	51 ① ② ③ ④ ⑤	64 ① ② ③ ④ ⑤
13 ① ② ③ ④ ⑤	26 ① ② ③ ④ ⑤	39 ① ② ③ ④ ⑤	52 ① ② ③ ④ ⑤	**STOP**

TEST CODE

Enter the test code from your test booklet. Then mark the circles below each box.

⓪ ⓪ ⓪
① ① ①
② ② ②
③ ③ ③
④ ④ ④
⑤ ⑤ ⑤
⑥ ⑥ ⑥
⑦ ⑦ ⑦
⑧ ⑧ ⑧
⑨ ⑨ ⑨

MAKE NO MARKS IN THIS AREA

0138622

TEST 3: SCIENCE

TEST CODE

0	0	0
1	1	1
2	2	2
3	3	3
4	4	4
5	5	5
6	6	6
7	7	7
8	8	8
9	9	9

Enter the test code from your test booklet. Then mark the circles below each box.

AA	AB	AC	AD	AE	AF	AG	AH	AI	AJ	AK	AL	AM	AN	AO	AP	AQ	AR	AS	AT	AU	AV	AW	AX	AY	AZ
○	○	○	○	○	○	○	○	○	○	○	○	○	○	○	○	○	○	○	○	○	○	○	○	○	○

TEST FORM

1 ①②③④⑤	11 ①②③④⑤	21 ①②③④⑤	31 ①②③④⑤	41 ①②③④⑤	51 ①②③④⑤	61 ①②③④⑤
2 ①②③④⑤	12 ①②③④⑤	22 ①②③④⑤	32 ①②③④⑤	42 ①②③④⑤	52 ①②③④⑤	62 ①②③④⑤
3 ①②③④⑤	13 ①②③④⑤	23 ①②③④⑤	33 ①②③④⑤	43 ①②③④⑤	53 ①②③④⑤	63 ①②③④⑤
4 ①②③④⑤	14 ①②③④⑤	24 ①②③④⑤	34 ①②③④⑤	44 ①②③④⑤	54 ①②③④⑤	64 ①②③④⑤
5 ①②③④⑤	15 ①②③④⑤	25 ①②③④⑤	35 ①②③④⑤	45 ①②③④⑤	55 ①②③④⑤	65 ①②③④⑤
6 ①②③④⑤	16 ①②③④⑤	26 ①②③④⑤	36 ①②③④⑤	46 ①②③④⑤	56 ①②③④⑤	66 ①②③④⑤
7 ①②③④⑤	17 ①②③④⑤	27 ①②③④⑤	37 ①②③④⑤	47 ①②③④⑤	57 ①②③④⑤	STOP
8 ①②③④⑤	18 ①②③④⑤	28 ①②③④⑤	38 ①②③④⑤	48 ①②③④⑤	58 ①②③④⑤	
9 ①②③④⑤	19 ①②③④⑤	29 ①②③④⑤	39 ①②③④⑤	49 ①②③④⑤	59 ①②③④⑤	
10 ①②③④⑤	20 ①②③④⑤	30 ①②③④⑤	40 ①②③④⑤	50 ①②③④⑤	60 ①②③④⑤	

TEST 4: INTERPRETING LITERATURE AND THE ARTS

TEST CODE

0	0	0
1	1	1
2	2	2
3	3	3
4	4	4
5	5	5
6	6	6
7	7	7
8	8	8
9	9	9

Enter the test code from your test booklet. Then mark the circles below each box.

AA	AB	AC	AD	AE	AF	AG	AH	AI	AJ	AK	AL	AM	AN	AO	AP	AQ	AR	AS	AT	AU	AV	AW	AX	AY	AZ
○	○	○	○	○	○	○	○	○	○	○	○	○	○	○	○	○	○	○	○	○	○	○	○	○	○

TEST FORM

1 ①②③④⑤	8 ①②③④⑤	15 ①②③④⑤	22 ①②③④⑤	29 ①②③④⑤	36 ①②③④⑤	43 ①②③④⑤
2 ①②③④⑤	9 ①②③④⑤	16 ①②③④⑤	23 ①②③④⑤	30 ①②③④⑤	37 ①②③④⑤	44 ①②③④⑤
3 ①②③④⑤	10 ①②③④⑤	17 ①②③④⑤	24 ①②③④⑤	31 ①②③④⑤	38 ①②③④⑤	45 ①②③④⑤
4 ①②③④⑤	11 ①②③④⑤	18 ①②③④⑤	25 ①②③④⑤	32 ①②③④⑤	39 ①②③④⑤	STOP
5 ①②③④⑤	12 ①②③④⑤	19 ①②③④⑤	26 ①②③④⑤	33 ①②③④⑤	40 ①②③④⑤	
6 ①②③④⑤	13 ①②③④⑤	20 ①②③④⑤	27 ①②③④⑤	34 ①②③④⑤	41 ①②③④⑤	
7 ①②③④⑤	14 ①②③④⑤	21 ①②③④⑤	28 ①②③④⑤	35 ①②③④⑤	42 ①②③④⑤	

TEST 5: MATHEMATICS

Enter the test code from your test booklet. Then mark the circles below each box.

TEST CODE

0	0	0
1	1	1
2	2	2
3	3	3
4	4	4
5	5	5
6	6	6
7	7	7
8	8	8
9	9	9

AA	AB	AC	AD	AE	AF	AG	AH	AI	AJ	AK	AL	AM	AN	AO	AP	AQ	AR	AS	AT	AU	AV	AW	AX	AY	AZ
○	○	○	○	○	○	○	○	○	○	○	○	○	○	○	○	○	○	○	○	○	○	○	○	○	○

TEST FORM

1 ①②③④⑤	9 ①②③④⑤	17 ①②③④⑤	25 ①②③④⑤	33 ①②③④⑤	41 ①②③④⑤	49 ①②③④⑤
2 ①②③④⑤	10 ①②③④⑤	18 ①②③④⑤	26 ①②③④⑤	34 ①②③④⑤	42 ①②③④⑤	50 ①②③④⑤
3 ①②③④⑤	11 ①②③④⑤	19 ①②③④⑤	27 ①②③④⑤	35 ①②③④⑤	43 ①②③④⑤	51 ①②③④⑤
4 ①②③④⑤	12 ①②③④⑤	20 ①②③④⑤	28 ①②③④⑤	36 ①②③④⑤	44 ①②③④⑤	52 ①②③④⑤
5 ①②③④⑤	13 ①②③④⑤	21 ①②③④⑤	29 ①②③④⑤	37 ①②③④⑤	45 ①②③④⑤	53 ①②③④⑤
6 ①②③④⑤	14 ①②③④⑤	22 ①②③④⑤	30 ①②③④⑤	38 ①②③④⑤	46 ①②③④⑤	54 ①②③④⑤
7 ①②③④⑤	15 ①②③④⑤	23 ①②③④⑤	31 ①②③④⑤	39 ①②③④⑤	47 ①②③④⑤	55 ①②③④⑤
8 ①②③④⑤	16 ①②③④⑤	24 ①②③④⑤	32 ①②③④⑤	40 ①②③④⑤	48 ①②③④⑤	56 ①②③④⑤

STOP

SOCIAL SECURITY NUMBER

WRITING SKILLS TEST - PART II

Write the letter of your essay topic in the box, then shade the corresponding circle.

TOPIC Ⓐ Ⓑ Ⓒ Ⓓ Ⓔ Ⓕ Ⓖ Ⓗ Ⓘ Ⓙ Ⓚ Ⓛ Ⓜ Ⓝ Ⓞ Ⓟ Ⓠ Ⓡ Ⓢ Ⓣ Ⓤ Ⓥ Ⓦ Ⓧ Ⓨ Ⓩ

Continue your essay on next page

USE A BALL POINT PEN TO WRITE YOUR ESSAY

TEST 1: WRITING SKILLS, PART I

Tests of General Educational Development

Directions

The Writing Skills Test is intended to measure your ability to use clear and effective English. It is a test of English as it should be written, not as it might be spoken. This test includes both multiple-choice questions and an essay. These directions apply only to the multiple-choice section; a separate set of directions is given for the essay.

The multiple-choice section consists of paragraphs with numbered sentences. Some of the sentences contain errors in sentence structure, usage, or mechanics (spelling, punctuation, and capitalization). After reading the numbered sentences, answer the multiple-choice questions that follow. Some questions refer to sentences that are correct as written. The best answer for these questions is the one which leaves the sentence as originally written. The best answer for some questions is the one which produces a sentence that is consistent with the verb tense and point of view used throughout the paragraph.

You should spend no more than 75 minutes on the multiple-choice questions and 45 minutes on your essay. Work carefully, but do not spend too much time on any one question. You may begin working on the essay part of this test as soon as you complete the multiple-choice section.

Do not mark in this test booklet. Record your answers on the separate answer sheet provided. Be sure that all requested information is properly recorded on the answer sheet.

To record your answers, mark one numbered space on the answer sheet beside the number that corresponds to the question in the test booklet.

FOR EXAMPLE:

Sentence 1: **We were all honored to meet governor Phillips.**

What correction should be made to this sentence?

(1) insert a comma after honored
(2) change the spelling of honored to honered
(3) change governor to Governor
(4) replace were with was
(5) no correction is necessary   ① ② ● ④ ⑤

In this example, the word "governor" should be capitalized; therefore, answer space 3 would be marked on the answer sheet.

Do not rest the point of your pencil on the answer sheet while you are considering your answer. Make no stray or unnecessary marks. If you change an answer, erase your first mark completely. Mark only one answer space for each question; multiple answers will be scored as incorrect. Do not fold or crease your answer sheet. All test materials must be returned to the test administrator.

Directions: Choose the one best answer to each item.

Items 1 to 6 refer to the following paragraph.

(1) According to a nationwide survey released by the National Federation of Independent Business, the cost of insurance is the greatest problem, for small business owners. (2) The most severe problem being the cost of liability insurance. (3) Many respondents cited the cost of health insurance as troublesome, but almost 40% called the costs and availability of liability insurance to be the most critical issue. (4) Cash flow, a perennial problem for small-business owners, are the fourth-ranked problem in the survey. (5) High telephone costs placing fifth on the survey. (6) Businessmen were asked to evaluate the severity of seventy-five potential problems. (7) This is the second survey done by the NFIB.

1. Sentence 1: **According to a nationwide survey released by the National Federation of Independent Business, the cost of insurance is the greatest problem, for small business owners.**

What correction should be made to this sentence?

(1) insert a comma after survey
(2) remove the comma after Business
(3) change the comma after Business to a semicolon
(4) remove the comma after problem
(5) no correction is necessary

2. Sentence 2: **The most severe problem being the cost of liability insurance.**

Which of the following is the best way to write the underlined portion of this sentence? If you think the original is the best way, choose option (1).

(1) most severe problem being the cost
(2) most severe being the problem of the cost
(3) most severe problem, the cost
(4) most severe is the cost
(5) most severe being the cost

3. Sentence 3: **Many respondents cited the cost of health insurance as troublesome, but almost 40% called the costs and availability of liability insurance to be the most critical issue.**

What correction should be made to this sentence?

(1) change cited to cite
(2) change the spelling of cited to sighted
(3) change called to call
(4) remove the to be
(5) no correction is necessary

4. Sentence 4: **Cash flow, a perennial problem for small-business owners, are the fourth-ranked problem in the survey.**

What correction should be made to this sentence?

(1) omit the comma after flow
(2) omit the comma after owners
(3) change are to is
(4) change are to were
(5) no correction is necessary

5. Sentences 4 and 5: **Cash flow, a perennial problem for small-business owners, are the fourth-ranked problem in the survey. High telephone costs placing fifth on the survey.**

The most effective combination of sentences 4 and 5 would include which of the following groups of words?

(1) the fourth-ranked problem in the survey, and high telephone costs placing
(2) the fourth-ranked problem of the survey; high telephone costs placing
(3) the fourth-ranked problem, with high telephone costs placing
(4) the fourth-ranked problem, and high telephone costs placing
(5) the fourth-ranked problem; high telephone costs placing

6. Sentences 6 and 7: **Businessmen were asked to evaluate the severity of seventy-five potential problems. This is the second survey done by the NFIB.**

An effective combination of sentences 6 and 7 beginning with

This second NFIB survey

would include which of the following groups of words?

(1) asked businessmen to evaluate
(2) in which businessmen were asked for an evaluation of
(3) asked businessmen for their evaluation of
(4) was done to ask businessmen to evaluate
(5) done to ask businessmen to evaluate

Items 7 to 13 refer to the following paragraph.

(1) One unexpected finding, was the low ranking of hazardous waste disposal, which ranked next to last. (2) Most respondents said it was not a problem at all. (3) A second surprise was the rise from twenty-fifth to tenth place of state taxes on business income, an example of how political change can effect small businesses. (4) With the reduction in federal aid to states, fees and state taxes have raised in many states. (5) The results of the survey are significant, because small business is one of the most important sectors of the nation's economy. (6) Since more than 90% of the non-farm businesses in the United States are small businesses. (7) It employs almost half of the private work force, accounting for 40% of the gross national product.

7. Sentence 1: **One unexpected finding, was the low ranking of hazardous waste disposal, which ranked next to last.**

   What correction should be made to this sentence?

   (1) remove the comma after finding
   (2) change the spelling of hazardous to hazerdous
   (3) change the spelling of disposal to disposel
   (4) remove the comma after disposal
   (5) no correction is necessary

8. Sentence 2: **Most respondents said it was not a problem at all.**

   What correction should be made to this sentence?

   (1) change said to say
   (2) change it to they
   (3) change was to were
   (4) change not a problem to not any problem
   (5) no correction is necessary

9. Sentence 3: **A second surprise was the rise from twenty-fifth to tenth place of state taxes on business income, an example of how political change can effect small businesses.**

   Which of the following is the best way to write the underlined portion of this sentence? If you think the original is the best way, choose option (1).

   (1) change can effect small businesses.
   (2) change can effect small business.
   (3) change can affect small businesses.
   (4) changes effect business.
   (5) changes effect small businesses.

10. Sentence 4: **With the reduction in federal aid to states, fees and state taxes have raised in many states.**

    What correction should be made to this sentence?

    (1) change <u>in</u> to <u>of</u>
    (2) change the comma after <u>states</u> to a semicolon
    (3) change <u>have raised</u> to <u>has raised</u>
    (4) change <u>have raised</u> to <u>have risen</u>
    (5) no correction is necessary

11. Sentence 5: **The results of the survey are significant because small business is one of the most important sectors of the nation's economy.**

    What correction should be made to this sentence?

    (1) change <u>business</u> to <u>businesses</u>
    (2) change <u>is</u> to <u>are</u>
    (3) change <u>sectors</u> to <u>sections</u>
    (4) change <u>nation's</u> to <u>nations</u>
    (5) no correction is necessary

12. Sentence 6: **Since more than 90% of the non-farm businesses in the United States are small businesses.**

    What correction should be made to this sentence?

    (1) remove the <u>Since</u>
    (2) change <u>more than</u> to <u>most of</u>
    (3) change <u>in</u> to <u>of</u>
    (4) change <u>are</u> to <u>have been</u>
    (5) no correction is necessary

13. Sentence 7: **It employs almost half of the private work force, accounting for 40% of the gross national product.**

    Which of the following is the best way to write the underlined portion of this sentence? If you think the original is the best way, choose option (l).

    (1) It employs almost half
    (2) They employ almost half
    (3) It will employ almost half
    (4) They will employ almost half
    (5) Employing almost half

Items 14 to 22 refer to the following paragraph.

(1) Thirty years ago, there were only two types of life insurance. (2) These were term and whole life. (3) Now there are three. (4) The latest offering in life insurance is called universal life, it is basically a blend of term and whole life. (5) Term insurance covers a buyers' life for a limited period of time for a fixed rate. (6) The cost of term insurance for a young man or woman in good health are low, but all the policy provides is protection in the event of death. (7) A whole life policy gives the same protection, and also an opportunity to save money and earn interest on that savings. (8) But the cost is certain to be higher. (9) A universal life policy, the insurance companies claim, combines the best of both the term and the whole life policies. (10) It earned interest at a higher rate than a whole life policy. (11) But consumer groups have warned that sales and adminstrative fees are often higher with universal life policies. (12) And the advertised higher interest rates are sometimes good for only the first year.

14. Sentence 1: **Thirty years ago, there were only two types of life insurance.**

Which of the following is the best way to write the underlined portion of this sentence? If you think the original is the best way, choose option (1).

(1) there were
(2) there was
(3) there is
(4) there are
(5) there will be

15. Sentences 1 and 2: **Thirty years ago, there were only two types of life insurance. These were term and whole life.**

The most effective combination of sentences 1 and 2 would include which of the following groups of words?

(1) insurance, and these were term and whole life.
(2) insurance, term and whole life.
(3) insurance, these being term and whole life.
(4) insurance, and these being term and whole life.
(5) insurance, and these are term and whole life.

16. Sentence 4: **The latest offering in life insurance is called universal life, it is basically a blend of term and whole life.**

Which of the following is the best way to write the underlined portion of this sentence? If you think the original is the best way, choose option (1)

(1) universal life, it is basically
(2) universal life and it is basically
(3) universal life. It is basically
(4) universal life and this is basically
(5) universal life it is basically

17. Sentence 5: **Term insurance covers a buyers' life for a limited period of time for a fixed rate.**

What correction should be made to this sentence?

(1) change the spelling of insurance to insurence
(2) change covers to cover
(3) change buyers' to buyer's
(4) add a comma after time
(5) no correction is necessary

18. Sentence 6: **The cost of term insurance for a young man or woman in good health are low, but all the policy provides is protection in the event of death.**

What correction should be made to this sentence?

(1) add a comma after insurance
(2) add a comma after man
(3) change are to is
(4) remove the comma after low
(5) change is to are

19. Sentence 7: **A whole life policy gives the same protection, and also an opportunity to save money and earn interest on that savings.**

If you rewrote sentence 7 beginning with

The same protection is given

the next word(s) should be

(1) a whole life policy
(2) so
(3) and
(4) and also
(5) by

20 Sentence 9: **A universal life policy, the insurance companies claim, combines the best of both the term and the whole life policies.**

What correction should be made to this sentence?

(1) remove the comma after policy
(2) remove the comma after claim
(3) remove the commas after policy and claim
(4) insert a comma after best
(5) no correction is necessary

21. Sentence 11: **But consumer groups have warned that sales and adminstrative fees are often higher with universal life policies.**

What correction should be made to this sentence?

(1) change the spelling of consumer to consumor
(2) change the spelling of groups to groops
(3) change the spelling of adminstrative to administrative
(4) change the spelling of often to offen
(5) change the spelling of universal to unversal

22. Sentence 12: **And the advertised higher interest rates are sometimes good for only the first year.**

What correction should be made to this sentence?

(1) add a comma after advertised
(2) add a comma after higher
(3) add a comma after interest
(4) add a comma after rates
(5) no correction is necessary

Items 23 to 31 refer to following paragraph.

(1) A movie that is very successful at the box-office is likely to inspire a sequel. (2) There was *Rocky,* then *Rocky II* then *Rocky III,* and *Rocky IV.* (3) There have been two films of *Jaws* and five *Friday the Thirteenth's.* (4) More often than not, the sequel is inferior from the original film, but not always. (5) Many moviegoers prefered *The Godfather, Part II,* to *The Godfather.* (6) The making of sequels are nothing new. (7) Many of the earliest films were repititions. (8) There were thirty-six Tarzan movies, and almost as many about Sherlock Holmes and Charlie Chan. (9) If moviegoers did not continue to pay to see sequels, would the studios go on making them. (10) There's no doubt at all. (11) But as long the public responds, there have been more and more of the same.

23. Sentence 2: **There was *Rocky,* then *Rocky II* then *Rocky III,* and *Rocky IV.***

What correction should be made to this sentence?

(1) remove the comma after *Rocky*
(2) insert a comma after *Rocky II*
(3) remove the comma after *Rocky III*
(4) omit the first then
(5) no correction is necessary

24. Sentence 4: **More often than not, the sequel is inferior from the original film, but not always.**

What correction should be made to this sentence?

(1) remove the comma after not
(2) change is to are
(3) change is to was
(4) change from to to
(5) no correction is necessary

25. Sentence 5: **Many moviegoers prefered *The Godfather, Part II,* to *The Godfather.***

What correction should be made to this sentence?

(1) change moviegoers to moviegoer
(2) change the spelling of prefered to preferred
(3) omit the comma between *Godfather* and *Part*
(4) change to to from
(5) change the period to a question mark

26. Sentence 6: **The making of sequels are nothing new.**

    Which of the following is the best way to write the underlined portion of this sentence? If you think the original is the best way, choose option (1).

    (1) making of sequels are nothing
    (2) making sequels are nothing
    (3) making of sequels are not
    (4) making of sequels is nothing
    (5) making of a sequel are not

27. Sentence 7: **Many of the earliest films were repititions.**

    What correction should be made to this sentence?

    (1) change many of the to many
    (2) change earliest to early
    (3) change were to are
    (4) change the spelling of repititions to repetitions
    (5) no correction is necessary.

28. Sentence 8: **There were thirty-six Tarzan movies, and almost as many about Sherlock Holmes and Charlie Chan.**

    If you rewrote sentence 8 beginning with

    Thirty-six Tarzan movies

    the next words should be

    (1) are there, and almost
    (2) were there, and almost
    (3) were made, and almost
    (4) are made, and almost
    (5) will be made, and almost

29. Sentence 9: **If moviegoers did not continue to pay to see sequels, would the studios go on making them.**

    What correction should be made to this sentence?

    (1) change did not to had not
    (2) change to see to and see
    (3) change the spelling of studios to studioes
    (4) change them to sequels
    (5) change the period to a question mark

30. Sentences 9 and 10: **If moviegoers did not continue to pay to see sequels, would the studios go on making them. There's no doubt at all.**

    If you combined sentences 9 and 10 beginning with

    There's no doubt that if moviegoers did not continue to pay to see sequels

    the next words should be

    (1) the studios would go on
    (2) the studios would stop
    (3) the studios will go on
    (4) the studios will continue
    (5) the studios would continue

31. Sentence 11: **But as long as the public responds, there have been more and more of the same.**

    Which of the following is the best way to write the underlined portion of this sentence? If you think the original is the best way, choose option (1).

    (1) responds, there have been
    (2) responds, there is
    (3) responds, there will be
    (4) responds, there are
    (5) responds there will be

Items 32 to 40 refer to following paragraph.

(1) According to the National Consumers League, consumer protection in many areas has not improved. (2) It has become weaker. (3) For example, the Enviromental Protection Agency's powers have decreased. (4) There are fewer inspectors at the Federal Aviation Administration, there are fewer air traffic controllers. (5) Improvements in health care are needed bad. (6) There are more than twenty-five million people in the United States who have no health insurance. (7) New spending cuts under the Gramm-Rudman bill will further weaken consumer protection programs. (8) Hoping to protect funding for health care, a new bill has been introduced by Senator Kennedy. (9) The proposal would exempt Medicare funding from the spending cuts required by the Gramm-Rudman legislation. (10) But the proposal may have come too late. (11) For consumers this has been a bad year in Congress.

32. Sentences 1 and 2: **According to the National Consumers League, consumer protection in many areas has not improved. It has become weaker.**

The most effective combination of sentences 1 and 2 would include which of the following groups of words?

(1) improved, and it has become
(2) improved, it has become
(3) improved, it having become
(4) improved, but has become
(5) improved, and so it has become

33. Sentence 3: **For example, the Enviromental Protection Agency's powers have decreased.**

What correction should be made to this sentence?

(1) remove the comma after example
(2) change the spelling of Enviromental to Environmental
(3) change Agency's to Agencies
(4) change have to has
(5) no correction is necessary

34. Sentence 4: **There are fewer inspectors at the Federal Aviation Administration, there are fewer air traffic controllers.**

Which of the following is the best way to write the underlined portion of the sentence? If you think the original is the best way, choose option (1).

(1) Administration, there are fewer
(2) Administration and there are fewer
(3) Administration there are fewer
(4) Administration. There are fewer
(5) Administration so there are fewer

35. Sentence 5: **Improvements in health care are needed bad.**

    What correction should be made to this sentence?

    (1) change Improvements to Improvement
    (2) change in to for
    (3) change are to is
    (4) change bad to badly
    (5) no correction is necessary

36. Sentence 6: **There are more than twenty-five million people in the United States who have no health insurance.**

    Which of the following is the best way to write the underlined portion of this sentence? If you think the original is the best way, choose option (1).

    (1) who have no
    (2) whom have no
    (3) whom has no
    (4) which have no
    (5) who has no

37. Sentence 7: **New spending cuts under the Gramm-Rudman bill will further weaken consumer protection programs.**

    What correction should be made to this sentence?

    (1) insert a comma after cuts
    (2) change under to underneath
    (3) change further to farther
    (4) change consumer to consumer's
    (5) no correction is necessary

38. Sentence 8: **Hoping to protect funding for health care, a new bill has been introduced by Senator Kennedy.**

    Which of the following is the best way to write the underlined portion of this sentence? If you think the original is the best way, choose option (1).

    (1) for health care, a new bill has been introduced by Senator Kennedy.
    (2) for health care a new bill has been introduced by Senator Kennedy.
    (3) for health care. A new bill has been introduced by Senator Kennedy.
    (4) for health care, Senator Kennedy has introduced a new bill.
    (5) for health care; Senator Kennedy has introduced a new bill.

39. Sentences 9 and 10: **The proposal would exempt Medicare funding from the spending cuts required by the Gramm-Rudman legislation. But the proposal may have come too late.**

    The most effective combination of sentences 9 and 10 would include which of the following groups of words?

    (1) legislation but the proposal
    (2) legislation, so the proposal
    (3) legislation, but it
    (4) legislation, and it
    (5) legislation, for the proposal

40. Sentence 11: **For consumers this has been a bad year in Congress.**

    What correction should be made to this sentence?

    (1) insert a comma after consumers
    (2) change has to had
    (3) insert a comma after year
    (4) change the period to a question mark
    (5) no correction is necessary

Items 41 to 49 refer to the following paragraph.

(1) Forty years ago, a steel mill operated not far from downtown Pittsburgh. (2) Where the mill once stands, the city is now developing an industrial park for high-technology companies. (3) In the last decade, dozens of mills and thousands of jobs have been lost. (4) As the number of steel jobs has declined, the number of jobs in high-tech industries has increased. (5) In fact, in metropolitan Pittsburgh more people now work in high-tech feilds than in steelmaking. (6) In 1984, the Pentagon decided to locate it's new national laboratory for computer software research in Pittsburgh. (7) And the city is also now a center for research and manufacture in automation technology. (8) One Pittsburgh firm is supplying robots to the auto industry. (9) Another has developed new technology for devices to monitor heartbeats. (10) Because few middle-aged steelworkers could take over computer jobs when they were laid off, the area still has unemployment problems. (11) But high-tech jobs have helped to lesson some of Pittsburgh's economic problems.

41. Sentence 1: **Forty years ago, a steel mill operated not far from downtown Pittsburgh.**

What correction should be made to this sentence?

(1) change the spelling of Forty to Fourty
(2) remove the comma after ago
(3) change the spelling of steel to steal
(4) change operated to operates
(5) no correction is necessary

42. Sentence 2: **Where the mill once stands, the city is now developing an industrial park for high-technology companies.**

Which of the following is the best way to write the underlined portion of this sentence? If you think the original is the best way, choose option (1).

(1) once stands, the city
(2) once stood the city
(3) once stood, the city
(4) once has stood, the city
(5) once has stood the city

43. Sentences 3 and 4: **In the last decade, dozens of mills and thousands of jobs have been lost. As the number of steel jobs has declined, the number of jobs in high-tech industries has increased.**

The most effective combination of sentences 3 and 4 as a single sentence would begin with which of the following groups of words?

(1) But in the last decade
(2) Although in the last decade
(3) Because in the last decade
(4) Yet in the last decade
(5) Since the last decade

44. Sentence 4: **As the number of steel jobs has declined, the number of jobs in high-tech industries has increased.**

What correction should be made to this sentence?

(1) change the first the number to the numbers
(2) change has declined to have declined
(3) change the second the number to the numbers
(4) change has increased to have increased
(5) no correction is necessary

45. Sentence 5: **In fact, in metropolitan Pittsburgh more people now work in high-tech feilds than in steelmaking.**

What correction should be made to this sentence?

(1) remove the comma after fact
(2) change people to peoples
(3) change the spelling of feilds to fields
(4) remove the in after than
(5) no correction is necessary

46. Sentence 6: **In 1984, the Pentagon decided to locate it's new national laboratory for computer software research in Pittsburgh.**

What correction should be made to this sentence?

(1) remove the comma after 1984
(2) change decided to has decided
(3) change it's to its
(4) change the spelling of laboratory to labratory
(5) insert a comma after research

47. Sentences 8 and 9: **One Pittsburgh firm is supplying robots to the auto industry. Another has developed new technology for devices to monitor heartbeats.**

The most effective combination of sentences 8 and 9 as a single sentence would include which of the following?

(1) industry, another
(2) industry and another
(3) industry; another
(4) industry? another
(5) industry: another

48. Sentence 10: **Because few middle-aged steelworkers could take over computer jobs when they were laid off, the area still has unemployment.**

Which of the following is the best way to write the underlined portion of this sentence? If you think the original is the best way, choose option (1).

(1) they were laid off, the area still
(2) they were laid off the area still
(3) having been laid off, the area still
(4) having been laid off the area still
(5) they laid off, the area still

49. Sentence 11: **But high-tech jobs have helped to lesson some of Pittsburgh's economic problems.**

What correction should be made to this sentence?

(1) change have helped to helped
(2) change the spelling of lesson to lessen
(3) remove the apostrophe in Pittsburgh's
(4) change Pittsburgh's to Pittsburghs'
(5) no correction is necessary

Items 50 to 55 refer to the following paragraph.

(1) How many times have you heard the phrase, "He can't even boil an egg" used to describe someone who can't cook? (2) More than once, probably. (3) But there's more to boiling an egg than dropping it into boiling water. (4) Experienced cooks recommend a hard-cooked, not a hard-boiled egg. (5) Once the water in which the eggs are cooking has reached the boiling point, you should reduce the heat and keep the water at a gentle simmer. (6) Prepared this way, hard-cooked eggs will take about twenty minutes. (7) The yolks will be a golden yellow, not that greenish black you sometimes see. (8) To prevent discoloring, plunge the eggs into cold water as soon as it is removed from the hot water. (9) Some chefs recommend cooking eggs in water in the top of a double boiler. (10) By using this method, you can be sure the water will not be too hot. (11) It seems that even some people who have been cooking for years can hardly boil an egg, at least as an egg should be boiled.

50. Sentence 1: **How many times have you heard the phrase, "He can't even boil an egg" used to describe someone who can't cook?**

What correction should be made to this sentence?

(1) remove the comma after <u>phrase</u>
(2) insert a comma after egg
(3) insert a comma after <u>egg"</u>
(4) insert a comma after <u>someone</u>
(5) change the question mark to a period

51. Sentence 4: **Experienced cooks recommend <u>a hard-cooked, not a hard-boiled egg.</u>**

Which of the following is the best way to write the underlined portion of this sentence? If you think the original is the best way, choose option (1).

(1) a hard-cooked, not a hard-boiled egg.
(2) a hard cooked, not a hard-boiled.
(3) a hard-cooked not a hard boiled.
(4) a hard cooked not hard boiled.
(5) a hard-cooked, not hard boiled.

52. Sentence 5: **Once the water in which the eggs are cooking has reached the boiling point, you should reduce the heat and keep the water at a gentle simmer.**

If you rewrote sentence 5 changing

<u>you should reduce the heat</u> to <u>the heat should be reduced</u>

the rest of the sentence would include which of the following groups of words?

(1) and you should keep
(2) and keep the water
(3) and keeping the water
(4) and the water kept
(5) and so you will keep

53. Sentence 6: **Prepared this way, hard-cooked eggs will take about twenty minutes.**

Which of the following is the best way to write the underlined portion of this sentence? If you think the original is the best way, choose option (1).

(1) way, hard-cooked eggs will take
(2) way, you will find that hard-cooked eggs take
(3) way, you will find hard-cooked eggs take
(4) way, you will see that hard-cooked eggs take
(5) way, hard-cooked eggs will have taken

54. Sentence 8: **To prevent discoloring, plunge the eggs into cold water as soon as it is removed from the hot water.**

What correction should be made to this sentence?

(1) remove the comma after discoloring
(2) change into to in
(3) change as soon as to when
(4) change it is to they have been
(5) no correction is necessary

55. Sentences 9 and 10: **Some chefs recommend cooking eggs in water in the top of a double boiler. By using this method, you can be sure the water will not be too hot.**

If sentences 9 and 10 are combined, the most effective version would include which of the following groups of words in place of these words?

By using this method, you can be sure

(1) to be sure
(2) so you can be sure
(3) a method that will make sure
(4) a means of making sure that
(5) and by using this method

END OF EXAMINATION

WRITING SKILLS: PART II

Tests of General Educational Development

Directions

This part of the Writing Skills Test is intended to determine how well you write. You are asked to write an essay that explains something or presents an opinion on an issue. In preparing your essay, you should take the following steps.

1. Read carefully the directions and the essay topic given below.

2. Plan your essay carefully before you write.

3. Use scratch paper to make any notes.

4. Write your essay on the lined pages of the separate answer sheet.

5. Read carefully what you have written and make any changes that will improve your essay.

6. Check your paragraphs, sentence structure, spelling, punctuation, capitalization, and usage, and make any necessary corrections.

Be sure you write the letter of the essay topic (given below) on your answer sheet. Write the letter in the box at the upper right-hand corner of the page where you write your essay.

You will have 45 minutes to write on the topic below. Write legibly and use a ballpoint pen so that the evaluators will be able to read your writing.

Write your essay on the lined pages of the separate answer sheet. The notes you make on scratch paper will not be scored.

Your essay will be scored by at least two trained evaluators who will judge it according to its overall effectiveness. They will judge how clearly you make the main point of your composition, how thoroughly you support your ideas, and how clearly and correctly you write throughout the essay.

TOPIC A

Many human inventions have had positive as well as negative effects on our everyday lives. One such invention, the automobile, has long been considered one of the great inventions of modern times.

In what ways has the automobile had positive and negative effects on our everyday lives? Write a composition of about 200 words explaining your answer to this question. Give reasons and examples to support your opinion.

TEST 2: SOCIAL STUDIES

Tests of General Educational Development

Directions

The Social Studies Test consists of multiple-choice questions intended to measure general social studies concepts. The questions are based on short readings which often include a graph, chart, or figure. Study the information given and then answer the question(s) following it. Refer to the information as often as necessary in answering the questions.

You should spend no more than 85 minutes answering the questions in this booklet. Work carefully, but do not spend too much time on any one question. Be sure you answer every question. You will not be penalized for incorrect answers.

Do not mark in this test booklet. Record your answers to the questions on the separate answer sheet provided. Be sure all requested information is properly recorded on the answer sheet.

To record your answers, mark the numbered space on the answer sheet beside the number that corresponds to the question in the test booklet.

FOR EXAMPLE:

Early colonists of North America looked for settlement sites that had adequate water supplies and were accessible by ship. For this reason, many early towns were built near

(1) mountains
(2) prairies
(3) rivers
(4) glaciers
(5) plateaus   ① ② ● ④ ⑤

The correct answer is "rivers"; therefore, answer space 3 would be marked on the answer sheet.

Do not rest the point of your pencil on the answer sheet while you are considering your answer. Make no stray or unnecessary marks. If you change an answer, erase your first mark completely. Mark only one answer space for each question; multiple answers will be scored as incorrect. Do not fold or crease your answer sheet. Return all test materials to the test administrator.

Directions: Choose the one best answer to each item.

Items 1 and 2 refer to the following information.

The equal pay principle states that all workers who perform the same job and have the same responsibilities should receive the same salary.

1. If a woman decides to sue her employer for violation of the equal pay principle, which of the following constitutional guarantees can be cited in support of the principle?

   (1) Sixth Amendment—right to a fair trial
   (2) Tenth Amendment—states' rights guarantees
   (3) Thirteenth Amendment—antislavery statutes
   (4) Fourteenth Amendment—equal protection of the law guarantees
   (5) Nineteenth Amendment—women's right to vote

2. Which of the following situations describes a violation of the equal pay principle?

   (1) Male locksmiths are paid more than female cafeteria workers in a school system.
   (2) Male filing clerks are paid less than female filing clerks whose responsibilities are the same.
   (3) Male and female nurses are paid the same wages in a large private hospital.
   (4) Female doctors are paid more than male nurses in a large private hospital.
   (5) Unionized male truck drivers are paid more than unionized female taxi drivers.

Items 3 to 6 refer to the following information.

A megalopolis is a continuous strip of urbanized settlement consisting of many different cities and communities. One such megalopolis in the United States runs for over 400 miles from Boston to Washington, D.C. This urban strip contains twenty percent of the nation's population and incorporates a number of states, cities, suburbs, and smaller local governments.

Although a megalopolis may have relative social integration because of physical proximity, political cooperation is uncommon. As a result, problems that these various communities face in common are difficult to resolve.

3. A second megalopolis in the United States could be found

   (1) along the Oregon-Washington coast
   (2) along the Arizona-New Mexico border
   (3) in central Oklahoma
   (4) along the northern Rocky Mountains
   (5) along the southern shores of the Great Lakes

4. The largest city that is part of the megalopolis described in the passage is

   (1) Boston
   (2) Providence
   (3) New York
   (4) Philadelphia
   (5) Newark

5. Communities in a megalopolis have difficulty in resolving common problems because with so many communities involved,

    (1) the administrators cannot all be well trained
    (2) some administrators have been elected, while others have been appointed
    (3) northerners and southerners rarely agree about anything
    (4) religious differences will make compromise impossible
    (5) it is difficult for all the different administering political bodies to reach any agreement

6. An example of a common problem these communities would find hard to resolve is

    (1) school bus safety
    (2) air pollution
    (3) city sales taxes
    (4) overcrowded courts
    (5) state income taxes

7. In 1781 the Articles of Confederation were adopted by the Second Continental Congress. The Articles strongly reflected the Americans' distrust of central power.

    Which of the following represents a provision in the Articles that reflects a distrust of central authority?

    (1) creating an independent executive with broad-based powers
    (2) allowing the national government to have broad taxing powers
    (3) providing the states with veto power over the national government
    (4) making the Articles the "supreme law of the land"
    (5) basing the President's power on the model of King George

Item 8 is based on the following paragraph.

    If one farmer produces an exceptionally large crop of corn in one year, we can correctly conclude that his or her income will rise. But if all farmers produced exceptionally large crops of corn, their incomes would probably fall if the price of corn was not supported by the government.

8. Which of the following best explains why all the farmers' income would fall as a result of their large harvests?

    (1) With so much corn available, the price of corn would fall.
    (2) With so much corn available, the price of corn would rise.
    (3) The corn could be sold at higher prices by exporting the surplus.
    (4) Corn prices fall at regular intervals.
    (5) Corn prices do not depend on supply and demand.

Items 9 and 10 are based on the following information.

    There are three common methods of choosing a leader. Leadership can be inherited, appointed, or elected.

9. Which of the following is an example of an elected leader?

    (1) the King of England
    (2) the President of the United States
    (3) the Chief Justice of the Supreme Court
    (4) the Prince of Wales
    (5) the Attorney General of the United States

10. Which of the following is an example of an appointed leader?

    (1) the Attorney General of the United States
    (2) the Queen of England
    (3) the President of the United States
    (4) the Pope
    (5) the Mayor of Chicago

Items 11 to 15 are based on the following graph.

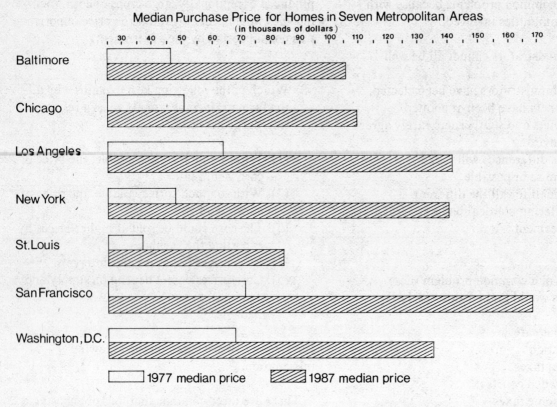

Median Purchase Price for Homes in Seven Metropolitan Areas
(in thousands of dollars)

☐ 1977 median price   ▨ 1987 median price

11. According to the graph, in 1977 the city with the lowest median purchase price for a home was

(1) Baltimore
(2) Chicago
(3) New York
(4) St. Louis
(5) Washington

12. In the ten years between 1977 and 1987, the median price of a home in Chicago increased by

(1) about 25%
(2) less than 75%
(3) less than 100%
(4) more than 100%
(5) more than 200%

13. According to the graph, in 1987 the median price of a home in the metropolitan areas listed was

(1) higher in east coast than in west coast cities
(2) higher in Midwest than in west coast cities
(3) higher in west coast than in east coast cities
(4) about the same in the cities of the east coast and the west coast
(5) about the same in the cities of the Midwest and the west coast.

14. In the ten years between 1977 and 1987, the largest dollar increase in the median price for a home was in

(1) Baltimore
(2) Chicago
(3) Los Angeles
(4) St. Louis
(5) San Francisco

15. The increase in median price between 1977 and 1987 was more than $50,000 in all of the following cities EXCEPT

   (1) Baltimore
   (2) Chicago
   (3) Los Angeles
   (4) New York
   (5) St. Louis

Item 16 is based on the following paragraph.

   According to some psychologists, the introvert is subjective, imaginative, and idealistic; the extrovert is practical, outward-oriented, and realistic. In fact, most people tend to fall somewhere between the extreme types.

16. According to the paragraph, most people are

   (1) subjective and imaginative
   (2) realistic and outward-oriented
   (3) idealistic and subjective
   (4) practical and realistic
   (5) neither wholly introvert nor wholly extrovert

17. Which of the following statements about President Reagan would be most difficult to prove or disprove?

   (1) He was the strongest anticommunist of all American Presidents.
   (2) In his term of office, the budget deficit reached its highest point.
   (3) His chief previous political experience was as Governor of California.
   (4) He was the first American President to belong to the screen actors' union.
   (5) He signed an arms-reduction treaty with the Soviet Union.

Items 18 to 20 refer to the following paragraph.

   Identification with a group frequently results in conformity. Those who want to be well liked by members of their family, gang, professional association, etc., will make a positive effort to conform with the norms of their reference group.

18. Which of the following social scientists would be most closely associated with the statement?

   (1) sociologist
   (2) political geographer
   (3) political scientist
   (4) demographer
   (5) historian

19. Which of the following is not consistent with the statement?

   (1) An individual will actually change his or her observations to agree with the group.
   (2) The desire to be accepted does not affect behavior.
   (3) Those who differ greatly with the values of their group will be rejected.
   (4) Abnormal behavior often results in social rejection.
   (5) By acting in an expected way, an individual can hope to obtain membership in a desired group.

20. According to the paragraph, conformity is

   (1) a benefit to society
   (2) a benefit to the independently minded individual
   (3) a result of the wish to be accepted
   (4) harmful to society
   (5) the result of group pressure on an individual

Items 21 and 22 refer to the following information.

A bill to increase the tax on oil produced from state-owned land is being debated in Congress. It appears that the bill will pass Congress by a substantial margin.

21. Which group of states would be most likely to vote against such a plan?

(1) Texas, Idaho, and Maine
(2) Alaska, Arizona, and Oregon
(3) Oklahoma, Texas, and Alaska
(4) California, Louisiana, and Indiana
(5) Texas, New York, and Pennsylvania

22. A Senator from a state opposed to the oil-tax plan realizes that the bill is going to pass Congress.

What constitutional privilege is available to the Senator to delay voting on the bill?

(1) cloture
(2) roll call
(3) veto
(4) filibuster
(5) habeas corpus

Item 23 refers to the following information.

An egalitarian society is one in which all persons in a given community have equal access to economic resources and to prestige. A stratified society is the opposite of an egalitarian society.

23. Which of the following would best describe a stratified society?

(1) There is equal access to economic resources.
(2) Positions of prestige are open to all persons capable of filling them.
(3) Status positions are not inheritable.
(4) There is unequal access to economic resources.
(5) Inequality is at minimal levels.

Items 24 to 27 refer to the following graphs.

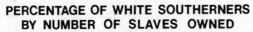

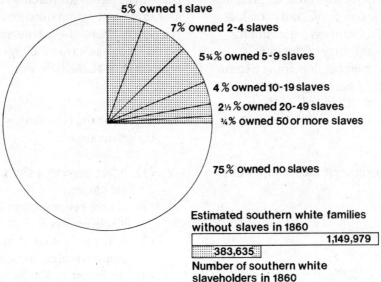

PERCENTAGE OF WHITE SOUTHERNERS
BY NUMBER OF SLAVES OWNED

5% owned 1 slave

7% owned 2-4 slaves

5¼% owned 5-9 slaves

4% owned 10-19 slaves

2½% owned 20-49 slaves

¼% owned 50 or more slaves

75% owned no slaves

Estimated southern white families
without slaves in 1860

| 1,149,979 |
| 383,635 |

Number of southern white
slaveholders in 1860

24. According to the graphs, the largest percentage of slaveowners owned

    (1) one slave
    (2) two to four slaves
    (3) five to nine slaves
    (4) ten to nineteen slaves
    (5) no slaves

25. According to the graphs, the smallest percentage of slaveowners owned

    (1) one slave
    (2) two to four slaves
    (3) five to nine slaves
    (4) ten to nineteen slaves
    (5) fifty or more slaves

26. Which of the following is supported by the data in the graphs?

    (1) More than one million white families did not own slaves.
    (2) More than five hundred thousand families owned at least one slave.
    (3) Of those who owned slaves, 5% owned one slave.
    (4) Of those who owned slaves, 7% owned two to four slaves.
    (5) Of those who owned slaves, 4% owned ten to nineteen slaves.

27. Which of the following is supported by the data in the graphs?

    (1) More than half of the slaveowners owned three or more slaves.
    (2) The lowest percentage of slaveowning southerners had only one slave.
    (3) The average white southerner was able to afford at least one slave.
    (4) The percentage of the population that did not own slaves was equal to the percentage of population that did own slaves.
    (5) The smallest percentage of the slaveowning population owned the smallest number of slaves.

Items 28 to 30 refer to the following paragraph.

A quorum by definition is the number of members of an organization who must be present in order for the organization to officially conduct business. In the U.S. Constitution a quorum for the Senate is fixed at a majority of the total membership. The total membership of the Senate is currently 100. A simple majority, like a quorum, is set at one more than half of the total membership.

28. Which of the following represents a quorum in the Senate?

    (1) 25
    (2) 26
    (3) 50
    (4) 51
    (5) 100

29. Which of the following best explains the purpose for requiring a quorum?

    (1) to make certain that all members of Congress must be present before legislation can be passed
    (2) to guarantee that a minimum number is present before legislation can be passed
    (3) to guarantee that all bills would be discussed by the House and Senate
    (4) to allow private citizens to oppose a bill to be heard
    (5) to allow time for the President to veto a bill

30. Which of the following events would account for a majority in the Senate increasing from 51 to 52?

    (1) an increase in the population of Florida
    (2) a decrease in the population of New York
    (3) the admission of a fifty-first state
    (4) Alaska's becoming the forty-ninth state
    (5) Hawaii's becoming the fiftieth state

Item 31 refers to the following information.

Aesop's fable about the fox who decided that the grapes out of his reach were probably sour is an example of rationalization. Rationalization is the concealment of the true motive for one's behavior or one's true feelings by assigning some other motive to the behavior.

31. Which of the following is an example of rationalization?

    (1) After missing a short putt, a golfer breaks his putter.
    (2) A shopper refuses to buy lettuce because it is overpriced.
    (3) A young woman dreams that she has hit a game-winning home run.
    (4) An investor who has lost money in stocks says he did so to have a tax deduction.
    (5) A man who has been divorced twice refuses a proposal of marriage from a rich woman.

Items 32 to 36 refer to the following information.

Listed below are five terms associated with some form of illegal activity, related to politics, public life, or finances. Each is followed by a brief definition.

(1) conflict of interest—a situation arising when a personal advantage, usually financial, is in conflict with unprejudiced performance of the duties or responsibility of office
(2) spoils system—the practice of treating appointed jobs or contracts as the prizes (spoils) of an election victory and distributing them to party workers and associates
(3) election fraud—the use of deception to affect the legitimate result of an election
(4) insider information—confidential information which can be used to allow the insider to make a profitable investment or avoid a loss
(5) consumer fraud—the use of deception to cheat the buyer of a product or service

Each of the five following sentences describes a situation which is an example of one of these five terms. Choose the term that best describes the situation. The terms may be used more than once in the set of items. No one question has more than one best answer.

32. After being elected mayor of a large city, the winning candidate appoints his brother as chief of police, his sister as chief of accounting, and eleven members of his election staff to well-paid city jobs.

    (1) conflict of interest
    (2) spoils system
    (3) election fraud
    (4) insider information
    (5) consumer fraud

33. A bank president buys a large piece of riverfront land when she learns from a confidential loan application that the construction company plans to use the money to develop shopping centers and homes on the riverfront.

    (1) conflict of interest
    (2) spoils system
    (3) election fraud
    (4) insider information
    (5) consumer fraud

34. A mail-order house advertises jewelry of eighteen carat gold, but the jewelry it sends to its customers contains no gold at all.

    (1) conflict of interest
    (2) spoils system
    (3) election fraud
    (4) insider information
    (5) consumer fraud

35. A city purchasing agent responsible for all paper products bought by the city is the part owner of a large office supplies company which is attempting to sell its products to the city.

    (1) conflict of interest
    (2) spoils system
    (3) election fraud
    (4) insider information
    (5) consumer fraud

36. The signatures gathered to qualify a candidate for the ballot in a mayoral election have been forged using the names of former voters who are now dead.

    (1) conflict of interest
    (2) spoils system
    (3) election fraud
    (4) insider information
    (5) consumer fraud

Item 37 refers to the following information.

Macro-economics emphasizes the study of aggregate, or total, economic activities affecting all aspects of a nation's economy. Micro-economics emphasizes the study of the actions of firms and individuals. The terms come from the Greek words makros (large) and mikros (small).

37. A macro-economics class would be likely to deal with all of the following EXCEPT

    (1) unemployment percentages
    (2) gross national product
    (3) international monetary policy
    (4) income theory
    (5) Orlando National Bank

Items 38 and 39 refer to the following information.

After the election of 1936, the Democrats controlled the White House, held a 322 to 103 majority in the House, and a 69 to 25 majority in the Senate.

38. Which of the following statements best reflects the most likely political consequences of the election of 1936?

    (1) A Republican would preside over the Senate.
    (2) The Republican party would be unable to prevent the passage of legislation favored by the Democrats.
    (3) The Republicans and the Democrats would divide committee chairmanships equally.
    (4) The Republican party would not be able to influence public opinion.
    (5) The two-party system would have to be abandoned.

39. Which of the following is the most probable result of the gubernatorial elections of 1936?

    (1) There were more Democratic governors than Republican governors elected.
    (2) There were more Republican governors than Democratic governors elected.
    (3) An equal number of Republican and Democratic governors were elected.
    (4) No Republican governors were elected.
    (5) No Democratic governors were elected.

Item 40 refers to the following information.

The middle class is characterized by deferred gratification, a pattern of behavior that greatly stresses postponement of immediate pleasures so that one can gain more in the end.

40. Which of the following is an example of an act of deferred gratification?

    (1) a businessman mortgages his home for $80,000
    (2) a family buys two small cars instead of one large car
    (3) an entrepreneur opens a fast food franchise
    (4) an art collector buys a painting by Andrew Wyeth
    (5) a family spends $8,000 each year on a daughter's education

Items 41 to 43 refer to the following time zone map.

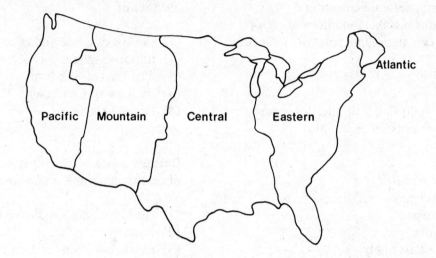

41. Georgia is located in which of the following time zones?

    (1) Pacific
    (2) Mountain
    (3) Central
    (4) Eastern
    (5) Atlantic

42. Which of the following states is not located in the geographical area depicted on this map?

    (1) Oregon
    (2) Louisiana
    (3) New York
    (4) Alaska
    (5) Maine

43. Missouri is located in which of the following time zones?

    (1) Pacific
    (2) Mountain
    (3) Central
    (4) Eastern
    (5) Atlantic

Items 44 and 45 refer to the following paragraph.

A norm is a rule of behavior defining how people ought to behave. Three main types of norm are folkways (customs, or traditional ways of doing things), mores (required ways of behaving regarded as necessary for the welfare of society), and laws (norms enacted and enforced by governmental authority).

44. Of the following, which is an example of the breaking of a folkway rather than of mores or laws?

    (1) an American teenage boy's shoplifting
    (2) an English girl's refusal to go to school
    (3) cannibalism
    (4) an American woman's refusal to wear makeup
    (5) a man's smoking in a no-smoking section of an airplane

45. All of the following are reasons for an individual's conformity to norms EXCEPT

    (1) the fear of punishment
    (2) habit
    (3) the desire to be accepted
    (4) the wish to assert one's individuality
    (5) the unquestioned acceptance of what one has been taught

Item 46 refers to the following information.

Video technology, personal computers, electronic data transmission, and information retrieval systems can all become potential tools for surveillance.

46. Which of the following civil liberties is most threatened by misuse of electronic technology?

    (1) right to counsel
    (2) right to privacy
    (3) habeas corpus
    (4) trial by jury
    (5) freedom of assembly

47. Dependence on foreign oil will create dramatic changes in both the location and construction of new housing.

If the price of gasoline increases and at the same time the government rations gasoline, which of the following would be the most likely effect on new housing construction?

    (1) Homes will become larger.
    (2) There will be a trend toward single-family homes.
    (3) Homes will be closer to major employment centers.
    (4) The suburbs will show a substantial increase in growth.
    (5) Mortgage rates will decrease.

Items 48 and 49 refer to the following information.

Imitative, or sympathetic, magic is based on the Law of Similarity. This law asserts there are underlying similarities in nature so that the human performance of one act will bring about a similar event in nature. A second kind of magic is based on the Law of Contagion. This law states that all objects that were once in contact retain some connection even when physically separated so that whatever is done to one will automatically happen to the other.

48. A medicine man's sprinkling water on the parched earth in order to cause rainfall is an instance of

    (1) the law of cause and effect
    (2) imitative magic
    (3) The Law of Similarity
    (4) the Law of Contagion
    (5) contagious magic

49. Burning a lock of an enemy's hair as a means of destroying him is an instance of

    (1) the law of cause and effect
    (2) imitative magic
    (3) magic based on the Law of Contagion
    (4) sympathetic magic
    (5) natural magic

50. The phrase "guns or butter" refers to priority decisions that a government must make.

If the government decides on a policy of "guns" rather than "butter," which of the following programs would most likely be cut?

    (1) military appropriations
    (2) government-sponsored educational loans
    (3) naval research-and-development programs
    (4) antiparticle missile development
    (5) increasing the nuclear submarine force

51. A regressive tax is one that is not based on one's ability to pay.

Which of the following taxes would fall most heavily on individuals who earn less than $8,000 per year?

    (1) a sales tax
    (2) a property tax
    (3) a federal income tax
    (4) a state income tax
    (5) an inheritance tax

Items 52 to 54 refer to the following graphs.

The following graphs record the interest rates paid over a five-month period.

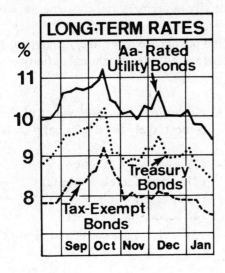

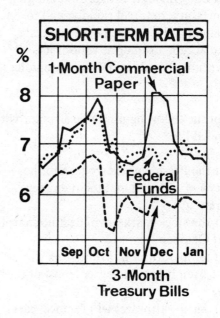

52. The highest average interest rate was paid by

    (1) utility bonds
    (2) treasury bonds
    (3) tax-exempt bonds
    (4) commercial paper
    (5) federal funds

54. The lowest long-term rates were reached on

    (1) September 30
    (2) October 31
    (3) November 30
    (4) December 31
    (5) January 31

53. On November 1st, the interest rate on treasury bonds was

    (1) 8%
    (2) 8.5%
    (3) 9%
    (4) 9.5%
    (5) 10%

Items 55 and 56 refer to the following paragraph.

Rumor is communication, the truth or falsity of which cannot be verified. It is likely to emerge in times of uncertainty, to travel rapidly, and to change in content as it is passed on. People are more likely to accept a rumor as valid if it is in agreement with their basic beliefs and prejudices.

55. Which of the following might be a rumor with an extended life?

  (1) that the President, the Pope, and the Queen of England met today in New York City
  (2) that the stock market will decline sharply next October
  (3) that temperatures in Miami this winter have been below 50 degrees most of the time
  (4) that warm salt water will remove warts
  (5) that a high jumper had jumped more than eight feet high

56. According to the paragraph, the person most likely to believe a rumor which claimed that the Virgin Mary had appeared to two children on Long Island is

  (1) a Buddhist
  (2) an agnostic
  (3) an atheist
  (4) a Jew
  (5) a Catholic

Items 57 to 59 refer to the following information.

A recent poll of 2,000 Iowa voters produced the following results:

Men are more likely than women to be politically active.

Protestants are more likely than Catholics to be politically active.

Young adults are more likely than elderly people to prefer the Democratic Party.

There is little or no difference in the political activity of farmers and construction workers.

Rich people are more likely than poor people to have a high rate of political activity.

57. According to the poll, which of the following is most likely to be politically active?

  (1) a female Catholic
  (2) a poor female Protestant
  (3) a young adult
  (4) a poor male farmer
  (5) a rich male construction worker

58. According to the poll, which of the following is least likely to be politically active?

  (1) a young adult
  (2) a rich Protestant female
  (3) a poor male construction worker
  (4) a rich Protestant male
  (5) a poor Catholic female

59. From the poll, we can be certain about all of the following EXCEPT

  (1) women are less likely than men to be politically active
  (2) Catholics are less likely than Protestants to be politically active
  (3) elderly people are more likely than young adults to prefer the Republican Party
  (4) the political activity of farmers is very like that of construction workers
  (5) poor people are less likely than rich people to have a high rate of political activity

Items 60 and 61 refer to the following information.

Water always has been precious in the American West. The scarcity of water in this brown and empty landscape has confined human occupation since the earliest Indian and Spanish settlements. Early nineteenth-century mapmakers described most of the region as the Great American Desert. Modern engineering has attempted to subdue the desert, but it endures and now threatens to cut short western economic progress.

Water use already has passed renewable natural supply in some western states, and the demand for water is accelerating. Irrigated farms, growing cities, and new industries are all competing for available water supplies. Entire states and regions are skirmishing over limited river flows, with economic survival at stake.

60. According to the information, which of the following is most likely to limit western economic development?

   (1) a population shift to the east
   (2) a demand for water greater than the supply
   (3) the rising population of coastal areas
   (4) urban industry
   (5) environment safeguards that inhibit growth

61. Which of the following is an example of "skirmishing over limited river flows"?

   (1) Arizona has sued California for a larger share of Colorado River water.
   (2) The cities of Phoenix and Tucson have established areas where desert plants are protected.
   (3) California has approved a plan to divert water from the Sacramento River delta.
   (4) The cities of Los Angeles and Riverside are quarreling about smog from Los Angeles which drifts east over the desert.
   (5) San Diego County has approved a new and very costly flood control program.

Item 62 is based on the following information.

Rats were placed in one feeding box after going without food for one hour and in a second feeding box after going without food for twenty hours. Later, after going without food for eleven hours and being placed in the one-hour and in the twenty-hour feeding boxes, the rats ate more food when placed in the twenty-hour box.

62. The results of this experiment suggest that

   (1) physical drives can be affected by the environment
   (2) hunger exists only in the mind
   (3) the sense of time is keener in humans than in animals
   (4) hunger cannot be influenced by the environment
   (5) conclusions drawn from animal experiments cannot be applied to humans

63. As long as the number of stock animals in a given area of farmland does not exceed the optimum level that the farm area can support, it can be said that the farm area is in balance.

Which of the following would be most likely to upset the balance in a farm area?

(1) overgrazing
(2) reducing the number of grazing animals
(3) expanding the grazing area
(4) introducing range-management techniques
(5) practicing mixed farming

Item 64 is based on the following information.

In 1906, the Food and Drug Administration (the F.D.A.) was set up to guarantee the "purity, safety, and truthful labeling of food, drugs, and cosmetics."

64. Which of the following products would be most likely to require F.D.A. approval?

(1) a new window cleaner advertised to work faster
(2) a shoe deodorizer advertised to smell cleaner
(3) a toothbrush advertised to reduce cavities
(4) an insecticide advertised to kill aphids
(5) a face cream advertised to reduce wrinkles

END OF EXAMINATION

TEST 3: SCIENCE

Tests of General Educational Development

Directions

The Science Test consists of multiple-choice questions intended to measure the general concepts in science. The questions are based on short readings which often include a graph, chart, or figure. Study the information given and then answer the question(s) following it. Refer to the information as often as necessary in answering the questions.

You should spend no more than 95 minutes answering the questions in this booklet. Work carefully, but do not spend too much time on any one question. Be sure you answer every question. You will not be penalized for incorrect answers.

Do not mark in this test booklet. Record your answers to the questions on the separate answer sheet provided. Be sure all requested information is properly recorded on the answer sheet.

To record your answers, mark the numbered space on the answer sheet beside the number that corresponds to the question in the test booklet.

FOR EXAMPLE:

Which of the following is the smallest unit in a living thing?

(1) tissue
(2) organ
(3) cell
(4) muscle
(5) capillary

The correct answer is "cell"; therefore, answer space 3 would be marked on the answer sheet.

Do not rest the point of your pencil on the answer sheet while you are considering your answer. Make no stray or unnecessary marks. If you change an answer, erase your first mark completely. Mark only one answer space for each question; multiple answers will be scored as incorrect. Do not fold or crease your answer sheet. Return all test materials to the test administrator.

Directions: Choose the one best answer to each item.

Items 1 and 2 refer to the following diagram of the human eye.

THE EYE

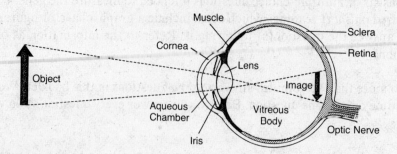

The diagram above shows how light rays are refracted as they pass through the cornea, lens, and vitreous body to focus on the retina, where an image is formed. The optic nerve then carries impulses from the retina to the brain.

1. The diagram shows how a human eye sees an object.

   In which part of the eye are the light-sensitive cells which pass the image on to the optic nerve?

   (1) cornea
   (2) iris
   (3) lens
   (4) retina
   (5) sclera

2. From the diagram, it appears that the image of the object is transposed, yet we see things right side up, not upside down.

   Which of the following best explains why we see the image in the correct position?

   (1) The image is actually transposed twice as it crosses through the vitreous body.
   (2) The image is not actually transposed on the retina, merely slightly refocused.
   (3) The image is transposed onto the retina, but the brain makes the proper adjustment as it reads the impulses.
   (4) The optic nerve transposes the upside down images before they reach the brain.
   (5) The image is transposed as it passes through the lens, then transposed again on the retina.

3. Alcohol dissolved in water is usually separated from the water by distillation. Distillation occurs when the solution is heated, because the alcohol is driven off as a vapor.

   What chemical property is the basis for this type of separation?

   (1) Alcohol has a lower boiling point than water does.
   (2) Alcohol has a slightly lower density than water does.
   (3) Alcohol is highly inflammable.
   (4) Water is much more viscous than alcohol is.
   (5) Water molecules are smaller than alcohol molecules.

Items 4 to 9 refer to the following five life zones.

(1) coniferous forest—evergreen forests where winters are cold, summers cool, with moderate rainfall
(2) deciduous forest—broadleaf forests where winters are cold, summers warm, with abundant rain
(3) desert—small number of plants spread over a large area, winters are cool, summers very hot, with little rainfall at any season
(4) prairie—grasslands where winters are cold, summers hot, with occasional thunderstorms
(5) tundra—bushes and other low-growing plants where only the surface soil thaws during the brief summer, below is permafrost

Each of the following items describes conditions that refer to one of the five life zones defined above. For each item, choose the one life zone that best meets the conditions given. Each of the life zones above may be used more than once in the following set of items.

4. Which of the life zones occupies the center of North America, from Saskatchewan southward through the Dakotas to Texas?

(1) coniferous forest
(2) deciduous forest
(3) desert
(4) prairie
(5) tundra

5. One of the life zones that is located in Canada and the northern United States is composed of cone-bearing trees: pines, firs, and spruces. Caribou, elk, lynx, red fox, and wolverine are also a part of this life zone. This same life zone presently has the largest numbers of moose, deer, mountain lion, and black bear.

In which of the life zones would you find the largest numbers of moose today?

(1) coniferous forest
(2) deciduous forest
(3) desert
(4) prairie
(5) tundra

6. Which of the life zones is most likely to have mosses, lichens, sedges, and grasses as its main plants?

(1) coniferous forest
(2) deciduous forest
(3) desert
(4) prairie
(5) tundra

7. In which of the life zones would the appearance of the plants change the most during the seasons of the year?

(1) coniferous forest
(2) deciduous forest
(3) desert
(4) prairie
(5) tundra

8. In which of the life zones would plants grow and flower most quickly after rains?

(1) coniferous forest
(2) deciduous forest
(3) desert
(4) prairie
(5) tundra

9. The region of the Great Lakes is a mixed forest of pines, maples, firs, and oaks.

Which of the five life zones would occur just to the north of the mixed forest?

(1) coniferous forest
(2) deciduous forest
(3) desert
(4) prairie
(5) tundra

Items 10 and 11 refer to the following information and diagram.

The great British physicist Ernest Rutherford discovered the basic structure of an atom. He performed a pioneering experiment in which a thin sheet of gold foil was bombarded with a beam of alpha particles. The foil was so thin that each alpha particle would meet only a few atoms of gold. Most of the particles passed through the foil with little or no deflection, as Rutherford had predicted. However, to his astonishment, some of the alpha particles rebounded backward. He compared that event to a cannonball bouncing off a sheet of paper!

The following diagram gives a close look at the gold atoms in the gold foil.

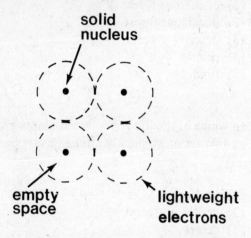

solid nucleus

empty space

lightweight electrons

10. Why did most of the alpha particles pass through the gold foil without rebounding backward?

   (1) The alpha particles had no electrical charge.
   (2) The gold atoms were widely separated in the foil.
   (3) Gold participates in few chemical reactions.
   (4) The high velocity of the beam prevented recoil.
   (5) Most of each gold atom is empty space.

11. Which of the following would best explain the surprising discovery that some of the alpha particles rebounded?

   (1) All substances are at least slightly radioactive.
   (2) A chemical reaction occurred in those cases.
   (3) The gold foil had acquired an electrostatic charge.
   (4) Hardness is known to be relative rather than absolute.
   (5) The tiny core of each gold atom could not be penetrated.

12. Most natural organisms depend on other organisms in the food chain for nutrition.

   Which of the following organisms is most truly independent in obtaining nourishment?

   (1) bighorn sheep
   (2) codfish
   (3) cougar
   (4) mosquito
   (5) palm tree

13. What part of the human body does about the same job as the gills of a fish?

   (1) ears
   (2) esophagus
   (3) lungs
   (4) neck
   (5) thyroid gland

14. Whipped cream, shaving foam, paint, and deodorant are among the household products that come in pressurized aerosol cans.

   Which of the following processes causes the ingredients to spray out when the top button is depressed?

   (1) the change from a gaseous to a liquid state
   (2) the expansion of a gas by being heated
   (3) the movement of molecules toward lower pressure
   (4) the multiplication of pressure inside a piston
   (5) the swelling of atoms to a larger size

Item 15 refers to the following chart.

	Eaten by monkey	Rejected by monkey
Insects of bright colors	23	120
Insects of dull colors	83	18

15. The chart sums up a study of 244 different species of insects offered to a monkey as food.

    Which of the following would be the most likely interpretation of the results in terms of animals adapting to their environment?

    A. Insects have adapted to have dull colors to avoid being eaten.
    B. Insects of bright colors must have adapted to have bitter tastes.
    C. Many insect species have adapted to have bright colors for protection.
    D. Monkeys have adapted to eat most species of insects.

    (1) A and B only
    (2) C and D only
    (3) B and C only
    (4) A and D only
    (5) B and D only

Item 16 and 17 refer to the following diagram.

FLOWER

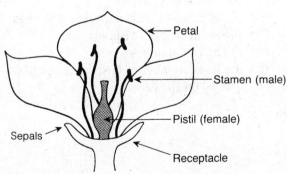

16. If this flower depends on bees to carry the pollen from one flower to another, the pollen would most likely be on the

    (1) receptacle
    (2) stamen
    (3) pistil
    (4) sepals
    (5) stem

17. Each flower species will be healthier if a flower gets its pollen from other flowers instead of getting pollen from itself. Cross-pollination is better than self-pollination. The wild sage salvia has developed a trigger that dusts visiting bees.

    This trigger mechanism provides a

    (1) good chance for cross-pollination
    (2) good chance for self-pollination
    (3) special means of feeding insects using the receptacle
    (4) method to discourage bees from stealing its nectar from the sepals
    (5) special means of attracting insects to the stamen

18. Today's lakes are young when compared to other features of the landscape. Each of the lakes was formed by some recent geological event, and each lake is being destroyed by present processes.

What is the main <u>natural</u> process that is destroying existing lakes?

(1) erosion of outlet
(2) evaporation
(3) faulting and folding
(4) pollution
(5) sedimentation

<u>Items 19 to 23</u> are based on the following paragraphs.

Evolution is the gradual changing of a species. This evolving depends on three items: (1) changes in chromosomes and genes, (2) isolation to establish new species, and (3) natural selection based upon different rates of reproduction. Successful organisms have more offspring than unsuccessful ones.

Evolution can vary in the time it takes for the process to occur. It does not proceed at the same rate for all organisms. In general, evolution happens more quickly when a new species appears, but slows down as the group becomes stable.

New species develop from unspecialized or simple forms within a group, not from the most advanced or complex forms. Sometimes evolution proceeds from the complex to simpler forms. This regressive evolution occurs when there is some special benefit to a species to simplify it's form. The return of mammals to the sea and the transformation of free-living worms to parasitic forms are examples of regressive evolution.

19. An example of regressive evolution is

(1) a whale
(2) a man
(3) a rose
(4) a cockroach
(5) an alligator

20. When a mutation or change in a gene occurs in an individual it will not have any effect on the group unless

(1) the individual lives to a great age
(2) the group stays in contact with almost all its members
(3) the environment changes
(4) it is a major gene change
(5) the individual lives long enough to breed

21. Scientists believe that mammals developed from reptiles.

Which of the following is the <u>most</u> likely reptile ancestor of mammals?

(1) the most successful and advanced of the dinosaurs
(2) the flying dinosaurs called archaeopteryx
(3) the specialized birds
(4) a primitive reptile with few special adaptations
(5) the fish-like dinosaurs of the ocean

22. Adaptive radiation is the evolution of many different species from the same ancestor.

What factor aided the evolution of the finch as it evolved into many species in the Galapagos Islands?

(1) the threat of predators
(2) the closeness to other species of finches
(3) the isolation of the islands
(4) the help of humans
(5) the large number of birds that already existed on the islands

23. Fruit flies are often used in the study of gene mutation <u>most</u> likely because

    A. they are rare
    B. they breed quickly
    C. many of their genetic characteristics are easy to see
    D. they seldom have changes in their genes
    E. they are small and easy to care for

    (1) A and D only
    (2) C and D only
    (3) A, C, and D only
    (4) B, C, and E only
    (5) A and E only

Items 24 and 25 refer to the following information.

The western coast of North America, from Mexico to Alaska, has a series of what seem to be former shorelines, each above the present sea level. These sculptured hills display flat terraces, cliffs, caves, and beach sands which testify to former erosion by the waves. Some areas have as many as twenty level terraces, ranging in altitude from 100 to 2000 feet above sea level. Also present are shells of marine creatures. Rocks and sands far above today's highest tide have remains of clams and barnacles.

24. The information gives several pieces of evidence for some coastal hills being ancient shorelines.

    All of the following points are evidence of a shoreline EXCEPT

    (1) high altitude
    (2) marine shells
    (3) parallel terraces
    (4) sand deposits
    (5) special landforms

25. What would <u>best</u> explain the former shorelines in the hills along the western coast of North America?

    (1) The coast has gradually grown by the accumulation of organic shells.
    (2) Deposits in the ocean basin have caused the sea level to rise.
    (3) Earth movements have lifted up the land along that coast.
    (4) Melting of the polar ice caps has flooded former shorelines.
    (5) Wave action has deposited huge volumes of material along that coast.

26. Junkyards often use large electromagnets to move pieces of scrap iron and steel. The magnetism is produced by a powerful electric current flowing through a large coil of wire.

    How would the operator most easily get the magnet to let go of an iron object?

    (1) by joggling the crane to shake off the object
    (2) by sending electricity through the coil in the other direction
    (3) by throwing a switch to interrupt the current
    (4) by turning on an opposing electromagnet
    (5) by using a transformer to change magnetism into electricity

27. Habit is present when an event is repeated again and again. Sometimes this habit is motivated by a reward.

    Which of the following animal experiments <u>most</u> clearly demonstrates the concept of <u>habit</u>?

    (1) a chimpanzee piling boxes up to reach a stalk of bananas
    (2) a dog growing on a meatless diet of vegetables and grains
    (3) a rat running through a maze faster each time
    (4) a rattlesnake vibrating its tail when poked by a stick
    (5) a young bird learning to fly without its mother

Items 28 to 31 refer to the following chart which describes the numbers of subatomic particles in five different atoms.

Atoms	Electrons (charge of −1)	Neutrons (no charge)	Protons (charge of +1)
A	19	21	19
B	18	22	18
C	18	20	17
D	18	20	19
E	18	18	16

Atomic weight of an atom is the sum of the protons and neutrons. The number of protons in each element is also the same as the number of the element in the periodic table. Two isotopes of one chemical element have the same number of protons but a different number of neutrons. The different number of neutrons causes the isotopes to have slightly different weights, but since both are the same element, they have the same chemical reactions.

28. Argon is the eighteenth element in the periodic table.

Which of the five atoms is argon?

(1) A
(2) B
(3) C
(4) D
(5) E

29. Which of the five atoms in the chart has a positive electrical charge?

(1) A
(2) B
(3) C
(4) D
(5) E

30. Which two atoms in the chart are isotopes of the same chemical element?

(1) A and B
(2) A and D
(3) B and E
(4) C and D
(5) C and E

31. What is the range of atomic weights for the five atoms in the chart?

(1) 16 to 22
(2) 34 to 38
(3) 34 to 40
(4) 36 to 40
(5) 52 to 59

32. Mitosis is simple cell-splitting, during which one parent cell divides into two new cells. Because the chromosomes duplicate themselves during mitosis, each new cell has the same chromosomes as the original cell. A mammalian cell contains 24 chromosomes in its normal diploid state.

After two generations of division by mitosis, how many chromosomes will be present in each new cell?

(1) 6
(2) 12
(3) 24
(4) 48
(5) 96

33. Sulfur dioxide is one of the main components of smog. The major source of that gas is the burning of coal containing traces of sulfur.

    Which of the following sources of air pollution probably contributes most to the sulfur dioxide problem?

    (1) automobile engines
    (2) electric power plants
    (3) garbage dumps
    (4) home furnaces
    (5) motorboats

34. Which of the following statements about cholesterol is a misconception, rather than a scientifically accurate statement?

    (1) The body needs cholesterol to produce many hormones.
    (2) Cholesterol is manufactured by a healthy body.
    (3) Cholesterol is an organic compound found in many animals.
    (4) Cholesterol is a toxic contaminant in many processed foods.
    (5) High blood cholesterol levels are associated with heart disease.

Item 35 refers to the following diagram.

DISPERSION OF SUNLIGHT

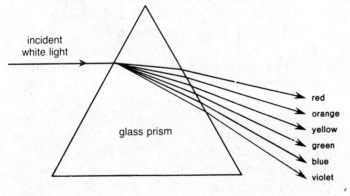

35. The diagram above shows the production of the color spectrum by shining sunlight through a glass prism.

    Which of the following is demonstrated by such an experiment?

    (1) The deflection of light rays is due to reflection.
    (2) The different atoms within glass emit separate colors.
    (3) Light is always deflected when passing through glass.
    (4) The reflection of white light yields many colors.
    (5) White light is a mixture of several colors.

Item 36 refers to the following graph.

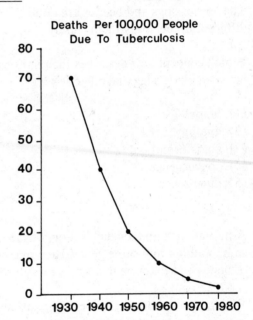

36. Based on the information in the graph above, the greatest decline in deaths per 100,000 people due to tuberculosis occurred from

    (1) 1930 to 1940
    (2) 1940 to 1950
    (3) 1950 to 1960
    (4) 1960 to 1970
    (5) 1970 to 1980

Items 37 to 42 refer to the following concepts which relate the structures of two animals to their evolutionary origins.

(1) homology—The two structures are similar because they are inherited from one feature of one ancestor.
(2) analogy—The two structures perform the same function but they are not inherited from one feature of one ancestor.
(3) transformation—The two structures perform different functions although they are inherited from one feature of one ancestor.
(4) convergence—Several similar structures have developed in two animals whose ancestors were less alike.
(5) divergence—Several different structures have developed in two animals whose ancestors were more alike.

Each of the following items describes a relationship that refers to one of the five concepts defined above. For each item, choose the one concept that best describes the relationship. Each of the categories above may be used more than once in the following set of items.

37. The legs of dogs and beetles are quite different if you study them closely.

Which concept best describes the relationship between a dog's leg and a beetle's leg?

(1) homology
(2) analogy
(3) transformation
(4) convergence
(5) divergence

38. A human arm and a whale's flipper have the same number and same general arrangement of bones and function in a similar way.

Which concept best describes the relationship between the two structures?

(1) homology
(2) analogy
(3) transformation
(4) convergence
(5) divergence

39. A dolphin is not a fish, but an air-breathing mammal with lungs. It bears live baby dolphins and suckles them like other mammals. The dolphin evolved from land-dwelling mammals.

Which of the following best describes the evolutionary relationship of dolphins and fishes?

(1) homology
(2) analogy
(3) transformation
(4) convergence
(5) divergence

40. The wing of a butterfly and the wing of a sparrow are very different in embryonic development and adult structure.

What concept best describes the relationship between the two wings?

(1) homology
(2) analogy
(3) transformation
(4) convergence
(5) divergence

41. Most fishes contain an air bladder that helps them control their depth in the water. The lungs of snakes evolved from an ancestral air bladder.

Which concept best describes the origin of such lungs?

(1) homology
(2) analogy
(3) transformation
(4) convergence
(5) divergence

42. All mammals are believed to have had one common ancestor, the earliest mammal, a reptile-like creature that developed better methods of caring for its young than simply leaving eggs like other reptiles.

Which of the concepts best explains the great variety of mammals on the Earth today, from mice to horses to humans?

(1) homology
(2) analogy
(3) transformation
(4) convergence
(5) divergence

43. In a legendary demonstration, the great scientist Galileo dropped two balls of different weights from the Leaning Tower of Pisa. They hit the ground at the same time. In later experiments by other scientists, feathers and lead balls fell at the same rate in a vacuum.

Which of the following did Galileo discover in his legendary demonstration with the two balls?

(1) Air resistance had a major effect on the falling rate.
(2) Direction of the fall had no effect on the falling rate.
(3) Distance of the fall had a major effect on the falling rate.
(4) Shape of the objects had a minor effect on the falling rate.
(5) Weight of the objects had no effect on the falling rate.

44. Over many generations, each organic species has tended to become better adapted to its place in the environment.

Which of the following features is least likely to be explained as adaptation?

(1) the bright color of flowers
(2) the eyes of a mole
(3) a flying squirrel
(4) the sting of a scorpion
(5) the webbed feet of ducks

45. Sugar is not a chemical element.

Which of the following experimental findings demonstrates that fact?

(1) Crystals of sugar are not uniform in color.
(2) Sugar burns to yield carbon dioxide and water vapor.
(3) Sugar does not conduct electricity like a metal.
(4) Sugar is highly soluble in water.
(5) Sugar is not known to occur in the gaseous state.

46. Many chemicals used in packaged foods are tested for safety by feeding them to laboratory mice.

Which of the following points is probably the most important scientific objection to such a testing method?

(1) The chemicals might behave differently in mice than in people.
(2) It is cruel to feed dangerous chemicals to helpless mice.
(3) It is too expensive to test all food ingredients in the laboratory.
(4) Mice can't eat enough to test a realistic amount of each chemical.
(5) People are mammals but mice are rodents.

47. Electromagnetic energy, such as X-rays, ultraviolet, infrared, and radar, is commonly used today. Much of the communication in our society is by energy traveling as electromagnetic waves.

All of the following means of communication are electromagnetic EXCEPT

(1) light
(2) microwaves
(3) radio
(4) sound
(5) television

Items 48 to 50 refer to the following chart.

Location of Water	Percent
oceans	97.1
saltwater lakes	0.008
freshwater lakes	0.009
rivers and streams	0.0001
polar ice caps	2.24
undergound water	0.61
water vapor in air	0.001
Total Water	100.0

48. The chart shows the distribution of water near the surface of the earth.

Which of the following events would cause a rise of sea level?

(1) the construction of more dams to generate electricity
(2) a fall in temperature leading to a renewed Ice Age
(3) an increase in the effectiveness of soil conservation programs
(4) the warming of the atmosphere due to higher carbon dioxide levels
(5) the widespread use of desalinization plants to obtain fresh water

49. Given our present technology and the prohibitive cost of using purification systems, the most likely sources of large amounts of drinking water for human use in the next twenty years are

(1) oceans and rivers and streams
(2) rivers and streams and water vapor
(3) underground water and fresh-water lakes
(4) oceans and polar ice caps
(5) fresh-water lakes, rivers and streams, and underground water.

50. Pollution is a threat to all the types of water shown on the chart. However, one water resource, although not one of the two largest, is in particular danger.

Which kind of water, once it is polluted, can spread pollution in an unseen and unpredictable way?

(1) oceans
(2) fresh-water lakes
(3) rivers and streams
(4) polar ice caps
(5) underground water

51. The space shuttle is designed to lift off the Earth's surface, carry astronauts and materials into space, and return to Earth as a glider so that it can be used again for another mission.

The space shuttle could perform all of the following tasks EXCEPT

(1) a landing on the moon
(2) helping in the building of a space station in Earth orbit
(3) servicing or repairing artificial satellites in Earth orbit
(4) taking pictures of the Earth's surface
(5) serving as a small laboratory in space for short-term experiments

52. The astronauts who visited the moon brought back many small rocks. The age of those samples from the moon has been estimated to be about 5 billion years old.

What information was used to estimate that age?

(1) the primitive nature of animal remains found in the rocks
(2) the ratio of fossil plants to fossil animals
(3) the relative abundance of radioactive elements
(4) the size of the crystals in the specimens
(5) the temperature of the rocks before being touched or collected

Items 53 and 54 refer to the following diagram showing the decomposition of water by an electric current.

ELECTROLYSIS

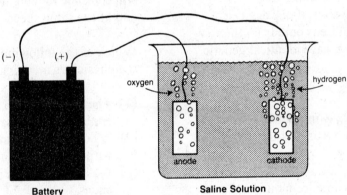

53. During the electrolysis shown in the diagram, why is hydrogen released at the negative cathode rather than the other electrode?

(1) Negatively charged hydrogen ions are attracted to the negative electrode.
(2) Negatively charged hydrogen ions are attracted to the positive electrode.
(3) Positively charged hydrogen ions are attracted to the negative electrode.
(4) The positive electrode attracts positive ions like hydrogen.
(5) The positive electrode attracts negative ions like hydrogen.

54. The purpose of the electrolytic experiment is to break down water (H_2O) into its elements, hydrogen and oxygen. If you examine the diagram carefully, you will see many more bubbles of hydrogen than of oxygen.

Why is more hydrogen released than oxygen?

(1) The battery pumps small hydrogen atoms much more efficiently than large oxygen atoms.
(2) The cathode material is considerably more porous than the anode material.
(3) Hydrogen gas is less dense than oxygen gas, so hydrogen bubbles rise faster.
(4) Some oxygen is dissolved into the solution, while all the insoluble hydrogen escapes.
(5) The water which is being decomposed has twice as much hydrogen as oxygen.

55. Arminta can float in a swimming pool. This is because the water has the power to exert an upward force on her body. The force of the water equals the weight of the water moved out of the way by her body.

What property of water best explains her ability to float?

(1) buoyancy
(2) mobility
(3) surface tension
(4) turbulence
(5) viscosity

Items 56 and 57 refer to the following passage.

When a woman has more than one child at a time during birth, each child commonly comes from a separate egg cell. The children are then genetically different. However, if one egg cell divides, and all of the children come from the same egg cell, the children have identical genetic heritage.

56. If a boy and a girl are twins, which of the following is the most accurate statement about their origin?

(1) They definitely came from one fertilized cell that divided.
(2) They probably came from one fertilized cell that divided.
(3) It is equally likely that they came from one or two cells.
(4) They probably came from two separately fertilized cells.
(5) They definitely came from two separately fertilized cells.

57. A woman taking a fertility drug gives birth to quintuplets. All of the babies are female, but three have pale skin and blue eyes, while the other two have dusky skin and brown eyes.

What is the smallest number of eggs that could have been fertilized to yield those five babies?

(1) 1
(2) 2
(3) 3
(4) 4
(5) 5

58. A physicist defines inertia as follows: Inertia refers to the motion of objects. Objects resist any change in their motion. An object at rest will continue at rest, while a moving object will continue moving in the the same direction and at the same speed.

Which of the following is the best example of the physicist's meaning of inertia?

(1) The great Egyptian pyramids have endured for thousands of years.
(2) A hockey puck slides in a straight line without slowing down.
(3) A skydiver feels a jerk as the parachute opens.
(4) A wrench dropped down an elevator shaft falls faster and faster.
(5) Each day is precisely the same length as the previous day.

59. Some beach sands in Alaska are currently being worked for gold. Because there are large gold deposits inland, the soils and sediments along the Alaskan coast contain traces of gold.

    Which of the following statements best explains why the gold is concentrated on those beaches?

    (1) Dense gold particles are left behind as the waves wash away other materials.
    (2) The gold was floated onto the shore in icebergs, which have completely melted.
    (3) The large "tidal" waves from frequent earthquakes wash the gold onto the shore.
    (4) Low water temperatures prevent the gold from dissolving as it does elsewhere.
    (5) Many treasure-laden ships have broken up on those dangerous shores.

60. Soft plant and animal tissues decompose quickly in the presence of decay bacteria. Such bacteria need oxygen to live.

    In which of the following locations would soft tissues be most likely to avoid decomposition and survive as fossils?

    (1) desert soil
    (2) beach sand
    (3) lake-bottom mud
    (4) offshore sandbar
    (5) river silt

Items 61 and 62 refer to the following paragraph.

   Dry wood is composed mainly of a stiff material called cellulose, a carbohydrate which cannot be digested by most animals. Even termites cannot directly dine on dry wood. However, termites have tiny one-celled parasites that live inside their intestines, and those protozoa can digest cellulose. Because of this, termites can live on dead wood, as they benefit from tiny creatures. Those creatures, in fair exchange, rely on the termite for most of their food supply.

61. According to the paragraph, what helps termites to derive nutrition from wood?

    (1) carbohydrates
    (2) dryness
    (3) enzymes
    (4) intestines
    (5) protozoa

62. Based on the information in the paragraph, which of the following best describes the relationship between the termite and its tiny inhabitants?

    (1) The inhabitants benefit at the expense of the termite.
    (2) The termite benefits at the expense of its inhabitants.
    (3) Both the termite and its inhabitants benefit from their association.
    (4) Both the termite and its inhabitants are harmed by their association.
    (5) There is neither benefit nor harm in this particular association.

63. Genetic scientists use the word characteristic to mean one feature of an organism. For example, eye color would be one characteristic.

    Which of the following possible relationships would make genetic research more difficult?

    A. One characteristic is controlled by several genes.
    B. One gene controls one characteristic.
    C. One gene controls several characteristics.

    (1) A only
    (2) B only
    (3) A and B only
    (4) A and C only
    (5) B and C only

Items 64 to 66 refer to the following paragraphs.

Many adults start their morning out with a cup of coffee. As a matter of fact, many coffee drinkers swear that they need a cup of coffee in the morning to get started. The reason that coffee gets them started is that it contains a large amount of caffeine, a potent stimulant. This stimulant is also found in tea, cocoa, some soft drinks, and some aspirin compounds.

Caffeine stimulates the intellectual part of the brain, producing a clearer, more efficient flow of thoughts and ideas. Caffeine also has many different effects on other parts of the body, making it of considerable value to groups ranging from athletes to migraine headache sufferers. Yet, caffeine is a nonessential chemical for human life. It is not a protein, fat, mineral, vitamin, or carbohydrate. And even though it is a natural, nonprescription substance that boosts performance and has many values, there are some dangers, especially when it is used in extreme amounts.

64. How much caffeine does the human body need?

   (1) The need is dependent upon the body weight of the individual.
   (2) The need is dependent upon the number of calories burned up by that particular body.
   (3) The need varies from person to person.
   (4) The amount of caffeine needed is in proportion to the vitamins needed.
   (5) The human body does not need caffeine.

65. Caffeine is found in

   (1) only natural substances
   (2) only artificial substances
   (3) vitamins
   (4) minerals
   (5) regular Pepsi-Cola

66. Some soft drink companies have made a special effort to publicize that their soft drink is caffeine free. Others have changed their product to remove any caffeine.

   Which of the following would be the best explanation for the action of these companies?

   (1) Caffeine-free drinks are easier to produce.
   (2) Caffeine-free drinks are cheaper to produce.
   (3) Research has shown that caffeine use has many negative side effects.
   (4) Research has shown that the value of using caffeine has been tremendously exaggerated.
   (5) The supply of caffeine is running very low.

END OF EXAMINATION

TEST 4: INTERPRETING LITERATURE AND THE ARTS

Tests of General Educational Development

Directions

The Interpreting Literature and the Arts Test consists of excerpts from classical and popular literature and articles about literature or the arts. Each excerpt is followed by multiple-choice questions about the reading material.

Read each excerpt first and then answer the questions following it. Refer back to the reading material as often as necessary in answering the questions.

Each excerpt is preceded by a "purpose question." The purpose question gives a reason for reading the material. Use these purpose questions to help focus your reading. You are not required to answer these purpose questions. They are given only to help you concentrate on the ideas presented in the reading materials.

You should spend no more than 65 minutes answering the questions in this booklet. Work carefully, but do not spend too much time on any one question. Be sure you answer every question. You will not be penalized for incorrect answers.

Do not mark in this test booklet. Record your answers on the separate answer sheet provided. Be sure all requested information is properly recorded on the answer sheet. To record your answers, mark the numbered space on the answer sheet beside the number that corresponds to the question in the test booklet.

FOR EXAMPLE:

It was Susan's dream machine. The metallic blue paint gleamed, and the sporty wheels were highly polished. Under the hood, the engine was no less carefully cleaned. Inside, flashy lights illuminated the instruments on the dashboard, and the seats were covered by rich leather upholstery.

The subject ("It") of this excerpt is most likely

(1) an airplane
(2) a stereo system
(3) an automobile
(4) a boat
(5) a motorcycle

The correct answer is "an automobile"; therefore, answer space 3 would be marked on the answer sheet.

Do not rest the point of your pencil on the answer sheet while you are considering your answer. Make no stray or unnecessary marks. If you change an answer, erase your first mark completely. Mark only one answer space for each question; multiple answers will be scored as incorrect. Do not fold or crease your answer sheet. Return all test materials to the test administrator.

Directions: Choose the <u>one best answer</u> to each item.

Items 1 to 5 refer to the following poem.

WHAT FASCINATES US ABOUT PENGUINS?

How is it these quilled milk-bottle
doorstops, straitjacketed in blubber,
without either knees or elbows, that
have to sleep standing, still seem
(5)   so hilarious a reflection of <u>us</u>, the
spoiled rich kids of natural history,
that notwithstanding our scant fondness
for other of our kind, we do love penguins?
They make us feel good about something,
(10)   and whatever it is, we've got to
look into it, we've got to have it.

So off go our spies into the daylong
dark of the Antarctic winter
to eavesdrop on what they do there—
(15)   foodless, fretful, shuffling to balance
an egg between foot and paunch until it hatches.

Shrug off that adventure as lunatic
or condemn it as invasion of privacy,
you'll find us at the penguinarium
(20)   staring rapt as they take their heartwarming
pratfalls on the ice, give vent to
gusts of head-shaking enmity, or stand
caricaturing the pathos of crowds
in wait for something or other
(25)   that never arrives—but that clearly,
whatever it is, is not us.

1. When she writes "quilled milk-bottle doorstops" (lines 1-2), the writer is referring to

(1) funny-looking elbows
(2) funny-looking knees
(3) penguin lovers
(4) penguins
(5) a new kind of doorstop

2. The writer would probably agree with which of the following conclusions?

(1) Most people love penguins.
(2) Penguins are afraid of humans.
(3) The penguinarium is not a popular place.
(4) Penguins fall on the ice as often as people do.
(5) Most penguins love people.

3. Which of the following best describes the structure of the first stanza (lines 1-11)?

    (1) beginning/middle/end
    (2) first/second/third
    (3) question/answer
    (4) past/present
    (5) positive/negative

4. According to the poem, what do the "spies" (line 12) do?

    (1) They go to the Antarctic to watch penguins.
    (2) They shuffle around, foodless and fretful.
    (3) They capture penguins for the penguinarium.
    (4) They slip upon the ice, in front of crowds.
    (5) They condemn penguins for invading their privacy.

5. With the phrase "scant fondness for others of our kind" (lines 7-8), the author suggests that

    (1) people tend to like only penguins
    (2) people tend not to like other people
    (3) there is no fondness in natural history
    (4) "spoiled rich kids" are not fond of penguins
    (5) penguins are the "spoiled rich kids of natural history."

Items 6 to 13 refer to the following excerpt from an essay.

WHY SHOULD A JUST MAN GO TO PRISON?

Under a government which imprisons any unjustly, the true place for a just man is also a prison. The proper place today, the only place which Massachusetts has
(5) provided for her freer and less desponding spirits is in her prisons, to be put out and locked out of the State by her own act, as they have already put themselves out by their principles. It is there that the fugitive
(10) slave and the Mexican prisoner on parole and the Indian come to plead the wrongs of his race should find them; on that separate but more free and honorable ground where the State places those who are not with her
(15) but against her—the only house in a slave State in which a free man can abide with honor. If any think that their influence would be lost there, and their voices no longer afflict the ear of the State, that they
(20) would not be as an enemy within its walls, they do not know by how much truth is stronger than error, nor how much more eloquently and effectively he can combat injustice who has experienced a little in his
(25) own person. Cast your whole vote, not a strip of paper merely, but your whole influence. A minority is powerless while it conforms to the majority; it is not even a minority then; but it is irresistible when it
(30) clogs by its whole weight. If the alternative is to keep all just men in prison or give up war and slavery, the State will not hesitate which to choose. If a thousand men were not to pay their tax-bills this year, that
(35) would not be a violent bloody measure, as it would be to pay them, and enable the State to commit violence and shed innocent blood. This is, in fact, the definition of a peaceable revolution, if any such is possible. If the
(40) tax-gatherer or any other public officer asks me, as one has done, "But what shall I do?" my answer is, "If you really wish to do anything, resign your office." When the subject has refused allegiance and the
(45) officer has resigned his office, then the revolution is accomplished.

6. The author would support which of the following methods of protest?

 (1) assassination of a government official
 (2) refusal to pay income tax
 (3) riots in the prisons
 (4) the assault of tax collectors
 (5) mob violence

7. Lines 1-25 make which of the following arguments?

 (1) Going to prison is advisable for those who wish to combat injustice.
 (2) Going to prison is only proper for slaves, Mexicans, and Indians.
 (3) In a just government, prisons do not exist.
 (4) All of the enemies of the government must destroy the prisons.
 (5) Going to prison is advisable only in Massachusetts.

8. What advice does the author give to the public official who asks what he should do to protest an unjust government?

 (1) Do your job as best you can.
 (2) Surrender yourself to a life in prison.
 (3) Refuse to pay your taxes.
 (4) Begin a revolution, by whatever means possible.
 (5) Quit your job.

9. The author would agree with which of the following conclusions?

 (1) Prisons must house the just as well as the unjust.
 (2) When just men are in the prisons, unjust men are outside, supporting the government.
 (3) When the prisons are full of just men, the government will start a revolution.
 (4) For a revolution to occur, the majority must go to prison, while the minority remains free.
 (5) Injustice will disappear, whether we protest it or not.

10. Lines 30-33 show that the author most likely believes that the following will take place if all just men choose prison to protest the government's participation in war and slavery:

    (1) The government will give up war and slavery.
    (2) The government will sell the prisoners into slavery.
    (3) The government will declare war on the prisoners.
    (4) The government will get rid of its prisons.
    (5) The government will ask the prisoners to vote on its policies.

11. When the author says "Cast your whole vote, not a strip of paper merely," (lines 25-26) he means

    (1) make sure to vote on election day
    (2) choose your candidate for public office wisely, and support him fully
    (3) take personal action, beyond just casting your vote, to affect the government
    (4) fill out the entire ballot, not just a small strip
    (5) realize that even those in prison should have the right to vote

12. According to the author, which of the following conditions make a peaceful revolution possible?

    A. citizens refusing to be loyal to the government
    B. complete participation by all voters in an election
    C. public officials resigning their jobs

    (1) A and B
    (2) A and C
    (3) A, B, and C
    (4) C only
    (5) A only

13. Which of the following are (is) probably the author's audience?

    (1) prisoners in Massachusetts
    (2) citizens of Massachusetts
    (3) government officials of Massachusetts
    (4) schoolchildren of Massachusetts
    (5) slaveholder in Massachusetts

Items 14 to 19 refer to the following article.

WHY ISN'T MODERNIST SCULPTURE POPULAR?

(5) If you asked a Parisian or a New Yorker in l886 what sculpture was, the answer (after a short blank stare) would have been: statues. Statuary, to borrow the mordant phrase of Claes Oldenburg many decades later, was "bulls and greeks and lots of nekkid broads." The sculptor of that day was responsible—as in the age of film, TV and other ways of mass-circulating the
(10) visual icon he is not—for commemorating the dead, illustrating religious myth or dogma and expressing social ideals. The aim and meaning of the work were rarely in doubt. With statues, good or bad, from
(15) garden gnome to Marcus Aurelius, you knew where you were.

In the 20th century, which, in cultural matters, really began around 1880, this changed. After 1910 the momentum of
(20) change was plain to all. Why do we always speak of "modern sculpture" but never of "modern statues"? Because one of the criteria of modernity itself was the degree to which sculptors angled their work away
(25) from the accepted forms of social communication via the human figure. Not because they lost interest in the figure—on the contrary, the years 1900-1950 were rich in figure sculpture and body-haunted
(30) objects by Matisse, Picasso, Archipenko, Brancusi, Miro, Calder, Giacometti and others—but because they did not want to serve the social consensus in the way that statuary did. Consequently, few public
(35) commemorative sculptures made in the past 75 years have any real importance in the modernist canon; and conversely, modern public sculpture is mostly banal in the extreme.
(40) Modern sculpture after 1910 wanted the liberty that painting had already claimed—the unobliged liberty of thought itself. It extracted new models from the changing culture around it, from painting
(45) and music, anthropology and

psychoanalysis, from the idea of the "primitive" (that escape route of a culture stuck in the gridlock of its own sophistication) and the dream of a utopian
(50) machine future. One could have a sculpture that was also a little building, like Alberto Giacometti's The Palace at 4 A.M., 1933, or a still life, like Henri Laurens's Dish with Grapes, 1918; an image of landscape, like
(55) David Smith's Australia, 1951, or for that matter a real landscape, like Robert Smithson's Spiral Jetty, 1970, a quarter-mile coil of rock now sunk in Utah's Great Salt Lake.   Marble, wood and
(60) bronze remained fundamental materials, but they were used in unorthodox ways; and in addition, a sculptor could use any kind of junk, from cardboard, tin and pine boards (the stuff of Picasso's and Laurens's cubist
(65) constructions) to the wire and celluloid favored by constructivists, the steel plates and boiler ends forged by Smith, and so on down to rocks, twigs, burlap, twine or even the artist's own dung, which, canned and
(70) labeled by the Italian Piero Manzoni in 1961, provided a nastily prophetic comment on fetishism in late modern art. On its road away from statuary, sculpture gained a new depth of cultural resonance, a flexibility of
(75) invention, an access to the inner self, a power of aggression and a weird, self-reflexive playfulness. All it lost was its audience.

The unpopularity of modernist sculpture,
(80) as compared with painting, is a fact of life.

14. The statement "All it lost was its audience" (lines 77-78) is another way of saying that

    (1) sculptors do most of their work in secret
    (2) modernist sculpture is unpopular
    (3) most people don't care about culture
    (4) the audience for sculpture has completely disappeared
    (5) modern sculptors do not need an audience

15. The third paragraph emphasizes which characteristic of modernist sculpture?

    (1) stupidity
    (2) beauty
    (3) ugliness
    (4) variety
    (5) largeness

16. According to the excerpt, one hundred years ago people thought sculpture was the same as

    (1) photography
    (2) drawing
    (3) painting
    (4) machines
    (5) statues

17. What does the writer mean, at the start of the second paragraph, when he says that "in cultural matters [the 20th century] really began around 1880"?

    (1) The cultural changes we associate with the 20th century began before 1900.
    (2) The 20th century did not really begin in 1900.
    (3) The lack of culture before 1880.
    (4) The 20th century began sometime between 1880 and 1910.
    (5) The production of statues stopped in 1880.

18. The writer identifies cardboard, tin, pine boards, rocks, twigs, and twine as

    (1) fundamental materials
    (2) traditional materials
    (3) junk parts
    (4) Picasso's materials
    (5) artistic toys

19. According to the third paragraph, changes in modern sculpture followed

    (1) the public demand for new art
    (2) the popular need for liberty
    (3) the demand by artists that art change
    (4) changes in modern painting
    (5) disgust with public sculpture

Items 20 to 24 refer to the following excerpt from a play.

WHAT HAPPENS WHEN TWO WOMEN THINK THEY ARE ENGAGED TO THE SAME MAN?

CECILY: (rather shy and confidingly) Dearest Gwendolen, there is no reason why I should make a secret of it to you. Our little country newspaper is sure to chronicle the fact next week. Mr. Ernest Worthing and I are engaged to be married.

(5) GWENDOLEN: (quite politely, rising) My darling Cecily, I think there must be some slight error. Mr. Ernest Worthing is engaged to me. The announcement will appear in the Morning Post on Saturday at the latest.

CECILY: (very politely, rising) I am afraid you must be under some misconception. Ernest proposed to me exactly ten minutes ago. (Shows diary.)

(10) GWENDOLEN: (examines diary through her lorgnette carefully) It is very curious, for he asked me to be his wife yesterday afternoon at 5:30. If you would care to verify the incident, pray do so. (Produces diary of her own.) I never travel without my diary. One should always have something sensational to read in the train. I am so sorry, dear Cecily, if it is any disappointment to you, but I am afraid I have

(15) the prior claim.

CECILY: It would distress me more than I can tell you, dear Gwendolen, if it caused you any mental or physical anguish, but I feel bound to point out that since Ernest proposed to you he clearly has changed his mind.

GWENDOLEN: (meditatively) If the poor fellow has been entrapped into any foolish promise I

(20) shall consider it my duty to rescue him at once, and with a firm hand.

CECILY: (thoughtfully and sadly) Whatever unfortunate entanglement my dear boy may have got into, I will never reproach him with it after we are married.

GWENDOLEN: Do you allude to me, Miss Cardew, as an entanglement? You are presumptuous. On an occasion of this kind it becomes more than a moral duty

(25) to speak one's mind. It becomes a pleasure.

CECILY: Do you suggest, Miss Fairfax, that I entrapped Ernest into an engagement? How dare you? This is no time for wearing the shallow mask of manners. When I see a spade I call it a spade.

GWENDOLEN: (satirically) I am glad to say that I have never seen a spade. It is obvious that

(30) our social spheres have been widely different.

20. In the course of this scene, the two women

    (1) become increasingly polite
    (2) become increasingly friendly
    (3) move from extreme politeness to open
        hostility
    (4) move from rage to quiet self-control
    (5) move from hostility to reconciliation

21. The changes in their attitudes are indicated
    by which of the following?

    A. They shift from the use of first names to
       <u>Miss</u>.
    B. They stop using terms of endearment.
    C. They accuse one another of entrapment.

    (1) A only
    (2) B only
    (3) A and C only
    (4) B and C only
    (5) A, B, and C

22. The scene is carefully balanced. That balance
    is reflected by both women's mentioning all of
    the following EXCEPT

    (1) a newspaper
    (2) an engagement announcement
    (3) a diary
    (4) the ensnaring of Ernest
    (5) a moral duty

23. In lines 27-28 when Cecily says "when I see a
    spade I call it a spade," she is

    (1) talking about gardening
    (2) talking about gambling
    (3) asserting her good nature
    (4) asserting her frankness
    (5) asserting her claim to marry Ernest

24. When Gwendolen replies "I have never seen a
    spade" (line 29), she intends to suggest that
    she

    (1) is socially superior to Cecily
    (2) seldom plays cards
    (3) knows little about gardening
    (4) is interested in astronomy
    (5) is more down to earth than Cecily

Items 25 to 32 refer to the following poem.

HOW SHOULD YOU DEAL WITH UNREQUITED LOVE?

       Why so pale and wan, fond lover?
          Prithee, why so pale?
       Will, when looking well can't move her,
          Looking ill prevail?
(5)   Prithee, why so pale?

       Why so dull and mute, young sinner?
          Prithee, why so mute?
       Will, when speaking well can't win her,
          Saying nothing do't?
(10)   Prithee, why so mute?

       Quit, quit, for shame, this will not move,
          This cannot take her.
       If of herself she will not love,
          Nothing can make her.
(15)   The devil take her!

25. The speaker of the poem is probably

(1) a former girlfriend of the lover
(2) the woman the lover is currently in love with
(3) a rival of the lover
(4) the lover
(5) a friend of the lover

26. In the first stanza (lines 1-5) of the poem, which lines are repeated?

(1) lines 1 and 2
(2) lines 1 and 4
(3) lines 2 and 4
(4) lines 2 and 5
(5) lines 4 and 5

27. What do all of the sentences in the first two stanzas (lines 1-10) of the poem have in common?

(1) They are all sentence fragments.
(2) They are all questions.
(3) They all describe the lady.
(4) They are all addressed to the lady.
(5) They all describe the appearance of the lover.

28. The third stanza (lines 11-15) is different from the first two because it

A. has no repeated lines
B. has no questions
C. is addressed to the lover

(1) A only
(2) B only
(3) C only
(4) A and B only
(5) A, B, and C

29. The underlying meaning of the first stanza
(lines 1-5) is

   (1) the lady may be won by pity
   (2) looking bad will not help win the lady
   (3) good looks are superficial
   (4) where love is concerned, appearance does
       not matter
   (5) the lady is not worth the effort it takes to
       win her

30. The argument of the last stanza (lines 11-15)
is

   (1) love is worth any sacrifice
   (2) the path of true love is never smooth
   (3) true love is worth waiting for
   (4) love that is not returned is not worth
       wasting time on
   (5) all women are fickle

31. In line 9, the word "do't" means

   (1) do not
   (2) don't
   (3) doubt
   (4) dote
   (5) do it

32. Which of the following pairs of words best
describe (1) the lover and (2) the speaker?

   (1) (1) romantic and (2) cynical
   (2) (1) realistic and (2) romantic
   (3) (1) unconventional and (2) conventional
   (4) (1) romantic and (2) sentimental
   (5) (1) cynical and (2) sentimental

Items 33 to 38 refer to the following excerpt from an article.

WHAT ARE THE WAYS OF THE SIERRA DEER?

The Sierra deer—the blacktail—spend the winters in the brushy and exceedingly rough region just below the main timber belt, and are less accessible to hunters there
(5) than when they are passing through the comparatively open forests to and from their summer pastures near the summits of the range. They go up the mountains early in the spring as the snow melts, not waiting
(10) for it all to disappear, reaching the high Sierra about the first of June and the coolest recesses at the base of the peaks a month or so later. I have tracked them for miles over compacted snow from three to
(15) ten feet deep.

Deer are capital mountaineers, making their way into the heart of the roughest mountains, seeking not only pasturage but a cool climate and safe, hidden places in
(20) which to bring forth their young. They are not supreme as rock-climbing animals; they take second rank, yielding the first to the mountain sheep, which dwell above them on the highest crags and peaks. Still, the two
(25) meet frequently; for deer climb all the peaks save the lofty summits above the glaciers, crossing piles of angular boulders, roaring swollen streams, and sheer-walled canyons by fords and passes that would try
(30) the nerves of the hardiest mountaineers—climbing with graceful ease and reserve of strength that cannot fail to arouse admiration. Everywhere some species of deer seems to be at home—on
(35) rough or smooth ground, lowlands or highlands, in swamps and barrens and the densest woods, in varying climates, hot or cold, over all the continent; maintaining glorious health, never making an awkward
(40) step. Standing, lying down, walking, feeding, running even for life, it is always invincibly graceful, and adds beauty and animation to every landscape—a charming animal, and a great credit to nature.

(45) I never see one of the common blacktail deer, the only species in the park, without fresh admiration, and since I never carry a gun I see them well: lying beneath a juniper or dwarf pine among the brown needles on
(50) the brink of some cliff, or at the end of a ridge commanding a wide outlook; feeding in sunny openings among chaparral, daintily selecting aromatic leaves and twigs; leading their fawns out of my way, or
(55) making them lie down and hide; bounding past through the forest, or curiously advancing and retreating again and again.

33. What does the writer probably mean when he says " since I never carry a gun I see them well" (lines 47-48)?

(1) Watching his gun distracts him from watching the deer.
(2) Deer hide from those who carry guns.
(3) For others, a gun makes up for poor eyesight.
(4) A gun tends to obstruct his vision.
(5) Those who carry guns shoot deer before they see them.

34. What can we conclude from the first sentence of the excerpt?

(1) Hunters do not hunt much in the winter.
(2) There are other animals besides deer that are easy to shoot in winter.
(3) Deer stay out of the timber belt because it is too rough.
(4) Wherever there is timber, there will be deer.
(5) Sierra deer are more likely to be shot in the summer than in the winter.

35. Which information in the passage suggests that the writer is a dedicated observer of blacktail deer?

    (1) He has tracked them for many miles through deep snow.
    (2) He has learned how to climb through rough mountain country.
    (3) He has captured a blacktail deer and confined it in a park.
    (4) He eats some of his own meals on the deer's feeding grounds.
    (5) He has watched the deer deliver their young.

36. According to the excerpt, the climbing ability of the Sierra deer is

    (1) supreme
    (2) equal to that of the mountain sheep
    (3) admirable, but second to that of the mountain sheep
    (4) very limited
    (5) not appreciated by the writer

37. When the writer says "Everywhere some species of deer seems to be at home," (lines 33-34) he indicates that

    (1) each deer finds a number of homes throughout its lifetime
    (2) deer who live in the highlands never travel to the lowlands
    (3) the life of a deer is always long and healthy
    (4) the deer makes its home at the spot that it loses strength
    (5) he is familiar with more than one species of deer

38. According to the excerpt, one reason that a deer ventures "into the heart of the roughest mountains" (lines 17-18) is for

    (1) the company of other deer
    (2) safety
    (3) solitude
    (4) exercise
    (5) recreation

Items 39 to 45 refer to the following excerpt from
a story.

IS THERE A LIQUOR
THIEF IN THE HOUSE?

Mr. Nonell had lunch in a Lebanese
restaurant with the man he considered his
best friend. They were celebrating Mr.
Nonell's seventy-third birthday. Since he
(5) hadn't been drinking or eating extravagant
meals for quite a while, he still felt a little
tipsy when he got home. Even so, he had no
trouble opening the door; he had realized on
leaving the restaurant that he had drunk too
(10) much, and all the way home he had been
picturing himself struggling to get the key
into the lock, just like in the movies.
Euphoria had put him in a state of mind
that seemed to call for one more drink. So
(15) he went into his bedroom (which doubled as
a study) and walked over to his formerly
well-stocked liquor cabinet to take out the
bottle of anisette, the only bottle in there
since his doctor had taken him off alcohol.
(20) It was empty. He had long suspected that
every now and then Matilde would sneak a
little swig. But he had never found the
bottle totally empty. And it was only empty
this time, he mused, because for the past
(25) few weeks—for the first time in decades,
and not without some sacrifice—Mr.
Nonell hadn't touched a drop of liquor. He
quickly put two and two together: Matilde
had been taking a little tipple now and then
(30) in the belief that, between one sip and the
next, Mr. Nonell was doing the same.
Confident that the level of liquid in the
bottle went down just a bit each time, she
hadn't realized that, since Mr. Nonell
(35) wasn't drinking at all, she had emptied it all
by herself.
Mr. Nonell had never given much
thought to those furtive swigs of anisette.
Matilde had been keeping house for him for
(40) forty-seven years, and she had always been
an ideal servant. That afternoon, though,
Mr. Nonell felt deeply hurt. Having found
the strength not to touch a single drop for

weeks, the least he could ask on coming
(45) home one day after a splendid meal, in the
mood for one last drink—just one—was to
have his way.

39. Which of the following probably caused Mr.
Nonell's happiness ("euphoria") mentioned in
the first paragraph?

(1) his difficulty opening the door upon
returning home
(2) his enjoyment of a fine meal with a good
friend
(3) his pride in his well-stocked liquor
cabinet
(4) his expectation of a surprise birthday
party
(5) his resolution to start drinking heavily
again

40. What does Mr. Nonell suspect that Matilde
has been doing?

(1) robbing his liquor cabinet of everything
but the anisette
(2) trying to hurt him for having lunch
without her
(3) pouring out all of his anisette
(4) drinking all of his anisette, little by little
(5) hiding the anisette in another room in the
house

41. Which of the following best expresses the
meaning of the final sentence of the excerpt?

(1) Mr. Nonell was so weak, upon returning
home, that he needed a drink.
(2) Because Mr. Nonell had successfully
stayed away from liquor for so long, he
was entitled to a drink.
(3) Because he successfully ate a good meal,
Mr. Nonell wanted to celebrate with one
drink.
(4) Mr. Nonell had really been drinking
constantly for weeks.
(5) Mr. Nonell was not interested in a drink,
just in the activities of Matilde.

42. Which of the following can be said about Matilde?

    (1) She had been a fine servant for a long time.
    (2) She had emptied all of his liquor bottles.
    (3) She did not like Mr. Nonell to be happy.
    (4) She did not know about Mr. Nonell's seventy-third birthday.
    (5) She had no interest in Mr. Nonell's health.

43. Which of the following does the writer emphasize throughout this excerpt?

    (1) The thoughts and feelings of Mr. Nonell.
    (2) The facts leading up to the disappearance of the anisette.
    (3) The reasons why Matilde might deceive Mr. Nonell.
    (4) The feebleness that had alarmed Mr. Nonell's doctor.
    (5) The sacrifices Mr. Nonell had made to avoid liquor.

44. Mr. Nonell suspects that Matilde did <u>not</u> know that he

    (1) had reached seventy-three years of age
    (2) had returned home that afternoon
    (3) had been to see his doctor
    (4) had gone to lunch for his birthday
    (5) had stopped drinking liquor

45. The excerpt suggests that

    (1) despite the advice of his doctor, Mr. Nonell has continued to drink excessively
    (2) Mr. Nonell still keeps a well-stocked liquor cabinet
    (3) Mr. Nonell limits himself to one daily drink of anisette
    (4) Mr. Nonell has never before suspected that Matilde is a liquor thief
    (5) anisette is a kind of liquor

END OF EXAMINATION

TEST 5: MATHEMATICS

Tests of General Educational Development

Directions

The Mathematics Test consists of multiple-choice questions intended to measure general mathematics skills and problem-solving ability. The questions are based on short readings which often include a graph, chart, or figure.

You should spend no more than 90 minutes answering the questions in this booklet. Work carefully, but do not spend too much time on any one question. Be sure you answer every question. You will not be penalized for incorrect answers.

Formulas you may need are given on the following page. Only some of the questions will require you to use a formula. Not all the formulas given will be needed.

Some questions contain more information than you will need to solve the problem. Other questions do not give enough information to solve the problem. If the question does not give enough information to solve the problem, the correct answer choice is "Not enough information is given."

The use of calculators is not allowed.

Do not mark in this test booklet. The test administrator will give you blank paper for your calculations. Record your answers on the separate answer sheet provided. Be sure all requested information is properly recorded on the answer sheet.

To record your answers, mark the numbered space on the answer sheet beside the number that corresponds to the question in the test booklet.

FOR EXAMPLE:

If a grocery bill totaling $15.75 is paid with a $20.00 bill, how much change should be returned?

(1) $5.26
(2) $4.75
(3) $4.25
(4) $3.75
(5) $3.25

The correct answer is "$4.25"; therefore, answer space 3 would be marked on the answer sheet.

Do not rest the point of your pencil on the answer sheet while you are considering your answer. Make no stray or unnecessary marks. If you change an answer, erase your first mark completely. Mark only one answer space for each question; multiple answers will be scored as incorrect. Do not fold or crease your answer sheet. Return all test materials to the test administrator.

FORMULAS

Description	Formula
AREA (A) of a:	
square	$A = s^2$; where s = side
rectangle	$A = lw$; where l = length, w = width
parallelogram	$A = bh$; where b = base, h = height
triangle	$A = \frac{1}{2}bh$; where b = base, h = height
circle	$A = \pi r^2$; where $\pi = 3.14$, r = radius
PERIMETER (P) of a:	
square	$P = 4s$; where s = side
rectangle	$P = 2l + 2w$; where l = length, w = width
triangle	$P = a + b + c$: where a, b, and c are the sides
circumference (C) of a circle	$C = \pi d$; where $\pi = 3.14$, d = diameter
VOLUME (V) of a:	
cube	$V = s^3$; where s = side
rectangular container	$V = lwh$; where l = length, w = width, h = height
cylinder	$V = \pi r^2 h$; where $\pi = 3.14$, r = radius, h = height
Pythagorean relationship	$c^2 = a^2 + b^2$; where c = hypotenuse, a and b are legs of a right triangle
distance (d) between two points in a plane	$d = \sqrt{(x_2 - x_1)^2 + (y_2 - y_1)^2}$; where (x_1, y_1) and (x_2, y_2) are two points in a plane
slope of a line (m)	$m = \dfrac{y_2 - y_1}{x_2 - x_1}$; where (x_1, y_1) and (x_2, y_2) are two points in a plane
mean	mean $= \dfrac{x_1 + x_2 + \cdots + x_n}{n}$; where the x's are the values for which a mean is desired, and n = number of values in the series
median	median = the point in an ordered set of numbers at which half of the numbers are above and half of the numbers are below this value
simple interest (i)	$i = prt$; where p = principal, r = rate, t = time
distance (d) as function of rate and time	$d = rt$; where r = rate, t = time
total cost (c)	$c = nr$; where n = number of units, r = cost per unit

Directions: Choose the one best answer to each item.

1. John worked 7 days last week. He worked 5½ hours each day. How many <u>hours</u> did John work last week?

   (1) 38½
   (2) 35½
   (3) 24½
   (4) 17½
   (5) 12½

Item 2 refers to the following triangle.

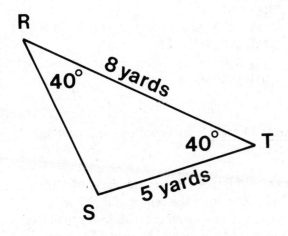

2. What is the <u>perimeter</u> (in yards) of the isosceles triangle RST pictured above?

   (1) 8
   (2) 13
   (3) 18
   (4) 20
   (5) Not enough information is given.

3. Alice wants to send 400 wedding invitations. She can do about 16 per day. If she begins on January 1st, when would she be expected to be finished?
   (1) January 25th
   (2) February 18th
   (3) March 30th
   (4) April 15th
   (5) May 1st

Item 4 is based on the following graph.

STUDENT BUDGET

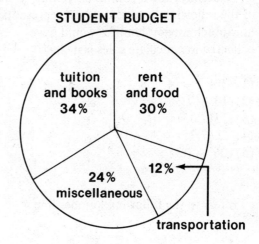

4. The graph above shows how a student spent his budget in a given year. According to the graph, what percent of his budget was <u>left</u> after rent, food, tuition, and book expenses?

   (1) 26%
   (2) 28%
   (3) 36%
   (4) 64%
   (5) 100%

5. Two glasses, identical except for height, were filled with water and left side by side on a picnic table. The water in the taller glass took 16 days to evaporate, while the water in the shorter glass took 10 days to evaporate. What is the height (in inches) of the <u>shorter</u> glass?

   (1) 10
   (2) 13
   (3) 16
   (4) 26
   (5) Not enough information is given.

6. Jennifer works in a candy store where she sells chocolate for $7.35 per pound. Last week she sold 3 pounds on Monday, 5 pounds on Tuesday, 4 pounds on Wednesday, 6 pounds on Thursday, and 8 pounds on Friday. Which of the following expressions best represents how much money Jennifer would have collected in chocolate sales last week?

(1) $3 + 5 + 4 + 6 + 8$
(2) $13 + 7.35$
(3) $13(7.35)$
(4) $26(7.35)$
(5) $26 + 7.35$

Item 7 refers to the following number line.

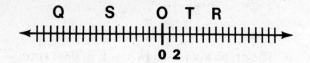

```
Q       S     O  T    R
<++++++++++++++|++++++++++++++>
              0 2
```

7. Which letter on the number line above represents 8?

(1) R
(2) O
(3) S
(4) T
(5) Q

8. Between which of the following pairs of numbers is the square root of 22?

(1) 2 and 4
(2) 4 and 5
(3) 5 and 8
(4) 8 and 10
(5) 10 and 12

9. You need to make 350 cupcakes for the bakesale. You can make an average of 45 cupcakes in an hour. Approximately how long will it take you to make the 350 cupcakes?

(1) between 4 and 5 hours
(2) between 5 and 6 hours
(3) between 6 and 7 hours
(4) between 7 and 8 hours
(5) between 8 and 9 hours

10. A motorcycle which usually sells for $1000.00 is discounted 10%. How much is the sale price?

(1) $10.00
(2) $90.00
(3) $100.00
(4) $900.00
(5) $990.00

Items 11 and 12 are based on the following information.

A crew of five people have six days to paint a divider line down the center of an 81-mile highway. Crew members with fewer than five years of experience will be paid $56.00 per day, while members with five or more years of experience will be paid $80.00 per day.

11. What is the minimum average number of miles the crew must paint each day to cover the 81 miles in the six days?

(1) 12.5
(2) 13.3
(3) 13.5
(4) 16.1
(5) 16.2

12. What is the crew's total earnings?

(1) $336.00
(2) $408.00
(3) $480.00
(4) $816.00
(5) Not enough information is given.

Item 13 refers to the following space module.

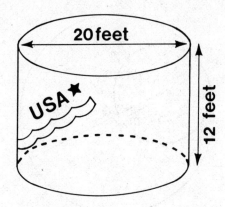

13. The dimensions of a cylindrical space module are shown above. Which one of the expressions below represents the maximum volume (in cubic feet) of air it can hold?

(1) $3.14(10)^2(12)$
(2) $3.14(10)(12)^2$
(3) $3.14(20)(12)$
(4) $3.14(20)^2(12)$
(5) $3.14(40)^2(12)$

14. Deana needs to make a dress for graduation, so she goes to the fabric store to get prices: pattern = $3.50, fabric = $16.00, notions = $4.75. A week later when Deana goes back to the store to buy what she needs, she finds the fabric on sale at 10% off. How much does Deana spend on her dress? (There is no sales tax.)

(1) $18.25
(2) $20.82
(3) $22.65
(4) $24.25
(5) $25.85

15. You wish to ship three packages—one worth $820, another worth $470, and the third worth $210. Shipping costs 15 percent of what the packages are worth. What will be your total shipping costs?

(1) $ 2.25
(2) $ 15.00
(3) $ 225.00
(4) $1500.00
(5) $1550.00

16. It takes Jean 45 minutes to mow her grandmother's lawn. After ¼ hour of mowing, Jean's grandmother asked her to run to the store for a carton of milk, which she gladly did. What fraction of the lawn-mowing job had Jean completed before she left?

(1) ¼
(2) ⅓
(3) ½
(4) ⅔
(5) ¾

17. Evaluate $3x^2 - 5y$, for $x = 4$ and $y = 2$.

(1)   14
(2)   38
(3) 119
(4) 134
(5) 290

18. Ericka's grandfather has a licorice rope 36 inches long, which he divides between Erika and her friend Tim. When he divides it, Tim gets 8 inches more of the licorice rope than Erika does. How many inches of the licorice rope does Erika get?

(1)   8
(2) 14
(3) 22
(4) 28
(5) 36

Item 19 refers to the following triangle.

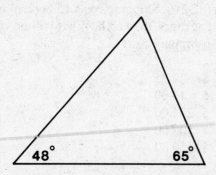

19. The triangle above has three interior angles. The measure of one angle is 48°, while the measure of another is 65°. What is the measure of the third interior angle?

    (1)   17°
    (2)   67°
    (3) 113°
    (4) 247°
    (5) Not enough information is given.

20. Rico went on a weekend car rally. He drove 120 miles on Friday, 210 miles on Saturday, and 180 miles on Sunday. What was his mean (average) daily mileage?

    (1) 120
    (2) 170
    (3) 180
    (4) 210
    (5) 510

Item 21 refers to the plane figure below.

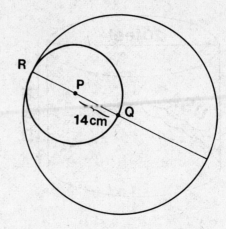

21. In the plane figure above, two circles have been drawn—the smaller circle with center at point P, the larger circle with center at point Q. The two circles intersect at point R, and PQ equals 14 cm. What is the diameter (in centimeters) of the larger circle?

    (1) 56
    (2) 28
    (3) 21
    (4) 14
    (5) Not enough information is given.

22. Keith appeared as a contestant on a television game show. All Keith had to do was correctly guess how many silver dollars were in the glass cookie jar, and he would win quadruple that amount. Keith won $388. Which equation below could be used to determine how many silver dollars were in the jar?

    (1) $d/4 = 388$
    (2) $d - 4 = 388$
    (3) $d + 4 = 388$
    (4) $4(d + 4) = 388$
    (5) $4d = 388$

23. Roberto and Linda were growing bacteria for a science experiment. At the end of the experiment, Roberto's culture had a population of 4×10^5, and Linda's culture had a population of 8×10^4. Which of the following statements would have been true at the end of the experiment?

(1) Linda's culture is 4 times Roberto's.
(2) Roberto's culture is 20 times Linda's.
(3) Linda's culture is twice Roberto's.
(4) Roberto's culture is 5 times Linda's.
(5) Roberto's culture and Linda's culture are of equal population.

24. Over the years, a dog named Abbey has had 48 puppies. Of these puppies, the number of females has been triple the number of males. How many of Abbey's puppies were <u>females</u>?

(1) 12
(2) 16
(3) 28
(4) 32
(5) 36

25. Miko gives Cecil a gumball machine for Cecil's birthday. He fills it with a mixture of <u>42 red</u> gumballs and <u>36 yellow</u> gumballs. What is the probability of getting a <u>yellow</u> gumball the first time the machine is used?

(1) $\dfrac{36}{42}$

(2) $\dfrac{36}{78}$

(3) $\dfrac{42}{78}$

(4) $\dfrac{(42 - 36)}{78}$

(5) $\dfrac{(42 + 36)}{78}$

Item 26 refers to the map below.

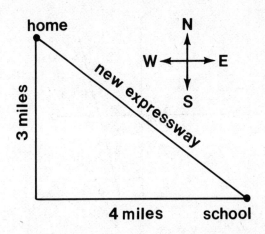

26. Russell now drives 7 miles to school by first traveling 3 miles south and then 4 miles east, as pictured above. Next month, the new expressway will be finished, and Russell can drive in a straight line directly to school. How many miles will Russell's trip to school be on the new expressway?

(1) 7
(2) 6
(3) 5.5
(4) 5
(5) 4.5

27. Kurt earned the following scores on his English tests:

90, 84, 77, 85, and 74

What is Kurt's <u>median</u> score?

(1) 74
(2) 77
(3) 82
(4) 84
(5) 90

Item 28 refers to the graph below.

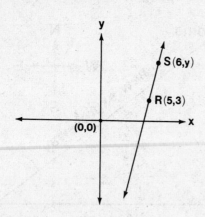

28. In the graph above, the slope of line RS is 4. What is the *y*-coordinate of point S?

(1)   3¼
(2)   4
(3)   7
(4)   9
(5)   10

29. Roy would like to reroof his house. He can buy asphalt shingles by the bundle. Each bundle weighs 50 pounds, and 3 bundles will cover 100 square feet. How many pounds of shingles will it take to reroof Roy's house?

(1)   150
(2)   500
(3)   750
(4)   2250
(5)   5000

30. Leona needs hay for her livestock. Grass hay sells for $5 per bale, and alfalfa hay sells for $7 per bale. Leona decides to buy 15 bales of grass hay and 20 bales of alfalfa hay. Which expression below could be used to calculate Leona's hay bill? (There is no sales tax.)

(1)   5(15) + 7(15)
(2)   5(15) + 7(20)
(3)   5(20) + 7(15)
(4)   5(20) + 7(20)
(5)   (5 + 7)(20 + 15)

31. Mike just got a job selling stereos, and he just made his first sale of $3600. Mike is to receive 8 percent commission for this sale. What will his commission be?

(1) $800
(2) $450
(3) $360
(4) $300
(5) $288

32. Dolores has materials for 100 linear feet of fencing plus a 4-foot-wide gate. She is planning an enclosed rectangular vegetable garden which, due to the size of her yard, needs to be 15 feet wide. What is the maximum length (in feet) of Dolores's vegetable garden?

(1)   37
(2)   38
(3)   44.5
(4)   85
(5)   Not enough information is given.

33. Pat's chickens eat 1¼ ounces of feed a day. How many days will 17½ ounces of feed last?

(1)   6
(2)   8½
(3)   14
(4)   17
(5)   18¾

34. Mario has three cats—Duke, Emily, and Frita. Emily weighs 4 pounds less than Duke, and Duke weighs 3 pounds more than Frita. Frita weighs 9 pounds. How much does Emily weigh?

(2)   12
(2)   10
(3)   8
(4)   4
(5)   2

35. Diane works 10 hours a day, four days a week—Monday through Thursday. On workdays, Diane drives her car 15 miles each day. On two of her days off, Diane drives a combined total of 13 miles, and one day she doesn't drive at all. How many miles will Diane drive from Monday, March 1st, through Wednesday, March 10th.

    (1) 146
    (2) 133
    (3) 120
    (4) 118
    (5) 105

36. Mr. Montoya, a local grocer, advertises that his prices are so low that you could save 25% off your present weekly grocery bill just by shopping at his store. If you now spend $140 per week for groceries somewhere else, how much would you be expected to spend if you shopped at Mr. Montoya's grocery store this week?

    (1) $125
    (2) $120
    (3) $115
    (4) $105
    (5) $100

37. To make 2 loaves of bread, a baker needs 5½ cups of flour. A large order just came in for 100 loaves. How many cups of flour will he need?

    (1) 11
    (2) 55
    (3) 110
    (4) 275
    (5) 550

38. Given the formula $w = 4x(y - 5)$, find w, for $x = 2$ and $y = 11$.

    (1) 48
    (2) 68
    (3) 83
    (4) 252
    (5) 451

39. Last month, Hometown High sponsored an invitational gymnastics meet. Four teams competed. Their team scores were 83.92, 57.30, 71.26, and 68.08. What was the average team score at the meet?

    (1) 64.28
    (2) 69.67
    (3) 70.14
    (4) 140.28
    (5) 280.56

Item 40 refers to the following graph.

milk consumed in California $\left(\begin{array}{c}\text{thousands}\\\text{of gallons}\end{array}\right)$

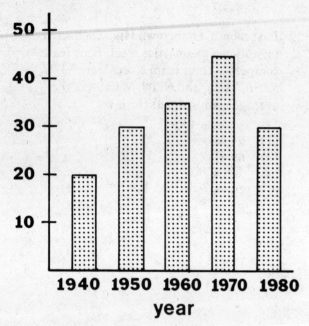

year

Item 41 refers to the enclosed rectangular box below.

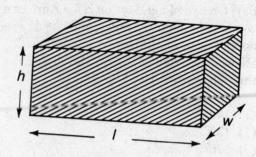

40. According to the graph above, by how many gallons did the milk consumption in California increase from 1950 to 1970?

   (1)   15
   (2)   20
   (3)   45
   (4) 15,000
   (5) 45,000

41. Which of these equations could be used to determine the surface area "S" of the enclosed rectangular box pictured above? The box's dimensions are l, by w, by h.

   (1) $S = 6(lwh)$
   (2) $S = 4(lwh)$
   (3) $S = 2(lw) + 2(wh) + 2(lh)$
   (4) $S = lwh$
   (5) $S = l^2 + w^2 + h^2$

42. Jan just got her paycheck. She finds that $30 has been deducted for union dues, $107 has been deducted for taxes; and she is pleasantly surprised to find that a $50 bonus has been included. If J represents Jan's original pay, which expression below would represent her net pay?

   (1) $J + 30 + 107 - 50$
   (2) $J - 30 + 107 + 50$
   (3) $J - 30 - 107 + 50$
   (4) $J + 30 - 107 + 50$
   (5) $J - 30 + 107 - 50$

Item 43 refers to the circle graph below.

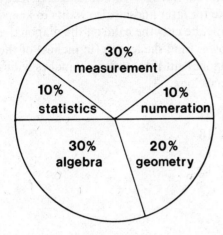

43. According to the graph above, if the test contains 5 numeration problems, then how many <u>algebra problems</u> should be expected?

    (1) 10
    (2) 15
    (3) 20
    (4) 25
    (5) 35

Item 44 refers to the following fruit stand price list.

FRIENDLY FRUIT STAND PRICE LIST

apples .... 60¢ each
bananas .... 20¢ each
cantaloupes .... 59¢ each or 2 for $1
oranges .... 39¢ each or 3 for $1

44. Mr. and Mrs. Adams are planning to attend a company picnic and need to make a fruit salad for the occasion. Their recipe calls for 5 apples, 10 bananas, 4 cantaloupes, and 5 oranges. What is the <u>least</u> amount they could spend at the fruit stand to buy all the fruit they need for their salad?

    (1) $11.00
    (2) $ 9.23
    (3) $ 9.00
    (4) $ 8.82
    (5) $ 8.78

45. Sunita notices that there are exactly three dozen daisies in the bunch she bought for her mother. In this bunch, there are three times more yellow daisies than white daisies, and no other colors. How many <u>yellow</u> daisies are in the bunch?

    (1) 9
    (2) 12
    (3) 24
    (4) 27
    (5) 33

46. Right now, Michelle makes $48 a day working on a road crew. Her employer has promised her a 12% raise beginning tomorrow. What will her new daily wage be, rounded to the nearest dollar, after she receives her raise?

    (1) $50
    (2) $53
    (3) $54
    (4) $56
    (5) $60

Item 47 refers to the following price list.

VITA-VALUE VENDING MACHINE PRICE LIST

soup .... 75¢
salad $1.00
sandwich $1.20
hot entree $1.45
beverage .... 50¢
dessert .... 80¢

47. Slim has decided to buy lunch from the Vita-Value Vending Machine. He has exactly $3.05 in change. If he buys a salad and a beverage, which of the following combinations could he also afford to buy?

    (1) sandwich and dessert
    (2) soup and dessert
    (3) soup and hot entree
    (4) soup and sandwich
    (5) hot entree and dessert

Item 48 refers to the diagram below.

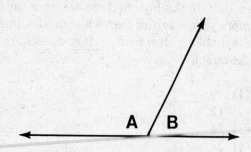

48. In the diagram above, if the degree measure of angle A is twice the degree measure of angle B, what is the degree measure of angle A?

    (1)   90
    (2) 100
    (3) 120
    (4) 160
    (5) Not enough information is given.

49. For which value of y below is the inequality $3y < 9$ true?

    (1) 6
    (2) 5
    (3) 4
    (4) 3
    (5) 2

Item 50 refers to the following diagram.

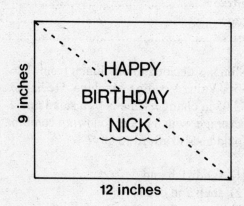

50. Nick has a rectangular birthday cake as pictured. Because he wants to save half of the cake for later and he also wants to keep his name, he cuts the cake on the diagonal as shown. Find the length (in inches) of the diagonal cut if the cake is 9 inches wide by 12 inches long.

    (1) 21
    (2) 18
    (3) 15
    (4) 12
    (5)   9

Item 51 refers to the following diagram.

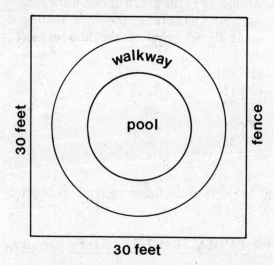

51. There is a 30-foot by 30-foot fenced in square at City Park. The Council would like to put a circular wading pool right in its center. Around the pool, there must be a 3-foot-wide walkway which can be no closer than 5 feet to the fence. What is the largest possible radius (in feet) of the pool?

    (1)   5
    (2)   7
    (3)   8
    (4) 11
    (5) Not enough information is given.

Item 52 refers to the drawing below.

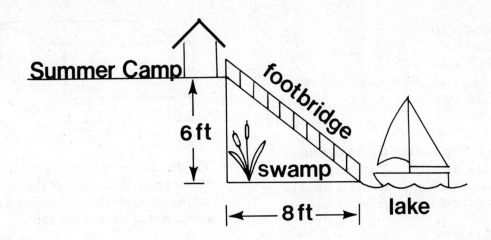

52. Camp Counselor Craig builds a footbridge from the summer camp to the lake so the campers will not have to crawl down a perpendicular 6-foot cliff and then trudge through 8 feet of swamp. How long (in feet) is the footbridge?

(1) 14
(2) 12
(3) 11
(4) 10
(5) 9

53. Which of the following expresses 485,362 in scientific notation?

(1) 4.85362×10^5
(2) 4.85362×10^6
(3) 48.5632×10^6
(4) 485.362×10^5
(5) 4853.62×10^3

54. Simon is buying a pickup truck that usually sells for $12,000 but which has been discounted 20%. Which expression could be used to represent the sale price?

(1) .20($12,000)
(2) ($12,000) − .20
(3) .20($12,000) + .02
(4) $12,000 − .20($12,000)
(5) ($12,000) − .02($12,000)

Item 55 refers to the triangle below.

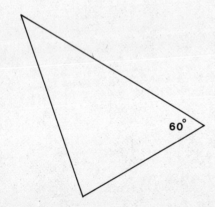

55. One angle of the above triangle is 60 degrees. Of the two remaining angles, one is twice the other. What are their measures (in degrees)?

(1) 100 and 200
(2) 60 and 120
(3) 50 and 100
(4) 40 and 80
(5) 30 and 60

Item 56 refers to the following fish tank.

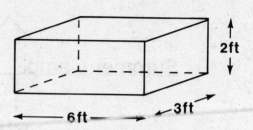

56. The dimensions of a rectangular fish tank are shown above. Which one of the expressions below represents the maximum volume (in cubic feet) of water it can hold?

(1) 6(3)(2)
(2) 6(3 + 2)
(3) 3(6 + 2)
(4) 2(6) + 2(3) + 2(2)
(5) 2(3) + 2(6)

END OF EXAMINATION

GED

SCORING AND EXPLANATIONS FOR PRACTICE EXAMINATION 1

Scoring Practice Examination 1

Score your GED Practice Examination 1 by following these steps:

1. Check the answers you marked on your answer sheet against the Answer Key that follows. Put a check mark in the box following any wrong answer.

2. Fill out the Scoring Chart (p. 396).

3. Estimate your score on each test using the Score Approximators (p. 397–399). Remember, these Score Approximators will give you a **very general** idea of how you are doing.

4. Read all of the explanations (pp. 401–436). Mark the boxes following the explanations as the directions there tell you. Go back to review any explanations that are not clear to you.

5. Finally, fill out the Reasons for Mistakes chart on p. 400.

Don't leave out any of these steps. They are very important in learning to do your best on the GED.

ANSWER KEY FOR PRACTICE EXAMINATION 1

TEST 1: WRITING SKILLS, PART I

1. (4) ☐	12. (1) ☐	23. (2) ☐	34. (2) ☐	45. (3) ☐
2. (4) ☐	13. (2) ☐	24. (4) ☐	35. (4) ☐	46. (3) ☐
3. (4) ☐	14. (1) ☐	25. (2) ☐	36. (1) ☐	47. (3) ☐
4. (3) ☐	15. (2) ☐	26. (4) ☐	37. (5) ☐	48. (1) ☐
5. (3) ☐	16. (3) ☐	27. (4) ☐	38. (4) ☐	49. (2) ☐
6. (1) ☐	17. (3) ☐	28. (3) ☐	39. (3) ☐	50. (2) ☐
7. (1) ☐	18. (3) ☐	29. (5) ☐	40. (1) ☐	51. (1) ☐
8. (5) ☐	19. (5) ☐	30. (2) ☐	41. (5) ☐	52. (4) ☐
9. (3) ☐	20. (5) ☐	31. (3) ☐	42. (3) ☐	53. (1) ☐
10. (4) ☐	21. (3) ☐	32. (4) ☐	43. (2) ☐	54. (4) ☐
11. (5) ☐	22. (5) ☐	33. (2) ☐	44. (5) ☐	55. (1) ☐

TEST 2: SOCIAL STUDIES

1. (4) ☐	14. (5) ☐	27. (1) ☐	40. (5) ☐	53. (3) ☐
2. (2) ☐	15. (5) ☐	28. (4) ☐	41. (1) ☐	54. (5) ☐
3. (5) ☐	16. (5) ☐	29. (2) ☐	42. (4) ☐	55. (2) ☐
4. (3) ☐	17. (1) ☐	30. (3) ☐	43. (3) ☐	56. (5) ☐
5. (5) ☐	18. (1) ☐	31. (4) ☐	44. (4) ☐	57. (5) ☐
6. (2) ☐	19. (2) ☐	32. (2) ☐	45. (4) ☐	58. (5) ☐
7. (3) ☐	20. (3) ☐	33. (4) ☐	46. (2) ☐	59. (3) ☐
8. (1) ☐	21. (3) ☐	34. (5) ☐	47. (3) ☐	60. (2) ☐
9. (2) ☐	22. (4) ☐	35. (1) ☐	48. (2) ☐	61. (1) ☐
10. (1) ☐	23. (4) ☐	36. (3) ☐	49. (3) ☐	62. (1) ☐
11. (4) ☐	24. (2) ☐	37. (5) ☐	50. (2) ☐	63. (1) ☐
12. (4) ☐	25. (5) ☐	38. (2) ☐	51. (1) ☐	64. (5) ☐
13. (3) ☐	26. (1) ☐	39. (1) ☐	52. (1) ☐	

TEST 3: SCIENCE

1. (4) ☐	15. (3) ☐	28. (2) ☐	41. (3) ☐	54. (5) ☐
2. (3) ☐	16. (2) ☐	29. (4) ☐	42. (5) ☐	55. (1) ☐
3. (1) ☐	17. (1) ☐	30. (2) ☐	43. (5) ☐	56. (5) ☐
4. (4) ☐	18. (5) ☐	31. (3) ☐	44. (2) ☐	57. (2) ☐
5. (1) ☐	19. (1) ☐	32. (3) ☐	45. (2) ☐	58. (2) ☐
6. (5) ☐	20. (5) ☐	33. (2) ☐	46. (1) ☐	59. (1) ☐
7. (2) ☐	21. (4) ☐	34. (4) ☐	47. (4) ☐	60. (3) ☐
8. (3) ☐	22. (3) ☐	35. (5) ☐	48. (4) ☐	61. (5) ☐
9. (1) ☐	23. (4) ☐	36. (1) ☐	49. (5) ☐	62. (3) ☐
10. (5) ☐	24. (1) ☐	37. (2) ☐	50. (5) ☐	63. (4) ☐
11. (5) ☐	25. (3) ☐	38. (1) ☐	51. (1) ☐	64. (5) ☐
12. (5) ☐	26. (3) ☐	39. (4) ☐	52. (3) ☐	65. (5) ☐
13. (3) ☐	27. (3) ☐	40. (2) ☐	53. (3) ☐	66. (3) ☐
14. (3) ☐				

TEST 4: INTERPRETING LITERATURE AND THE ARTS

1. (4) ☐	10. (1) ☐	19. (4) ☐	28. (4) ☐	37. (5) ☐
2. (1) ☐	11. (3) ☐	20. (3) ☐	29. (2) ☐	38. (2) ☐
3. (3) ☐	12. (2) ☐	21. (5) ☐	30. (4) ☐	39. (2) ☐
4. (1) ☐	13. (2) ☐	22. (5) ☐	31. (5) ☐	40. (4) ☐
5. (2) ☐	14. (2) ☐	23. (4) ☐	32. (1) ☐	41. (2) ☐
6. (2) ☐	15. (4) ☐	24. (1) ☐	33. (2) ☐	42. (1) ☐
7. (1) ☐	16. (5) ☐	25. (5) ☐	34. (5) ☐	43. (1) ☐
8. (5) ☐	17. (1) ☐	26. (4) ☐	35. (1) ☐	44. (5) ☐
9. (2) ☐	18. (3) ☐	27. (2) ☐	36. (3) ☐	45. (5) ☐

TEST 5: MATHEMATICS

1. (1) ☐	13. (1) ☐	24. (5) ☐	35. (4) ☐	46. (3) ☐
2. (3) ☐	14. (3) ☐	25. (2) ☐	36. (4) ☐	47. (2) ☐
3. (1) ☐	15. (3) ☐	26. (4) ☐	37. (4) ☐	48. (3) ☐
4. (3) ☐	16. (2) ☐	27. (4) ☐	38. (1) ☐	49. (5) ☐
5. (5) ☐	17. (2) ☐	28. (3) ☐	39. (3) ☐	50. (3) ☐
6. (4) ☐	18. (2) ☐	29. (4) ☐	40. (4) ☐	51. (2) ☐
7. (1) ☐	19. (2) ☐	30. (2) ☐	41. (3) ☐	52. (4) ☐
8. (2) ☐	20. (2) ☐	31. (5) ☐	42. (3) ☐	53. (1) ☐
9. (4) ☐	21. (1) ☐	32. (1) ☐	43. (2) ☐	54. (4) ☐
10. (4) ☐	22. (5) ☐	33. (3) ☐	44. (5) ☐	55. (4) ☐
11. (3) ☐	23. (4) ☐	34. (3) ☐	45. (4) ☐	56. (1) ☐
12. (5) ☐				

SCORING CHART

Use your marked Answer Key to fill in the following Scoring Chart.

	Possible	Completed	Right	Wrong
Test 1: Writing Skills, Part I	55			
Test 2: Social Studies	64			
Test 3: Science	66			
Test 4: Interpreting Literature and the Arts	45			
Test 5: Mathematics	56			
TOTAL	286			

Now, use this Scoring Chart to approximate your score on the following pages.

APPROXIMATING YOUR SCORE

The following Score Approximators will help you evaluate your skills and give you a very *general* indication of your scoring potential.

Test 1: Writing Skills

To approximate your Writing Skills score

1. Using the Scoring Chart, fill in the blank below with the number of questions you answered *correctly* on Part I: Multiple Choice.

2. Have an English teacher, tutor, or someone else with good writing skills read and evaluate your essay using the Checklists given in Part 3, How to Start Reviewing. Have your reader evaluate the complete essay as *good* or *poor*. Note that your paper would actually be scored from 1 to 6 by two trained readers. But since we are trying only for a rough approximation, the simple *good* or *poor* evaluation will give you a general feeling for your score range.

3. Use the following table to get an approximate score. Notice that the left-hand column shows the number of correct answers on Part I: Multiple Choice. The right-hand column lists your approximate score range with a poor essay and your approximate score range with a good essay.

Right answers on Part I _____
Essay evaluation   Poor   Good

Number of Right Answers on Part I: Multiple Choice	Approximate Score Range with Essay Evaluation	
	Poor Essay	Good Essay
0–10	21–31	32–42
11–20	32–35	43–47
21–30	36–39	48–51
31–40	40–43	52–55
41–50	44–51	56–63
51–54	52–60	64–72

Remember, this is only an *approximate score range*. When you take the GED Writing Skills Test, some of the multiple-choice questions may be easier or more difficult. The essay will be scored accurately by trained readers.

Test 2: Social Studies

To approximate your Social Studies score

1. Using the Scoring Chart, fill in the blank below with the number of questions you answered *correctly*.

2. Use the following table to match the number of right answers and the approximate score range.

Right answers _____

Number of Right Answers	Approximate Score Range
0–10	20–32
11–20	33–41
21–30	42–47
31–40	48–53
41–50	54–63
51–64	64–80

Remember, this is only an *approximate score range*. When you take the GED Social Studies Test, you will have questions that are similar to those in this book. Some questions, however, may be slightly easier or more difficult.

Test 3: Science

To approximate your Science score

1. Using the Scoring Chart, fill in the blank below with the number of questions you answered *correctly*.

2. Use the following table to match the number of right answers to the approximate score range.

Right answers _____

Number of Right Answers	Approximate Score Range
0–10	20–30
11–20	31–37
21–30	38–43
31–40	44–49
41–50	50–56
51–60	57–68
61–66	69–80

Remember, this is only an *approximate score range*. When you take the GED Science Test, you will have questions that are similar to those in this book. Some questions, however, may be slightly easier or more difficult.

Test 4: Interpreting Literature and the Arts

To approximate your Interpreting Literature and the Arts score

1. Using the Scoring Chart, fill in the blank below with the number of questions you answered *correctly*.

2. Use the following table to match the number of right answers to the approximate score range.

Right answers _____

Number of Right Answers	Approximate Score Range
0–10	20–34
11–20	35–43
21–30	44–52
31–40	53–68
41–45	69–80

Remember, this is only an *approximate score range*. When you take the GED Interpreting Literature and the Arts Test, you will have questions that are similar to those in this book. Some questions, however, may be slightly easier or more difficult.

Test 5: Mathematics

To approximate your Mathematics score

1. Using the Scoring Chart, fill in the blank below with the number of questions you answered *correctly*.

2. Use the following table to match the number of right answers to the approximate score range.

Right answers _____

Number of Right Answers	Approximate Score Range
0–10	20–32
11–20	33–39
21–30	40–45
31–40	46–51
41–50	52–60
51–56	61–80

Remember, this is only an *approximate score range*. When you take the GED Mathematics Test, you will have questions that are similar to those in this book. Some questions, however, may be slightly easier or more difficult.

REASONS FOR MISTAKES

Fill out the following chart *only after you have read all the explanations that follow*. This chart will help you spot your strengths and weaknesses and your repeated errors or trend in types of errors.

	Total Missed	Simple Mistake	Misread Problem	Lack of Knowledge
Test 1: Writing Skills, Part I				
Test 2: Social Studies				
Test 3: Science				
Test 4: Interpreting Literature and the Arts				
Test 5: Mathematics				
TOTAL				

Examine your results carefully. Reviewing the above information will help you pinpoint your common mistakes. Focus on avoiding your most common mistakes as you practice. If you are missing a lot of questions because of "Lack of Knowledge," you should go back and review the basics.

Explanations for Practice Examination 1

Each explanation is followed by two boxes, OK and ?. After you read each explanation, mark box OK if you understand the answer, and if you missed the question, why you did. Mark box ? if you do not understand the answer. After you complete each section, go back and review the explanations that you marked ?.

TEST 1: WRITING SKILLS, PART 1

1. (4) The only comma needed in this sentence is the one which follows the long introductory phrase (*According . . . Business*). OK ?

2. (4) Only answer (4) has a main verb (*is*). All of the other answers produce a sentence fragment because they have no main verb. OK ?

3. (4) The *to be* is not needed and does not fit with the verb *called*. OK ?

4. (3) The singular verb *is* is needed to agree with the singular subject, *Cash flow*. OK ?

5. (3) Only answer (3), which uses a prepositional phrase (*with high telephone . . .*) is correct. In all four other versions, the second half of the sentence is a fragment. OK ?

6. (1) The grammar in this version is correct, and it makes its point with fewer words than any of the others. OK ?

7. (1) The comma between the subject of the sentence (*finding*) and the verb (*was*) is incorrect. OK ?

8. (5) The sentence is correct as written. OK ?

9. (3) The verb *affect* means to *influence*. The verb *effect* means to *bring about*. OK ?

10. (4) The verb *raise-raised-raised* takes a direct object. The correct verb here is *rise-rose-risen,* which does not take a direct object. OK ?

11. (5) The sentence is correct as written. OK ?

12. (1) Unless the *Since* is removed, the sentence is not a complete sentence. OK ?

13. (2) The previous sentence is about small businesses (a plural), so the pronoun here must be plural (*they*) to agree with *businesses,* the word the pronoun refers to. The present tense (*employ*) is correct. OK ?

14. (1) The plural *were* is correct here, to agree with the plural *two types*. The past tense is needed because the sentence refers to a time *thirty years ago*.   OK   ?

15. (2) Although in answers (1), (3), and (5) the grammar is correct, answer (2) is the shortest and clearest version. Answer (4) is not a complete sentence. Answer (5) is also wrong because it changes from the past tense (*were*) to the present tense (*are*), which does not agree with the first verb.   OK   ?

16. (3) Answer (3) ends the first complete sentence with a period and begins a second complete sentence with *It*. Answer (2) or (4) would be right if there were a comma after *life*.   OK   ?

17. (3) Since *a buyer* is singular, the apostrophe to show possession must come before the final *s*.   OK   ?

18. (3) The subject of sentence is the singular *cost*. So the verb must be the singular *is* to agree in number.   OK   ?

19. (5) The revision changes the verb *is* (active) to *is given* (passive). The subject (*a whole life policy*) of a sentence in the active voice will become the object of the preposition *by* (*by a whole life policy*) in the sentence in the passive voice.   OK   ?

20. (5) The sentence is correct as written.   OK   ?

21. (3) The spelling error in the sentence leaves out the letter *i* from the word *administrative*.   OK   ?

22. (5) The sentence is correct as written.   OK   ?

23. (2) The sentence tests the use of the comma in a series. The comma after *Rocky III* may be used or it may be left out, but there *must* be commas after *Rocky* and *Rocky II*.   OK   ?

24. (4) The sentence tests your knowledge of what words in English belong together (idiom). We say something is *inferior to,* not *inferior from*. The verb *is* is in the correct tense (present) and number (singular). The comma after *not* is right. It sets off the introductory phrase.   OK   ?

25. (2) Though the word *prefer* has only one *r*, the *r* is doubled in *preferred*.   OK   ?

26. (4) The sentence tests subject and verb agreement. Since the subject (*making*) is singular, the verb must be singular (*is*). *Are* is the plural form.   OK   ?

27. (4) The error in the sentence is the incorrect spelling of *repetition*.   OK   ?

28. (3) The revision requires changing the verb from *were* (active) to *were made* (passive). Answers (4) and (5) cannot be correct because the sentence is in the past tense not the present or the future.   OK   ?

29. (5) The sentence asks a question (*would the studios go on making them?*) and so must end with a question mark.

OK ?

30. (2) The original sentences ask a question and clearly make you think that the answer is *no*. The revised single sentence needs a verb like *stop*, a negative word. The studios would not continue to make films if no audience paid to see them.

OK ?

31. (3) This sentence tests verb tense. *But as long as the public responds* tells you that the sentence is talking about an action that will go on into the future. The *there will be* in answer (3) is right because it is in the future tense. Answer (5) is in the future tense too, but it leaves out the comma that belongs after *responds*.

OK ?

32. (4) Answer (2) is wrong because it uses a comma where a semicolon is needed. Answers (1) and (5) use correct grammar, but they are more wordy than the original version. Answer (4) uses the conjunction *but*, which is logical after the *not* in the first sentence. Answer (4) is the clearest way of combining the two sentences.

OK ?

33. (2) The *n* is sometimes not heard when the word is spoken, but the correct spelling is *environmental*.

OK ?

34. (2) The punctuation is correct only in answer (4).

OK ?

35. (4) The adjective *bad* should be changed to the adverb *badly*. To modify the verb *are needed*, you must use an adverb.

OK ?

36. (1) The correct pronoun here is *who*. The subject form (*who*) is correct here because *who* is the subject of the clause *who have no health insurance*. The plural *have* is correct because *who* refers to the plural *people*. *Which* is also a pronoun, but *which* is generally not used to refer to persons.

OK ?

37. (5) The sentence is correct as it is written.

OK ?

38. (4) The error in this sentence is called a dangling participle. The sentence begins with *Hoping*, a participle, that is, a verb used as an adjective. *Who* is hoping, the bill or Senator Kennedy? The Senator, of course. To make it clear that the participle modifies the man, his name must come as close to the participle as possible. Answer (5) cannot be correct because a semicolon is like a period, and a sentence ending after *care* would be a fragment because it has no main verb.

OK ?

39. (3) Since the second sentence shows a contrast with the first, the best connecting word here is *but*. Answer (3) is better than answer (1) because it avoids the punctuation error and, by using the pronoun *it*, it avoids repeating the word *proposal*.

OK ?

40. (1) The comma here sets off the introductory words *For consumers*.

OK ?

41. (5) The sentence is correct as written.

OK ?

42. (3) The past tense verb *stood* is needed here. The comma sets off the introductory clause. *Has stood* describes an action that began in the past and is still going on in the present. For example, if the mill is still there, we would say, "The mill has stood for forty years." But in the passage, it is clear that the mill is gone.

OK ?

43. (2) Of the five first words, only *Although* which means *in spite of the fact that* logically introduces the second sentence, which describes a change for the better.

OK ?

44. (5) The sentence is correct as written. The phrase *the number* is singular and so the verbs (*has declined, has increased*) must also be singular. If *the numbers were used,* the verbs would have to be plurals (*have declined, have increased*). In each of the four changes, the subject and the verb do not agree.

OK ?

45. (3) There are a few exceptions to the *i* before *e* except after *c* rule, but *fields* follows the rule.

OK ?

46. (3) The possessive of the pronoun *it* is *its* without an apostrophe. With the apostrophe, *it's* means *it is*.

OK ?

47. (3) A semicolon is used in the same way as a period, and you should use it here to combine the two sentences. It is possible to use *and*, but you would have to put a comma between *industry* and *and*.

OK ?

48. (1) The original version is correct. The correct verb form is *were laid off* (past tense, passive voice); the comma is needed after *off*.

OK ?

49. (2) The noun *lesson* (something to be learned) ends in *on*. The verb *lessen* (to decrease) ends in *en*..

OK ?

50. (2) The sentence needs a comma after *egg*. Both commas and periods are placed inside quotation marks.

OK ?

51. (1) The comma after *cooked* is needed. In the first version, both *hard-cooked* and *hard-boiled* have a hyphen, as they should, and both have an *a* before them. Two items like this should be in the same form. You need to keep the word *egg* in order to make clear *what* is hard-cooked and hard-boiled.

OK ?

52. (4) The second phrase should have the same verb form as the first (passive)—*reduced, kept*.

OK ?

53. (1) The *eggs* are prepared, not *you*. To prevent this misunderstanding, *hard-cooked eggs* must follow *way*. The form of the verb in answer (5) is wrong. *Will take* (future tense) is right.

OK ?

54. (4) The pronoun and verb (*They have been*) must agree in number with the plural word they refer to, *eggs*.

OK ?

55. (1) The *to be sure* is the clearest and shortest revision.

OK ?

TEST 2: SOCIAL STUDIES

1. (4) The Fourteenth Amendment's equal protection of the law guarantees have been the constitutional basis for ending management practices that result in unequal pay for persons performing the same job. Notice that both the question and the correct answer use the word *equal* (*equal pay—equal protection*).

OK ?

2. (2) Though it is unusual for male workers to be paid less than female workers doing the same job, such a situation would violate the equal pay principle. In choices (1), (4), and (5) the pay is unequal, but the jobs are not the same. In choice (3), the pay and jobs are the same.

OK ?

3. (5) A second heavily populated area is in the Midwest and includes the cities of Cleveland, Chicago, Detroit, and many others. The other choices are sparsely populated areas.

OK ?

4. (3) New York is the country's largest city, and the largest in the northeast corridor.

OK ?

5. (5) Since the megalopolis would include large cities, suburbs, small cities, and small towns, as well as at least seven different states, there would be hundreds of different political bodies, all with different needs and interests. It would be very difficult for so many different administrations to agree on policies.

OK ?

6. (2) Air pollution would not respect city or state boundary lines and would be a problem all the communities in the area would face. The other options are sometimes problems, but each can be handled by an individual city, town, or state.

OK ?

7. (3) Allowing states to veto (that is, to block) national legislation is the only choice that limits the power of the central government. The other choices do just the opposite and reduce the power of the states.

OK ?

8. (1) One successful producer cannot alone produce an oversupply, but if all the farmers have larger than usual crops, there will be more corn than buyers, and the price of corn will fall. Corn prices *do* depend on supply and demand.

OK ?

9. (2) The United States President is elected. The Chief Justice and Attorney General are appointed by the President. The King of England and Prince of Wales are inherited titles.

OK ?

10. (1) The Attorney General, a Cabinet member, is appointed. The Pope, the President, and the Mayor of Chicago are elected. The Queen of England is an inherited title.

OK ?

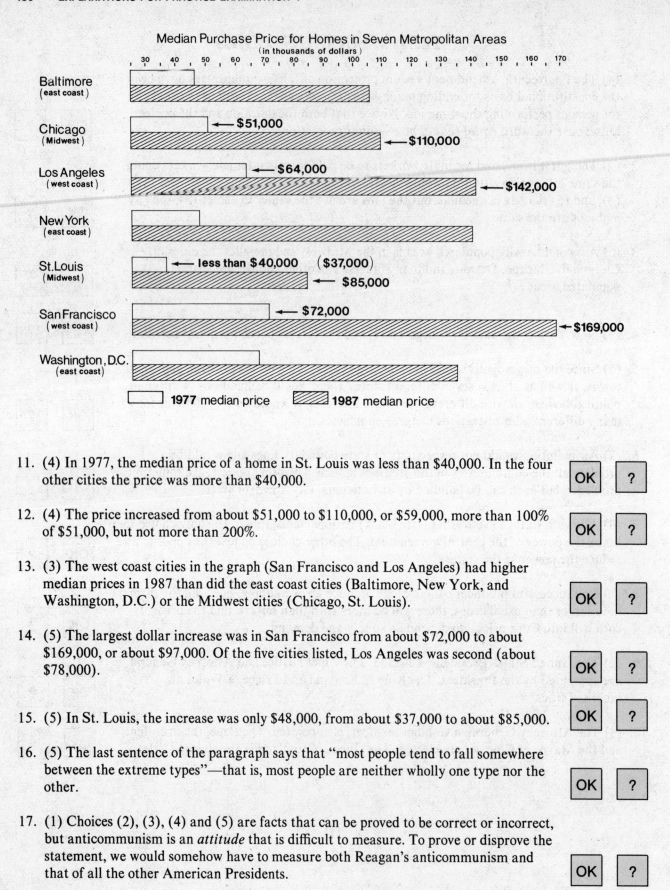

Median Purchase Price for Homes in Seven Metropolitan Areas
(in thousands of dollars)

11. (4) In 1977, the median price of a home in St. Louis was less than $40,000. In the four other cities the price was more than $40,000.

12. (4) The price increased from about $51,000 to $110,000, or $59,000, more than 100% of $51,000, but not more than 200%.

13. (3) The west coast cities in the graph (San Francisco and Los Angeles) had higher median prices in 1987 than did the east coast cities (Baltimore, New York, and Washington, D.C.) or the Midwest cities (Chicago, St. Louis).

14. (5) The largest dollar increase was in San Francisco from about $72,000 to about $169,000, or about $97,000. Of the five cities listed, Los Angeles was second (about $78,000).

15. (5) In St. Louis, the increase was only $48,000, from about $37,000 to about $85,000.

16. (5) The last sentence of the paragraph says that "most people tend to fall somewhere between the extreme types"—that is, most people are neither wholly one type nor the other.

17. (1) Choices (2), (3), (4) and (5) are facts that can be proved to be correct or incorrect, but anticommunism is an *attitude* that is difficult to measure. To prove or disprove the statement, we would somehow have to measure both Reagan's anticommunism and that of all the other American Presidents.

18. (1) A sociologist studies human interaction. The subject here is not politics, geography, or history. A demographer studies vital statistics, such as births and deaths, of populations.   OK   ?

19. (2) Since the wish for acceptance by a group leads to a "positive effort to conform," the desire to be accepted clearly does affect behavior. The other four choices give examples or possible results in accordance with the statement.   OK   ?

20. (3) The passage says nothing about the benefit or harm of conformity. Though choice (5) may be true, it is not, like choice (3), clearly stated in the paragraph. So choice (3) is the *best* choice.   OK   ?

21. (3) Since the tax will fall on states in which oil is produced, we can expect the states most likely to vote against the bill to be oil producing states like Alaska, Texas, California, Louisiana, and Oklahoma. At least one, and sometimes two, of the states in the incorrect options do not produce oil.   OK   ?

22. (4) The vote on a bill can be delayed by filibuster, the right of a Senator to hold the floor so long as he or she talks without interruption.   OK   ?

23. (4) Since a stratified society is the opposite of an egalitarian society, a stratified society would *not* have equal access to economic resources.   OK   ?

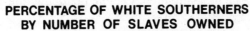

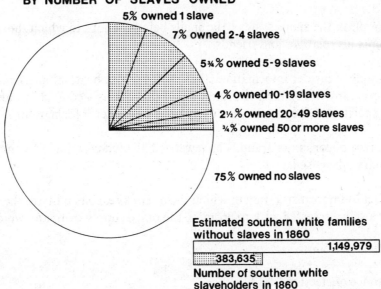

PERCENTAGE OF WHITE SOUTHERNERS
BY NUMBER OF SLAVES OWNED

5% owned 1 slave
7% owned 2-4 slaves
5¾% owned 5-9 slaves
4% owned 10-19 slaves
2½% owned 20-49 slaves
¾% owned 50 or more slaves

75% owned no slaves

Estimated southern white families
without slaves in 1860
1,149,979
383,635
Number of southern white
slaveholders in 1860

24. (2) Slaveowners make up 25% of the graph. Of these, the largest share is the 7% of all white southerners who owned two to four slaves. Those southerners who owned *no* slaves make up the largest part of the graph, but the question asks only about *slaveowners*.   OK   ?

25. (5) The smallest percentage is the three-quarters of one percent who owned fifty or more slaves.   OK   ?

26. (1) The small bar graph gives the number of families who did not own slaves as 1,149,979. Choice (2) is wrong because the small bar graph gives the number of slaveowners as 383,635, fewer than five hundred thousand (500,000). At first glance, you might think that choices (3), (4), and (5) are true. But notice that the percentages given are percentages of the *total number of white southerners,* not the *total number of slaveowners.*

27. (1) Of the 25% of the population who were slaveowners, 5% owned one slave and 7% owned two to four. Even if all of this 7% owned only two, there would still be more than half the slave owners who owned five or more slaves.

28. (4) Since there are two Senators from each of the fifty states, a quorum (one more than half the total membership) would be fifty-one.

29. (2) The quorum requirement will make sure that least fifty-one Senators are present before legislation can be passed. The other options are not true or have nothing to do with the purpose of a quorum requirement.

30. (3) To change the majority of the Senate from fifty-one to fifty-two would require an increase in the size of the Senate from 100 to 102. Of the five choices, only the admission of a fifty-first state would have this effect.

31. (4) Only in choice (4) does a person conceal his real feelings or motive (he invested his money in hope of earning more, not in hope of losing money). The tax deduction will not be equal to his loss.

32. (2) This is an example of the spoils system, the spoils being the jobs to which the mayor-elect appoints his relatives and friends.

33. (4) This is an example of insider information (that the land is to be developed) being used for personal profit by the banker. It could be said that this is a conflict of interest situation, but the specifics of the case more clearly refer to insider information.

34. (5) This is an instance of consumer fraud. The jewelry delivered was not of the high quality of the jewelry advertised.

35. (1) This is a conflict of interest situation in which the agent's responsibility to the city may conflict with a self-interested wish to promote the office supply company which he or she owns.

36. (3) This is an instance of election fraud.

37. (5) A single bank is the area of study of micro-economics. All of the first four choices are subjects of national or international importance.

38. (2) With such majorities in the House and Senate, the Democrats would be able to pass any legislation they could agree upon. But it does not follow that simply because their numbers are fewer that Republicans could not influence public opinion (choice 4).

39. (1) Though it is not certain, it is probable that in an election in which the Democrats won large majorities in the national election, the Democrats would do better in state elections than the Republicans. OK ?

40. (5) The investment in education, which gives no immediate reward, is expected to assure the daughter of a better future. OK ?

41. (1) Georgia is on the Atlantic Ocean just north of Florida. OK ?

42. (4) Alaska is further north than the area covered by this map. OK ?

43. (3) Missouri is in the Midwest, the central part of the United States, which is in the Central time zone. OK ?

44. (4) Since most American women do wear makeup, a woman who refuses to do so breaks no laws or mores, but does violate a folkway. OK ?

45. (4) The wish to assert one's individuality is a good reason for refusing to conform to norms. OK ?

46. (2) Unauthorized (illegal) surveillance (close watch kept on a person) of an individual is a violation of the right to privacy. OK ?

47. (3) If gasoline is expensive and in short supply, commuters will not be able to drive long distances to their jobs. As a result, homes will be in demand closer to the places of employment. OK ?

48. (2) The action is an instance of imitative (or sympathetic) magic, which is believed to work *because of* the Law of Similarity. OK ?

49. (3) The magic here is based on the Law of Contagion and assumes if the hair is destroyed, the enemy will also be destroyed. OK ?

50. (2) "Guns" is really another way of saying military priorities. Of the five choices, only the educational loan is an expenditure not related to the military.

OK   ?

51. (1) A low income person or family must spend all of its money. With sales taxes, nearly everything it buys is taxed. Income, property, and inheritance taxes are less likely to affect individuals earning less than $8,000 a year.

OK   ?

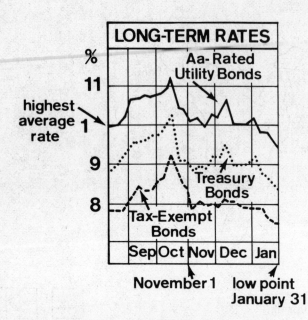

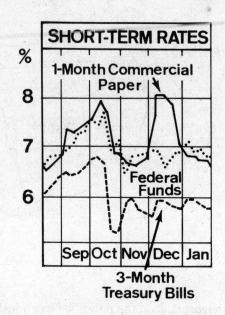

52. (1) The average rate for utility bonds was above 10%.

OK   ?

53. (3) November first is the perpendicular line before November.

OK   ?

54. (5) All of the long-term rates were at their lowest on January 31.

OK   ?

55. (2) Choices (1), (3), (4), and (5) could be easily proved or disproved, but what might happen in the future could continue as rumor because it cannot be disproved until the month is reached.

OK   ?

56. (5) Since people are more likely to accept a rumor that agrees with their beliefs, a Catholic, whose religion believes in the Virgin and the possibility of her appearances, is the most likely to accept this rumor.

OK   ?

57. (5) According to the poll, the rich and male are more likely to be active than the poor and female. The information about the young adults tells us about party preference but *not* about political activity.

OK   ?

58. (5) According to the poll, the poor, the Catholic, and the female are all less likely to be active than the rich, the Protestant, and the male.

OK   ?

59. (3) Choices (1), (2), (4), and (5) can all be supported by the data in the poll. Though we are told young adults are more likely than the elderly to prefer the Democratic party, we are *not* told that elderly people are more likely to prefer the Republican Party. It may be true, but the results of this poll do not make it clear.

OK   ?

60. (2) The first paragraph speaks of the threat of a lack of water to economic progress in the West.

OK   ?

61. (1) A "skirmish" is a fight or encounter. The law suits between California and Arizona are examples of the contests over river flows.

OK   ?

62. (1) That the rats appeared to associate the box with a length of time without food suggests that the environment (in this case, the feeding boxes) affects physical drives (hunger).

OK   ?

63. (1) Overgrazing would produce a situation where the land could not support all the animals. All of the four other options would *increase* the food supply.

OK   ?

64. (5) Though all of the advertising claims may be untrue, the F.D.A. is concerned with food, drugs, or cosmetics. There are no foods or drugs listed, and only the face cream is a cosmetic.

OK   ?

TEST 3: SCIENCE

THE EYE

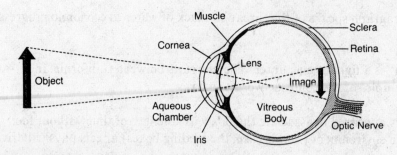

1. (4) The image of the object forms on the retina, a light-sensitive tissue which produces electrical signals to be sent on to the optic nerve. The purpose of the iris, cornea, and lens is to focus the light onto the retina so that a sharp image is formed.   OK   ?

2. (3) When the retina gets the image, it has been transposed (turned upside down). The optic nerve sends the image as it is to the brain. The brain makes the adjustment by transposing the image so that it is right side up.   OK   ?

3. (1) Because alcohol has a lower boiling temperature than water does, when the solution is heated, the alcohol boils first.   OK   ?

4. (4) The center of North America is prairie, in which grasses are the chief plants. This almost treeless region runs along the valley of the Mississippi River. East of the prairie lies forested land, while to the west are the desert plains.   OK   ?

5. (1) The information given with this question says that the "largest numbers of moose" are found in the "cone-bearing" (coniferous) area of "Canada and the northern United States."   OK   ?

6. (5) The tundra is the treeless Arctic region with a brief, cool summer. Such a cold area can support only small plants that are unusually resistant to low temperatures. The information tells you that the tundra has "bushes and other low-growing plants." "Mosses, lichens, sedges, and grasses" are all low-growing plants. Since the question did not mention any trees, you should have quickly decided against the first two answers.   OK   ?

7. (2) The deciduous forest is made up of oaks, maples, elms, and walnuts. Those broad-leafed trees turn bright red or yellow each fall, then lose their leaves for the winter. The coniferous forest is different; it has needle-bearing trees which are rightly called "evergreen."   OK   ?

8. (3) Plants must grow and flower to produce seeds to keep the species alive. The rare rainstorms in the desert require plants to reproduce quickly or die.   OK   ?

9. (1) The mixed forest contains some coniferous trees (pines, firs) and some deciduous trees (maples, oaks). So it is logical to decide the mixed forest is the area where the coniferous forest meets the deciduous forest. Since evergreen trees tend to live in colder regions, they would be found north of the mixed forest.   OK   ?

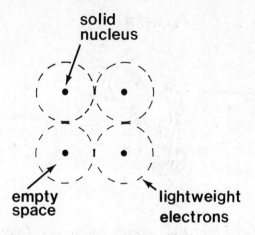

solid
nucleus

empty
space

lightweight
electrons

10. (5) As in any metal, and as the diagram shows, the gold atoms are touching, and so the alpha particles had to pass through the gold atoms. Since most of the particles passed straight through the foil, you can think of each gold atom as mostly empty space. We now know that an atom has a few electrons revolving around a very small nucleus.

OK ?

11. (5) The alpha particles that rebounded from the gold atoms must have hit something. The diagram shows a nucleus that is labeled "solid," so you can see that this is the most likely thing that could not be penetrated (gone through). Since only a few of the alpha particles rebounded, or bounced back, the core must be very small compared to the entire gold atom, as you can see in the diagram.

OK ?

12. (5) The palm tree is most truly independent. Green plants get their energy from sunlight and store that energy as sugar. Animals cannot be independent because they get their energy either by eating plants (as sheep do) or other animals (as codfish, cougars, and mosquitoes do).

OK ?

13. (3) The job, or function, of the lungs in a person is similar to the function of the gills in a fish. Human lungs allow oxygen from the air to enter the bloodstream. Almost all animals require oxygen to live.

OK ?

14. (3) Inside the aerosol can is the actual product and a compressed gas. That gas is stored under high pressure. Notice that the question mentions "pressurized" cans. Pressing the top button allows the gas to escape toward lower pressure in the surrounding air. As the gas escapes to the lower pressure it also pushes out the product (like cream or hair spray).

OK ?

	Eaten by monkey	Rejected by monkey
Insects of bright colors	23	120
Insects of dull colors	83	18

15. (3) It is to the advantage of each insect species to avoid being eaten. Many insect species have adapted to have bright colors for protection. Apparently many of their enemies (like monkeys) have learned that bright colors mean a bad taste. Even insects that don't taste bad to monkeys would find bright colors a helpful protection.

OK ?

FLOWER

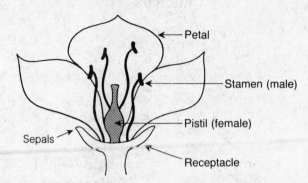

16. (2) The several stamens are the source of the male pollen cells. The bee gets coated with pollen as it enters and leaves the flower in search of nectar. It is logical that the pollen would be between the bee and the nectar.   OK   ?

17. (1) It seems that the wild sage has developed a trigger that dusts bees with pollen to have its pollen taken on to other sage blossoms. The trigger mechanism provides a good chance for cross-pollination.   OK   ?

18. (5) All lakes are gradually filling up with sediments. Rivers and streams wash particles of clay, silt, and sand into the lakes, where the particles settle in the still water. Choice (4) is incorrect because pollution is not a *natural* process.   OK   ?

19. (1) The paragraph mentions the simplifying of form as an example of regressive evolution. Whales have no hind legs but they developed from a mammal with two pairs of legs. The whale's streamlined body is simpler than its ancestor but better adapted to its environment.   OK   ?

20. (5) The change or mutation of a gene must be passed on to the offspring of a plant or animal if that characteristic is to be spread to the whole group.   OK   ?

21. (4) The paragraph says that "new species develop from unspecialized or simple forms" of animals or plants. Highly adapted animals like the dinosaurs rarely are the ancestors of new species.   OK   ?

22. (3) The paragraph says that "evolving depends on . . . isolation to establish new species." Isolation, such as that on islands, gives an opportunity for characteristics to concentrate and become established in a given population.   OK   ?

23. (4) All flies reproduce rapidly, but fruit flies have two additional advantages; they have genetic variations that are easy to see, like eye color and wing type, and they are small and easy to care for, growing happily in bottles of mashed bananas. Choices A and D would be good reasons *not* to use a species to study gene mutation.   OK   ?

24. (1) The high altitude of such land features is not evidence in favor of a shoreline origin. Instead, the high altitude of the features is a puzzle to be solved.   OK   ?

25. (3) Along the west coast of North America, earth movements have been slowly lifting the land upward for millions of years. Thus old shorelines that formed at past sea level have been lifted hundreds of feet above the present sea level.   OK   ?

26. (3) Since the magnetism is "produced by a powerful electric current," interrupting the current would cause the magnetism to disappear. Choice (2) is wrong because the magnetism is caused by any electric current that changes its strength or direction of flow.

OK   ?

27. (3) Habit requires repeating an event again and again. The rat runs through the maze a little faster as it learns by habit. The chimpanzee wants to eat the bananas, so its learning would be called problem solving or *motivation*. Both the rattlesnake (4) and the bird (5) behave by *instinct* without having to repeat the event. (A rat in an experiment is also often motivated by a reward at the end of the maze.)

OK   ?

Atoms	Electrons (charge of −1)	Neutrons (no charge)	Protons (charge of +1)
A	19	21	19
B	18	22	18
C	18	20	17
D	18	20	19
E	18	18	16

28. (2) Argon is atom B in the chart. Each element is defined by the number of protons in the atomic nucleus. The eighteenth element, argon, has 18 protons in each atom. In the same way, the last column of the chart reveals atoms of elements number 16, 17, and 19.

OK   ?

29. (4) The electrical charges on the three types of subatomic particles, as shown at the top of the chart, are electron −1, neutron 0, and proton +1. An atom with a positive charge has more protons than electrons, so the right answer is atom D (19 protons and 18 electrons). Atoms A and B are electrically neutral, because the number of protons equal the number of electrons. Atom C has a charge of −1, and atom E has a charge of −2.

OK   ?

30. (2) The information below the chart says that "isotopes of one chemical element have the same number of protons but a different number of neutrons." Only atoms A and D have the same number of protons (19). Also, the second column shows that their number of neutrons is different (21 and 20).

OK   ?

31. (3) The information below the chart says that the "atomic weight of an atom is the sum of the protons and neutrons." Here are the five atomic weights: A is 40, B is 40, C is 37, D is 39, and E is 34. The range from lowest to highest is 34 to 40.

OK   ?

32. (3) The question says, "Each new cell has the same chromosomes as the original cell." So there will be 24 chromosomes in each of the new cells.

OK   ?

33. (2) Electric power plants are the main source of sulfur dioxide pollution. Coal is the most common fuel in electric power plants, where the heat from burning the coal produces steam which is used to turn the electric generators. Some electric power plants burn oil or natural gas, which also yield sulfur dioxide fumes.

OK   ?

34. (4) Cholesterol could not be described as a toxic contaminant in foods. It occurs naturally in a wide variety of foods, so it is not a contaminant added during processing.

OK   ?

DISPERSION OF SUNLIGHT

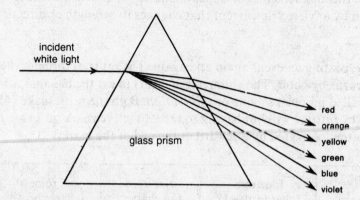

incident
white light

glass prism

red
orange
yellow
green
blue
violet

35. (5) White light enters the glass prism, but several colors leave the prism. The prism has separated white light into its basic colors, showing that white light is a mixture. Choice (4) is wrong because the experiment does not show any reflection of light backward.

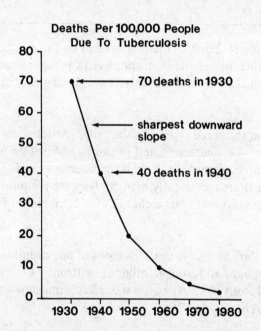

**Deaths Per 100,000 People
Due To Tuberculosis**

70 deaths in 1930

sharpest downward
slope

40 deaths in 1940

1930 1940 1950 1960 1970 1980

36. (1) The sharpest downward slope in the graph is from 1930 to 1940. This sharp slope shows the greatest decline (drop). By reading the numbers, you can see that the number of deaths dropped from 70 to 40, a drop of 30, which is greater than any of the other drops.

37. (2) We are thinking about two structures (the legs) which perform the same function (walking). Only the first two answer choices might be right, so we must decide whether the legs came from one ancestor. Since the two legs are so different in detail, there probably were two different ancestors. This is an example of *analogy*.

38. (1) The fact that the number and the arrangement of bones are the same could not be a coincidence. The two structures must be inherited from the front limb of a mammal that is an ancestor of both humans and whales. The relationship is best described as *homology*.

39. (4) This is a case of two animals of similar lifestyles and many structures which seem very much alike. Both animals live in water, they are streamlined for swimming, and they use fins and flippers to control their movements. These similarities have appeared despite their different ancestors. So this is best described as *convergence*.

OK ?

40. (2) The two wings both perform the same function, letting the animal fly. But the difference between the two wings is so great that there must have been different ancestors. The relationship is one of *analogy*.

OK ?

41. (3) Both the air bladder of a fish and the lungs of a snake developed from the air bladder of an ancestral fish. The two structures perform very different functions, depth control and breathing. The origin of the lungs is best explained as *transformation*. The word *transformation* means *change,* and the air bladder has changed into lungs.

OK ?

42. (5) The passage states that the great variety of mammals has come from one ancestor, the earliest mammal. So all the differences between mammals have developed with the passing of time. The origin of such differences is called *divergence*. It is the most obvious and basic feature of the evolution of life.

OK ?

43. (5) The two balls had the same shape but were of different weights. So Galileo discovered that the time of falling did not depend on weight. The experiments in a vacuum to avoid air resistance showed that feathers and lead balls fell at exactly the same rate.

OK ?

44. (2) Adaptation(s) described in choices (1), (3), (4), and (5) show the development of a feature that helps a plant or animal to perform better in its environment. Flowers need to be seen by bees for pollination. Some squirrels use flight to escape enemies. Scorpions defend themselves by stinging. Ducks use their feet to swim. However, a mole lives underground, and its eyes are almost useless; the eyes are explained as being inherited from some ancestor that lived on the surface.

OK ?

45. (2) The definition of a chemical element is that it cannot be separated into simpler substances. The burning of sugar to give carbon dioxide (CO_2) and water vapor (H_2O) shows that sugar must contain at least two simpler substances, carbon and hydrogen. The oxygen in those gases comes from both the air and the sugar.

OK ?

46. (1) Mice and people are not the same, so a chemical might affect them differently. The question asked for a *scientific* objection, but choice (3) concerns ethics and choice (4) concerns economics. Choice (5) is not right because all rodents are mammals too.

OK ?

47. (4) Sound travels as a pattern of vibrating molecules, so it does not use electromagnetic waves. The other four choices—light, microwaves, radio, and television—are all electromagnetic.

OK ?

48. (4) The chart shows the second largest amount of water is in ice near the North and South Poles. A warmer atmosphere would melt some of that ice, causing a rise of sea level. The theory that more carbon dioxide could cause that warming is called the Greenhouse Effect. Choices (2) and (5) could lead to a lower sea level.

OK ?

49. (5) Although most of the water is in the oceans, it is not useful because of the salt. The cost of removing the salt makes it, economically, a poor source for large amounts of water. The water of the polar ice caps is fresh but it is too far from the places it would be needed. Choice (5) contains all the major sources of fresh water.   OK   ?

50. (5) Once underground water is poisoned, it is almost impossible to clean up. Also the connections between underground resources are not well understood. While pollution is a problem in all water sources, it is easier to discover and clean up in surface waters. Because the question mentions the word *unseen,* you could decide on choice (5) because it is the only water source that we cannot easily *see.*   OK   ?

51. (1) The space shuttle could not land on the moon since the moon lacks an atmosphere to glide down on and a runway for landing. All the other choices given are regular functions of the space shuttle.   OK   ?

52. (3) Since the moon never had any living animals or plants, the first two answer choices are wrong. The age of the rocks was found by studying the radioactive elements in great detail.   OK   ?

ELECTROLYSIS

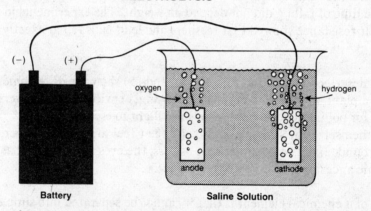

Battery   **Saline Solution**

53. (3) The question says that the cathode is negative (−). The diagram also shows that the cathode is negative and that the anode is positive (+). If you remember that charges that are alike repel each other and that charges that are different attract each other, you can see that the negative cathode will attract something that is positive. So the hydrogen must be positive.   OK   ?

54. (5) Each molecule of water (H_2O) contains two hydrogen atoms and one oxygen atom. So the decomposition of water gives exactly twice as much hydrogen as oxygen.   OK   ?

55. (1) Buoyancy is the power of a fluid to exert an upward force on any body placed in the fluid. The force equals the weight of the fluid moved out of the way by the body. When she gets into a swimming pool, she moves away water that weighs as much as she does, so she floats. Choice (3) is wrong because most of her body is below the surface.   OK   ?

56. (5) A boy and a girl cannot have the same genetic makeup because their sex chromosomes are different. They cannot be identical twins. The boy and the girl came from two separately fertilized cells, and that conclusion is definite rather than only probable.

OK   ?

57. (2) The five babies are not identical, so more than one egg cell must have been fertilized. Because the brief description of the babies given in the question suggests the babies fall into two groups, there must have been at least two egg cells that were fertilized by sperm. One egg cell could have divided into three cells, while the second egg cell could have divided into two cells.

OK   ?

58. (2) The question says that inertia means that a "moving object will continue moving in the same direction and at the same speed." A hockey puck sliding on ice is a fine example of the inertia of a moving object because the friction is so low it slows down very gradually.

OK   ?

59. (1) On some beaches, the wave action is just right to wash away the mud and sand, leaving the heavy gold particles behind. Without the sorting action of the waves, the percent of gold would be too low to be worth mining. The question mentions the gold deposits "inland," so choices (2), (3), and (5), which mention gold coming from the sea, are not good choices.

OK   ?

60. (3) The soft tissues would break down and disappear if decay bacteria were present. These bacteria exist wherever some oxygen is present, and those locations are near the air. The most isolated material of the five choices would be the mud at the bottom of a lake. The water and the mud would prevent air from reaching the organic tissues.

OK   ?

61. (5) The little parasites that live inside termites are able to break down cellulose into useful food. The third sentence of the paragraph says that the one-celled parasites are also called *protozoa*.

OK   ?

62. (3) Both creatures benefit from their association. The termite gets food from the cellulose that is digested by its tiny inhabitants. Those little parasites get much of their food from the termite. Such a relationship of benefit to both animals is called *symbiosis*.

OK   ?

63. (4) The simplest relationship is case B, where one gene controls one characteristic. Anything more complicated makes research much more difficult. Biologists have discovered that the complicated cases A and C are very common.

OK   ?

64. (5) The human body does not *need* caffeine. The second paragraph says that "caffeine is a nonessential [unneeded] chemical for human life. It is not a protein, fat, mineral, vitamin, or carbohydrate."

OK   ?

65. (5) Caffeine is found in some soft drinks—regular Pepsi-Cola is one of them.

OK   ?

66. (3) If research has shown that caffeine use has many negative side effects, then soft drink companies would fear a drop in sales of their soft drinks that contain caffeine. This potential loss of sales would force them to change their product and publicize the change.

OK   ?

TEST 4: INTERPRETING LITERATURE AND THE ARTS

1. (4) By line 8, it becomes clear that the writer has been referring to penguins since the beginning of the poem. `OK` `?`

2. (1) When the writer says "we do love penguins" (line 8) and goes on to describe what is attractive about them, she suggests that most people love penguins. `OK` `?`

3. (3) The first eight lines end with a question mark, and line 9, "They make us feel good about something," begins to answer that question. `OK` `?`

4. (1) The spies go to the Antarctic "to eavesdrop on [watch] what they [penguins] do there." `OK` `?`

5. (2) The writer is writing here about *us* (people—see line 5), so the *our* in line 7 also refers to people; *scant fondness* means *little* or *not much* fondness. `OK` `?`

6. (2) The author does not support violence in the excerpt, so (1), (3), (4), and (5) are not good choices. He does suggest, from line 33 on, that refusing to pay taxes is a good way to protest. `OK` `?`

7. (1) In lines 17–25, the author says that one who has experienced prison can more effectively *combat injustice*. `OK` `?`

8. (5) In lines 42–43, the author replies "If you really wish to do anything, resign your office." `OK` `?`

9. (2) In the first sentence, the author says that "the true place for a just man is also a prison" and later continues that these just men in prison are "put out and locked out of the State." So it is likely that the author believes that those who remain in the State (or government), not locked away in prison, are the unjust rather than the just. `OK` `?`

10. (1) Throughout the excerpt, the author is making the point that peaceful protest against the government can be effective in changing the government's policies. Here he says that the State "will not hesitate which to choose," and because of the author's belief, it is very likely that he is suggesting that the State will choose to "give up war and slavery" before it will allow all its just citizens to remain in prison `OK` `?`

11. (3) The whole excerpt speaks about the importance of taking personal action against injustice, and this statement ends by urging the citizen to "use your whole influence." `OK` `?`

12. (2) The last sentence says "When the subject has refused allegiance" (refused to be loyal—choice A) and "has resigned his office" (job—choice C), the "revolution is accomplished." The revolution is a peaceful one because refusing to be loyal and leaving a job are not violent acts. `OK` `?`

13. (2) Throughout the excerpt, the author seems to be speaking to citizens, encouraging them to protest government policies; you can see this best in line 25, when he says "Cast your whole vote," talking to citizens (voters) directly with the word "your." `OK` `?`

14. (2) The sentence that follows lines 77–78 talks about "unpopularity of modernist sculpture," which explains why the sculpture "lost . . . its audience." **OK** **?**

15. (4) The writer gives several examples of very different kinds of sculpture and by doing that emphasizes its variety. **OK** **?**

16. (5) The first sentence says that a *Parisian* or *New Yorker* (people) in *1886* (about a hundred years ago) would have said that sculpture was *statues* (choice 5). **OK** **?**

17. (1) None of the other choices is a logical or sensible meaning for this statement. **OK** **?**

18. (3) The writer says that "a sculptor could use any kind of junk" (lines 62–63) and goes on to identify the materials mentioned in this question as junk. **OK** **?**

19. (4) The third paragraph says that sculpture "wanted the liberty that painting had already claimed." Choice 2 is wrong because *popular need* means a need of the general public, and the sentence talks about only what *sculpture* wants. **OK** **?**

20. (3) In their first two speeches, both women are very polite, but by the time the scene ends, they are insulting one another. **OK** **?**

21. (5) The two women do all three of the things listed, and by changing the way they behave, they show the change in the way they feel (attitudes). **OK** **?**

22. (5) Each woman mentions a newspaper, an engagement announcement, a diary, and the ensnaring (entanglement, entrapment) of Ernest. But only Gwendolen refers to *moral duty* (line 24). **OK** **?**

23. (4) Cecily uses the phrase to tell Gwendolen that she is speaking plainly and truthfully and is not pretending that something is what it isn't. **OK** **?**

24. (1) Gwendolen pretends that Cecily's figurative language (She isn't really talking about a spade. She is talking about being truthful.) is literal (which would mean that she really *is* talking about a shovel). Gwendolen is suggesting that a person in her high social class would never come in contact with anything so low class as a spade. The effect of the line, and of the whole scene, is comic. **OK** **?**

25. (5) The speaker who gives friendly, if unromantic, advice to the lover is probably a friend. **OK** **?**

26. (4) Lines 2 and 5 are exactly the same in both the first and the second stanzas of the poem. **OK** **?**

27. (2) All of the sentences in lines 1–10 are questions. **OK** **?**

28. (4) Unlike the first two stanzas, the third verse of the poem has no questions and no repeated lines (A and B). But all three stanzas are addressed to the lover. **OK** **?**

29. (2) The friend argues, sensibly, that if the lover cannot win the lady when he is looking his best, then he will have no chance at all if he allows his love to make him pale and wan.   OK   ?

30. (4) The speaker says the woman who won't love should go to the devil, because nothing the lover can do will change her mind.   OK   ?

31. (5) *Do't* is a contraction for *do it*—that is, being speechless won't do it (win the lady). You don't have to know the meaning of *do't* to answer this question. You can try each of the answer choices in the line. When you do that, you will see that only *do it* makes sense.   OK   ?

32. (1) The lover, pale and speechless with love could be described as *romantic* or *sentimental* or *conventional* (doing what is expected), while the friend could be called *realistic* or *cynical* or *unconventional*.   OK   ?

33. (2) None of the other choices is a reasonable or logical interpretation of this statement. You might be tempted to choose (4) because a gun held in the firing position would sometimes obstruct the vision. But (4) is not the best choice because it is not likely that the gun would be held up all of the time.   OK   ?

34. (5) The sentence says that deer are "less accessible to [able to be reached by] hunters" in the winter than in the summer. So if the hunters can't reach the deer, they are less likely to shoot them in the winter and more likely to shoot them in the summer (5). Choice (3) contradicts information in the sentence; the sentence doesn't say anything at all about (1), (2), and (4).   OK   ?

35. (1) This is the only information actually mentioned in the article (lines 13–15).   OK   ?

36. (3) The writer tells us that "deer are capital [excellent] mountaineers," but not as capable as the mountain sheep (lines 16–24).   OK   ?

37. (5) None of the other choices is supported by the excerpt. It is logical that if the author is able to comment on more than one species of deer, he is familiar with more than one species.   OK   ?

38. (2) The excerpt mentions that the deer seeks "safe, hidden places" in the mountains (line 19).   OK   ?

39. (2) Since Mr. Nonell's *euphoria* follows soon after his *extravagant meal*, you can conclude that the lunch contributed to his happiness. You might think, also, that the drinks he had at lunch were responsible, but that is not one of the answer choices.   OK   ?

40. (4) In the second paragraph, we are told Mr. Nonell's conclusion that Matilde "had been taking a little tipple now and then" until "she had emptied it all by herself."   OK   ?

41. (2) This choice summarizes the meaning of the final sentence.   OK   ?

42. (1) The last paragraph says that Matilde had been an *ideal servant* for forty-seven years.

    <kbd>OK</kbd> <kbd>?</kbd>

43. (1) The first paragraph emphasizes how Mr. Nonell feels after his lunch with a friend, and the rest of the passage emphasizes what he thinks about the disappearance of the anisette.

    <kbd>OK</kbd> <kbd>?</kbd>

44. (5) Mr. Nonell suspects that Matilde has been sipping his anisette "in the belief that . . . Mr. Nonell was doing the same"; she does not know (he thinks) that Mr. Nonell has given up liquor.

    <kbd>OK</kbd> <kbd>?</kbd>

45. (5) Line 16 says that Mr. Nonell takes the bottle of anisette out of the formerly "well-stocked liquor cabinet," and the excerpt goes on to describe Matilde's "little tipple now and then." (line 29) "Tipple" is a word that is used for drinking liquor. So it is logical to decide that anisette is a kind of liquor.

    <kbd>OK</kbd> <kbd>?</kbd>

TEST 5: MATHEMATICS

1. (1) You should multiply 7 (the number of days John worked) by 5½ (the number of hours he worked each day) to find the total number of hours he worked.

$$7 \times 5\frac{1}{2} =$$

$$\frac{7}{1} \times \frac{11}{2} =$$

$$\frac{77}{2} =$$

38½

2. (3) Since angle R and angle T have equal measures (40°), the sides opposite them have equal measures. So RS = 5 yards. (An isosceles triangle has 2 equal sides.) To finds the perimeter (the distance around the triangle), we add the three sides:

$$8 \text{ yards} + 5 \text{ yards} + 5 \text{ yards} = 18 \text{ yards}$$

3. (1) You want to find how many groups of 16 it takes to make 400, so divide 16 into 400.

$$\begin{array}{r} 25 \\ 16\overline{)400} \\ \underline{32} \\ 80 \\ \underline{80} \\ 0 \end{array}$$

So it will take Alice about 25 days to do 400 invitations. If she starts on January 1st, she should be finished by about January 25th.

4. (3) Add 30% + 34% = 64% spent on rent, food, tuition, and books. Since the entire graph equals 100%,

$$100\% - 64\% = 36\% \text{ remaining}$$

You can also find the answer by noticing that after tuition, books, rent, and food are taken away, only two wedges of the graph are left. You can add the amounts in these two wedges to get the answer.

$$24\% + 12\% = 36\% \text{ remaining}$$

5. (5) To answer this question, you would need to know the height of the taller glass so you could set up a proportion. Because the height of the taller glass is not given, this problem cannot be solved.

6. (4) To find Jennifer's total sales, you could add together all the pounds she sold:

$$3 + 5 + 4 + 6 + 8 = 26 \text{ pounds}$$

Then multiply the 26 pounds by the price for each pound:

$$26(7.35)$$

Remember that 26(7.35) is the same as 26 × 7.35.

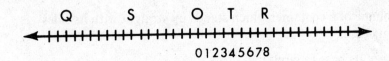

```
Q    S   O  T    R
012345678
```

7. (1) 0 is the origin of the number line, with positive numbers to the right and negative numbers to the left. So the right answer is R because it is 8 units to the right of 0.

8. (2) The square root of a number is a number which, when multiplied by itself produces the number. Example: The square root of 9 is 3 because $3 \times 3 = 9$.

$$4 \times 4 = \underline{16} \text{ and } 5 \times 5 = \underline{25}$$

So the square root of 22 must be between 4 and 5 because 22 is between 16 and 25.

9. (4) You want to know how many 45-cupcake groups it's going to take to make 350 cupcakes, so divide 45 into 350.

$$
\begin{array}{r}
7 \\
45{\overline{\smash{\big)}\,350}} \\
\underline{315} \\
35
\end{array}
$$

So you know that it will take you more than 7 hours but fewer than 8 hours (because only 35 is left over).

10. (4) Since the motorcycle is discounted 10%, the buyer will pay 90%. So you need to find 90% of $1000. "%" means *out of 100*, "of" means *multiply*, and "is" means =.

So if you want to use fractions:

$$90\% \text{ of } 1000 = \frac{90}{\cancel{100}_{1}} \times \frac{\cancel{1000}^{10}}{1} = 90 \times 10 = 900$$

If you want to use decimals:

$90\% \text{ of } 1000 = .90 \times 1000 = 900$

11. (3) The crew is to paint 81 miles in six days. To find the average number of miles they must paint per day, you need to divide 81 by 6.

$$
\begin{array}{r}
13.5 \\
6{\overline{\smash{\big)}\,81.0}} \\
\underline{6} \\
21 \\
\underline{18} \\
30 \\
\underline{30} \\
0
\end{array}
$$

12. (5) In order to find a correct answer to this question, you would have to know how many of the crew have less than five years of experience and how many have five years of experience or more. Since this information is not given, this problem cannot be solved.

13. (1) To find the volume of a container which stands up straight with its sides perpendicular to its base,

First find the area of its base (a circle):

pi times (radius)^2 [A = πr^2]

Then multiply this by its height. So

Volume = pi × (radius)^2 × height = 3.14(10)^2(12)

Reminder: Radius is the distance from the center to the circle (halfway across), and the formula for finding the area of a circle is

$$A = \pi r^2$$

pi, or π, is approximately 3.14

14. (3) Since the fabric was on sale at 10% off, this means that Deana paid 90% of the price.

90% of the price = .90 × $16.00 = $14.40

Reminder: "%" means *out of 100* and "of" means *multiply*. So

pattern + fabric + notions =

$3.50 + $14.40 + $4.75 = $22.65

15. (3) Since you need to find 15% of what the packages are worth, you could begin by finding their total worth:

$820 + $470 + $210 = $1500

And then find 15% of $1500 ("%" means *out of 100*, "of" means *multiply*):

15% of $1500 = .15 × $1500 = $225.00

Or if you prefer fractions:

$$\frac{15}{\cancel{100}_{1}} \times \frac{\cancel{1500}^{15}}{1} = \$225$$

16. (2) At the time she stopped mowing, Jean had mowed 15 out of the 45 minutes necessary to complete the job:

$$\frac{15}{45} = \frac{1}{3}$$

Reminder: There are 60 minutes in one hour, 30 minutes in ½ hour, and 15 minutes in ¼ hour.

17. (2) Substituting 4 for x, and 2 for y:

$3x^2 - 5y = 3(4)^2 - 5(2)$ $[(4)^2 = 4 \times 4 = 16]$
$\qquad\qquad = 3(16) - 5(2)$
$\qquad\qquad = 48 - 10$
$\qquad\qquad = 38$

18. (2) If we let

E = Erika's

Then   E + 8 = Tim's (Tim got 8 more inches than Erika did)

And   Erika's + Tim's = 36

So   E + (E + 8) = 36

$$2E + 8 = 36$$
$$\underline{-8 \quad -8}$$
$$2E \quad = 28$$

$$E = 14$$

Or

If they split the licorice rope evenly, they each would receive 18 inches. A difference of 8 inches is split, and half is added to Tim's and half is subtracted from Erika's.

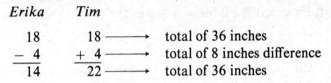

Erika	Tim	
18	18 ⟶	total of 36 inches
− 4	+ 4 ⟶	total of 8 inches difference
14	22 ⟶	total of 36 inches

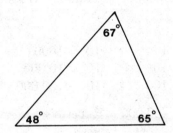

19. (2) The sum of the three interior angles of any triangle is 180°. So, to find the measure of the missing angle in this problem, you need to find out how many degrees you have already:

$$48° + 65° = 113°$$

And then you need to find out how many more degrees are needed to equal 180°:

$$180° - 113° = 67°$$

20. (2) To find the mean (average)

Add all values: $120 + 210 + 180 = 510$

Divide your total by the number of values (in this case, 3):

$$\begin{array}{r} 170 \\ 3\overline{)510} \\ \underline{3} \\ 21 \\ \underline{21} \\ 0 \\ \underline{0} \\ 0 \end{array}$$

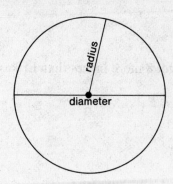

21. (1) RP = PQ = 14 cm.
    RP + PQ = 14 + 14 = 28 cm.

    RQ is the radius of the larger circle, so the diameter must be 56.

    Reminder: The radius of a circle is the distance from the center to the circle (halfway across), while the diameter is the distance all the way across the circle through its center.

    OK   ?

22. (5) *Quadruple* means to *multiply by 4,* so equation (5) describes this:

    Four times the number of silver dollars is $388.
    $$4 \qquad\qquad\qquad d \quad = \quad 388$$

    OK   ?

23. (4)

$10^0 = 1$	$10^3 = 1000$
$10^1 = 10$	$10^4 = 10,000$
$10^2 = 100$	$10^5 = 100,000$

    So $4 \times 10^5 = 4 \times 100,000 = 400,000 =$ Roberto's
    And $8 \times 10^4 = 8 \times 10,000 = 80,000 =$ Linda's

    And $80,000 \times 5 = 400,000$

    So   Roberto's (400,000) is 5 times Linda's (80,000).

    OK   ?

24. (5) *Triple* means *three times.*

    So
    $$m = \text{males}$$
    $$3m = \text{females}$$

    Altogether she had 48 puppies:

    $$\text{males} + \text{females} = m + 3m = 48$$
    $$4m = 48$$
    $$m = \frac{48}{4}$$
    $$m = 12$$

    So, if Abbey had 12 males, she must have had 36 females.
    $$48 - 12 = 36$$

    OK   ?

25. (2) There are 36 yellow gumballs out of a total of 78 gumballs, so the chance of getting a yellow gumball is 36 out of 78 or 36/78.

    OK

26. (4) The Pythagorean theorem states that given a right triangle with legs a and b, and hypotenuse c:

Using Russell's mileage

$$a^2 + b^2 = c^2$$
$$3^2 + 4^2 = c^2$$
$$9 + 16 = c^2$$
$$25 = c^2$$
$$5^2 = c^2$$
$$5 = c$$

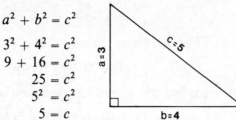

OK   ?

27. (4) *Median* means the *middle value* in a list which has been arranged in numerical order:

$$90, 85, \underline{84}, 77, 74$$

The list above is in descending order (highest to lowest). You may prefer ascending order (lowest to highest):

$$74, 77, \underline{84}, 85, 90$$

Whichever way you prefer, the answer is 84.

OK   ?

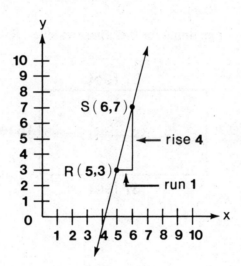

28. (3) Slope =

$$4 = \frac{4}{1} = \frac{\text{rise}}{\text{run}}$$

This means that for every unit you "run" to the right, you "rise" 4 units. So, if you begin at point R (5, 3) and run one unit to the right, then rise 4 units straight up, this will put you at point S (6, 7).

OK   ?

29. (4) Roy's roof has *15 hundred* (1500) square feet.

$$1500 \div 100 = 15$$

For each hundred Roy needs 3 bundles, so he will need

$$15 \times 3 = 45 \text{ bundles}$$

Because each bundle weighs 50 pounds, the total weight of the shingles will be

$$45 \times 50 = 2250 \text{ pounds}$$

OK   ?

30. (2) Fifteen bales of grass hay *at* $5 per bale means that you should multiply to get the total cost for grass hay:

$$5 \times 15$$

20 bales of alfalfa hay *at* $7 per bale is

$$7 \times 20$$

To find the total cost of grass hay *and* alfalfa hay, you need to add the two costs:

$$(5 \times 15) + (7 \times 20) = 5(15) + 7(20)$$

31. (5) Mike's commission is 8% of $3600. Remember that "%" means *out of 100,* and "of" means *multiply.* So

$$8\% \text{ of } 3600 = .08 \times 3600 = 288$$

32. (1) Dolores has 100 + 4 = 104 feet of materials. Therefore, the perimeter of her garden will be 104. (Remember that *perimeter* means *distance around.*) Dolores will have two sections that are 15 feet:

$$2 \times 15 = 30$$

This leaves 104 − 30 = 74 feet remaining for the other two sides. So 74 ÷ 2 = 37 feet for each side

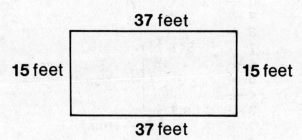

To check:

15 + 15 + 37 + 37 = 104

33. (3) You need to find how many 1¼'s there are in 17½, so divide:

$$17\tfrac{1}{2} \div 1\tfrac{1}{4} = \frac{35}{2} \div \frac{5}{4} = \frac{\overset{7}{\cancel{35}}}{\underset{1}{\cancel{2}}} \times \frac{\overset{2}{\cancel{4}}}{\underset{1}{\cancel{5}}} = 14$$

Or in decimals:

$$1\tfrac{1}{4} = 1.25 \qquad \text{and} \qquad 17\tfrac{1}{2} = 17.5$$

$$
\begin{array}{r}
14. \\
1.25\overline{)17.50.} \\
\underline{12\ 5} \\
5\ 00 \\
\underline{5\ 00} \\
0
\end{array}
$$

34. (3) If Frita weighs 9 pounds, then Duke must weigh 9 + 3 = 12 pounds. If Duke weighs 12 pounds, then Emily must weigh 12 − 4 = 8 pounds.

35. (4) Let's take a look at March 1st through March 10th.

Mon		Tues		Wed		Thurs		Fri Sat Sun		Mon		Tues		Wed	
15	+	15	+	15	+	15	+	13	+	15	+	15	+	15	= 118

36. (4) If you save 25%, then you pay 75%. This means that you want to find 75% of $140. ("%" means *out of 100*, and "of" means *multiply*.)

$$75\% \text{ of } 140 = .75 \times 140 = \$105.00$$

37. (4)

If   5½ cups ⟶ 2 loaves

Then ? cups ⟶ 100 loaves

Because 50 × 2 = 100, you will need 50 of these 2-loaf batches. In other words, you will need 50 × 5½ cups of flour:

$$50 \times 5\tfrac{1}{2} = \frac{\overset{25}{\cancel{50}}}{1} \times \frac{11}{\underset{1}{\cancel{2}}} = 25 \times 11 = 275$$

Or in decimals: $50 \times 5\tfrac{1}{2} = 50 \times 5.5 = 275$

38. (1) Substitute 2 for *x* and 11 for *y*:

$$w = 4x(y - 5)$$
$$w = 4(2)(11 - 5)$$
$$= 4 \times 2 \times 6$$
$$= 8 \times 6$$
$$= 48$$

Reminder: Do the math in this order (order of operations).

1. parentheses [do the work within them—for example, 6(2 + 1) = 6(3)]

2. powers (for example, $2 + 2^2 = 2 + 4$)

3. multiply and divide—from left to right (for example, 2 + 2 × 5 = 2 + 10)

4. add and subtract—from left to right (for example, 2 + 2 − 1 = 3)

39. (3) To find the average, first you add the four scores:

$$83.92 + 57.30 + 71.26 + 68.08 = 280.56$$

Then divide by the number of items you added (in this case, 4).

$$
\begin{array}{r}
70.14 \\
4\overline{)280.56} \\
\underline{28} \\
00 \\
\underline{00} \\
5 \\
\underline{4} \\
16 \\
\underline{16} \\
0
\end{array}
$$

OK   ?

40. (4) Note that the scale on the left says "thousands of dollars." So

$$1950 = 30{,}000 \quad \text{and} \quad 1970 = 45{,}000$$

$$
\begin{array}{r}
45{,}000 \\
-\ 30{,}000 \\
\hline
15{,}000 \text{ increase}
\end{array}
$$

OK   ?

41. (3) To find the surface area, you must find the area of each of the faces, then add them all together. Since each face is a rectangle, to find the area of each, we simply multiply its two dimensions:

top face $= l \times w$
right face $= w \times h$
front face $= l \times h$

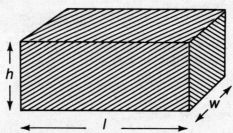

There is a bottom face to match the top face.
There is a left face to match the right face.
There is a back face to match the front face.

So we need:

$$2(l \times w) + 2(w \times h) + 2(l \times h) = 2(lw) + 2(wh) + 2(lh)$$

OK   ?

42. (3) To *deduct* means to *subtract,* so each of the two deductions need to be subtracted from J. Of course, when a bonus is received, this is added.

So $\qquad\qquad J - 30 - 107 + 50 = $ net pay

Note: *Net* means the *resulting amount*—in this case, "take-home" pay.

OK   ?

43. (2) Numeration is 10%. Algebra is 30%. This means that there should be three times as many algebra problems. So if there are 5 numeration problems, there should be

$$5 \times 3 = 15 \text{ algebra problems}$$

OK   ?

44. (5)

5 apples:	$5 \times .60 = \$3.00$
10 bananas:	$10 \times .20 = \$2.00$
4 cantaloupes:	$2 \times 1.00 = \$2.00$　(4 = 2 × 2 for $1)
5 oranges:	$\$1.00 + 2 \times .39 = \$1.78$　(3 for $1 and 39¢ each for the other 2)

To find the total we add:

$$\$3.00 + \$2.00 + \$2.00 + \$1.78 = \$8.78$$

OK 　 ?

45. (4) Since there are 12 daisies in a dozen, there are $3 \times 12 = 36$ daisies in three dozen. There were three times more yellow daisies:

$$\text{yellow} + \text{white} = 3(\text{white}) + \text{white} = 36 \text{ daisies}$$

So

$$4(\text{white}) = 36$$

$$\frac{\cancel{4}(\text{white})}{\cancel{4}} = \frac{36}{4}$$

$$\text{white} = 9$$

Finally, if there are 9 white daisies, there must be 27 yellow daisies.

$$36 - 9 = 27$$

OK 　 ?

46. (3) You need to find 12% of $48 ("%" means *out of 100*, "of" means *multiply*):

12% of $48 = $.12 \times \$48 = \$5.76 = \$6.00$ raise (to the nearest dollar)

Now add her raise to her wage:

$$\$48 + \$6 = \$54$$

OK 　 ?

47. (2) Slim buys a salad + beverage = $1.00 + .50 = \$1.50$. So he has left

$$\$3.05 - \$1.50 = \$1.55$$

The only combination that Slim can buy is the one in answer choice (2):

$$\text{soup} + \text{dessert} = .75 + .80 = \$1.55$$

Each of the other answer choices would cost more than the $1.55 that Slim has remaining.

OK 　 ?

48. (3) Since angle A and angle B form a straight line, their sum must equal 180 degrees.

So 　　　　　　　$A + B = 180$

And since A is twice B 　$2B + B = 180$
　　　　　　　　　　$3B = 180$

$$B = \frac{180}{3}$$

$$B = 60$$

Because $A + B = 180$, and $B = 60$, A must equal 120 degrees.

OK 　 ?

49. (5) $3y < 9$ will be true only when y is less than three.

$$\text{If } 3y < 9$$

$$\text{then } y < \frac{9}{3}$$

$$\text{or } y < 3$$

$$3(2) < 9 \text{ because } 6 < 9$$

Reminder: $<$ means *less than*
$>$ means *greater than*
$\leq$ means *less than or equal to*
$\geq$ means *greater than or equal to*
$\neq$ means *not equal to*

50. (3) When Nick makes the diagonal cut, right triangles are formed. To find the length of the diagonal cut, we must use the Pythagorean theorem:

$$a^2 + b^2 = c^2$$
$$9^2 + 12^2 = c^2$$
$$81 + 144 = c^2$$
$$225 = c^2$$
$$(15)^2 = c^2$$
$$15 = c$$

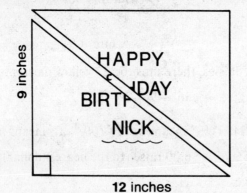

51. (2) If the dimensions of the square are 30 feet by 30 feet, then the distance to a side from the center is 15 feet. And if the walkway is 5 feet from the fence, and it is 3 feet across, that's 8 feet of the radius already spoken for.

So $15 - 8 = 7$ feet remain for the radius of the pool

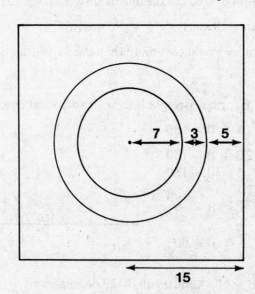

52. (4) To solve this, you need to find the hypotenuse (the footbridge) of the right triangle, using the Pythagorean theorem:

$$a^2 + b^2 = c^2$$
$$(6)^2 + (8)^2 = c^2$$
$$36 + 64 = c^2$$
$$100 = c^2$$
$$10 = c$$

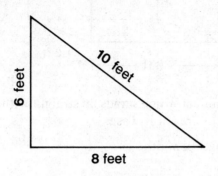

53. (1)

$$10^0 = 1 \qquad\qquad 10^4 = 10,000$$
$$10^1 = 10 \qquad\qquad 10^5 = 100,000$$
$$10^2 = 100 \qquad\qquad 10^6 = 1,000,000$$
$$10^3 = 1000$$

So $\qquad\qquad 4.85362 \times 10^5 = 4.85362 \times 100,000 = 485,362$

54. (4) Find 20% of $12,000:

$$.20(\$12,000)$$

Then subtract this discount from the original price:

$$\$12,000 - .20(\$12,000)$$

55. (4) The sum of the three interior angles of any triangle is 180°. So, if one angle is 60°, that leaves

$$180° - 60° = 120°$$

Because one angle is twice the other

$$\text{angle} + 2(\text{angle}) = 120°$$

$$\frac{3(\text{angle})}{3} = \frac{120°}{3}$$

$$\text{angle} = 40°$$
$$\text{and } 2(\text{angle}) = 80°$$

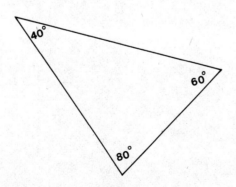

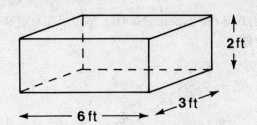

56. (1) To find the volume of a container which stands up straight with its sides perpendicular to its base, find the area of its base.

$$\text{length} \times \text{width}$$

Then multiply this by its height:

$$\text{Volume} = \text{length} \times \text{width} \times \text{height} = 6(3)(2)$$

OK   ?

GED

PRACTICE EXAMINATION 2

When you take Practice Examination 2, try to duplicate the test conditions by using only the time allowed.

TEST 1: WRITING SKILLS		
Part I: Multiple-Choice	55 questions	75 minutes
Part II: Essay	1 essay	45 minutes

TEST 2: SOCIAL STUDIES	64 questions	85 minutes

TEST 3: SCIENCE	66 questions	95 minutes

TEST 4: INTERPRETING LITERATURE AND THE ARTS	45 questions	65 minutes

TEST 5: MATHEMATICS	56 questions	90 minutes

Since this test is new, times and numbers of questions may be adjusted slightly in later testings.

Before you take Practice Examination 2, cut out the answer sheets and the lined essay sheets that you'll find following and use them to mark your answers. Use a single sheet of your own paper for scratch paper for your essay. On the actual test, scratch paper will be given to you along with the answer sheets.

Be sure to mark the answers for the test you are taking in the correct section of the answer sheet. For each test, find the "form" on your test booklet cover, and mark the circle corresponding to the form in the box labelled Test Form.

TEST 1: WRITING SKILLS - PART 1

TEST FORM

AA AB AC AD AE AF AG AH AI AJ AK AL AM AN AO AP AQ AR AS AT AU AV AW AX AY AZ
○ ○

1 ① ② ③ ④ ⑤   12 ① ② ③ ④ ⑤   23 ① ② ③ ④ ⑤   34 ① ② ③ ④ ⑤   45 ① ② ③ ④ ⑤
2 ① ② ③ ④ ⑤   13 ① ② ③ ④ ⑤   24 ① ② ③ ④ ⑤   35 ① ② ③ ④ ⑤   46 ① ② ③ ④ ⑤
3 ① ② ③ ④ ⑤   14 ① ② ③ ④ ⑤   25 ① ② ③ ④ ⑤   36 ① ② ③ ④ ⑤   47 ① ② ③ ④ ⑤
4 ① ② ③ ④ ⑤   15 ① ② ③ ④ ⑤   26 ① ② ③ ④ ⑤   37 ① ② ③ ④ ⑤   48 ① ② ③ ④ ⑤
5 ① ② ③ ④ ⑤   16 ① ② ③ ④ ⑤   27 ① ② ③ ④ ⑤   38 ① ② ③ ④ ⑤   49 ① ② ③ ④ ⑤
6 ① ② ③ ④ ⑤   17 ① ② ③ ④ ⑤   28 ① ② ③ ④ ⑤   39 ① ② ③ ④ ⑤   50 ① ② ③ ④ ⑤
7 ① ② ③ ④ ⑤   18 ① ② ③ ④ ⑤   29 ① ② ③ ④ ⑤   40 ① ② ③ ④ ⑤   51 ① ② ③ ④ ⑤
8 ① ② ③ ④ ⑤   19 ① ② ③ ④ ⑤   30 ① ② ③ ④ ⑤   41 ① ② ③ ④ ⑤   52 ① ② ③ ④ ⑤
9 ① ② ③ ④ ⑤   20 ① ② ③ ④ ⑤   31 ① ② ③ ④ ⑤   42 ① ② ③ ④ ⑤   53 ① ② ③ ④ ⑤
10 ① ② ③ ④ ⑤   21 ① ② ③ ④ ⑤   32 ① ② ③ ④ ⑤   43 ① ② ③ ④ ⑤   54 ① ② ③ ④ ⑤
11 ① ② ③ ④ ⑤   22 ① ② ③ ④ ⑤   33 ① ② ③ ④ ⑤   44 ① ② ③ ④ ⑤   55 ① ② ③ ④ ⑤

TEST CODE

Enter the test code from your test booklet. Then mark the circles below each box.

⓪ ⓪ ⓪
① ① ①
② ② ②
③ ③ ③
④ ④ ④
⑤ ⑤ ⑤
⑥ ⑥ ⑥
⑦ ⑦ ⑦
⑧ ⑧ ⑧
⑨ ⑨ ⑨

GO ON TO WRITING SKILLS - PART II

TEST 2: SOCIAL STUDIES

TEST FORM

AA AB AC AD AE AF AG AH AI AJ AK AL AM AN AO AP AQ AR AS AT AU AV AW AX AY AZ
○ ○

1 ① ② ③ ④ ⑤   14 ① ② ③ ④ ⑤   27 ① ② ③ ④ ⑤   40 ① ② ③ ④ ⑤   53 ① ② ③ ④ ⑤
2 ① ② ③ ④ ⑤   15 ① ② ③ ④ ⑤   28 ① ② ③ ④ ⑤   41 ① ② ③ ④ ⑤   54 ① ② ③ ④ ⑤
3 ① ② ③ ④ ⑤   16 ① ② ③ ④ ⑤   29 ① ② ③ ④ ⑤   42 ① ② ③ ④ ⑤   55 ① ② ③ ④ ⑤
4 ① ② ③ ④ ⑤   17 ① ② ③ ④ ⑤   30 ① ② ③ ④ ⑤   43 ① ② ③ ④ ⑤   56 ① ② ③ ④ ⑤
5 ① ② ③ ④ ⑤   18 ① ② ③ ④ ⑤   31 ① ② ③ ④ ⑤   44 ① ② ③ ④ ⑤   57 ① ② ③ ④ ⑤
6 ① ② ③ ④ ⑤   19 ① ② ③ ④ ⑤   32 ① ② ③ ④ ⑤   45 ① ② ③ ④ ⑤   58 ① ② ③ ④ ⑤
7 ① ② ③ ④ ⑤   20 ① ② ③ ④ ⑤   33 ① ② ③ ④ ⑤   46 ① ② ③ ④ ⑤   59 ① ② ③ ④ ⑤
8 ① ② ③ ④ ⑤   21 ① ② ③ ④ ⑤   34 ① ② ③ ④ ⑤   47 ① ② ③ ④ ⑤   60 ① ② ③ ④ ⑤
9 ① ② ③ ④ ⑤   22 ① ② ③ ④ ⑤   35 ① ② ③ ④ ⑤   48 ① ② ③ ④ ⑤   61 ① ② ③ ④ ⑤
10 ① ② ③ ④ ⑤   23 ① ② ③ ④ ⑤   36 ① ② ③ ④ ⑤   49 ① ② ③ ④ ⑤   62 ① ② ③ ④ ⑤
11 ① ② ③ ④ ⑤   24 ① ② ③ ④ ⑤   37 ① ② ③ ④ ⑤   50 ① ② ③ ④ ⑤   63 ① ② ③ ④ ⑤
12 ① ② ③ ④ ⑤   25 ① ② ③ ④ ⑤   38 ① ② ③ ④ ⑤   51 ① ② ③ ④ ⑤   64 ① ② ③ ④ ⑤
13 ① ② ③ ④ ⑤   26 ① ② ③ ④ ⑤   39 ① ② ③ ④ ⑤   52 ① ② ③ ④ ⑤   **STOP**

TEST CODE

Enter the test code from your test booklet. Then mark the circles below each box.

⓪ ⓪ ⓪
① ① ①
② ② ②
③ ③ ③
④ ④ ④
⑤ ⑤ ⑤
⑥ ⑥ ⑥
⑦ ⑦ ⑦
⑧ ⑧ ⑧
⑨ ⑨ ⑨

MAKE NO MARKS IN THIS AREA

0138622

TEST 3: SCIENCE

TEST CODE		
⓪	⓪	⓪
①	①	①
②	②	②
③	③	③
④	④	④
⑤	⑤	⑤
⑥	⑥	⑥
⑦	⑦	⑦
⑧	⑧	⑧
⑨	⑨	⑨

Enter the test code from your test booklet. Then mark the circles below each box.

AA	AB	AC	AD	AE	AF	AG	AH	AI	AJ	AK	AL	AM	AN	AO	AP	AQ	AR	AS	AT	AU	AV	AW	AX	AY	AZ
○	○	○	○	○	○	○	○	○	○	○	○	○	○	○	○	○	○	○	○	○	○	○	○	○	○

TEST FORM

1 ①②③④⑤	11 ①②③④⑤	21 ①②③④⑤	31 ①②③④⑤	41 ①②③④⑤	51 ①②③④⑤	61 ①②③④⑤
2 ①②③④⑤	12 ①②③④⑤	22 ①②③④⑤	32 ①②③④⑤	42 ①②③④⑤	52 ①②③④⑤	62 ①②③④⑤
3 ①②③④⑤	13 ①②③④⑤	23 ①②③④⑤	33 ①②③④⑤	43 ①②③④⑤	53 ①②③④⑤	63 ①②③④⑤
4 ①②③④⑤	14 ①②③④⑤	24 ①②③④⑤	34 ①②③④⑤	44 ①②③④⑤	54 ①②③④⑤	64 ①②③④⑤
5 ①②③④⑤	15 ①②③④⑤	25 ①②③④⑤	35 ①②③④⑤	45 ①②③④⑤	55 ①②③④⑤	65 ①②③④⑤
6 ①②③④⑤	16 ①②③④⑤	26 ①②③④⑤	36 ①②③④⑤	46 ①②③④⑤	56 ①②③④⑤	66 ①②③④⑤
7 ①②③④⑤	17 ①②③④⑤	27 ①②③④⑤	37 ①②③④⑤	47 ①②③④⑤	57 ①②③④⑤	STOP
8 ①②③④⑤	18 ①②③④⑤	28 ①②③④⑤	38 ①②③④⑤	48 ①②③④⑤	58 ①②③④⑤	
9 ①②③④⑤	19 ①②③④⑤	29 ①②③④⑤	39 ①②③④⑤	49 ①②③④⑤	59 ①②③④⑤	
10 ①②③④⑤	20 ①②③④⑤	30 ①②③④⑤	40 ①②③④⑤	50 ①②③④⑤	60 ①②③④⑤	

TEST 4: INTERPRETING LITERATURE AND THE ARTS

TEST CODE		
⓪	⓪	⓪
①	①	①
②	②	②
③	③	③
④	④	④
⑤	⑤	⑤
⑥	⑥	⑥
⑦	⑦	⑦
⑧	⑧	⑧
⑨	⑨	⑨

Enter the test code from your test booklet. Then mark the circles below each box.

AA	AB	AC	AD	AE	AF	AG	AH	AI	AJ	AK	AL	AM	AN	AO	AP	AQ	AR	AS	AT	AU	AV	AW	AX	AY	AZ
○	○	○	○	○	○	○	○	○	○	○	○	○	○	○	○	○	○	○	○	○	○	○	○	○	○

TEST FORM

1 ①②③④⑤	8 ①②③④⑤	15 ①②③④⑤	22 ①②③④⑤	29 ①②③④⑤	36 ①②③④⑤	43 ①②③④⑤
2 ①②③④⑤	9 ①②③④⑤	16 ①②③④⑤	23 ①②③④⑤	30 ①②③④⑤	37 ①②③④⑤	44 ①②③④⑤
3 ①②③④⑤	10 ①②③④⑤	17 ①②③④⑤	24 ①②③④⑤	31 ①②③④⑤	38 ①②③④⑤	45 ①②③④⑤
4 ①②③④⑤	11 ①②③④⑤	18 ①②③④⑤	25 ①②③④⑤	32 ①②③④⑤	39 ①②③④⑤	STOP
5 ①②③④⑤	12 ①②③④⑤	19 ①②③④⑤	26 ①②③④⑤	33 ①②③④⑤	40 ①②③④⑤	
6 ①②③④⑤	13 ①②③④⑤	20 ①②③④⑤	27 ①②③④⑤	34 ①②③④⑤	41 ①②③④⑤	
7 ①②③④⑤	14 ①②③④⑤	21 ①②③④⑤	28 ①②③④⑤	35 ①②③④⑤	42 ①②③④⑤	

TEST 5: MATHEMATICS

Enter the test code from your test booklet. Then mark the circles below each box.

TEST CODE		
⓪	⓪	⓪
①	①	①
②	②	②
③	③	③
④	④	④
⑤	⑤	⑤
⑥	⑥	⑥
⑦	⑦	⑦
⑧	⑧	⑧
⑨	⑨	⑨

AA	AB	AC	AD	AE	AF	AG	AH	AI	AJ	AK	AL	AM	AN	AO	AP	AQ	AR	AS	AT	AU	AV	AW	AX	AY	AZ
○	○	○	○	○	○	○	○	○	○	○	○	○	○	○	○	○	○	○	○	○	○	○	○	○	○

TEST FORM

1 ①②③④⑤	9 ①②③④⑤	17 ①②③④⑤	25 ①②③④⑤	33 ①②③④⑤	41 ①②③④⑤	49 ①②③④⑤
2 ①②③④⑤	10 ①②③④⑤	18 ①②③④⑤	26 ①②③④⑤	34 ①②③④⑤	42 ①②③④⑤	50 ①②③④⑤
3 ①②③④⑤	11 ①②③④⑤	19 ①②③④⑤	27 ①②③④⑤	35 ①②③④⑤	43 ①②③④⑤	51 ①②③④⑤
4 ①②③④⑤	12 ①②③④⑤	20 ①②③④⑤	28 ①②③④⑤	36 ①②③④⑤	44 ①②③④⑤	52 ①②③④⑤
5 ①②③④⑤	13 ①②③④⑤	21 ①②③④⑤	29 ①②③④⑤	37 ①②③④⑤	45 ①②③④⑤	53 ①②③④⑤
6 ①②③④⑤	14 ①②③④⑤	22 ①②③④⑤	30 ①②③④⑤	38 ①②③④⑤	46 ①②③④⑤	54 ①②③④⑤
7 ①②③④⑤	15 ①②③④⑤	23 ①②③④⑤	31 ①②③④⑤	39 ①②③④⑤	47 ①②③④⑤	55 ①②③④⑤
8 ①②③④⑤	16 ①②③④⑤	24 ①②③④⑤	32 ①②③④⑤	40 ①②③④⑤	48 ①②③④⑤	56 ①②③④⑤

STOP

Write the letter of your essay topic in the box, then shade the corresponding circle.

TOPIC Ⓐ Ⓑ Ⓒ Ⓓ Ⓔ Ⓕ Ⓖ Ⓗ Ⓘ Ⓙ Ⓚ Ⓛ Ⓜ Ⓝ Ⓞ Ⓟ Ⓠ Ⓡ Ⓢ Ⓣ Ⓤ Ⓥ Ⓦ Ⓧ Ⓨ Ⓩ

Continue your essay on next page

USE A BALL POINT PEN TO WRITE YOUR ESSAY

TEST 1: WRITING SKILLS, PART I

Tests of General Educational Development

Directions

The Writing Skills Test is intended to measure your ability to use clear and effective English. It is a test of English as it should be written, not as it might be spoken. This test includes both multiple-choice questions and an essay. These directions apply only to the multiple-choice section; a separate set of directions is given for the essay.

The multiple-choice section consists of paragraphs with numbered sentences. Some of the sentences contain errors in sentence structure, usage, or mechanics (spelling, punctuation, and capitalization). After reading the numbered sentences, answer the multiple-choice questions that follow. Some questions refer to sentences that are correct as written. The best answer for these questions is the one which leaves the sentence as originally written. The best answer for some questions is the one which produces a sentence that is consistent with the verb tense and point of view used throughout the paragraph.

You should spend no more than 75 minutes on the multiple-choice questions and 45 minutes on your essay. Work carefully, but do not spend too much time on any one question. You may begin working on the essay part of this test as soon as you complete the multiple-choice section.

Do not mark in this test booklet. Record your answers on the separate answer sheet provided. Be sure that all requested information is properly recorded on the answer sheet.

To record your answers, mark one numbered space on the answer sheet beside the number that corresponds to the question in the test booklet.

FOR EXAMPLE:

Sentence 1: **We were all honored to meet governor Phillips.**

What correction should be made to this sentence?

(1) insert a comma after <u>honored</u>
(2) change the spelling of <u>honored</u> to <u>honered</u>
(3) change <u>governor</u> to <u>Governor</u>
(4) replace <u>were</u> with <u>was</u>
(5) no correction is necessary   

In this example, the word "governor" should be capitalized; therefore, answer space 3 would be marked on the answer sheet.

Do not rest the point of your pencil on the answer sheet while you are considering your answer. Make no stray or unnecessary marks. If you change an answer, erase your first mark completely. Mark only one answer space for each question; multiple answers will be scored as incorrect. Do not fold or crease your answer sheet. All test materials must be returned to the test administrator.

Directions: Choose the one best answer to each item.

Items 1 to 6 refer to the following paragraph.

(1) Recently, mutual funds have become an increasing popular investment. (2) With five hundred to one thousand dollars to invest, you can choose from a broad range of investment possibilities. (3) For example, you could invest in precious metals, tax-free bonds, mortgage securities, or over-the-counter stocks. (4) The interest rate you receive depends on how much that funds securities are earning. (5) Some funds specialize in only one kind of security or industry, most offer a variety and, therefore, a means to minimize your risk. (6) If your fund is sold by an investment group that offers several types of funds, one can usually move money from one fund to another to take advantage of changes in market conditions.

1. Sentence 1: **Recently, mutual funds have become an increasing popular investment.**

Which of the following is the best way to write the underlined portion of this sentence? If you think the original is the best way, choose option (1).

(1) an increasing popular
(2) a increasing popular
(3) increasing and popular
(4) an increasingly and popular
(5) an increasingly popular

2. Sentence 2: **With five hundred to one thousand dollars to invest, you can choose from a broad range of investment possibilities.**

What correction should be made to this sentence?

(1) change to invest to for investing
(2) remove the comma after invest
(3) change the spelling of choose to chose
(4) change possibilities to possibility
(5) no correction is necessary

3. Sentences 2 and 3: **With five hundred to one thousand dollars to invest, you can choose from a broad range of investment possibilities. For example, you could invest in precious metals, tax-free bonds, mortgage securities, or over-the-counter stocks.**

The most effective combination of sentences 2 and 3 would include which of the following groups of words?

(1) possibilities, for example, you could
(2) possibilities; for example, you could
(3) possibilities, including, for example,
(4) possibilities; and these include, for example,
(5) possibilities, and these would include

4. Sentence 4: **The interest rate you receive depends on how much <u>that funds securities are</u> earning.**

   Which of the following is the best way to write the underlined portion of this sentence? If you think the original is the best way, choose option (1).

   (1) that funds securities are
   (2) that funds securities is
   (3) that funds' securities are
   (4) that fund's securities are
   (5) that fund's securities is

5. Sentence 5: **Some funds specialize in only one kind of security or industry, most offer a variety and, therefore, a means to minimize your risk.**

   What correction should be made to this sentence?

   (1) move <u>only</u> to before <u>in</u>
   (2) insert a comma after <u>security</u>
   (3) remove the comma after <u>industry</u>
   (4) insert a <u>but</u> before <u>most</u>
   (5) no correction is necessary

6. Sentence 6: **If your fund is sold by an investment group that offers several types of funds, one can usually move money from one fund to another to take advantage of changes in market conditions.**

   What correction should be made to this sentence?

   (1) change <u>is sold</u> to <u>has been sold</u>
   (2) change <u>offers</u> to <u>offer</u>
   (3) change the comma after <u>funds</u> to a semicolon
   (4) change <u>one</u> to <u>you</u>
   (5) no correction is necessary

Items 7 to 12 refer to the following paragraph.

(1) One popular type of fund is the money market mutual fund. (2) It may invest in a variety of securities or in only one type, such as treasury bills. (3) Like with a money market deposit account, you can withdraw your money without penalty at any time. (4) You can also write checks, usually for a minimum amount, such as $250. (5) But one shall keep in mind that your money may not be protected by federal insurance in this type of fund. (6) Since mutual funds are required by law to declare its investment policies, you can use these statements to select funds that match your investment goals. (7) You can buy mutual funds either through brokers or mutual fund corporations directly.

7. Sentences 1 and 2: **One popular type of fund is the money market mutual fund. It may invest in a variety of securities or in only one type, such as treasury bills.**

The most effective combination of sentences 1 and 2 would include which of the following groups of words?

(1) One of the popular types of fund is the
(2) A type of fund that is popular is the
(3) A popular fund is the
(4) One popular type of fund, the money market mutual fund
(5) One popular type, which is the money market mutual fund

8. Sentence 3: **Like with a money market deposit account, you can withdraw your money without penalty at any time.**

What correction should be made to this sentence?

(1) change Like to As
(2) change you to one
(3) change your to one's
(4) insert any after without
(5) no correction is necessary

9. Sentence 4: **You can also write checks, usually for a minimum amount, such as $250.**

What correction should be made to this sentence?

(1) change can to could
(2) remove the comma after checks
(3) change minimum to minimal
(4) change the spelling of amount to ammount
(5) no correction is necessary

10. Sentence 5: **But one shall keep in mind that your money may not be protected by federal insurance in this type of fund.**

    Which of the following is the best way to write the underlined portion of this sentence? If you think the original is the best way, choose option (1).

    (1) But one shall keep in mind
    (2) But, one shall keep in mind
    (3) But, one should keep in mind
    (4) But you should keep in mind
    (5) But you shall keep in mind

11. Sentence 6: **Since mutual funds are required by law to declare its investment policies, you can use these statements to select funds that match your investment goals.**

    What correction should be made to this sentence?

    (1) change its to their
    (2) change the comma after policies to a semicolon
    (3) remove the comma after policies
    (4) change your to one's
    (5) no correction is necessary

12. Sentence 7: **You can buy mutual funds either through brokers or mutual fund corporations directly.**

    Which of the following is the best way to write the underlined portion of this sentence? If you think the original is the best way, choose option (1).

    (1) either through brokers or mutual fund corporations
    (2) either through brokers or you can buy through mutual fund corporations
    (3) through either brokers or through mutual fund corporations
    (4) either through broker or mutual fund corporation
    (5) through either brokers or mutual fund corporations

Items 13 to 24 refer to the following paragraphs.

(1) You must be sixty-two years old to qualify for the Social Security retirement benefits you have earned, but most workers do not begin to receive they're benefits until they are sixty-five. (2) If you retire earlier and elect to collect Social Security at sixty-two, your benefits will be lesser. (3) Usually, a person must have worked for ten years to qualify for benefits. (4) The Social Security office can provide an estimate of the amount you received if you are approaching retirement age. (5) This estimate will not include whatever additional contributions you will make between the time your estimate is figured and the time of your retirement.

(6) If you have an income from investments retirement funds, or any sources other than a paying job or self-employment your Social Security benefits will not be affected. (7) It may, however, be subject to income taxes, at least in part. (8) If your gross income exceed a certain amount, a portion of your Social Security payment will be taxed. (9) And if you return to work after you've begun to receive benefits, you will loose one dollar in benefits for every two dollars you earn above a certain amount. (10) Currently, for a worker over sixty-five, this limit is $7,320. (11) For someone under sixty-five, $5,400. (12) If your over seventy, you can earn as much as you like without any reduction in Social Security benefits.

13. Sentence 1: **You must be sixty-two years old to qualify for the Social Security retirement benefits you have earned, but most workers do not begin to receive they're benefits until they are sixty-five.**

    What correction should be made to this sentence?

    (1) change have earned to will have earned
    (2) omit the comma after earned
    (3) change the spelling of receive to recieve
    (4) change they're to their
    (5) no correction is necessary

14. Sentence 2: **If you retire earlier and elect to collect Social Security at sixty-two, your benefits will be lesser.**

    Which of the following is the best way to write the underlined portion of this sentence? If you think the original is the best way, choose option (1).

    (1) sixty-two, your benefits will be lesser.
    (2) sixty-two, then your benefits will be lesser.
    (3) sixty-two your benefits are less.
    (4) sixty-two your benefits will be less.
    (5) sixty-two, your benefits will be smaller.

15. Sentence 3: **Usually, a person must have worked for ten years to qualify for benefits.**

    Which of the following is the best way to write the underlined portion of this sentence? If you think the original is the best way, choose option (1).

    (1) Usually, a person must have worked
    (2) Usually, a person must be working
    (3) Usually, you must have worked
    (4) Usually, you must work
    (5) Usually, you work

16. Sentence 4: **The Social Security office can provide an estimate of the amount you received if you are approaching retirement age.**

    What correction should be made to this sentence?

    (1) change can provide to provides
    (2) change received to receive
    (3) change received to will receive
    (4) change are approaching to approach
    (5) no correction is necessary

17. Sentence 5: **This estimate will not include whatever additional contributions you will make between the time your estimate is figured and the time of your retirement.**

    What correction should be made to this sentence?

    (1) change will not include to do not include
    (2) change you will make to you are making
    (3) change is figured to was being figured
    (4) change your retirement to you retiring
    (5) no correction is necessary

18. Sentence 6: **If you have an income from investments retirement funds, or any sources other than a paying job or self-employment your Social Security benefits will not be affected.**

    What correction should be made to this sentence?

    (1) insert commas after investments and self-employment
    (2) remove the comma after funds
    (3) insert a semicolon after self-employment
    (4) change the period to a question mark
    (5) no correction is necessary

19. Sentence 7. **It may, however, be subject to income taxes, at least in part.**

    Which of the following is the best way to write the underlined portion of this sentence? If you think the original is the best way, choose option (1).

    (1) It may, however, be
    (2) However, it may be
    (3) It may be however,
    (4) They may, however, be
    (5) However they may be

20. Sentence 8: **If your gross income exceed a certain amount, a portion of your Social Security payment will be taxed.**

    What correction should be made to this sentence?

    (1) change your to one's
    (2) change exceed to exceeds
    (3) omit the comma after amount
    (4) change will be to is
    (5) no correction is necessary

21. Sentence 9: **And if you return to work after you've begun to receive benefits, you will loose one dollar in benefits for every two dollars you earn above a certain amount.**

    What correction should be made to this sentence?

    (1) omit the And
    (2) change you've to you
    (3) change the spelling of loose to lose
    (4) change every to each
    (5) no correction is necessary

22. Sentence 10: **Currently, for a worker over sixty-five, this limit is $7,320.**

    Which of the following is the best way to write the underlined portion of this sentence? If you think the original is the best way, choose option (1).

    (1) Currently, for a worker over
    (2) Currently for a worker over
    (3) For a worker currently over
    (4) For a worker currently above
    (5) For a worker, currently above

23. Sentence 11: **For someone under sixty-five, $5,400.**

    What correction should be made to this sentence?

    (1) add who is after someone
    (2) change the comma to a colon
    (3) add it is after sixty-five
    (4) remove the comma after sixty-five
    (5) no correction is necessary

24. Sentence 12: **If your over seventy, you can earn as much as you like without any reduction in Social Security benefits.**

    What correction should be made to this sentence?

    (1) change your to a person is
    (2) change your to you're
    (3) insert money after as much
    (4) change you like to one likes
    (5) no correction is necessary

Items 25 to 32 refer to the following paragraph.

(1) In 1952, when Kate Nelson and Jane Gilbertson began their work as independent architects, woman in the profession were as rare in San Diego as high-rise buildings. (2) There are many more tall buildings now. (3) But women architects are still scarce. (4) Less than seven percent of the 50,000 current members of the American Institute of Architects were female. (5) The new formed Nelson-Gilbertson company is one of a very small number of women-owned architecture firms in California. (6) It has, however already begun work on several large projects with a value of more than twenty-five million dollars. (7) Nelson had owned her own company for ten years before she teamed with Gilbertson. (8) Gilbertson, one of the first black women architects to practice in the United States and a fellow of the American Institute of Architects. (9) The new firm's projects include the San Diego center, a large retail complex two shopping malls in Oceanside, and a high school in Long Beach. (10) "Though the profession is still dominated by males," Nelson said, "it is possible for a woman to find a place."

25. Sentence 1: **In 1952, when Kate Nelson and Jane Gilbertson began their work as independent architects, woman in the profession were as rare in San Diego as high-rise buildings.**

What correction should be made to this sentence?

(1) remove the comma after 1952
(2) replace their with there
(3) change the spelling of independent to independant
(4) change woman to women
(5) no correction is necessary

26. Sentences 2 and 3: **There are many more tall buildings now. But women architects are still scarce.**

The most effective combination of sentences 2 and 3 would include which of the following groups of words?

(1) tall buildings now and women
(2) tall buildings now, women
(3) tall buildings, now women
(4) tall buildings now, but women
(5) tall buildings now, and women

27. Sentence 4: **Less than seven percent of the 50,000 current members of the American Institute of Architects were female.**

What correction should be made to this sentence?

(1) change than to then
(2) change the spelling of current to currant
(3) change Architects to architects
(4) change were to are
(5) no correction is necessary

28. Sentence 5: **The new formed Nelson-Gilbertson company is one of a very small number of women-owned architecture firms in California.**

What correction should be made to this sentence?

(1) change new to newly
(2) change is to are
(3) insert the after number of
(4) change in to of
(5) no correction is necessary

29. Sentence 6: **It has, however already begun work on several large projects with a value of more than twenty-five million dollars.**

Which of the following is the best way to write the underlined portion of this sentence? If you think the original is the best way, choose option (1).

(1) It has, however already
(2) It has, however, already
(3) However it has already
(4) It, however has already
(5) Already, however it has

30. Sentence 7: **Nelson had owned her own company for ten years before she teamed with Gilbertson.**

What correction should be made to this sentence?

(1) change had owned to has owned
(2) change had owned to having owned
(3) change had owned to will have owned
(4) change teamed to teams
(5) no correction is necessary

31. Sentence 8: **Gilbertson, one of the first black women architects to practice in the United States and a fellow of the American Institute of Architects.**

What correction should be made to this sentence?

(1) replace the comma after Gilbertson with is
(2) remove the comma after Gilbertson
(3) change to practice to to have practiced
(4) insert a comma after practice
(5) no correction is necessary

32. Sentence 9: **The new firm's projects include the San Diego Center, a large retail complex two shopping malls in Oceanside, and a high school in Long Beach.**

What correction should be made to this sentence?

(1) change firm's to firms'
(2) remove the comma after Center
(3) insert a comma after complex
(4) remove the comma after Oceanside
(5) no correction is necessary

Items 33 to 40 refer to the following paragraph.

(1) With consumer's increasingly concerned about calories, it is no surprise that poultry and beef producers have developed lower calorie products. (2) Like the makers of light beer, light maple syrup, or light mayonnaise, low-fat beef and low-fat chicken are appearing more and more in supermarkets and on restaurant menus. (3) But many consumers do not know exactly what they are paying a higher price for. (4) Low-fat beef comes from a cattle breed who is about 30% lower in fat than other breeds. (5) Beef lower in fat content is likely to be least tender. (6) Producers solve this problem by using younger cattle. (7) Health-conscious consumers are also attracted by natural beef that is, beef that has been raised without the use of hormones, steroids, or antibiotics. (8) Of course, they'res a much easier way to cut down on fat intake. (9) Eat smaller portions. (10) The National Beef Council insists that there is nothing at all wrong with regular beef. (11) The trouble is that some of us just eat too much of it.

33. Sentence 1: **With consumer's increasingly concerned about calories, it is no surprise that poultry and beef producers have developed lower calorie products.**

Which of the following is the best way to write the underlined portion of this sentence? If you think the original is the best way, choose option (1).

(1) With consumer's increasingly concerned about calories
(2) With consumers increasingly concerned about calories
(3) With consumers increased concerned about calories
(4) With consumers increasingly concern about calories
(5) With consumers increased concern about calories

34. Sentence 2: **Like the makers of light beer, light maple syrup, or light mayonnaise, low-fat beef and low-fat chicken are appearing more and more in supermarkets and on restaurant menus.**

What correction should be made to this sentence?

(1) remove the phrase the makers of
(2) remove the commas after beer and syrup
(3) remove the comma after mayonnaise
(4) change are appearing to appears
(5) no correction is necessary

35. Sentence 3: **But many consumers do not know exactly what they are paying a higher price for.**

What correction should be made to this sentence?

(1) change many to much
(2) change do to does
(3) change the spelling of know to no
(4) remove the for at the end of the sentence
(5) no correction is necessary

36. Sentence 4: **Low-fat beef comes from a cattle breed who is about 30 % lower in fat than other breeds.**

    Which of the following is the best way to write the underlined portion of this sentence? If you think the original is the best way, choose option (1).

    (1) cattle breed who is about
    (2) cattle breed, who is about
    (3) cattle breed that is about
    (4) cattle breed which are about
    (5) cattle breed that are about

37. Sentence 5: **Beef lower in fat content is likely to be least tender.**

    What correction should be made to this sentence?

    (1) insert a comma after Beef
    (2) insert a comma after content
    (3) change is to are
    (4) change least to less
    (5) no correction is necessary

38. Sentence 7: **Health-conscious consumers are also attracted by natural beef that is, beef that has been raised without the use of hormones, steroids, or antibiotics.**

    What correction should be made to this sentence?

    (1) insert a comma after natural beef
    (2) remove the comma after is
    (3) remove the comma after hormones
    (4) remove the comma after steroids
    (5) no correction is necessary

39. Sentence 8: **Of course, they're a much easier way to cut down on fat intake.**

    Which of the following is the best way to write the underlined portion of this sentence? If you think the original is the best way, choose option (1).

    (1) Of course, they'res
    (2) Of course, theres
    (3) Of course, theirs
    (4) Of course theres
    (5) Of course, there's

40. Sentences 10 and 11: **The National Beef Council insists that there is nothing at all wrong with regular beef. The trouble is that some of us just eat too much of it.**

    The most effective combination of sentences 10 and 11 would include which of the following groups of words?

    (1) and the trouble is
    (2) the trouble being
    (3) but the trouble is
    (4) except that
    (5) except for the fact that

Items 41 to 48 refer to the following paragraph.

(1) The nonpartisan Center for Responsive Politics has recently issued a report severely criticizing of the runaway spending of political action committees, better known as PACs. (2) Campaign spending for federal, state, and local elections in 1984 was $1.8 billion, in 1972, it was only $425 million. (3) Congressmen running for election in 1984 spent nearly $400 million. (4) The average costs of a single campaign for the Senate is now nearly $5 million. (5) By 1992, some Senate races have cost as much as $30 million. (6) As expenditures has grown, so has the PACs. (7) Does a PAC contributor expect some return on their investment? (8) So it seems. (9) As defense spending grew during the early 1980s, the largest defense contractors tripled their contributions. (10) A lion's share of this money went to members of the Senate Armed Services Committee. (11) Unless Congress reforms the system of campaign contributions, things can only become worse.

41. Sentence 1: **The nonpartisan Center for Responsive Politics has recently issued a report severely criticizing of the runaway spending of political action committees, better known as PACs.**

Which of the following is the best way to write the underlined portion of this sentence? If you think the original is the best way, choose option (1).

(1) severely criticizing of
(2) severe critical of
(3) severely critical of
(4) severe criticizing
(5) criticizing severely of

42. Sentence 2: **Campaign spending for federal, state, and local elections in 1984 was $1.8 billion, in 1972, it was only $425 million.**

What correction should be made to this sentence?

(1) remove the comma after federal
(2) remove the comma after state
(3) change the comma after billion to a colon
(4) change the comma after billion to a semicolon
(5) remove the comma after 1972

43. Sentence 4: **The average costs of a single campaign for the Senate is now nearly $5 million.**

What correction should be made to this sentence?

(1) change costs to cost
(2) change the spelling of single to signal
(3) change the spelling of Senate to senate
(4) change nearly to near
(5) no correction is necessary

44. Sentence 5: **By 1992, some Senate races have cost as much as $30 million.**

What correction should be made to this sentence?

(1) remove the comma after 1992
(2) change the spelling of Senate to senate
(3) change the spelling of races to Races
(4) change have cost to will cost
(5) no correction is necessary

45. Sentence 6: **As expenditures has grown, so has the PACs.**

Which of the following is the best way to write the underlined portion of this sentence? If you think the original is the best way, choose option (1).

(1) has grown, so has
(2) have grown, so has
(3) have grown so have
(4) have grown so, has
(5) have grown, so have

46. Sentence 7: **Does a PAC contributor expect some return on their investment?**

What correction should be made to this sentence?

(1) change Does to Do
(2) change their to there
(3) change their to his
(4) change the question mark to a period
(5) no correction is necessary

47. Sentences 9 and 10: **As defense spending grew during the early 1980s, the largest defense contractors tripled their contributions. A lion's share of this money went to members of the Senate Armed Services Committee.**

The most effective combination of sentences 9 and 10 would include which of the following groups of words?

(1) and they gave a lion's share of this money to members
(2) and a lion's share of this money went to members
(3) a lion's share going to members
(4) their contributions to members
(5) and a lion's share goes to

48. Sentence 11: **Unless Congress reforms the system of campaign contributions, things can only become worse.**

What correction should be made to this sentence?

(1) change reforms to reform
(2) remove the comma after contributions
(3) move the only to before things
(4) change can to can't
(5) no correction is necessary

Items 49 to 55 refer to the following paragraph.

(1) Honest car repair is sometimes hard to find. (2) According to the Office of Consumer affairs, auto-related problems always outnumber all other complaints. (3) How widespread the automobile repair problem is hard to determine. (4) There's no denying the problem exists. (5) Causes include the shortage of qualified auto service technicians. (6) And the difficulty of attracting skilled workers to enter careers in auto repair. (7) Some mechanics who have not kept up with the new technology. (8) But there are some hopeful signs. (9) A non-profit organization, the NIASE, now provide voluntary competency testing for mechanics nationwide. (10) The AAA investigated and approves car repair facilities across the country. (11) Motorists themselves by recognizing the need for preventive maintenance, are doing more to keep their cars in good condition.

49. Sentence 2: **According to the Office of Consumer affairs, auto-related problems always outnumber all other complaints.**

What correction should be made to this sentence?

(1) change the spelling of affairs to Affairs
(2) remove the comma after affairs
(3) insert a hyphen between related and problems
(4) change the spelling of outnumber to out number
(5) no correction is necessary

50. Sentence 3: **How widespread the automobile repair problem is hard to determine.**

What correction should be made to this sentence?

(1) change the spelling of widespread to wide spread
(2) change is to are
(3) insert a second is after is
(4) change the period to a question mark
(5) no correction is necessary

51. Sentences 5 and 6: **Causes include the shortage of qualified auto technicians. And the difficulty of attracting skilled workers to enter careers in auto repair.**

Which of the following is the best way to write the underlined portion of these sentences? If you think the original is the best way, choose option (1).

(1) technicians. And the difficulty
(2) technicians; and the difficulty
(3) technicians: and the difficulty
(4) technicians and the difficulty
(5) technicians. The difficulty

52. Sentence 7: **Some mechanics who have not kept up with the new technology.**

    Which of the following is the best way to write the underlined portion of this sentence? If you think the original is the best way, choose option (1).

    (1) mechanics who have not kept up
    (2) mechanics, who have not kept up
    (3) mechanics have not kept up
    (4) mechanics who had not kept up
    (5) mechanics not having kept up

53. Sentence 9: **A nonprofit organization, the NIASE, now provide voluntary competency testing for mechanics nationwide.**

    What correction should be made to this sentence?

    (1) remove the comma after organization
    (2) remove the comma after NIASE
    (3) change provide to provides
    (4) change the spelling of competency to compatancy
    (5) no correction is necessary

54. Sentence 10: **The AAA investigated and approves car repair facilities across the country.**

    What correction should be made to this sentence?

    (1) change investigated to investigates
    (2) change approves to approve
    (3) change approves to will approve
    (4) insert a comma after approves
    (5) insert a comma after facilities

55. Sentence 11: **Motorists themselves by recognizing the need for preventive maintenance, are doing more to keep their cars in good condition.**

    What correction should be made to this sentence?

    (1) insert a comma after themselves
    (2) change for to to
    (3) remove the comma after maintenance
    (4) change the spelling of their to there
    (5) no correction is necessary

END OF EXAMINATION

WRITING SKILLS: PART II

Tests of General Educational Development

Directions

This part of the Writing Skills Test is intended to determine how well you write. You are asked to write an essay that explains something or presents an opinion on an issue. In preparing your essay, you should take the following steps.

1. Read carefully the directions and the essay topic given below.

2. Plan your essay carefully before you write.

3. Use scratch paper to make any notes.

4. Write your essay on the lined pages of the separate answer sheet.

5. Read carefully what you have written and make any changes that will improve your essay.

6. Check your paragraphs, sentence structure, spelling, punctuation, capitalization, and usage, and make any necessary corrections.

Be sure you write the letter of the essay topic (given below) on your answer sheet. Write the letter in the box at the upper right-hand corner of the page where you write your essay.

You will have 45 minutes to write on the topic below. Write legibly and use a ballpoint pen so that the evaluators will be able to read your writing.

Write your essay on the lined pages of the separate answer sheet. The notes you make on scratch paper will not be scored.

Your essay will be scored by at least two trained evaluators who will judge it according to its overall effectiveness. They will judge how clearly you make the main point of your composition, how thoroughly you support your ideas, and how clearly and correctly you write throughout the essay.

TOPIC B

In our society today, we need a great deal of energy. Some of our sources of energy have caused alarm among those concerned about our health and environment.

Identify a source or sources of energy that cause you concern. Write a composition of about 200 words explaining why you have this concern. Provide reasons and examples to support your view.

458

TEST 2: SOCIAL STUDIES

Tests of General Educational Development

Directions

The Social Studies Test consists of multiple-choice questions intended to measure general social studies concepts. The questions are based on short readings which often include a graph, chart, or figure. Study the information given and then answer the question(s) following it. Refer to the information as often as necessary in answering the questions.

You should spend no more than 85 minutes answering the questions in this booklet. Work carefully, but do not spend too much time on any one question. Be sure you answer every question. You will not be penalized for incorrect answers.

Do not mark in this test booklet. Record your answers to the questions on the separate answer sheet provided. Be sure all requested information is properly recorded on the answer sheet.

To record your answers, mark the numbered space on the answer sheet beside the number that corresponds to the question in the test booklet.

FOR EXAMPLE:

Early colonists of North America looked for settlement sites that had adequate water supplies and were accessible by ship. For this reason, many early towns were built near

(1) mountains
(2) prairies
(3) rivers
(4) glaciers
(5) plateaus

The correct answer is "rivers"; therefore, answer space 3 would be marked on the answer sheet

---

Do not rest the point of your pencil on the answer sheet while you are considering your answer. Make no stray or unnecessary marks. If you change an answer, erase your first mark completely. Mark only one answer space for each question; multiple answers will be scored as incorrect. Do not fold or crease your answer sheet. Return all test materials to the test administrator.

Directions: Choose the one best answer to each item.

Items 1 to 3 refer to the following information.

The federal government is sovereign in certain areas such as the regulation of interstate commerce. State governments control certain other areas, such as regulation of intrastate (within a state) commerce or the police. An intermingling of powers can be seen in some railroad traffic. If a train crosses a state line, it constitutes interstate commerce. Rail shipments originating and ending within a single state constitute intrastate commerce and therefore are regulated by state governments. However, the intrastate and interstate traffic may have moved over the same rails.

1. Which of the following is an example of intrastate commerce?

   (1) an oil shipment transported from New Jersey to Michigan
   (2) air shipment of computer chips from California to Oregon
   (3) a utility company operating solely in New Hampshire
   (4) a rail shipment from Chicago to St. Louis
   (5) shipping Florida citrus to other sunbelt states

2. Which of the following is an issue more likely to concern a member of a state legislature than a member of the United States Congress?

   (1) federal income tax exemptions
   (2) airline routes throughout New England
   (3) transcontinental interstate highways
   (4) fishing rights in the Gulf of Mexico
   (5) the selection of an official state flower

3. Over which of the following would the federal rather than the state government have control?

   (1) state wildlife refuges
   (2) colleges and universities
   (3) transcontinental bus routes
   (4) intrastate canals
   (5) city and county jails

Item 4 refers to the following information.

Although education provides an avenue of upward social mobility for a few persons, it also acts to maintain the existing racial and class structure. In the 1980s, about 85 percent of sons of fathers in the upper and upper-middle classes entered college, compared to 6 percent of the sons of unskilled worker fathers.

4. An example of upward mobility made possible by education would be

   (1) a successful professional teenage baseball player
   (2) a miner's son who became a famous biochemist
   (3) a doctor's son who became a lawyer
   (4) a doctor's daughter who became a doctor
   (5) a successful circus performer

Items 5 to 7 refer to the following definitions of government systems.

gerontocracy—a government ruled by elders

theocracy—a government ruled by religious functionaries

monarchy—a government ruled by a king or queen

aristocracy—a government ruled by a small hereditary nobility

democracy—a government ruled by the citizens

The following items relate to one of the five government systems described above. Choose the government system that best fits the circumstances given. The categories may be used more than once in the set of items. No one question has more than one best answer.

5. In which of the five forms of government does the power reside in the smallest number of people?

    (1) gerontocracy
    (2) theocracy
    (3) monarchy
    (4) aristocracy
    (5) democracy

6. The form of government of Tibet in which the Dalai Lama and other monks held power is an example of

    (1) gerontocracy
    (2) theocracy
    (3) monarchy
    (4) aristocracy
    (5) democracy

7. In the Renaissance, the system of government most common in European countries was

    (1) gerontocracy
    (2) theocracy
    (3) monarchy
    (4) aristocracy
    (5) democracy

Items 8 and 9 refer to the following information.

    The Constitution gives the Senate the power to advise and consent to the President's treaty making and appointment power. The Senate must ratify all international treaties and appointments to the Cabinet, Supreme Court, and ambassadorships.

8. In which of the following situations would the Senate use its authority to advise and consent?

    (1) a presidential proposal for a new national holiday
    (2) a presidential proposal for an arms-limitation treaty with the Soviet Union
    (3) a House of Representatives proposal for a trade agreement with Japan
    (4) the Governor of California asks for disaster relief after an earthquake
    (5) a candidate is nominated for Circuit Court Judge

9. All of the following presidential appointments would require Senate confirmation EXCEPT

    (1) Ambassador to Mexico
    (2) Secretary of Defense
    (3) White House Press Secretary
    (4) Supreme Court Chief Justice
    (5) Attorney General

Item 10 refers to the following information.

    Obsessions are excessive thinking and doubting without being able to get one's mind off a subject. Compulsions are ritualistic behaviors that cannot be ended without extreme discomfort.

10. Which of the following is an example of compulsive behavior?

    (1) washing vegetables before cooking
    (2) never stepping on a crack in the sidewalk while walking
    (3) brushing one's teeth before going to bed
    (4) tying one's shoes
    (5) fear of heights

Items 11 to 14 are based on the following graph and information.

A favorable balance of trade results when exports are greater than imports; an unfavorable balance of trade results when imports are greater than exports.

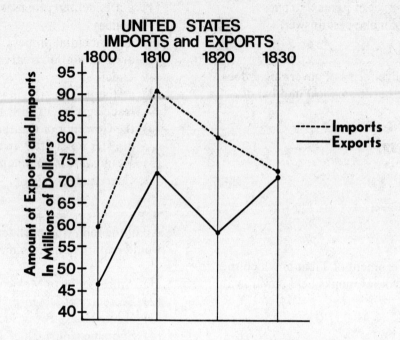

11. From the graph and information it can be concluded that

    (1) exports and imports increased during each ten-year period
    (2) in 1810 exports were approximately twice as great as imports
    (3) exports and imports nearly equaled each other in 1830
    (4) the greatest growth in exports was between 1810 and 1820
    (5) the amount of exports and imports in 1810 and 1820 nearly equaled each other

12. The year in which the United States experienced the most nearly favorable balance of trade was

    (1) 1830
    (2) 1825
    (3) 1820
    (4) 1810
    (5) 1800

13. In 1820, the value of goods imported by the United States was approximately

    (1) $93 million
    (2) $82 million
    (3) $74 million
    (4) $60 million
    (5) $48 million

14. In 1800, the balance of trade was unfavorable by approximately

    (1) $12 million
    (2) $21 million
    (3) $26 million
    (4) $47 million
    (5) $59 million

Items 15 and 16 refer to the following paragraph.

The divorce rate in the United States and other western countries has risen, and the United States is not the only country with a high rate of marital dissolution. Good economic conditions and high employment are factors that encourage divorce. In states or countries where it is difficult to obtain a divorce, there are especially high rates of desertion.

15. From the information in the passage we can conclude that one result of making divorce easier to obtain is

(1) an increase in teenage marriages
(2) a decrease in teenage marriages
(3) a decrease in the number of desertions
(4) a decrease in unemployment
(5) a decrease in the divorce rate

16. Divorces are probably more common in times of economic prosperity than in times of economic depression because

(1) people have the money to pay the legal expenses
(2) people are happier when they have an assured income
(3) people become selfish in times of prosperity
(4) people are less content when they worry about money
(5) divorce is more socially acceptable at such times

Item 17 refers to the following information.

The Spanish American War demonstrated the ineffectiveness of the American Navy in two oceans separated by a continent. In response to this problem the United States acquired the Panama Canal Zone, and subsequently built the Panama Canal.

17. According to the information, which of the following statements best explains the acquisition of the Panama Canal Zone?

(1) the need for a strategic and mobile navy
(2) the delay in completing the transcontinental railroad
(3) the weakness of any South American country in preventing the acquisition
(4) the pro-navy attitude of Teddy Roosevelt
(5) the discovery of gold in California

Items 18 to 20 refer to the following situation.

Before a jury is picked to hear a controversial murder case, a judge issues a "gag" order restricting the press from reporting about the case.

18. Which of the following best explains the reason for issuing "gag" orders?

(1) The press is often sensational in its reporting of murder cases.
(2) Pretrial media publicity can often prejudice potential jurors.
(3) Judges distrust aggressive media reporting.
(4) Judges have the power to issue "gag" orders.
(5) Mass media in the electronic age have little impact on public opinion.

19. Which constitutional guarantees are most likely to be in conflict when a judge issues a "gag" order?

(1) freedom of assembly and the right to an impartial jury
(2) due process of the law and the freedom of religion
(3) freedom of the press and the right to a fair trial
(4) freedom of speech and the right to appeal court decisions
(5) the right to remain silent and the freedom of the press

20. Which of the following is a question most likely to be asked all of the prospective jurors in this case?

    (1) Do you believe the judge in this case to be fair?
    (2) What is your educational background?
    (3) For how many years have you held your present job?
    (4) Have you read about or seen coverage of this case on television?
    (5) For how many years have you lived at your present address?

Items 21 and 22 are based on the following paragraph.

A folk society has a number of traits that set it off from a modern society. A folk society is small, stable, and agricultural, with little differentiation of occupation. Family and kinship groups, customs, and traditions are highly valued.

21. Which of the following statements is supported by the paragraph?

    (1) A folk society is a hunting society.
    (2) A modern society is stable and agricultural.
    (3) A folk society respects family ties.
    (4) A modern society values tradition highly.
    (5) A folk society depends upon many different occupations.

22. Which of the following is likely to be characteristic of a modern society?

    (1) a small size
    (2) large occupational differentiation
    (3) stability
    (4) respect for tradition
    (5) respect for kinship groups

23. "Geography molds history."

    Which of the following would be the best explanation of this statement?

    (1) Natural disasters influence history.
    (2) Geography has little impact on world history.
    (3) History can never be fully interpreted because the events in question are part of the past.
    (4) Natural resources can directly affect historical developments.
    (5) Geography, like history, is constantly changing.

24. In 1974 the western world was faced with an Arab oil embargo.

    Which industry was not negatively affected by the reduction in oil supplies?

    (1) auto industry
    (2) leisure time industry
    (3) coal industry
    (4) housing industry
    (5) construction industry

Items 25 and 26 refer to the following graphs.

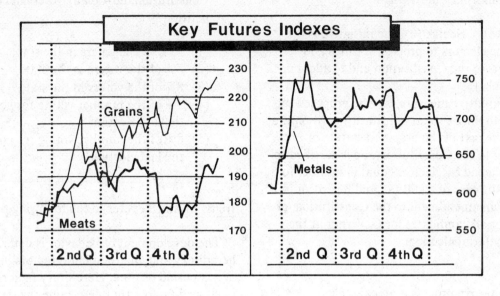

25. According to the graphs, at the end of the second quarter, metals were at

    (1) 190
    (2) 200
    (3) 650
    (4) 700
    (5) 750

26. According to the graphs, at the end of the third quarter, the difference between the price of meats and the price of grains was

    (1) 5
    (2) 10
    (3) 15
    (4) 20
    (5) 25

Item 27 refers to the following paragraph.

In the Zuni and Hopi Indian tribes, competition and attempts to perform better than one's peers are regarded as deviant behavior (that is, differing from the normal). But they are looked upon as normal in contemporary American life.

27. This paragraph was probably written by a(n)

    (1) anthropologist
    (2) economist
    (3) historian
    (4) geographer
    (5) political scientist

Items 28 to 30 refer to the following section of the State of California Constitution.

[Initiative]   Sec. 8. (a) The initiative is the power of the electors to propose statutes and amendments to the Constitution and to adopt or reject them.

(b) An initiative measure may be proposed by presenting to the Secretary of State a petition that sets forth the text of the proposed statute or amendment to the Constitution and is certified to have been signed by electors equal in number to 5 percent in the case of a statute, and 8 percent in the case of an amendment to the Constitution, of the votes for all candidates for Governor at the last gubernatorial election.

28. The initiative process is an example of

   (1) the power of the state legislature to make laws
   (2) a constitutional guarantee that both federal and state government possess
   (3) the right of the people to directly propose state legislation
   (4) a constitutional check on the electors of a state
   (5) the power of the state legislature to amend the Constitution

29. All of the following accurately describe a California initiative EXCEPT

   (1) an initiative may amend the state Constitution
   (2) an initiative may amend the federal Constitution
   (3) an initiative must be supported by at least 5% or 8% of voters in the last election for Governor
   (4) a statute is easier to qualify than an amendment
   (5) an initiative is submitted to the Secretary of State

30. To qualify an initiative to amend the State Constitution, how many voters must sign the petition?

   (1) 52% of the voters in the state
   (2) 5% of the voters in the state
   (3) 8% of the voters in the state
   (4) 5% of the number voting for governor in the last election
   (5) 8% of the number voting for governor in the last election

Items 31 and 32 refer to the following paragraph.

The development of behavior is determined by hereditary and environmental factors interacting over a period of time. Hereditary factors are those biological factors that determine the structure and the function of the body. Environmental factors are those stimulating factors that act upon the organism.

31. The passage was probably written by which of the following social scientists?

   (1) a historian
   (2) a geographer
   (3) a psychologist
   (4) an economist
   (5) a political scientist

32. Which of the following is an environmental rather than a hereditary factor?

   (1) eye color
   (2) height
   (3) religion
   (4) sex
   (5) weight

Items 33 to 36 refer to the following information.

Propaganda is the manipulation of public opinion, or the attempt to influence people to adopt a particular point of view. Listed below are five propaganda techniques:

(1) name-calling—giving a negative or unpopular label to a person, group, or concept
(2) technical jargon—using technical language or unfamiliar words for the purpose of impressing people
(3) plain folks—identifying one's positions as representative of views commonly held and accepted by the majority of people
(4) band wagon—suggesting that the majority of people have already shifted to the propagandist's position
(5) card stacking—manipulating fact and fiction in such a way that a person must reach a desired conclusion

In each of the following situations, one of the five techniques described above is used. Identify the technique that best characterizes the statement. The categories may be used more than once in the set of items. No one question has more than one best answer.

33. A Senator urges the passage of a tax cut on the grounds that "95% of the people in the East and 98% of the people in the West support the legislation."

(1) name calling
(2) technical jargon
(3) plain folks
(4) band wagon
(5) card stacking

34. A candidate for governor tells the voters he is just a "simple, honest farm boy who favors prosperity, honesty, and democracy."

(1) name calling
(2) technical jargon
(3) plain folks
(4) band wagon
(5) card stacking

35. A Presidential candidate is quoted as saying, "The only way to ensure prosperity is to be sure that Ginnie Maes and Fannie Maes do not decline to a point below the average total of the prime, and MMA and LD rates."

(1) name calling
(2) technical jargon
(3) plain folks
(4) band wagon
(5) card stacking

36. A candidate for office who has never played baseball says the following: "Do you want a senator who has served time in prison for mail fraud or do you want an honest, church-going, baseball-playing, hard-working family man like me?"

(1) name calling
(2) technical jargon
(3) plain folks
(4) band wagon
(5) card stacking

Item 37 is based on the following paragraph.

The first sentence of the Fourteenth Amendment (1868) undertakes to define United States citizenship in these words: "All persons born or naturalized in the United States, and subject to the jurisdiction thereof, are citizens of the United States and of the State wherein they reside."

37. If a man was born in New York of parents who were both French citizens and who subsequently moved to live in Florida, that man would

(1) not be an American citizen nor a citizen of New York
(2) not be an American citizen but would be a citizen of Florida
(3) be an American citizen and a citizen of both New York and Florida
(4) be an American citizen and a citizen of Florida
(5) be an American citizen and a citizen of New York

Item 38 refers to the following information.

Discovery is the realization of something that was unknown before even though it existed all along.

Invention is the combining of existing elements and knowledge to create new and different forms.

38. Which of the following is an example of a discovery?

   (1) the telescope
   (2) the planet Pluto
   (3) the hot air balloon
   (4) radar
   (5) dynamite

Items 39 and 40 refer to the following paragraph.

   A popular character in oral literature is the trickster. Sometimes the trickster is an animal, rather than a man, who relies on craftiness to accomplish his ends. Another popular type is Foolish Jack, the village idiot who proves to be much wiser than people thought.

39. The animal that most often plays the trickster in western literature is

   (1) the fox
   (2) the mouse
   (3) the fish
   (4) the tiger
   (5) the dog

40. An example of oral literature is

   (1) a best-selling novel
   (2) a play by Shakespeare
   (3) a work by Dickens
   (4) a comic strip
   (5) a fairy tale

Items 41 to 44 are based on the following map.

ELECTION OF 1868

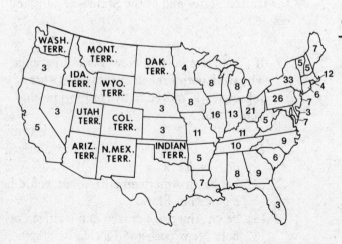

CANDIDATES	ELECTORAL VOTE	POPULAR VOTE
REPUBLICAN Ulysses S. Grant	214	3,013,421
DEMOCRATIC Horatio Seymour	80	2,706,829
NOT VOTED	23	
	317	5,720,250

The numbers refer to the number of electoral votes of each state.
Those areas without numbers had not become states in 1868.

41. According to this map, which of the following had achieved statehood in 1868?

    (1) Utah
    (2) Arkansas
    (3) New Mexico
    (4) Washington
    (5) North Dakota

42. Of the five following states, which one had the largest number of electoral votes in 1868?

    (1) California
    (2) Michigan
    (3) New York
    (4) Pennsylvania
    (5) Illinois

43. Which of the following statements is supported by the data in the map?

    (1) The South voted solidly Democratic in the election of 1868.
    (2) The potential for future statehood was greater in the southeast than in the southwest
    (3) Grant received more than twice as many electoral and popular votes as did Seymour
    (4) More than six million people voted in the election of 1868.
    (5) Not all of the electoral votes were voted in the election of 1868.

44. Which of the following states had not achieved statehood by 1868?

    (1) South Dakota
    (2) Oregon
    (3) Nevada
    (4) Illinois
    (5) Missouri

Items 45 and 46 are based on the following information.

   Economic sanctions are enacted to prevent another nation from conducting normal commerce and to force a change in its policies.

45. Which of the following is the best example of economic sanctions?

    (1) The United States sells surplus wheat to the Soviet Union.
    (2) The government outlaws the hiring of undocumented foreign workers by American companies.
    (3) The United States refuses to allow South African companies that practice apartheid to sell goods in the United States.
    (4) Massachusetts enacts a state tax on tobacco.
    (5) Great Britain joins the Common Market.

46. All of the following might be employed to enforce economic sanctions EXCEPT

    (1) an embargo
    (2) high import taxes
    (3) high export taxes
    (4) an import ban
    (5) a state income tax

Item 47 is based on the following information.

   There are two basic ways of obtaining food. Collecting (or foraging) includes the gathering of vegetables and hunting and trapping. Food producing (or domestication) includes the cultivation of plants and the keeping and breeding of animals.

47. Agriculture is an example of

    (1) collecting
    (2) foraging
    (3) gathering
    (4) food producing
    (5) breeding

Item 48 is based on the following information.

The term institutional racism implies that government agencies such as the army, state and federal governments, and large business concerns that serve the public, such as banks and corporations, follow policies that discriminate against a minority or race.

48. According to the information, which of the following is the best example of a federal policy that attempts to end institutional racism?

(1) All large corporations are requested by the federal government to end discrimination in hiring voluntarily.
(2) Discriminatory membership policies by organized church groups are ordered to stop.
(3) The federal government, by executive order, ends segregation in the armed forces.
(4) A world-wide corporation is ordered by the federal government to stop administering lie detector tests to its employees.
(5) A federal statute institutes a 10-year phased-in plan to reserve top management positions for college-educated workers.

Items 49 and 50 are based upon the following statement.

It is important to consider that the world population problem cannot be adequately resolved by simply producing more food. Increased food production cannot keep pace with current increases in world population.

49. Which of the following would most help the problem of dwindling food supplies?

(1) a sharp decrease in the birth rate
(2) a sharp increase in the food supply
(3) a sharp decrease in birth rate and a decrease in the food supply
(4) a decrease in the birth rate and an increase in the food supply
(5) a sharp increase in the food supply and a sharp decrease in the birth rate

50. Which of the following programs would the author of this statement be most likely to favor?

(1) government-sponsored soil research programs
(2) government price supports for wheat
(3) state-supported insect control programs
(4) government incentives to reduce the birth rate
(5) cooperative sharing of the world's farm products

Item 51 is based on the following information.

The Fourth Amendment limits government agencies in searching and seizing people or property. The key to Fourth Amendment legal controversy is the extent of "reasonable cause" for search and seizure.

51. Which of the following examples would most likely be considered an unreasonable search?

(1) A person gives his consent for the police to search his automobile.
(2) A police officer searches a car after smelling the odor of marijuana on the driver.
(3) A warrant is issued by a judge to search a home for stolen automobile tires.
(4) A person is searched for weapons after threatening a police officer with a knife.
(5) The police enter a home without a court order because they suspect that the owner is selling illegal drugs.

Items 52 to 55 are based on the four following graphs which deal with economic indicators in the American Depression years.

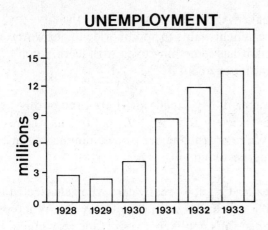

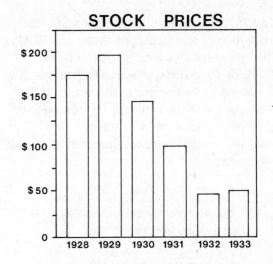

52. In the years between 1928 and 1933, the American economy was most prosperous in

(1) 1928
(2) 1929
(3) 1930
(4) 1931
(5) 1933

53. Farm prices were at their lowest point in

(1) 1928
(2) 1930
(3) 1931
(4) 1932
(5) 1933

54. According to the Prices Index graph, between 1930 and 1932 farm prices

(1) rose by 40 points
(2) rose by 60 points
(3) were unchanged
(4) fell by 40 points
(5) fell by 60 points

55. According to the graph, unemployment declined in the year

(1) from 1928 to 1929
(2) from 1929 to 1930
(3) from 1930 to 1931
(4) from 1931 to 1932
(5) from 1932 to 1933

Items 56 and 57 are based on the following paragraph.

In 1787, the Connecticut Compromise resolved the question of representation in the new Congress by providing for a bicameral, or two-house, legislature. Regardless of size, each state is represented by two people in the Senate. The representation in the House of Representatives is based upon population, with states with a larger population having a higher number of Representatives.

56. The Connecticut Compromise was a way of solving a dispute between

    (1) northern states and southern states
    (2) slave states and non-slave states
    (3) large population states and small population states
    (4) farm states and industrialized states
    (5) states large in area and states small in area

57. The size of the United States Senate has grown from

    (1) 13 to 50
    (2) 26 to 96
    (3) 26 to 98
    (4) 26 to 100
    (5) 26 to 435

Items 58 to 61 are based on the following information.

Speaker A: Someone told me that the city government wants to add fluoride to our water. I think it has something to do with teeth. I don't know much about it.

Speaker B: My friends and I are tired of this phony society and the phony politicians who run it. We're organizing our own commune on some wilderness land.

Speaker C: I don't really care who gets elected to public office. I'm satisfied with my life. Whatever happens, it's not likely to affect me very much. I'll still have my family, my job, my home.

Speaker D: The whole society is sick. It has to be torn apart and rebuilt. That's the only political program that's worth anything.

Speaker E: Most public officials in this state are socialist traitors who have forgotten the true American heritage. No peaceful efforts can make these public officials change their ways. I have started an underground organization of true patriots who will save this country from socialism.

58. Which of the speakers are political activists?

    (1) A and B
    (2) B and C
    (3) A and D
    (4) D and E
    (5) C and E

59. Which speakers appear to be most indifferent to politics?

    (1) A and E
    (2) A and C
    (3) B and D
    (4) C and D
    (5) B and E

60. Which speaker best represents the self-centered, so-called "me generation"?

    (1) A
    (2) B
    (3) C
    (4) D
    (5) E

61. The speaker most likely to belong to a right-wing group is

    (1) A
    (2) B
    (3) C
    (4) D
    (5) E

Items 62 to 64 are based on the following information.

    Studies indicate that the most effective propaganda messages are those (1) that come from a credible source, (2) that include some arguments for the opposite side, (3) that make their appeal indirectly, (4) that actively involve the recipient, and (5) that require a large rather than a small change of opinion.

62. According to the details of the passage, which of the following would be the most effective spokesperson for a cigarette manufacturer trying to convince high school students to smoke cigarettes?

    (1) a famous young athlete well known for his previous antismoking views and his sincerity
    (2) a high school principal
    (3) a talk show host famous for insulting his guests
    (4) a famous singer well known for his smoking commercials in magazines
    (5) a trial lawyer

63. The purpose of a propagandist's including some arguments for the opposite side is probably

    (1) so he or she can disagree with those arguments later
    (2) to give an impression of impartiality
    (3) to be as fair as possible at all times
    (4) because those arguments cannot be avoided
    (5) because the propagandist doesn't really want to convince the audience

64. Of the five qualities listed, all but one emphasize the credibility of the source or the tactful involving of the listener.

    The surprising exception is

    (1) a credible source
    (2) arguments for the opposite side
    (3) indirect appeal
    (4) involving the recipient
    (5) a large change of opinion

END OF EXAMINATION

TEST 3: SCIENCE

Tests of General Educational Development

Directions

The Science Test consists of multiple-choice questions intended to measure the general concepts in science. The questions are based on short readings which often include a graph, chart, or figure. Study the information given and then answer the question(s) following it. Refer to the information as often as necessary in answering the questions.

You should spend no more than 95 minutes answering the questions in this booklet. Work carefully, but do not spend too much time on any one question. Be sure you answer every question. You will not be penalized for incorrect answers.

Do not mark in this test booklet. Record your answers to the questions on the separate answer sheet provided. Be sure all requested information is properly recorded on the answer sheet.

To record your answers, mark the numbered space on the answer sheet beside the number that corresponds to the question in the test booklet.

FOR EXAMPLE:

Which of the following is the smallest unit in a living thing?

(1) tissue
(2) organ
(3) cell
(4) muscle
(5) capillary   ① ② ● ④ ⑤

The correct answer is "cell"; therefore, answer space 3 would be marked on the answer sheet.

Do not rest the point of your pencil on the answer sheet while you are considering your answer. Make no stray or unnecessary marks. If you change an answer, erase your first mark completely. Mark only one answer space for each question; multiple answers will be scored as incorrect. Do not fold or crease your answer sheet. Return all test materials to the test administrator.

Directions: Choose the one best answer to each item.

1. As a covered kettle of vegetable soup continues to boil gently on the stove, what happens to the temperature of the soup?

   (1) It falls very slowly.
   (2) It is slightly less than 212 degrees Fahrenheit.
   (3) It remains the same.
   (4) It rises very slowly.
   (5) It rises quite rapidly.

Items 2 and 3 refer to the following diagram and information.

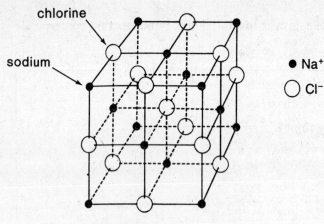

● Na⁺

○ Cl⁻

**CRYSTAL STRUCTURE
OF SODIUM CHLORIDE**

The diagram above shows the crystal structure of sodium chloride, ordinary table salt, with the atoms greatly magnified to show their arrangement. Table salt is made up of equal numbers of sodium and chlorine atoms. This solid keeps its shape because the bonding holds the atoms in a rigid, stable arrangement.

2. Based on the diagram and information given, which of the following statements is accurate?

   A. Atoms of opposite charge are closer than atoms of the same charge.
   B. Each atom could vibrate in only three directions.
   C. The crystal faces would be slightly rounded.
   D. The pattern could be continued in all directions.

   (1) A and B only
   (2) A and D only
   (3) B and C only
   (4) B and D only
   (5) C and D only

3. A spoonful of table salt is stirred into a pot of water until it is all dissolved.

   Which of the following is the best description of how the salt occurs within the solution?

   (1) atoms
   (2) crystals
   (3) enzymes
   (4) molecules
   (5) polymers

Items 4 to 9 refer to the following methods of respiration for animals.

Method A: Respiration from air through moist lung surfaces to blood vessels.
Method B: Respiration from air or water to a system of air ducts to the body tissues.
Method C: Respiration from water through gill surfaces to blood vessels.
Method D: Respiration from air or water by diffusion through a moist surface into the body tissues.
Method E: Respiration from air or water by diffusion through thin membrane to blood vessels.

Note: The simplest way to understand the five methods of respiration is to realize that four (A, B, D, E) are from air, and four (B, C, D, E) are from water.
Each of the following items describes a situation that refers to one of the methods of respiration mentioned above. For each item, choose the one method of respiration that best fits the situation described. Each of the categories above <u>may</u> be used more than once in the following set of items.

4. Which of the methods of respiration is used by a fox to breathe?

   (1) A
   (2) B
   (3) C
   (4) D
   (5) E

5. In an earthworm, oxygen passes directly through the body wall into shallow blood vessels.

   Which method of respiration is used by an earthworm?

   (1) A
   (2) B
   (3) C
   (4) D
   (5) E

6. A trout must obtain its oxygen from the surrounding water.

   Which method of respiration is used by a trout?

   (1) A
   (2) B
   (3) C
   (4) D
   (5) E

7. Beetles obtain their oxygen by means of a network of tiny tubes that begin at the surface and branch to all interior organs and tissues.

   Which method of respiration is used by beetles?

   (1) A
   (2) B
   (3) C
   (4) D
   (5) E

8. Some internal parasites are immersed in the body fluids of their hosts, and from those fluids they absorb oxygen and give up carbon dioxide.

   Which method of respiration is used by these parasites?

   (1) A
   (2) B
   (3) C
   (4) D
   (5) E

9. Of the five methods of respiration, which three could most probably be used only by small organisms?

   (1) A, B, and D
   (2) A, C, and E
   (3) B, C, and E
   (4) B, D, and E
   (5) C, D, and E

10. Here are four plants with very different organization and reproduction: a fern, a moss, a pine, and a rose.

    What is the order of their appearance by evolution, from earliest to latest?

    (1) fern, moss, rose, pine
    (2) fern, rose, moss, pine
    (3) moss, fern, pine, rose
    (4) pine, fern, moss, rose
    (5) rose, moss, fern, pine

Items 11 to 13 refer to the diagrams on the effects of Boyle's Law and Charles' Law.

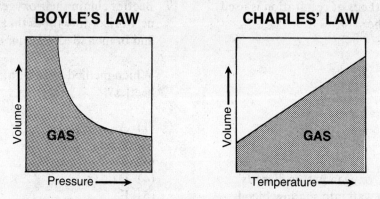

BOYLE'S LAW   CHARLES' LAW

Gases can be compressed to small volumes by pressure or they can expand to fill any available space. Higher temperature makes gas molecules move faster and hit the walls of their container.

11. Which of the following sentences best summarizes Charles' Law?

    (1) As the temperature increases, the volume of a gas increases.
    (2) As the temperature decreases, the volume of a gas increases.
    (3) As the pressure increases, the volume of a gas increases.
    (4) The temperature has no direct effect on volume.
    (5) The volume of a gas increases only when new molecules are added.

12. Boyle's Law shows that

    (1) as the volume of a gas increases, the pressure increases
    (2) as the temperature of a gas increases, the volume decreases
    (3) as the volume of a gas decreases, the pressure decreases
    (4) as the pressure of a gas increases, the volume decreases
    (5) the pressure of a gas has no effect on the volume

13. If a car is driven at high speed for a long time, the volume, or size, of the tires will

    (1) temporarily increase due to inertia
    (2) temporarily decrease due to pressure
    (3) stay the same
    (4) last a long time due to use
    (5) temporarily increase due to pressure

Items 14 to 18 refer to the following optical processes.

(1) absorption—light of certain colors is captured by the atoms within a substance
(2) emission—the atoms of a substance are forced to radiate, or give off, light of certain colors
(3) linear propagation—the movement of light in a straight line
(4) reflection—the rebounding of light off the boundary between two substances
(5) refraction—the change in direction of light when it passes through the boundary between two substances

Each of the following items describes occurrences that relate to one of the optical processes defined above. For each item choose the optical process that best describes the occurrence. Each of the categories above may be used more than once in the following set of items.

14. Which of the five optical processes produces an image when you look at a mirror?

    (1) absorption
    (2) emission
    (3) linear propagation
    (4) reflection
    (5) refraction

15. Which optical process explains why a teaspoon appears bent when it is immersed halfway into a cup of weak tea?

    (1) absorption
    (2) emission
    (3) linear propagation
    (4) reflection
    (5) refraction

16. Which optical process best explains the origin of shadows?

    (1) absorption
    (2) emission
    (3) linear propagation
    (4) reflection
    (5) refraction

17. Which optical process explains the cause of the glow when a fireplace poker is heated red-hot?

    (1) absorption
    (2) emission
    (3) linear propagation
    (4) reflection
    (5) refraction

18. Which two optical processes explain why a ripe apple appears red in sunlight?

    (1) absorption and reflection
    (2) emission and linear propagation
    (3) reflection and emission
    (4) refraction and absorption
    (5) linear propagation and refraction

Item 19 refers to the following diagram of the circulatory system.

THE CIRCULATORY SYSTEM

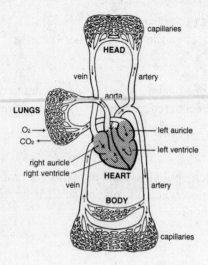

19. Which of the following sequences within the human circulatory system best describes the circulation of blood specifically to the body?

    (1) lungs → body → lungs
    (2) lungs → body → heart → lungs
    (3) lungs → heart → body → lungs
    (4) lungs → body → heart → body → lungs
    (5) lungs → heart → body → heart → lungs

20. Which of the following is the best explanation of the fact that a rubber band may be stretched and then return to its original size?

    (1) The actual length of the band cannot be altered because it forms a loop.
    (2) Each long molecule in the band can be deformed but recovers its original shape.
    (3) Most natural rubber of prime quality has a very high content of gas.
    (4) The unusual strength of the bonding makes the rubber band unbreakable.
    (5) Rubber can be melted.

Items 21 to 23 refer to the following information.

Most of the higher animals are described as mobile because each individual moves about by its own efforts. On the other hand, many primitive marine animals are described as sessile if they are more or less permanently fixed to some rock, plant, or larger animal. Another distinction that may be made involves their independence. A solitary animal is basically capable of surviving alone for some time, while a colonial animal always lives in a group.

21. Based on the information, how should a hawk be classified?

    (1) colonial and mobile
    (2) mobile and sessile
    (3) mobile and solitary
    (4) sessile and colonial
    (5) solitary and sessile

22. A reef coral is a small cup-shaped animal that looks similar to a flower blossom.

    Based on the information, how should a reef-building coral be classified?

    (1) colonial and mobile
    (2) mobile and sessile
    (3) mobile and solitary
    (4) sessile and colonial
    (5) solitary and sessile

23. Based on the information, how should a honey bee be classified?

    (1) colonial and mobile
    (2) mobile and sessile
    (3) mobile and solitary
    (4) sessile and colonial
    (5) solitary and sessile

24. Marble is a metamorphic rock that formed at very high temperature, in excess of 300 degrees centigrade. Yet, that rock type is found at hundreds of locations on the Earth's surface, from Italy to California.

Which of the following best explains the occurrences of marble in places that have normal temperature?

(1) The Earth's surface was much colder in the past than it is today.
(2) Impacts of giant meteorites have baked the rocks in certain localities.
(3) The high pressures during earthquakes have squeezed some rocks into marble.
(4) Long periods of erosion have exposed rocks that formed at great depth.
(5) Volcanoes bring heat to the surface and erupt flows of marble lavas.

Item 25 refers to the following chart.

	Horse	Cow	Sheep	Pig	Rabbit	Mouse
Horse	0	18	18	17	25	23
Cow	18	0	13	17	26	20
Sheep	18	13	0	18	29	24
Pig	17	17	18	0	26	24
Rabbit	25	26	29	26	0	28
Mouse	23	20	24	24	28	0

25. The chart above shows the number of amino acid differences between portions of the hemoglobin molecule in selected animals.

Using only the data given in the chart, which of the two animals are most similar?

(1) horse and cow
(2) cow and sheep
(3) sheep and pig
(4) pig and rabbit
(5) rabbit and mouse

Items 26 to 28 refer to the following figure.

REFLECTION AND REFRACTION

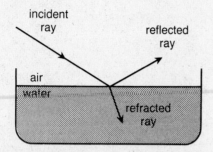

Light rays normally travel in a straight line, but when they pass through a material like glass they slow down and bend, or refract. When the ray leaves the glass it speeds up and refracts again. Prisms bend light in a particular way to create spectrums.

26. Which materials below would refract light?

 A. diamond
 B. steel
 C. water
 D. alcohol
 E. snow

 (1) A, C, and E only
 (2) B, C, and E only
 (3) B, C, and D only
 (4) A, C, and D only
 (5) A, B, and C only

27. Which of the following statements about light is the most correct?

 (1) When light slows down, it refracts.
 (2) When light is colored, it bends.
 (3) When the speed of light increases, it refracts.
 (4) When the speed of light changes, it refracts.
 (5) When prisms are used, there is no refraction.

28. Prisms have been used since the time of the Greeks, but it was Sir Isaac Newton who first used them in his classic experiment to change our understanding of light.

 Newton used them to prove that

 A. white light is made of several colors that could be separated and then recombined to form white light
 B. $E = mc^2$ (where c equals the speed of light)
 C. prisms cannot refract light

 (1) A only
 (2) B only
 (3) C only
 (4) A and B only
 (5) B and C only

29. Kilauea volcano in Hawaii erupts lava as relatively peaceful, nondangerous fountains and flows. By contrast, Mount Saint Helens in Washington erupted very violently, blowing off the mountaintop and spewing ash for many miles. The difference in volcanic style is due to the difference in composition of the lavas.

 A comparison of the lava of Mount Saint Helens to that of Kilauea shows that the Washington lava

 (1) was considerably hotter
 (2) flowed more freely
 (3) was more abundant
 (4) was richer in gases
 (5) was somewhat denser

Item 30 refers to the following diagram of an eclipse of the sun.

SOLAR ECLIPSE

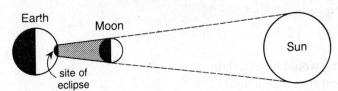

30. The diagram above shows the relationship of the Earth, moon, and sun during an eclipse of the sun.

 Which of the following conditions are <u>true</u> for such an eclipse?

 A. The earth's shadow covers half of the moon.
 B. The eclipse would occur in the middle of the night.
 C. For someone watching from the Earth, at the site of the eclipse, the moon's disk would seem to cover the sun's disk.
 D. A total eclipse would be seen from a small area only.

 (1) A and B only
 (2) A and D only
 (3) B and C only
 (4) B and D only
 (5) C and D only

31. Two parents with brown eyes give birth to a blue-eyed baby.

 Which of the following possibilities could <u>best</u> explain the appearance of the blue eyes?

 A. The baby has genes for blond hair.
 B. The gene for blue eyes is recessive compared to the gene for brown eyes.
 C. A gene for brown eyes has undergone mutation.

 (1) A only
 (2) C only
 (3) A and B only
 (4) A and C only
 (5) B and C only

Items 32 and 33 refer to the following information.

 The acid or alkaline strength of a solution is measured on the pH scale. The term "pH" has a capital H to represent hydrogen, because acids and alkalis have different hydrogen concentrations. The pH scale runs from 1 to 14, from acid to alkaline.
 The pH of a solution is commonly measured by a colored indicator, like litmus paper. Litmus paper changes color when dipped into acidic or alkaline solutions. It turns red in acids and blue in bases.

32. Which of the following best describes a chemical solution that has a pH equal to 8.5?

 (1) very acidic
 (2) slightly acidic
 (3) neutral
 (4) slightly alkaline
 (5) very alkaline

33. In which of the following solutions would litmus paper turn red?

 (1) liquid drain opener
 (2) pancake syrup
 (3) saltwater
 (4) vinegar
 (5) vodka

34. The wild fruit fly <u>Drosophila</u> has red eyes. Some biologists bred that fly in captivity through many generations. Among thousands of red-eyed flies, the scientists found one fly with white eyes.

    Which of the following would best explain what caused the appearance of the unusual fly?

    (1) adaptation
    (2) competition
    (3) evolution
    (4) mutation
    (5) natural selection

<u>Items 35 to 37</u> refer to the following chart listing properties of the five alkali metals.

Metal Element	Melting Point in °C	Boiling Point in °C
cesium	29	670
lithium	186	1336
potassium	62	760
rubidium	39	700
sodium	98	880

35. Which alkali metal is <u>most</u> likely to exist as a liquid at 84° F, the temperature of a warm room?

    (1) cesium
    (2) lithium
    (3) potassium
    (4) rubidium
    (5) sodium

36. Which alkali metal has the <u>greatest</u> temperature range in the liquid state?

    (1) cesium
    (2) lithium
    (3) potassium
    (4) rubidium
    (5) sodium

37. As a general rule in chemistry, the bonds between atoms are strongest for solids and weakest for gases. The strength of bonds varies <u>inversely</u> with the size of atoms. "Inversely" means that they vary in opposite directions. Strong bonds go with small atoms, and weak bonds go with large atoms.

    Which of the five alkali elements has the largest atoms?

    (1) cesium
    (2) lithium
    (3) potassium
    (4) rubidium
    (5) sodium

Items 38 to 41 refer to the following diagram and information.

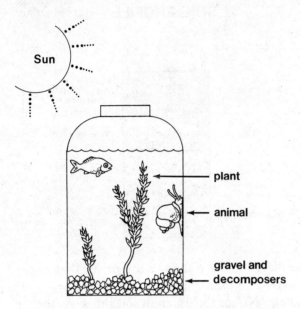

Sun

plant

animal

gravel and decomposers

In a sealed jar, a complete world can be created. The organisms supply the needs of each other, and the system can go on for months.

38. In this system, what is the major contribution of the plants to the welfare of the whole?

(1) They produce carbon dioxide needed by the animals.
(2) They are a major source of new water.
(3) They produce oxygen needed by the animals.
(4) They produce carbon dioxide needed by the other plants.
(5) They filter the water to maintain cleanliness.

39. Every system of plants and animals needs an input of energy to continue life.

What is the energy input in this system?

(1) The growth of the plants continues to supply the energy needed.
(2) The heat and motion of the animals provide the needed energy.
(3) The gravel in the floor of the container radiates energy.
(4) As plants and animals decompose they give off the needed energy.
(5) Sunlight provides energy to the system through the glass walls of the container.

40. Which of the following best shows the flow of energy through the system?

(1) animal to plant to sun to decomposers
(2) sun to plant to animal to decomposers
(3) decomposers to sun to animal to plant
(4) sun to animal to plant to decomposers
(5) plant to animal to sun to decomposers

41. This system could

(1) continue if the animals were removed but not the plants
(2) continue if the plants were removed but not the animals
(3) continue if the sun were removed but not the animals
(4) continue if the sun and the gravel were removed
(5) not survive if any part of the system were removed

42. During exploration for petroleum, it is found that an underground reservoir in porous rock usually contains some oil, some water, and some natural gas. Those three substances don't mix and occur as separate horizontal layers.

   In what order would a drill hole find those three substances?

   (1) first gas, second water, third oil
   (2) first gas, second oil, third water
   (3) first oil, second water, third gas
   (4) first water, second oil, third gas
   (5) first water, second gas, third oil

43. Dogs, cats, and horses are among the group of warm-blooded animals that have body temperatures that generally remain constant. Snakes and lizards are among the group of cold-blooded animals.

   Which of the following is the best definition of a cold-blooded animal?

   (1) It has a low body temperature.
   (2) It lives in the deserts or warm regions.
   (3) It has the temperature of its environment.
   (4) It lives in mountains or polar regions.
   (5) Its skin feels cold to the touch.

44. The new biotechnology industry is mainly concerned with proteins. It has discovered how to mass-produce many rare natural proteins and, on a more advanced level, has begun to change some proteins in the hope of obtaining new and useful effects.

   All of the following goals are being pursued by the biotechnology industry EXCEPT

   (1) a cheaper method for producing Portland cement
   (2) crop plants that can be irrigated with sea water
   (3) laboratory tests for disorders that are inherited
   (4) leaner beef that is unusually tender
   (5) treatments or cures for some cancers

Item 45 refers to the following diagram.

SOIL PROFILE

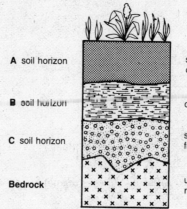

A soil horizon — sand rich in dark organic matter

B soil horizon — clay and sand

C soil horizon — sand and rock fragments

Bedrock — unweathered rock

The diagram above shows a soil profile that might be exposed on the side of a recent trench or roadcut. Notice the different soil zones. At the top of the profile, a long period of weathering has produced fine soil. Deeper into the profile, weathering is just beginning to produce fragments which will eventually become sand.

45. What does the profile above suggest about the origin of soil?

   (1) An accumulation of organic matter leads to soil.
   (2) The soil forms by the breakdown of bedrock.
   (3) Soil occurs where much clay has been deposited.
   (4) Soil requires an underground source of water.
   (5) Soil was laid down beneath a lake or ocean.

46. The household glass thermometer is partially filled with mercury and is scaled with marks along the side.

    What physical principle justifies the use of that instrument to measure temperature?

    (1) The change in air pressure upon heating moves the mercury.
    (2) Heat produces magnetic fields within a metallic liquid.
    (3) The heated glass contracts to squeeze mercury up from the bulb.
    (4) Liquid mercury expands in a regular manner when heated.
    (5) A solid like glass expands more rapidly than a liquid like mercury.

Items 47 to 52 refer to the following classes of chemical compounds in the human body.

(1) <u>Carbohydrates</u> are medium-size molecules, including starches and sugars, that are involved in metabolism.
(2) <u>Lipids</u> are medium-size molecules, including fats and oils, that are needed for tissues and membranes.
(3) <u>Nucleic acids</u> are long molecules, including DNA and RNA, that are used to store genetic information.
(4) <u>Phosphates</u> are medium-size molecules, including ATP and ADP, that provide the energy for many chemical reactions.
(5) <u>Proteins</u> are long molecules, built as chains of amino acids, that are necessary for many body functions.

Each of the following items describes conditions that relate to one of the classes of chemical compounds in the human body defined above. For each item, choose the one class that best meets the conditions given. Each of the classes of chemical compounds above <u>may</u> be used more than once in the following set of items.

47. Which class of compounds explains why children resemble their parents?

    (1) carbohydrates
    (2) lipids
    (3) nucleic acids
    (4) phosphates
    (5) proteins

48. Which class of compounds includes sucrose (from such things as sugar beets), lactose (from milk), and dextrose (from such things as grapes)?

    (1) carbohydrates
    (2) lipids
    (3) nucleic acids
    (4) phosphates
    (5) proteins

49. Which class of compounds is needed to build tubes for blood and other fluids to circulate through the body?

    (1) carbohydrates
    (2) lipids
    (3) nucleic acids
    (4) phosphates
    (5) proteins

50. Every day the human body uses about 90 pounds of Molecule X to move muscles, to amplify signals from the senses, and to produce other molecules. Fortunately, the body readily produces this medium size molecule during metabolism.

    Which class of compounds includes Molecule X?

    (1) carbohydrates
    (2) lipids
    (3) nucleic acids
    (4) phosphates
    (5) proteins

51. The polypeptides are large molecules constructed from 20 standard building blocks according to an inherited plan. The building blocks are obtained by the disintegration of dietary protein during digestion.

What is another name for the polypeptides?

(1) carbohydrates
(2) lipids
(3) nucleic acids
(4) phosphates
(5) proteins

52. The amount of energy in food is measured in calories. The average diet gets calories from sources such as bread, potatoes, butter, steak, bacon, chicken, milk, and so on.

All of the following classes of compounds are important as sources of energy in the food we eat EXCEPT

(1) carbohydrates and lipids
(2) lipids and nucleic acids
(3) nucleic acids and phosphates
(4) phosphates and proteins
(5) proteins and carbohydrates

53. Natural selection is commonly explained as "the survival of the fittest." For any organic change to affect an entire species, a change in one individual must be inherited by its offspring.

Which of the following choices is necessary for natural selection to alter a species from one superior animal?

(1) The animal cannot die from famine, drought, or disease.
(2) The animal must eat other animals.
(3) The animal should be fully adapted to its environment.
(4) The animal must outwit its natural predators.
(5) The animal must participate in reproduction.

Items 54 to 56 refer to the following diagram.

THE CELL

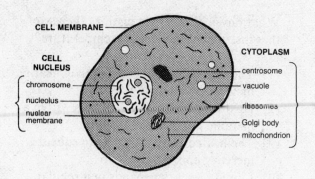

54. What part of a cell allows nutrients to enter and wastes to leave?

(1) cell membrane
(2) chromosome
(3) Golgi body
(4) mitochondrion
(5) nucleolus

55. In what part of the cell is the genetic material?

(1) centrosome
(2) chromosome
(3) nucleolus
(4) ribosome
(5) vacuole

56. The cytoplasm is one of the three essential subdivisions of any cell.

Which of the following best describes the basic characteristics of this essential subdivision?

(1) The cytoplasm varies in consistency from a fluid to a semi-solid.
(2) The cytoplasm is a consistent fluid.
(3) The cytoplasm is composed of only two items.
(4) The cytoplasm occurs within the nucleus.
(5) The cytoplasm is not present in plant cells.

57. Within a natural community of many different plant and animal species, which statement is most likely to be true?

(1) Competition is mostly between different species.
(2) Each species occupies its own place in the environment.
(3) Environmental conditions will not change significantly.
(4) The largest meat-eater should have the longest lifespan.
(5) One species will drive the others to extinction.

58. A geological principle is that rocks and structures formed long ago are best explained by studying earth processes now happening. This is sometimes stated as "the present is the key to the past."

All of the following conclusions are based on that principle EXCEPT

(1) almost all valleys were slowly carved out by stream erosion
(2) the extinction of dinosaurs was caused by a gigantic meteorite
(3) a layer of rock salt records an ancient episode of evaporation
(4) most limestone beds were deposited by organisms
(5) the rocky soil called "till" was left by melting glaciers

59. The Scottish scientist Robert Brown discovered that very small particles suspended in a liquid are continually moving in an irregular, zig-zag fashion.

What causes that unceasing "Brownian Movement" of small particles?

(1) cosmic rays
(2) electromagnetism
(3) molecular impacts
(4) ultrasonic sound
(5) the Uncertainty Principle

60. Enzymes are proteins which act as catalysts during metabolism. For each reaction there is usually only one enzyme that allows it to go forward. The body uses enzymes to control all of its many thousands of chemical reactions.

Which of the following statements best summarizes the contribution of these enzymes?

(1) They are secreted by endocrine glands and regulate many functions of the body.
(2) They convert the energy of sunlight into the chemical energy of glycogen.
(3) They permit certain chemical reactions to proceed at significant speeds.
(4) They release stored heat at a slow but useful pace.
(5) They transfer energy from one complex molecule to another complex molecule.

61. Most bodies of ore that are rich in copper, lead, zinc, or silver are believed to have formed by underground deposits from hot water solutions.

All of the following facts support that understanding EXCEPT

(1) magnetic properties are useful in finding such ore deposits
(2) many bodies of ore are located along fissures and faults
(3) the nearby rocks display intense changes due to water
(4) similar deposits have been seen to form in hot springs
(5) the ore crystals contain microscopic bubbles filled with water

Items 62 to 66 refer to the diagram and table below.

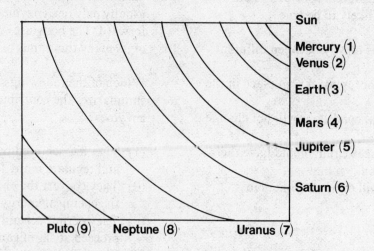

	Average Density in Grams per Cubic Centimeter	Surface Temperature in Degrees Centigrade	Diameter at the Equator in Kilometers
(1)	5.3	345 to −175	5,000
(2)	5.2	500	12,100
(3)	5.6	10	12,800
(4)	4.0	−30 to −90	6,787
(5)	1.34	−150	142,800
(6)	0.70	−180	120,000
(7)	1.3	−190	51,800
(8)	1.7	−215	49,000
(9)	?	−230	6,000

62. Objects float in water if they are lighter than an equal volume of water. An object with a density of 1 g/cm³ has a volume equal to that of the water it displaces.

Which planet or planets would be able to float if there were a lake large enough?

(1) Mercury
(2) Earth
(3) Mercury and Earth
(4) Jupiter and Uranus
(5) Saturn

63. Which of the following is (are) generally true concerning the position of the planets as they orbit the sun?

A. Low temperature planets are found furthest from the sun.
B. Dense planets orbit closer to the sun.
C. Planets of greater size are closer to the sun.

(1) A only
(2) B only
(3) C only
(4) A and B only
(5) B and C only

64. On which planet or group of planets would you be likely to find the largest amounts of liquid water?

    (1) Mars and Jupiter
    (2) Neptune
    (3) Earth
    (4) Saturn and Jupiter
    (5) Saturn, Jupiter, and Uranus

65. Venus has the

    A. second highest density of the planets
    B. highest surface temperature of the planets
    C. second smallest diameter of the planets

    (1) A only
    (2) B only
    (3) C only
    (4) A and B only
    (5) B and C only

66. Which of the following can be concluded from the information given?

    (1) The average density of a planet is in direct proportion to the surface temperature.
    (2) The surface temperature of the planet is in direct proportion to the diameter at the equator.
    (3) The diameter at the equator of the planet is in direct proportion to the average density.
    (4) The average density of a planet is inversely proportional to the surface temperature.
    (5) No direct or inverse proportions can be concluded from the information given.

END OF EXAMINATION

TEST 4: INTERPRETING LITERATURE AND THE ARTS

Tests of General Educational Development

Directions

The Interpreting Literature and the Arts Test consists of excerpts from classical and popular literature and articles about literature or the arts. Each excerpt is followed by multiple-choice questions about the reading material.

Read each excerpt first and then answer the questions following it. Refer back to the reading material as often as necessary in answering the questions.

Each excerpt is preceded by a "purpose question." The purpose question gives a reason for reading the material. Use these purpose questions to help focus your reading. You are not required to answer these purpose questions. They are given only to help you concentrate on the ideas presented in the reading materials.

You should spend no more than 65 minutes answering the questions in this booklet. Work carefully, but do not spend too much time on any one question. Be sure you answer every question. You will not be penalized for incorrect answers.

Do not mark in this test booklet. Record your answers on the separate answer sheet provided. Be sure all requested information is properly recorded on the answer sheet. To record your answers, mark the numbered space on the answer sheet beside the number that corresponds to the question in the test booklet.

FOR EXAMPLE:

It was Susan's dream machine. The metallic blue paint gleamed, and the sporty wheels were highly polished. Under the hood, the engine was no less carefully cleaned. Inside, flashy lights illuminated the instruments on the dashboard, and the seats were covered by rich leather upholstery.

The subject ("It") of this excerpt is most likely

(1) an airplane
(2) a stereo system
(3) an automobile
(4) a boat
(5) a motorcycle

The correct answer is "an automobile"; therefore, answer space 3 would be marked on the answer sheet.

Do not rest the point of your pencil on the answer sheet while you are considering your answer. Make no stray or unnecessary marks. If you change an answer, erase your first mark completely. Mark only one answer space for each question; multiple answers will be scored as incorrect. Do not fold or crease your answer sheet. Return all test materials to the test administrator.

Directions: Choose the one best answer to each item.

Items 1 to 5 refer to the following poem.

DOES THE HARD LIFE OF A CHIMNEY SWEEP HAVE ANY REWARD?

When my mother died I was very young,
And my Father sold me while yet my tongue
Could scarcely cry "'weep! 'weep! 'weep! 'weep!"
So your chimneys I sweep, and in soot I sleep.

(5)   There's little Tom Dacre, who cried when his head,
That curled like a lamb's back, was shaved: so I said,
"Hush, Tom! never mind it, for when your head's bare
You know that the soot cannot spoil your white hair."

And so he was quiet and that very night
(10) As Tom was a-sleeping, he had such a sight!
That thousands of sweepers, Dick, Joe, Ned, and Jack,
Were all of them locked up in coffins of black.

And by came an Angel who had a bright key,
And he opened the coffins and set them all free;
(15) Then down a green plain leaping, laughing, they run,
And wash in a river, and shine in the Sun.

Then naked and white, all their bags left behind,
They rise upon clouds and sport in the wind;
And the Angel told Tom, if he'd be a good boy,
(20) He'd have God for his father, and never want joy.

And so Tom awoke; and we rose in the dark,
And got with our bags and our brushes to work.
Though the morning was cold, Tom was happy and warm;
So if all do their duty they need not fear harm.

1. When the author writes "'weep!" (line 3), he suggests with an apostrophe (') that a letter is missing from the beginning of the word. That letter is most probably

   (1) s
   (2) q
   (3) w
   (4) d
   (5) p

2. The "bags left behind" mentioned in line 17 are probably

   (1) bags of groceries, which the boys will not need in heaven
   (2) bags of equipment used in the job of chimney-sweeping
   (3) luggage in which the boys keep their traveling clothes
   (4) bags that had been taken out of the coffins
   (5) sleeping bags

3. Which of the following best characterizes Tom's dream?

   (1) It has a happy beginning and a horrible ending.
   (2) It is the dream that many chimney sweeps have.
   (3) It portrays the happy life of a chimney sweep.
   (4) It has a scary beginning and a happy ending.
   (5) It shows that chimney sweeps are really God's favorite workers.

4. In line 20, the phrase "and never want joy" probably means

   (1) have enough joy
   (2) look for joy forever
   (3) never have any joy
   (4) give all joy away
   (5) only have joy in his dreams

5. What time of day does Tom awaken, in line 21?

   (1) just after sundown
   (2) close to midnight
   (3) at mid-day
   (4) at the break of dawn
   (5) very early in the morning, before dawn

Items 6 to 13 refer to the following excerpt from an essay.

ARE INSECTS AS WARLIKE AS HUMANS?

One day when I went out to my wood pile, or rather my pile of stumps, I observed two large ants, the one red, the other much larger, nearly half an inch long, and black,
(5) fiercely contending with one another. Having once got hold they never let go, but struggled and wrestled and rolled on the chips incessantly. Looking farther, I was surprised to find that the chips were covered
(10) with such combatants, that it was not a duellum, but a bellum, a war between two races of ants, the red always pitted against the black, and frequently two red ones to one black. The legions of these Myrmidons
(15) covered all the hills and vales in my wood-yard, and the ground was already strewn with the dead and dying, both red and black. It was the only battle which I have ever witnessed, the only battle-field I
(20) ever trod while the battle was raging; internecine war; the red republicans on the one hand, and the black imperialists on the other.

On every side they were engaged in
(25) deadly combat, yet without any noise that I could hear, and human soldiers never fought so resolutely. I watched a couple that were fast locked in each other's embraces, in a little sunny valley amid the
(30) chips, now at noonday prepared to fight till the sun went down, or life went out. The smaller red champion had fastened himself like a vice to his adversary's front, and through all the tumblings on that field
(35) never for an instant ceased to gnaw at one of his feelers near the root, having already caused the other to go by the board; while the stronger black one dashed him from side to side, and, as I saw on looking nearer, had
(40) already divested him of several of his members. They fought with more pertinacity than bulldogs. Neither manifested the least disposition to retreat.

It was evident that their battle-cry was
(45) "Conquer or die." In the meanwhile there came along a single red ant on the hillside of this valley, evidently full of excitement, who either had despatched his foe, or had not yet taken part in the battle; probably
(50) the latter, for he had lost none of his limbs; whose mother had charged him to return with his shield or upon it.

6. In the excerpt, the author compares

(1) the strength of ants with the strength of other insects
(2) ants with human soldiers
(3) the battle that takes place around his woodpile with battles he has witnessed elsewhere
(4) the republicans and the imperialists
(5) the struggle for survival with the struggle for victory

7. The writing style in this passage would probably be appropriate in a(n)

(1) journal of personal experiences
(2) army recruiting advertisement
(3) history book
(4) scientific study of ants and their behavior
(5) news story

8. The "single red ant" which the author describes at the end of the passage is spoken of as a warrior who has

(1) lost his shield
(2) been seriously injured
(3) not been hurt in the battle
(4) left his shield with his mother
(5) just fought another ant and lost

9. As used in this excerpt, what does "pertinacity" (line 42) mean?

   (1) defending weakly
   (2) pressing hard
   (3) reacting calmly
   (4) holding firmly
   (5) shouting angrily

10. Why does the author use the phrase "red republicans" (line 21)?

   (1) to suggest a possible comparison between the ant army and a human army
   (2) to suggest that even creatures as tiny as ants probably belong to political parties
   (3) to lead to a discussion of the actual battle between the republicans and the imperialists
   (4) to express his own political views
   (5) to warn the reader that she or he should view any battle in the animal kingdom as a political battle

11. Which of the following terms best describes the author's description of the battle between the red and black ants?

   (1) factual
   (2) comical
   (3) simple
   (4) angry
   (5) imaginative

12. The author is likely to agree with which of the following statements?

   (1) A writer must be a neutral observer.
   (2) When writing about nature, one must use the language of science.
   (3) A writer can describe an ordinary situation in an extraordinary way.
   (4) Facts and statistics are important tools for any writer.
   (5) If a writer cannot write with cool objectivity, he had better not write at all.

13. When the author says "that it was not a duellum, but a bellum" (line 11), he means

   (1) it was not a duel, but a war
   (2) the war of ants was a series of duels
   (3) this was not wrestling, but rather combat
   (4) each of the duels led to a battle
   (5) winning the war meant winning the duels

Items 14 to 18 refer to the following excerpt from a novel

HOW IS ELINOR DIFFERENT
FROM HER MOTHER AND SISTER?

Elinor, the eldest daughter whose advice was so effectual, possessed a strength of understanding and coolness of judgment which qualified her, though only nineteen,

(5)   to be the counsellor of her mother, and enabled her frequently to counteract, to the advantage of them all, that eagerness of mind in Mrs. Dashwood which must generally have led to imprudence. She had

(10) an excellent heart; her disposition was affectionate, and her feelings were strong; but she knew how to govern them; it was a knowledge which her mother had yet to learn, and which her sister, Marianne, had

(15) resolved never to be taught.

Marianne's abilities were in many respects quite equal to Elinor's. She was lively and clever, but eager in everything; her sorrows, her joys, could have no

(20) moderation. She was generous, amiable, interesting: she was everything but prudent. The resemblance between her and her mother was strikingly great.

Elinor saw with concern the excess of her

(25) sister's sensibility, but by Mrs. Dashwood it was valued and cherished. They encouraged each other now in the violence of their feelings. Elinor, too, was deeply afflicted; but still she could struggle, she could exert

(30) herself.

14. Listed according to age with the oldest first, the three characters mentioned are

    (1) Elinor, Mrs. Dashwood, Marianne
    (2) Mrs. Dashwood, Elinor, Marianne
    (3) Mrs. Dashwood, Marianne, Elinor
    (4) Elinor, Marianne, Mrs. Dashwood
    (5) Marianne, Mrs. Dashwood, Elinor

15. The excerpt suggests that Elinor

    (1) is cold and unfeeling
    (2) feels less strongly than Marianne
    (3) feels more strongly than Marianne
    (4) unlike Marianne, controls her feelings
    (5) like Marianne, controls her feelings

16. Mrs. Dashwood and Marianne share all of the following qualities EXCEPT

    (1) eagerness
    (2) imprudence
    (3) affection
    (4) impulsiveness
    (5) moderation

17. A story about Elinor and Marianne might best be titled

    (1) Hope and Hatred
    (2) Pride and Prejudice
    (3) Sadness and Sorrow
    (4) Sense and Sensibility
    (5) Happiness and Hope

18. The passage suggests that strong feelings are

    (1) important, but must be controlled
    (2) dangerous, and to be avoided at all costs
    (3) characteristic of the young but not the old
    (4) characteristic of the old but not the young
    (5) usually accompanied by prudence

Items 19 to 23 are based on the following excerpt from a play.

IS VIVIE WARREN A MODERN WOMAN?

<u>Scene</u>: By a cottage in the country, a young lady lies in a hammock reading and making notes. A large pile of books and papers are on a wooden chair nearby. A carefully dressed middle-aged man enters and looks over the fence.

	THE GENTLEMAN:	(taking off his hat) I beg your pardon. Can you direct me to
(5)		Hindview—Mrs. Alison's?
	THE YOUNG LADY:	(glancing up from her book) This is Mrs. Alison's. (She resumes her work.)
	THE GENTLEMAN:	Indeed! Perhaps—may I ask are you Miss Vivie Warren?
	THE YOUNG LADY:	(sharply, as she turns on her elbow to get a good look at him) Yes.
(10)	THE GENTLEMAN:	(daunted and conciliatory) I'm afraid I appear intrusive. My name is Praed. (Vivie at once throws her books upon the chair, and gets out of the hammock) Oh, pray don't let me disturb you.
	VIVIE:	(striding to the gate and opening it for him) Come in, Mr. Praed. (He comes in.) Glad to see you. (She proffers her hand and takes his with a
(15)		resolute and hearty grip. She is an attractive, young, middle-class Englishwoman. Age 22.)
	PRAED:	Very kind of you indeed, Miss Warren. (She shuts the gate with a vigorous slam. He passes in to the middle of the garden, exercising his fingers, which are slightly numbed by her greeting.) Has your mother
(20)		arrived?
	VIVIE:	Is she coming?
	PRAED:	(surprised) Didn't you expect us?
	VIVIE:	No.
	PRAED:	Now, goodness me, I hope I've not mistaken the day. That would be just
(25)		like me, you know. Your mother arranged that she was to come down from London and that I was to come over from Horsham to be introduced to you.
	VIVIE:	Did she? H'm! My mother has rather a trick of taking me by surprise—to see how I behave myself when she's away, I suppose. I fancy I shall take
(30)		my mother very much by surprise one of these days, if she makes arrangements that concern me without consulting me beforehand. She hasn't come.
	PRAED:	(embarrassed) I'm really very sorry.
	VIVIE:	It's not your fault, Mr. Praed, is it? And I'm very glad you've come. You
(35)		are the only one of my mother's friends I have ever asked her to bring to see me.
	PRAED:	Oh, now this is really very good of you, Miss Warren!
	VIVIE:	Will you come indoors; or would you rather sit out here and talk?
	PRAED:	It will be nicer out here, don't you think?
(40)	VIVIE:	Then I'll go and get you a chair. (She goes to the porch for a garden chair.)
	PRAED:	(following her) Oh, pray, pray! Allow me. (He lays hands on the chair.)
	VIVIE:	(letting him take it) Take care of your fingers: they're rather dodgy things, those chairs. (She goes across to the chair with the books on it;
(45)		pitches them into the hammock.)

PRAED: (who has just unfolded his chair) Oh, now do let me take that hard chair. I like hard chairs.

VIVIE: So do I. Sit down, Mr. Praed.

PRAED: By the way, though, hadn't we better go to the station to meet your

(50) mother?

VIVIE: (coolly) Why? She knows the way.

PRAED: (disconcerted) Er—I suppose she does. (He sits down.)

19. The first impression of Vivie that the scene conveys is that she is

(1) lazy
(2) shy
(3) studious
(4) athletic
(5) vain

20. A piece of visually comic action in this scene is Vivie's

(1) reading
(2) getting out of the homework
(3) closing the gate
(4) handshake
(5) walking to the porch

21. Vivie's response to Praed's remarks about her mother in this scene suggests that

(1) Praed has never met her mother
(2) Praed dislikes her mother
(3) Vivie and her mother are very alike
(4) Vivie and her mother get along well
(5) Vivie and her mother do not get along well

22. Compared to Vivie, Mr. Praed is more

(1) authoritative
(2) conventional
(3) earnest
(4) successful
(5) musical

23. Which of the following of Vivie's actions probably do not agree with Praed's expectations of how a female should behave?

A. her handshake
B. her allowing him to unfold the garden chair
C. her not wishing to meet her mother's train

(1) A only
(2) B only
(3) C only
(4) A and B
(5) A, B, and C

<u>Items 24 to 29</u> refer to the following excerpt from an article.

DOES "COLORIZING" OLD MOVIES MAKE THEM BETTER?

When the film fans dream of old movies, they dream in black and white. They think of Lillian Gish's <u>Scarlet Letter</u> emblazoned in gray. For them the true colors of <u>Red</u>
(5) <u>River</u>, <u>Blue Denim</u>, <u>Golden Boy</u> and <u>Green Pastures</u> are those shades of pearl and ivory determined by the films' cinematographers. And when Bogie says, "here's looking at you, kid," movie lovers gaze at Ingrid
(10) Bergman in glorious monochrome.

But who cares about the visual integrity of Hollywood movies when there is a buck to be made? Not the studios or the TV networks. For them the golden oldies are
(15) either profitable inventory or chopped celluloid. And now the archives are being raided by technicians with a new idea: "colorizing" the black-and-white films of Hollywood's Golden Age through computer
(20) wizardry. The film is copied onto video and broken down into gradations of gray. An "art director" sits at a console and chooses the colors for each face, dress and prop, which the computerized "paintbrush" adds
(25) frame by frame. (Cost per film about $180,000.) Voila! Jimmy Stewart's Christmas tree in "It's a Wonderful Life" is as green as greenbacks.

Some people, especially young people
(30) nurtured on color TV, like the idea. In a poll by Ted Turner's Cable News Network the day the colorized <u>Yankee Doodle Dandy</u> premiered on Turner's SuperStation WTBS last month, 61% of the call-in respondents
(35) preferred to see old films in color. Good thing: the Turner Broadcasting System has ordered the coloring of 100 black-and-whites from the MGM and Warner Bros. libraries. "We're not trying to
(40) make bad films great," says Jack Petrik, executive vice president of WTBS. "We're trying to make great films better." Charles Powell, executive vice president of Color Systems Technology, which provides the

(45) new versions to TBS, calls the process "simply another state-of-the-art enhancement. Would you rather have a film sit on the shelf in its 'pure' form or be seen by large numbers of people only because it
(50) was colored?"

24. The question that begins with line 11 indicates which of the following about the writer of this excerpt?

(1) The writer is most interested in making a buck.
(2) The writer is on the side of the studios and TV networks.
(3) The writer thinks that "visual integrity" is more important than "making a buck."
(4) The writer often dreams of old movies.
(5) The writer thinks that old movies are no more than "chopped celluloid."

25. Which of the following conclusions is expressed in the excerpt?

(1) People who grew up watching color TV are in favor of "colorizing."
(2) Ted Turner is one of those movie fans who "dream in black and white."
(3) <u>Yankee Doodle Dandy</u> is available only in black and white.
(4) 39% of those who called WTBS are not movie fans.
(5) Most black-and-white movies were made by MGM and Warner Brothers.

26. What is the writer probably trying to indicate by putting quotation marks around the term "art director" in line 22?

(1) The writer is using the art director's own words.
(2) "Art director" is another name for "paintbrush."
(3) The art director is the most important person in the colorizing process.
(4) There are as many art directors as there are paintbrushes.
(5) "Art director" is a title that doesn't really describe the actual job.

27. Which of the following does the first paragraph suggest?

   (1) Ingrid Bergman objected to making films in color.
   (2) Film fans rarely choose to watch a movie in color.
   (3) Red River was a black-and-white film.
   (4) Most cinematographers dream in black and white.
   (5) No old movies were made in color.

28. With which of the following would Jack Petrik probably agree?

   (1) Color films are better than black-and-white films.
   (2) WTBS should not colorize more than 100 films.
   (3) Yankee Doodle Dandy was the best choice for the first colorized film.
   (4) Colorizing films does not affect their quality.
   (5) More people today prefer black-and-white films over color films.

29. Based on the information in the article, which of the following is probably true about colorization?

   (1) Only WTBS is able to do it.
   (2) It relies upon computer technology.
   (3) Most actors are likely to approve of it.
   (4) It will not result in profit for the studios or networks.
   (5) It will not change the dreams of film fans.

Items 30 to 33 refer to the following poem

HOW DOES THE AUTHOR REGARD CHILD LABOR?

The golf links lie so near the mill
That almost every day
The laboring children can look out
And see the men at play.

30. The best synonym for "golf links" would be

   (1) golf cart
   (2) golf course
   (3) golf players
   (4) fence
   (5) joint

31. Which of the following normal expectations of the reader does the poem deliberately upset?

   (1) that children wish to appear older than they really are
   (2) that parents must sometimes be strict with children
   (3) that men work while children play
   (4) that some children enjoy both work and play
   (5) that golf is a game for grownups, not for children

32. The poem probably takes place in which of the following time periods?

   (1) the 1980s
   (2) the 1940s
   (3) 1914-1918
   (4) the nineteenth century
   (5) the Middle Ages

33. Which of the following adjectives best describes this poem?

   (1) nostalgic
   (2) ironic
   (3) genial
   (4) optimistic
   (5) pious

Items 34 to 39 refer to the following excerpt.

WHAT DETAILS MAKE UP
THE BEAUTY OF AUTUMN?

Waking in late September, in New
Hampshire, we gaze south toward Mt.
Kearsarge from the dawn window under the
great maple that torches the hillside. Each
(5)   morning is more outrageous than the one
before, days outdoing their predecessors as
sons outdo their fathers. We walk out, over
the chill dew, to audit glorious wreckage
from the night's cold passage—new
(10) branches suddenly turned, others gone
deeper into ranges of fire, trees vying to
surpass one another and their yester-selves.
In the afternoon we take long walks with
Gus the dog, who is the color of oak leaves,
(15) who bounds ahead of us and leaps to chase
a leaf falling. Maybe we walk up New
Canada, the dirt road that climbs the
northwest slope of Ragged Mountain, and
walk in a tunnel of red shade under oak and
(20) maple, under wide old birches with leaves a
delicate yellow. On the downslope, as leaves
fall away, the valley opens, and on the
clearest days for the first time since April
we can look across and see the hills of
(25) Vermont. As the dog bounces our hearts
bounce also with a happy overload, our
landscape turned into sensuous Italian
crockery or grand opera.

Or we walk on the low dirt road that
(30) skirts Eagle Pond, and on the rattling
bridge at the south end—over the
Blackwater River's tributaries exiting the
pond, by the beaver's bog where wet earth
stabs upward with cone-shaped, gnawed
(35) stumps of poplar—we stand and stare with
our jaws gaped at the tweedy circumference
of the pond, low trees turned orange,
Chinese red, pink, russet, together with
silver-gray trunk and evergreen green,
(40) weaving the universe's most outlandish
fabric, the whole more purple than not,
although no part of it is purple. Walking
back to our house, from any direction, we
know again, and always for the

(45) heart-stopping first time, that our house sits
floating in the center of autumn's flood:
yellow candle leaves against unpainted
barn; fiery wild maple shooting up against
the sprawling old white house with green
(50) shutters; the slope of Ragged rising behind
with its crazy anthology of color, shade, and
texture. We inhabit the landscape's
brightest and briefest flesh.

34. What is the "glorious wreckage" (line 8) that
the writer walks out to "audit"?

(1) the results of a giant forest fire
(2) animals playing around campfires at
sunrise
(3) destruction from a storm that passed
overnight
(4) branches of trees filled with the colors of
autumn
(5) fathers and sons who have been walking
through the countryside for days

35. According to the excerpt, the bouncing along
of Gus the dog can be compared to

(1) the happiness of the writer and his
companion
(2) the falling of oak leaves
(3) the music of Italian grand opera
(4) the excitement of the writer running
along a dirt road
(5) the heavy load of crockery that the writer
and his companion carry with them

36. ". . . we stand and stare with our jaws
gaped. . ." (lines 35–36) The writer probably
includes this remark to suggest that he is

(1) ready to shout out loud
(2) near to the outer edge of the pond
(3) imitating the behavior of his companion
(4) stuck in the beaver's bog
(5) amazed by the beautiful sights he beholds

37. "Anthology" in line 51 probably means

    (1) scenery
    (2) pile
    (3) combination
    (4) sounds
    (5) reds

38. One characteristic of this passage which
    stands out is its

    (1) witty use of dialogue
    (2) persistent description of noises
    (3) emphasis on the comedy of the landscape
    (4) repeated reference to places familiar to
        most readers
    (5) vivid use of visual details

39. What information does the writer
    communicate in the first sentence?

    (1) the thesis that he expects to prove
    (2) the precise location of Mt. Kearsarge
    (3) the time of year and the general location
    (4) the time of day, the time of year, and the
        general location
    (5) the reason for his awakening so early

Items 40 to 45 refer to the following excerpt.

SHOULD CHIEF SEATTLE
SELL INDIAN LAND
TO THE U.S. GOVERNMENT?

Yonder sky that has wept tears of
compassion upon my people for centuries
untold, and which to us appears changeless
and eternal, may change. Today is fair.
(5)   Tomorrow may be overcast with clouds. My
words are like the stars that never change.
Whatever Seattle says the great chief at
Washington can rely upon with as much
certainty as he can upon the return of the
(10) sun or the seasons. The White Chief says
that Big Chief at Washington sends us
greetings of friendship and goodwill. That is
kind of him for we know he has little need
of our friendship in return. His people are
(15) many. They are like the grass that covers
vast prairies. My people are few. They
resemble the scattering trees of a
storm-swept plain. The great, and—I
presume—good, White Chief sends us word
(20) that he wishes to buy our lands but is
willing to allow us enough to live
comfortably. This indeed appears just, even
generous, for the Red Man no longer has
rights that he need respect, and the offer
(25) may be wise also, as we are no longer in
need of an extensive country. . . . I will not
dwell on, nor mourn over, our untimely
decay, nor reproach our paleface brothers
with hastening it, as we too may have been
(30) somewhat to blame.

40. When the speaker (Chief Seattle) says, "They
are like the grass that covers vast prairies"
(lines 15–16), he means

   (1) the White people can be found only on
the prairies
   (2) the White people rely on the prairie
grasses for food
   (3) there are huge numbers of White people
   (4) the White people, like the prairie grasses,
will die out
   (5) the cities of the White people are
covering the prairies

41. According to Chief Seattle, how much of the
Indian land does the "White Chief" wish to
buy?

   (1) all except a portion large enough for the
Indians to "live comfortably"
   (2) only a small portion, rather than an
"extensive country"
   (3) enough for a few Indians
   (4) only as much as the Indians have a right
to
   (5) as much land as Seattle wishes to sell

42. Which of the following is characteristic of the
unique style of this excerpt?

   (1) complete sentences
   (2) formal English
   (3) references to Washington
   (4) images from nature
   (5) occasional profanity

43. Chief Seattle's attitude toward the White
Chief's desire to buy Indian land is

   (1) accepting
   (2) hostile
   (3) amused
   (4) confused
   (5) desperate

44. Who, according to Seattle, may be to blame
for the "untimely decay" of his people?

   (1) The White people are entirely to blame.
   (2) No one is really to blame.
   (3) Blame rests with Seattle and the White
Chief.
   (4) Blame rests partly with the White people
and partly with the Indians.
   (5) Seattle alone is to blame.

45. When Chief Seattle compares his words to
stars (lines 5–6), he means that his words are

   (1) always brilliant
   (2) trustworthy
   (3) unreachable
   (4) distant
   (5) cold

END OF EXAMINATION

TEST 5: MATHEMATICS

Tests of General Educational Development

Directions

The Mathematics Test consists of multiple-choice questions intended to measure general mathematics skills and problem-solving ability. The questions are based on short readings which often include a graph, chart, or figure.

You should spend no more than 90 minutes answering the questions in this booklet. Work carefully, but do not spend too much time on any one question. Be sure you answer every question. You will not be penalized for incorrect answers.

Formulas you may need are given on the following page. Only some of the questions will require you to use a formula. Not all the formulas given will be needed.

Some questions contain more information than you will need to solve the problem. Other questions do not give enough information to solve the problem. If the question does not give enough information to solve the problem, the correct answer choice is "Not enough information is given."

The use of calculators is not allowed.

Do not mark in this test booklet. The test administrator will give you blank paper for your calculations. Record your answers on the separate answer sheet provided. Be sure all requested information is properly recorded on the answer sheet.

To record your answers, mark the numbered space on the answer sheet beside the number that corresponds to the question in the test booklet.

FOR EXAMPLE:

If a grocery bill totaling $15.75 is paid with a $20.00 bill, how much change should be returned?

(1) $5.26
(2) $4.75
(3) $4.25
(4) $3.75
(5) $3.25

The correct answer is "$4.25"; therefore, answer space 3 would be marked on the answer sheet.

Do not rest the point of your pencil on the answer sheet while you are considering your answer. Make no stray or unnecessary marks. If you change an answer, erase your first mark completely. Mark only one answer space for each question; multiple answers will be scored as incorrect. Do not fold or crease your answer sheet. Return all test materials to the test administrator.

FORMULAS

Description	Formula

AREA (A) of a:

- square — $A = s^2$; where s = side
- rectangle — $A = lw$; where l = length, w = width
- parallelogram — $A = bh$; where b = base, h = height
- triangle — $A = \frac{1}{2}bh$; where b = base, h = height
- circle — $A = \pi r^2$; where π = 3.14, r = radius

PERIMETER (P) of a:

- square — $P = 4s$; where s = side
- rectangle — $P = 2l + 2w$; where l = length, w = width
- triangle — $P = a + b + c$: where a, b, and c are the sides
- circumference (C) of a circle — $C = \pi d$; where π = 3.14, d = diameter

VOLUME (V) of a:

- cube — $V = s^3$; where s = side
- rectangular container — $V = lwh$; where l = length, w = width, h = height
- cylinder — $V = \pi r^2 h$; where π = 3.14, r = radius, h = height

Pythagorean relationship — $c^2 = a^2 + b^2$; where c = hypotenuse, a and b are legs of a right triangle

distance (d) between two points in a plane — $d = \sqrt{(x_2 - x_1)^2 + (y_2 - y_1)^2}$; where (x_1, y_1) and (x_2, y_2) are two points in a plane

slope of a line (m) — $m = \dfrac{y_2 - y_1}{x_2 - x_1}$; where (x_1, y_1) and (x_2, y_2) are two points in a plane

mean — $\text{mean} = \dfrac{x_1 + x_2 + \cdots + x_n}{n}$; where the x's are the values for which a mean is desired, and n = number of values in the series

median — median = the point in an ordered set of numbers at which half of the numbers are above and half of the numbers are below this value

simple interest (i) — $i = prt$; where p = principal, r = rate, t = time

distance (d) as function of rate and time — $d = rt$; where r = rate, t = time

total cost (c) — $c = nr$; where n = number of units, r = cost per unit

Directions: Choose the one best answer to each item.

1. Alex has a job working for the Adams Apple Orchard. Two hundred new apple trees just arrived, which Mr. Adams would like Alex to plant. Alex can plant an average of 15 trees per work day. At this rate, approximately how many work days will it take Adam to plant the 200 trees?

(1) between 7 and 9
(2) between 9 and 11
(3) between 11 and 13
(4) between 13 and 15
(5) between 15 and 17

2. A car which usually sells for $10,000 is discounted 20%. What is the sale price?

(1) $ 20.00
(2) $ 80.00
(3) $2000.00
(4) $8000.00
(5) $8800.00

3. Lorene jogs 1½ hours each day. Last week she jogged 5 days. How many hours did Lorene jog last week?

(1) 6½
(2) 7
(3) 7½
(4) 8
(5) 8½

Item 4 refers to the number line below.

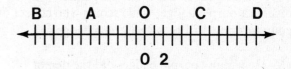

4. Which letter on the number line above represents −6?

(1) A
(2) B
(3) O
(4) C
(5) D

Item 5 refers to the triangle below.

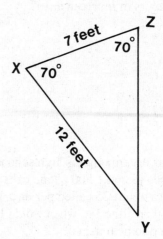

5. Triangle XYZ above is isosceles. What is its perimeter (in feet)?

(1) 19
(2) 21
(3) 26
(4) 31
(5) Not enough information is given.

Items 6 and 7 refer to the following information.

A den of 8 cub scouts has fourteen days to collect 301 pounds of newspapers for the paper drive. Scouts who collect more than 50 pounds will receive a purple badge, while scouts who collect 50 pounds or less will receive a green badge.

6. How many purple badges did the den of scouts receive?

   (1) 50
   (2) 14
   (3)   8
   (4)   6
   (5) Not enough information is given.

7. What is the minimum average number of pounds of newspapers per day that the den must collect in order to have 301 pounds of newspapers in fourteen days?

   (1) 13.7
   (2) 21.5
   (3) 37.6
   (4) 42.8
   (5) 50.1

8. Jamal is organizing his high school reunion. He needs to make 500 phone calls and averages about 25 called per day. If he begins phoning on June 1st, when would he be expected to be finished?

   (1) June 5th
   (2) June 10th
   (3) June 15th
   (4) June 20th
   (5) June 25th

Item 9 refers to the circle graph below.

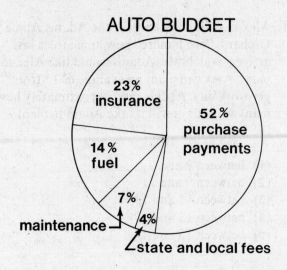

9. The circle graph above shows how the average adult spends his or her auto budget. According to the graph, what percent of the auto budget is left after purchase payments and insurance?

   (1) 100
   (2)   75
   (3)   50
   (4)   25
   (5)   0

10. Between which of the following pairs of numbers is the square root of 40?

   (1) 2 and 6
   (2) 6 and 7
   (3) 14 and 18
   (4) 18 and 22
   (5) 22 and 26

Item 11 refers to the two similar triangles below.

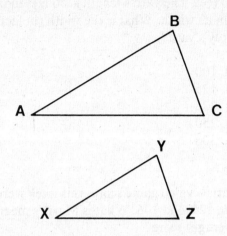

11. In the figure above, triangle ABC is similar to triangle XYZ. The perimeter of triangle ABC is 14 inches, while the perimeter of triangle XYZ is 8 inches. What is the <u>length of side AB</u> (in inches)?

(1) 4
(2) 6
(3) 7
(4) 14
(5) Not enough information is given.

12. When Gary rides his bicycle, he burns 3.3 calories per minute. Last week Gary rode his bicycle 45 minutes on Monday, 30 minutes on Tuesday, 40 minutes on Wednesday, and 50 minutes on Thursday. Which of the following expressions best represents how many <u>calories</u> Gary burned riding his bicycle last week?

(1) 45 + 30 + 40 + 50
(2) 165 + 3.3
(3) 165(3.3)
(4) 330(3.3)
(5) 330 + 3.3

Item 13 refers to the triangle below.

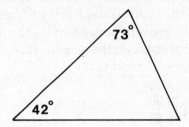

13. The triangle above has three interior angles. The measure of one is 73 degrees, and the measure of another is 42 degrees. What is the measure (in degrees) of the third interior angle?

(1) 42
(2) 65
(3) 73
(4) 115
(5) 145

Item 14 refers to the following juice package.

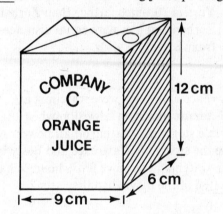

14. Pictured above is the new rectangular package Company C is considering for their orange juice. Because of the structure of the package, it can be filled to only 3/4 of its capacity without bursting. Given the dimensions above, which of the following expressions represents the <u>maximum volume</u> (in cubic centimeters) of orange juice that the package can hold <u>without bursting</u>?

(1) (9)(6)(12)
(2) (3/4)(9)(6)(12)
(3) (3/4)(6)(12 + 9)
(4) 2(6) + 2(12) + 2(9)
(5) Not enough information is given.

15. Last summer Arnie traveled to China. He bought silk fabric for $250 and jade jewelry for $380. As Arnie was leaving China, the customs agent informed him that he must pay 15% export tax on these items. How much was Arnie's <u>export tax</u>?

(1) $630.00
(2) $535.50
(3) $150.00
(4) $ 94.50
(5) $ 15.00

16. If the distance from Earth to the planet Zorbon is 9×10^6 light years away, and the distance from Earth to the planet Yeva is 3×10^5 light years away, which of the following statements would be <u>true</u> concerning the planets' distances from Earth?

(1) Zorbon is 3 times farther than Yeva.
(2) Yeva is 3 times farther than Zorbon.
(3) Zorbon is 30 times farther than Yeva.
(4) Yeva is 30 times farther than Zorbon.
(5) Zorbon and Yeva are equal distances from Earth.

17. Lawrence and Betty were watching a 105-minute movie on television when a terrible storm hit, cutting off all power. At the time the storm hit, Lawrence and Betty had been watching the move for ¼ hour. What <u>fraction</u> of the movie had they <u>seen</u>?

(1) $\dfrac{1}{105}$

(2) $\dfrac{1}{7}$

(3) $\dfrac{1}{5}$

(4) $\dfrac{1}{4}$

(5) Not enough information is given.

18. The perimeter of Leroy's rectangular yard is 600 feet. The yard's length is 50 feet more than its width. What is the <u>width</u> (in feet) of Leroy's yard?

(1) 100
(2) 125
(3) 225
(4) 250
(5) 300

19. Maria's video game scores this week were 186, 124, and 146. What is Maria's <u>mean</u> (average) score?

(1) 456
(2) 186
(3) 152
(4) 146
(5) 124

20. Luke went to the store and bought celery priced at $.29, lettuce priced at $.69, a chicken priced at $2.68, and dish soap priced at $1.50. There is no tax on food items. Nonfood items are taxed 6%. What was Luke's <u>total bill</u>?

(1) $5.47
(2) $5.25
(3) $5.16
(4) $3.66
(5) $1.50

21. This year Tina's father is 39 years old. He is triple her age. Which equation below could be used to determine <u>Tina's age</u>?

(1) $39 = 3T$
(2) $39 = 3 + T$
(3) $39 = T - 3$
(4) $39 = T/3$
(5) $39 = 3/T$

Item 22 refers to the graph below.

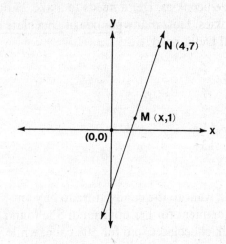

22. In the graph above, the slope of line MN is 3. What is the x-coordinate of point M?

(1) 1
(2) 2
(3) 3
(4) 4
(5) 5

23. Evaluate $7y + 6y^2$, for $x = 3$ and $y = 4$.

(1) 13
(2) 64
(3) 82
(4) 300
(5) 352

24. Dmitri bought 10 dozen tulip bulbs last fall and planted them in his garden. This spring, when his tulips bloomed, he noticed that they all were either red or yellow and that there were twice as many red as yellow. How many red tulips does he have in this assortment?

(1) 10
(2) 12
(3) 40
(4) 80
(5) 120

25. Mr. Spears baked cookies on Thursday. He baked the following assortment: 3 dozen chocolate chip, 2 dozen oatmeal, and 4 dozen peanut butter. After all the cookies were cool, Mr. Spears mixed them all up and put them in his grandmother's big ceramic cookie jar. His youngest son, who is not yet tall enough to look into the jar, took the first cookie. What was the probability that it was oatmeal?

(1) 1/12
(2) 2/9
(3) 2/7
(4) 1/3
(5) 2/3

Item 26 refers to the figure below.

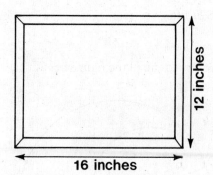

26. Sonya is building a picture frame as a gift for her aunt and uncle. To make sure that the corners meet squarely, Sonya must check the diagonals of the frame. If the diagonals are equal, then the corners meet squarely (are square). What should the length (in inches) of each diagonal be so that Sonya can be sure that the corners are square?

(1) 18
(2) 20
(3) 22
(4) 24
(5) Not enough information is given.

27. Marie is collecting information for a research project for her economics class at school, so she interviews her seven favorite teachers. Marie finds that their annual incomes are

    $25,000
    $17,000
    $20,000
    $25,000
    $27,000
    $21,000
    $22,000

    What is their median income?

    (1) $17,000
    (2) $22,000
    (3) $23,000
    (4) $24,000
    (5) $27,000

Item 28 refers to the plane figure below.

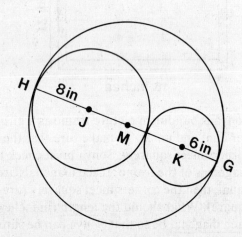

28. In the plane figure above, two smaller circles with centers at points J and K have been drawn inside a larger circle with center at point M. If JH = 8 inches and KG = 6 inches, what is the diameter (in inches) of the larger circle with center at point M?

    (1) 12
    (2) 14
    (3) 16
    (4) 22
    (5) 28

29. It takes 2 pounds of chocolate chips to make 6 dozen cookies. Delta needs to make 27 dozen cookies. How many pounds of chocolate chips will Delta need?

    (1) 5
    (2) 7
    (3) 9
    (4) 11
    (5) 13

30. Ella went to the candy store to buy an assortment for her boyfriend. She found that milk chocolates sold for 50¢ each, while semisweet chocolates sold for 40¢ each. Ella decided to buy 12 milk chocolates and 8 semisweet chocolates. Which expression below could be used to calculate Ella's bill? (There is no sales tax.)

    (1) 12(50) + 8(40)
    (2) 12(40) + 8(50)
    (3) 12(50) + 8(50)
    (4) 12(40) + 8(40)
    (5) Not enough information is given.

31. Julie just bought a car for $5800. The insurance fee will be 8% of the selling price. What will the fee be?

    (1) $800.00
    (2) $725.00
    (3) $580.00
    (4) $464.00
    (5) $ 8.00

32. Paul and Pam have just purchased their first home. They would like to weather strip around the perimeter of their big picture window. The window is a rectangle 10 feet wide and 8 feet tall. How many feet of weather stripping do they need?

    (1) 18
    (2) 36
    (3) 40
    (4) 72
    (5) 80

33. Lavell's baby eats 5½ ounces of cereal each day. How many days will a 44-ounce box of cereal last?

    (1) 49½
    (2) 38½
    (3) 20
    (4) 10
    (5) 8

34. Sam has 4 brothers—Tom, Joe, Chet, and Al. Tom and Joe are twins. Al is 5 years younger than Chet, and Chet is 2 years older than Tom. How old will Joe be when Al is 21?

    (1) 12
    (2) 14
    (3) 18
    (4) 22
    (5) 24

35. The O'Brien family takes the local paper every day. It costs 25¢ each weekday, 50¢ on Saturday, and 75¢ on Sunday. The O'Brien family always pays in advance. This month they are going on vacation from Wednesday the 8th through Monday the 20th and will not be receiving the paper those days. If they will receive a full refund, how much will it be?

    (1) $5.00
    (2) $4.75
    (3) $4.50
    (4) $4.25
    (5) $4.00

36. Ahmed's parents were shopping around for a wood stove for their house in the mountains, so they attended the Energy Fair. They found the stove they wanted. The Energy Fair gave them a coupon which they could take to the store to receive a 15% discount on the stove. If the stove regularly sold for $500, what would the discounted price be?

    (1) $515
    (2) $485
    (3) $470
    (4) $450
    (5) $425

37. 420 pounds of lawn seed will plant 2 acres of lawn. How many pounds of seed are needed to plant 12 acres?

    (1) 840
    (2) 1260
    (3) 2520
    (4) 5040
    (5) Not enough information is given.

38. Find x, for $y = 3$ and $z = 7$, if $x = 5y(z - 1)$.

    (1) 90
    (2) 94
    (3) 104
    (4) 114
    (5) 318

39. Frank goes grocery shopping once a week. Last month Frank spent $82.96 the first week, $58.34 the second week, $70.25 the third week, and $62.49 the fourth week. What was Frank's average weekly grocery bill?

    (1) $ 62.49
    (2) $ 68.51
    (3) $ 70.25
    (4) $145.45
    (5) $274.04

Item 40 refers to the graph below.

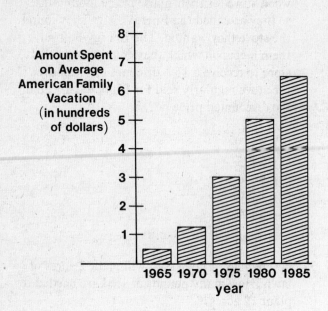

40. According to the graph above, by how much did the amount spent on the average American family vacation increase from 1970 to 1985?

(1) $ 5.25
(2) $ 6.50
(3) $ 65.00
(4) $525.00
(5) $650.00

Item 41 refers to the drawing below.

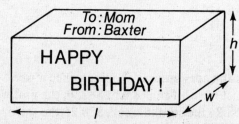

41. Baxter is going to decorate the closed gift box above by glueing gold braid along each of the edges. If the dimensions of the box are l by w by h, which equation below could be used to determine the amount of braid that Baxter (B) will need?

(1) $B = 4(lwh)$
(2) $B = 4l + 4w + 4h$
(3) $B = 2l + 2w + 2h$
(4) $B = 2(lwh)$
(5) $B = 3(l + w + h)$

42. Andre is fighting the battle of the bulge. He is counting calories consumed and calories burned. Today Andre ate 250 calories of fruits and vegetables, 500 calories of meat, 125 calories of cereals, and 275 calories of dairy products. Andre burned 980 calories today. Which expression below could be used to express his net calorie count for the day?

(1) $250 + 500 + 125 + 275 - 980$
(2) $980 - 250 - 500 - 125 - 275$
(3) $250 + 500 - 125 - 275 + 980$
(4) $250 - 500 + 125 + 275 - 980$
(5) $250 + 500 + 125 + 275 + 980$

Item 43 refers to the circle graph below.

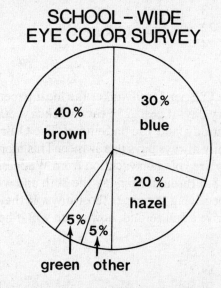

SCHOOL–WIDE EYE COLOR SURVEY

43. Annette does a school-wide survey and publishes her results in the circle graph above. If 62 people at Annette's school have hazel eyes, how many have brown eyes?

(1)   20
(2)   40
(3)   62
(4) 124
(5) 248

Item 44 refers to the following price list.

PRICE LIST

Top Sirloin .... $2.99 per pound
                or 2 pounds for $5.00
Filet Mignon .... $4.00 per pound
London Broil .... $1.79 per pound
                or 3 pounds for $5.00

44. Randy owns and manages Randy's Steakhouse. He needs to buy the following meats in order to have enough for the weekend business: 9 pounds of Top Sirloin, 8 pounds of Filet Mignon, and 7 pounds of London Broil. What is the least amount Randy can spend to buy the meat he needs for the weekend business?

(1) $97.00
(2) $71.44
(3) $66.78
(4) $54.99
(5) $34.78

45. Mrs. Schmidt bought an assortment of cookies for the tenants' meeting in her apartment house. The assortment consisted of 6 dozen cookies, some chocolate and some vanilla. There were twice as many chocolate cookies as there were vanilla cookies. How many chocolate cookies were in the assortment?

(1) 6
(2) 12
(3) 24
(4) 48
(5) 72

46. Due to a slow-down at the lumber mill, the wages of all employees will be reduced 10%. Before the slow-down, Jason was making $321 a week. What will Jason's new approximate wage be?

(1) $310
(2) $290
(3) $160
(4) $ 30
(5) Not enough information is given.

Item 47 refers to the following calorie chart.

CALORIE CHART

slice of bread 70
glass of milk 120
apple 60
orange 50
4 ounces of lean meat 200
1 cup of steamed vegetables 75
baked potato 80
bowl of soup 90
cookie 95
ice cream sundae 800

47. Chuck is watching his weight and is limiting his daily calorie intake to 1200 calories. Today, he has had 2 slices of bread, a bowl of soup, 2 glasses of milk, 2 cookies, and an orange. Which of the following combinations could he also eat and be within his 1200 calorie limit?

(1) 8 ounces of lean meat, baked potato, 1 cup of steamed vegetables
(2) apple, ice cream sundae
(3) 2 glass of milk, 4 ounces of lean meat, ice cream sundae
(4) 2 cups of steamed vegetables, 1 glass of milk, ice cream sundae
(5) 4 ounces of lean meat, baked potato, 1 cup of steamed vegetables, glass of milk

Item 48 refers to the plane figure shown below.

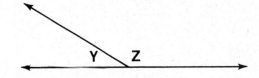

48. In the plane figure above, if the degree measure of angle Z is 5 times that of angle Y, what is the degree measure of angle Z?

(1) 30
(2) 60
(3) 150
(4) 180
(5) Not enough information is given.

49. Which of the values of *j* given below will make the inequality $2j \geq 9$ true?

    (1) 1
    (2) 2
    (3) 3
    (4) 4
    (5) 5

Item 50 refers to the map below.

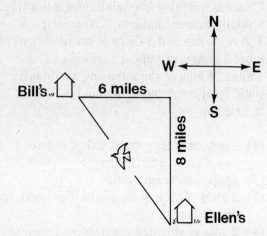

50. Ellen can get to Bill's house by driving 8 miles north, then 6 miles west. Tomorrow is Bill's birthday, and Ellen plans to send a birthday greeting by way of a messenger pigeon. If the messenger pigeon flies directly from Ellen's house to Bill's house, how many miles does the messenger pigeon fly?

    (1) 7
    (2) 8
    (3) 9
    (4) 10
    (5) Not enough information is given.

51. What is the radius (in inches) of the largest circle that can be drawn on a piece of paper 8½ inches by 11 inches?

    (1) 11
    (2) 8½
    (3) 5½
    (4) 4¼
    (5) 2¾

Item 52 refers to the figure below.

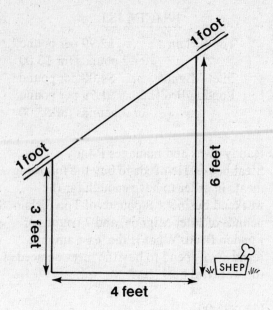

52. Pictured above is a side view of the doghouse that Wendy is building for her dog, Shep. She has it completely built except for the roof. What is the entire length of the roof (in feet) if it is to have a 1-foot overhang in the front and in the back?

    (1) 5
    (2) 6
    (3) 7
    (4) 8
    (5) Not enough information is given.

53. Which of the following expresses 269,753 in scientific notation?

    (1) 2.69753×10^5
    (2) 2.69753×10^6
    (3) 26.9753×10^6
    (4) 269.753×10^5
    (5) 2697.53×10^3

54. Hal was doing such a good job as a day care instructor, he was offered an 18% raise. If Hal's yearly salary before the raise was $14,000, which expression below could be used to represent his new salary?

(1) .18($14,000)
(2) $14,000 ÷ .18
(3) $14,000 + .18($14,000)
(4) $14,000 − .18($14,000)
(5) $14,000 + ($14,000 ÷ .18)

Item 55 refers to the triangle below.

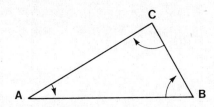

55. The above triangle contains three interior angles. The second angle is double the first, and the third angle is triple the first. What are the degree measures of the angles?

(1) 10, 20, 30
(2) 20, 40, 60
(3) 30, 60, 90
(4) 40, 80, 120
(5) 60, 120, 180

Item 56 refers to the diagram below.

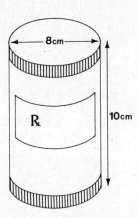

56. Jorge works as a pharmacist. A customer purchases the cylindrical container of medication pictured above. Which expression below could be used to calculate the maximum volume (in cubic centimeters) that this container can hold?

(1) $\pi(8^2)(10)$
(2) $\pi(4^2)(10)$
(3) $2\pi(8)(10)$
(4) $2\pi(4)(10)$
(5) Not enough information is given.

END OF EXAMINATION

GED

SCORING AND EXPLANATIONS FOR PRACTICE EXAMINATION 2

Scoring Practice Examination 2

Score your GED Practice Examination 2 by following these steps:

1. Check the answers you marked on your answer sheet against the Answer Key that follows. Put a check mark in the box following any wrong answer.

2. Fill out the Scoring Chart (p. 524).

3. Estimate your score on each test using the Score Approximators (p. 525–527). Remember, these Score Approximators will give you a **very general** idea of how you are doing.

4. Read all of the explanations (pp. 529–566). Mark the boxes following the explanations as the directions there tell you. Go back to review any explanations that are not clear to you.

5. Finally, fill out the Reasons for Mistakes chart on p. 528.

Don't leave out any of these steps. They are very important in learning to do your best on the GED.

ANSWER KEY FOR PRACTICE EXAMINATION 2

TEST 1: WRITING SKILLS, PART I

1. (5) ☐	12. (5) ☐	23. (3) ☐	34. (1) ☐	45. (5) ☐
2. (5) ☐	13. (4) ☐	24. (2) ☐	35. (5) ☐	46. (3) ☐
3. (3) ☐	14. (5) ☐	25. (4) ☐	36. (3) ☐	47. (3) ☐
4. (4) ☐	15. (3) ☐	26. (4) ☐	37. (4) ☐	48. (5) ☐
5. (4) ☐	16. (3) ☐	27. (4) ☐	38. (1) ☐	49. (1) ☐
6. (4) ☐	17. (5) ☐	28. (1) ☐	39. (5) ☐	50. (3) ☐
7. (4) ☐	18. (1) ☐	29. (2) ☐	40. (4) ☐	51. (4) ☐
8. (1) ☐	19. (4) ☐	30. (5) ☐	41. (3) ☐	52. (3) ☐
9. (5) ☐	20. (2) ☐	31. (1) ☐	42. (4) ☐	53. (3) ☐
10. (4) ☐	21. (3) ☐	32. (3) ☐	43. (1) ☐	54. (1) ☐
11. (1) ☐	22. (1) ☐	33. (2) ☐	44. (4) ☐	55. (1) ☐

TEST 2: SOCIAL STUDIES

1. (3) ☐	14. (1) ☐	27. (1) ☐	40. (5) ☐	53. (4) ☐
2. (5) ☐	15. (3) ☐	28. (3) ☐	41. (2) ☐	54. (5) ☐
3. (3) ☐	16. (1) ☐	29. (2) ☐	42. (3) ☐	55. (1) ☐
4. (2) ☐	17. (1) ☐	30. (5) ☐	43. (5) ☐	56. (3) ☐
5. (3) ☐	18. (2) ☐	31. (3) ☐	44. (1) ☐	57. (4) ☐
6. (2) ☐	19. (3) ☐	32. (3) ☐	45. (3) ☐	58. (4) ☐
7. (3) ☐	20. (4) ☐	33. (4) ☐	46. (5) ☐	59. (2) ☐
8. (2) ☐	21. (3) ☐	34. (3) ☐	47. (4) ☐	60. (3) ☐
9. (3) ☐	22. (2) ☐	35. (2) ☐	48. (3) ☐	61. (5) ☐
10. (2) ☐	23. (4) ☐	36. (5) ☐	49. (5) ☐	62. (1) ☐
11. (3) ☐	24. (3) ☐	37. (4) ☐	50. (4) ☐	63. (2) ☐
12. (1) ☐	25. (4) ☐	38. (2) ☐	51. (5) ☐	64. (5) ☐
13. (2) ☐	26. (4) ☐	39. (1) ☐	52. (2) ☐	

TEST 3: SCIENCE

1. (3) ☐	15. (5) ☐	28. (1) ☐	41. (5) ☐	54. (1) ☐
2. (2) ☐	16. (3) ☐	29. (4) ☐	42. (2) ☐	55. (2) ☐
3. (1) ☐	17. (2) ☐	30. (5) ☐	43. (3) ☐	56. (1) ☐
4. (1) ☐	18. (1) ☐	31. (5) ☐	44. (1) ☐	57. (2) ☐
5. (5) ☐	19. (5) ☐	32. (4) ☐	45. (2) ☐	58. (2) ☐
6. (3) ☐	20. (2) ☐	33. (4) ☐	46. (4) ☐	59. (3) ☐
7. (2) ☐	21. (3) ☐	34. (4) ☐	47. (3) ☐	60. (3) ☐
8. (4) ☐	22. (4) ☐	35. (1) ☐	48. (1) ☐	61. (1) ☐
9. (4) ☐	23. (1) ☐	36. (2) ☐	49. (2) ☐	62. (5) ☐
10. (3) ☐	24. (4) ☐	37. (1) ☐	50. (4) ☐	63. (4) ☐
11. (1) ☐	25. (2) ☐	38. (3) ☐	51. (5) ☐	64. (3) ☐
12. (4) ☐	26. (4) ☐	39. (5) ☐	52. (3) ☐	65. (2) ☐
13. (5) ☐	27. (4) ☐	40. (2) ☐	53. (5) ☐	66. (5) ☐
14. (4) ☐				

TEST 4: INTERPRETING LITERATURE AND THE ARTS

1. (1) ☐	10. (1) ☐	19. (3) ☐	28. (1) ☐	37. (3) ☐
2. (2) ☐	11. (5) ☐	20. (4) ☐	29. (2) ☐	38. (5) ☐
3. (4) ☐	12. (3) ☐	21. (5) ☐	30. (2) ☐	39. (4) ☐
4. (1) ☐	13. (1) ☐	22. (2) ☐	31. (3) ☐	40. (3) ☐
5. (5) ☐	14. (2) ☐	23. (4) ☐	32. (4) ☐	41. (1) ☐
6. (2) ☐	15. (4) ☐	24. (3) ☐	33. (2) ☐	42. (4) ☐
7. (1) ☐	16. (5) ☐	25. (1) ☐	34. (4) ☐	43. (1) ☐
8. (3) ☐	17. (4) ☐	26. (5) ☐	35. (1) ☐	44. (4) ☐
9. (4) ☐	18. (1) ☐	27. (3) ☐	36. (5) ☐	45. (2) ☐

TEST 5: MATHEMATICS

1. (4) ☐	13. (2) ☐	24. (4) ☐	35. (2) ☐	46. (2) ☐
2. (4) ☐	14. (2) ☐	25. (2) ☐	36. (5) ☐	47. (5) ☐
3. (3) ☐	15. (4) ☐	26. (2) ☐	37. (3) ☐	48. (3) ☐
4. (1) ☐	16. (3) ☐	27. (2) ☐	38. (1) ☐	49. (5) ☐
5. (4) ☐	17. (2) ☐	28. (5) ☐	39. (2) ☐	50. (4) ☐
6. (5) ☐	18. (2) ☐	29. (3) ☐	40. (4) ☐	51. (4) ☐
7. (2) ☐	19. (3) ☐	30. (1) ☐	41. (2) ☐	52. (3) ☐
8. (4) ☐	20. (2) ☐	31. (4) ☐	42. (1) ☐	53. (1) ☐
9. (4) ☐	21. (1) ☐	32. (2) ☐	43. (4) ☐	54. (3) ☐
10. (2) ☐	22. (2) ☐	33. (5) ☐	44. (3) ☐	55. (3) ☐
11. (5) ☐	23. (3) ☐	34. (5) ☐	45. (4) ☐	56. (2) ☐
12. (3) ☐				

SCORING CHART

Use your marked Answer Key to fill in the following Scoring Chart.

	Possible	Completed	Right	Wrong
Test 1: Writing Skills, Part I	55			
Test 2: Social Studies	64			
Test 3: Science	66			
Test 4: Interpreting Literature and the Arts	45			
Test 5: Mathematics	56			
TOTAL	286			

Now, use this Scoring Chart to approximate your score on the following pages.

APPROXIMATING YOUR SCORE

The following Score Approximators will help you evaluate your skills and give you a very *general* indication of your scoring potential.

Test 1: Writing Skills

To approximate your Writing Skills score

1. Using the Scoring Chart, fill in the blank below with the number of questions you answered *correctly* on Part I: Multiple Choice.

2. Have an English teacher, tutor, or someone else with good writing skills read and evaluate your essay using the Checklists given in Part 3, How to Start Reviewing. Have your reader evaluate the complete essay as *good* or *poor*. Note that your paper would actually be scored from 1 to 6 by two trained readers. But since we are trying only for a rough approximation, the simple *good* or *poor* evaluation will give you a general feeling for your score range.

3. Use the following table to get an approximate score. Notice that the left-hand column shows the number of correct answers on Part I: Multiple Choice. The right-hand column lists your approximate score range with a poor essay and your approximate score range with a good essay.

Right answers on Part I _____
Essay evaluation   Poor   Good

Number of Right Answers on Part I: Multiple Choice	Approximate Score Range with Essay Evaluation	
	Poor Essay	Good Essay
0–10	21–31	32–42
11–20	32–35	43–47
21–30	36–39	48–51
31–40	40–43	52–55
41–50	44–51	56–63
51–54	52–60	64–72

Remember, this is only an *approximate score range*. When you take the GED Writing Skills Test, some of the multiple-choice questions may be easier or more difficult. The essay will be scored accurately by trained readers.

Test 2: Social Studies

To approximate your Social Studies score

1. Using the Scoring Chart, fill in the blank below with the number of questions you answered *correctly*.

2. Use the following table to match the number of right answers and the approximate score range.

Right answers ____

Number of Right Answers	Approximate Score Range
0–10	20–32
11–20	33–41
21–30	42–47
31–40	48–53
41–50	54–63
51–64	64–80

Remember, this is only an *approximate score range*. When you take the GED Social Studies Test, you will have questions that are similar to those in this book. Some questions, however, may be slightly easier or more difficult.

Test 3: Science

To approximate your Science score

1. Using the Scoring Chart, fill in the blank below with the number of questions you answered *correctly*.

2. Use the following table to match the number of right answers to the approximate score range.

Right answers ____

Number of Right Answers	Approximate Score Range
0–10	20–30
11–20	31–37
21–30	38–43
31–40	44–49
41–50	50–56
51–60	57–68
61–66	69–80

Remember, this is only an *approximate score range*. When you take the GED Science Test, you will have questions that are similar to those in this book. Some questions, however, may be slightly easier or more difficult.

Test 4: Interpreting Literature and the Arts

To approximate your Interpreting Literature and the Arts score

1. Using the Scoring Chart, fill in the blank below with the number of questions you answered *correctly*.

2. Use the following table to match the number of right answers to the approximate score range.

Right answers _____

Number of Right Answers	Approximate Score Range
0–10	20–34
11–20	35–43
21–30	44–52
31–40	53–68
41–45	69–80

Remember, this is only an *approximate score range*. When you take the GED Interpreting Literature and the Arts Test, you will have questions that are similar to those in this book. Some questions, however, may be slightly easier or more difficult.

Test 5: Mathematics

To approximate your Mathematics score

1. Using the Scoring Chart, fill in the blank below with the number of questions you answered *correctly*.

2. Use the following table to match the number of right answers to the approximate score range.

Right answers _____

Number of Right Answers	Approximate Score Range
0–10	20–32
11–20	33–39
21–30	40–45
31–40	46–51
41–50	52–60
51–56	61–80

Remember, this is only an *approximate score range*. When you take the GED Mathematics Test, you will have questions that are similar to those in this book. Some questions, however, may be slightly easier or more difficult.

REASONS FOR MISTAKES

Fill out the following chart *only after you have read all the explanations that follow*. This chart will help you spot your strengths and weaknesses and your repeated errors or trend in types of errors.

	Total Missed	Simple Mistake	Misread Problem	Lack of Knowledge
Test 1: Writing Skills, Part I				
Test 2: Social Studies				
Test 3: Science				
Test 4: Interpreting Literature and the Arts				
Test 5: Mathematics				
TOTAL				

Examine your results carefully. Reviewing the above information will help you pinpoint your common mistakes. Focus on avoiding your most common mistakes as you practice. If you are missing a lot of questions because of "Lack of Knowledge," you should go back and review the basics.

Explanations for Practice Examination 2

Each explanation is followed by two boxes, OK and ?. After you read each explanation, mark box OK if you understand the answer, and if you missed the question, why you did. Mark box ? if you do not understand the answer. After you complete each section, go back and review the explanations that you marked ?.

TEST 1: WRITING SKILLS, PART 1

1. (5) Use the adverb, *increasingly,* to modify the adjective, *popular.*   OK ?

2. (5) The sentence is correct as written.   OK ?

3. (3) The correct, shortest, and clearest version of the sentence would replace *you could invest in* with the single word *including.* The punctuation in (2) is not wrong (the semicolon can separate the two sentences), but this choice is no real improvement on the original and is not the most effective combination.   OK ?

4. (4) The word *fund* is singular. You can be sure it is meant to be singular because of the word *that.* If the writer meant the word to be plural, *those* would be used instead of *that.* You must also notice in this question that the word *fund* should be possessive. In other words, the *securities* belong to the fund. So, to make the possessive of a singular word, add *'s, fund's* (choice 4). The plural verb *are* is right because it refers to *securities,* which is plural.   OK ?

5. (4) The sentence can be corrected either by changing the comma after *industry* to a semicolon (a punctuation mark that can separate two complete sentences) or by adding the conjunction *but* and keeping the comma. Remember, a semicolon is correct between two sentences that are not joined by a conjunction (such as *and, but,* and *so*). A comma is correct between two sentences that *are* joined by a conjunction.   OK ?

6. (4) The paragraph and the first part of this sentence use the second person pronoun (*you, your*); the second part of this sentence should also use *you,* not *one.*   OK ?

7. (4) The best combination of the two sentences would use the main verb of the second sentence: *One popular type of fund, the money market mutual fund, may invest in a variety of securities. . . .*   OK ?

8. (1) *Like* is a preposition and takes an object. (*Like other people, you can . . .* This sentence is correct because the object of the preposition *like* is *other people. Like with a money market . . .* is not correct because there is no object for *like.*) *As,* a conjunction, is necessary here to introduce the prepositional phrase beginning with *with.*   OK ?

9. (5) The sentence is correct as written.   OK ?

10. (4) As in question 6, use the pronoun *you* because the rest of the paragraph uses *you*. The correct verb is *should*. *Should* suggests an obligation, something you ought to do. *Shall* is the future tense and suggests that this is something that you will definitely do at some time.   `OK` `?`

11. (1) The plural *their* agrees in number with the word it refers to, the plural *funds*.   `OK` `?`

12. (5) With *either . . . or*, you should use as close to the same structure as possible after each of the two conjunctions. In answer (5), a noun (*brokers*) follows *either* and a noun (*corporations*) with two modifying words (*mutual fund*) follows *or*. None of the four other answers has the same structure after *either* and *or*.

    Choice (1) *either through/or mutual*
    Choice (2) *either through/or you*
    Choice (3) *either brokers/or through*
    Choice (4) *either through/or mutual*   `OK` `?`

13. (4) The possessive form of *they* is *their*. *They're* means *they are*.   `OK` `?`

14. (5) Either *less* or *smaller* is better here than *lesser*. Options (3) and (4) leave out the needed comma, and the present tense verb in (3), *are,* is wrong because the sentence is speaking about something that may happen in the future.   `OK` `?`

15. (3) The passage uses the second person pronoun (*you*) throughout. The perfect tense *have worked* is necessary because the action of working will have been completed.   `OK` `?`

16. (3) The correct verb tense here is the future, *will receive,* because the sentence says that you are *approaching retirement age*. In other words, you are still working. So, you *will receive* the benefits in the future.   `OK` `?`

17. (5) The verbs in this sentence are correct, and the sentence is correct as written.   `OK` `?`

18. (1) Two commas are missing. The first comma is needed to separate part of a series (*investments, . . . funds, . . . sources*). The second comma is needed to separate a dependent clause (*If . . . self-employment*) from the main clause of the sentence (*Your Social . . . affected*).   `OK` `?`

19. (4) Wherever the *however* is placed, it must be set off by a comma or commas. The correct pronoun is *they*, not *it*, because the word refers to the plural *benefits* in sentence 6.   `OK` `?`

20. (2) The correct verb form is the singular *exceeds*, to agree with the singular *income*.   `OK` `?`

21. (3) The correct spelling here is *lose*.   `OK` `?`

22. (1) In this sentence, *currently* means *at the present time*, and it refers to the *limit* at this time. In options (3), (4), and (5), *currently* describes the *worker* rather than the *law*. This introductory adverb should be set off by a comma.   `OK` `?`

23. (3) The original sentence is a fragment. Adding a subject and verb (*it is*) makes it a complete sentence.   `OK` `?`

24. (2) *You're,* which means *you are,* is needed here because the clause must have a subject and verb (*If you are over seventy*). Since the paragraph uses the pronoun *you* throughout, there is no reason to change to *one.*   `OK` `?`

25. (4) With the plural verb *were,* the subject must be the plural *women.*   `OK` `?`

26. (4) Use a conjunction preceded by a comma to link the two sentences. Both *but* (4) and *and* (5) are possible, but since the second sentence draws a contrast with the first, *but* is a better choice.   `OK` `?`

27. (4) The sentence uses the word *current* (which means *at the present time*), and so it is clear that the sentence is about the membership in the *present*. The verb should be in the present tense (*are*).   `OK` `?`

28. (1) Use the adverb (*newly*) not the adjective (*new*) to modify *formed,* a verbal adjective. Adjectives modify nouns; adverbs modify verbs, adjectives, and other adverbs.   `OK` `?`

29. (2) Use commas both before and after *however* to set it off.   `OK` `?`

30. (5) The past perfect tense (*had owned*) is correct. The past perfect tense describes an action further in the past than another action in the past (*teamed*).   `OK` `?`

31. (1) As it is written, the sentence has no main verb and is a fragment. The *is* supplies the verb that makes the sentence complete.   `OK` `?`

32. (3) The sentence presents a series. Separate parts of a series with commas (*Center, . . . complex, . . . Oceanside*).   `OK` `?`

33. (2) There are several ways to write this phrase. Of the five versions here, only (2) is correct. In (2), *consumers* is a plural noun, the object of *with,* and modified by the adjective *concerned.* The adverb *increasingly* modifies *concerned.* The phrase might have been written *with consumers' increased concern,* in which case *consumers'* is a possessive plural, *concern,* is a noun, and *increased* is an adjective modifying the noun *concern.*   `OK` `?`

34. (1) The phrase *the makers of* should be removed, or the comparison introduced by *Like* makes no sense. As it now stands, the sentence compares the *manufacturers* to *low-fat beef and chicken.* The right comparison is between light beer, maple syrup, or mayonnaise and low-fat meats.   `OK` `?`

35. (5) The sentence is correct as written.   OK   ?

36. (3) Use the pronoun *who* to refer only to people. Use *that* to refer to people, animals, or things. Use *which* to refer to animals or things. Since a *cattle breed* is singular, the verb must be *is* not *are*.   OK   ?

37. (4) In this sentence, the comparative *less tender* makes more sense than the superlative *least*. Since the sentence begins with the comparative *lower,* we can expect a second adjective to be parallel to the first.   OK   '?

38. (1) Use two commas to set off *that is*. The two commas in the series at the end of the sentence are right.   OK   ?

39. (5) Set off the introductory *of course* with a comma. The correct contraction for *there is* is *there's*. *They're* is the contraction of *they are,* and *theirs* is a possessive form.   OK   ?

40. (4) If you use the phrase *except that* after *regular beef,* the two sentences can be combined using fewer words (*nothing at all wrong with regular beef, except that some of us . . .*). All of the other answers are longer, and (2) is not grammatically correct.   OK   ?

41. (3) The correct usage is either *criticizing the spending* or *critical of the spending*. The adverb *severely* should be used to modify the adjective *critical*.   OK   ?

42. (4) All of the commas in the sentence are necessary except the comma after *billion*. This should be a semicolon, dividing the two sentences not joined by a conjunction. You could also divide the sentences by using a period and beginning the new sentence with *In*.   OK   ?

43. (1) The sentence uses the singular verb *is,* so the subject must be the singular *cost*. The use of *nearly* (an adverb) is correct in the sentence.   OK   ?

44. (4) Since 1992 is in the future, the verb should be in the future tense (*will cost*).   OK   ?

45. (5) There are two agreement errors in the original sentence. Both *expenditures* and *the PACs* are plural, so both verbs (*have grown, have*) must also be plural. The dependent clause that begins the sentence (*As expenditures have grown*) must be set off by a comma.   OK   ?

46. (3) The singular subject (*a contributor*) should be followed by a singular verb (*does*) and a singular possessive pronoun (*his* or *her* or *his or her*).   OK   ?

47. (3) By making the second sentence subordinate, and making *a lion's share* refer to *contributions,* none of the original meaning is lost, and three fewer words are used (*. . . tripled their contributions, a lion's share going to members . . .*). Answers (1) and (2) are grammatically correct but wordier than the original sentences. Option (4) is the shortest possible version of the sentence, but it would change the meaning of the sentence if it reads *tripled their contributions to members*. The original sentences say only that *a lion's share*, not three times as much money, went to the committee members. Option (5) incorrectly combines a past and a present tense.   OK   ?

48. (5) The sentence is correct as written.

    OK   ?

49. (1) Since the full title is *Office of Consumer Affairs,* all the important words in the name should begin with a capital letter.

    OK   ?

50. (3) The subject of the sentence is the clause *How widespread the automobile repair problem is,* and the *is* belongs to this clause. If the sentence is to be complete, it must have a main verb. A second *is* must follow the first.

    OK   ?

51. (4) If either a period or a semicolon is used after *technicians,* the second sentence is a fragment; it lacks a main verb. Only option (4) solves this problem by using the conjunction *and.*

    OK   ?

52. (3) If the *who* clause is kept, the sentence is a fragment, lacking a main verb. The *having* in (5) is a participle, not a main verb. Only (3) supplies a main verb (*have*) and gets rid of the dependent clause.

    OK   ?

53. (3) The subject of the sentence is the singular *A nonprofit organization.* The verb must be the singular *provides.*

    OK   ?

54. (1) Most of the paragraph is written in the present tense, and in this sentence, the verb *approves* is also present tense. *Investigates* should also be in the present.

    OK   ?

55. (1) The phrase *by recognizing the need for preventive maintenance,* which separates the subject and verb, should be set off by commas before and after.

    OK   ?

TEST 2: SOCIAL STUDIES

1. (3) A company operating solely within (*intra*) a state, in this case, New Hampshire, is intrastate commerce. `OK` `?`

2. (5) A state flower is an issue confined to a single state. All of the other choices have to do with issues that would concern several states and so would be a more likely concern of the United States Congress rather than a concern of a member of a state legislature. `OK` `?`

3. (3) The federal government would oversee transcontinental (across a continent) bus routes because they cross several state lines. `OK` `?`

4. (2) To become a biochemist, the miner's son would need much more education than a miner does. The other answers are examples of no upward mobility at all or of positions gained without formal education. `OK` `?`

5. (3) Though there have been rare cases in which two monarchs ruled (King William and Queen Mary, for example), a monarchy is normally ruled by one person, a king or queen. `OK` `?`

6. (2) The Dalai Lama and monks are members of a religious order. `OK` `?`

7. (3) Most European nations in the Renaissance (14th–17th centuries) were monarchies. `OK` `?`

8. (2) An arms-limitation treaty is an international treaty requiring ratification by the Senate. `OK` `?`

9. (3) The Secretary of Defense and Attorney General are Cabinet appointments. Only the Press Secretary would not require Senate confirmation. `OK` `?`

10. (2) Three of the choices (1, 3, 4) are normal human activities, but superstitiously avoiding a sidewalk crack all the time (*never*) is compulsive behavior. `OK` `?`

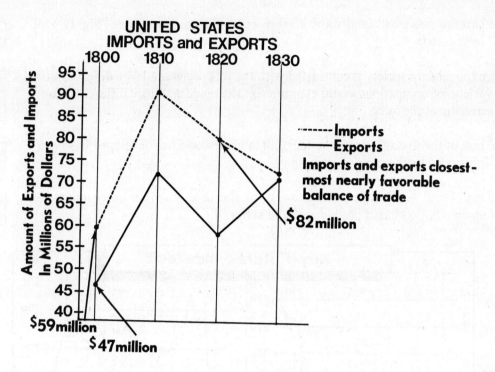

UNITED STATES
IMPORTS and EXPORTS

------ Imports
—— Exports

Imports and exports closest—
most nearly favorable
balance of trade

$82 million

$59 million

$47 million

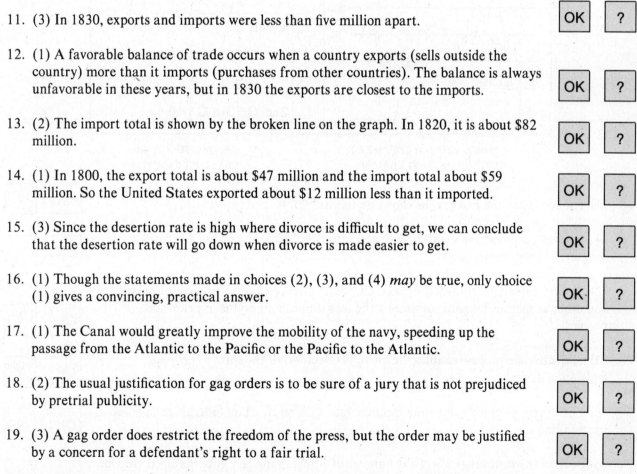

11. (3) In 1830, exports and imports were less than five million apart.   OK   ?

12. (1) A favorable balance of trade occurs when a country exports (sells outside the country) more than it imports (purchases from other countries). The balance is always unfavorable in these years, but in 1830 the exports are closest to the imports.   OK   ?

13. (2) The import total is shown by the broken line on the graph. In 1820, it is about $82 million.   OK   ?

14. (1) In 1800, the export total is about $47 million and the import total about $59 million. So the United States exported about $12 million less than it imported.   OK   ?

15. (3) Since the desertion rate is high where divorce is difficult to get, we can conclude that the desertion rate will go down when divorce is made easier to get.   OK   ?

16. (1) Though the statements made in choices (2), (3), and (4) *may* be true, only choice (1) gives a convincing, practical answer.   OK   ?

17. (1) The Canal would greatly improve the mobility of the navy, speeding up the passage from the Atlantic to the Pacific or the Pacific to the Atlantic.   OK   ?

18. (2) The usual justification for gag orders is to be sure of a jury that is not prejudiced by pretrial publicity.   OK   ?

19. (3) A gag order does restrict the freedom of the press, but the order may be justified by a concern for a defendant's right to a fair trial.   OK   ?

20. (4) Some of the five questions may or may not be asked, but in a case where pretrial publicity is an issue, it is certain that jurors will be asked about their knowledge of the case before the trial begins.   OK   ?

21. (3) The passage says that "family and kinship groups" (family ties) are "highly valued" (respected). OK ?

22. (2) Since the modern society is contrasted with the folk society, a large differentiation, a wide variety, of occupations would characterize the modern; "little differentiation" is characteristic of the folk. OK ?

23. (4) The best of the five answers is the fourth. How the world has developed has been greatly influenced by the facts of geography. OK ?

24. (3) The use of coal would increase at a time of oil shortage. The four other industries, which rely on oil or oil-based products, would suffer. OK ?

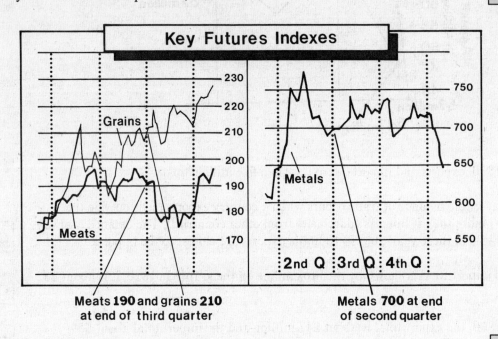

Meats **190** and grains **210**
at end of third quarter

Metals **700** at end
of second quarter

25. (4) The second of the two graphs shows metals at 700. OK ?

26. (4) The first graph shows meats at 190 and grains at 210 at the end of the third quarter. The difference is 20. OK ?

27. (1) An anthropologist studies the races, characteristics, customs, social relationships, and other aspects of humans, especially the institutions and myths of primitive peoples. OK ?

28. (3) The initiative process enables the citizens (electors) of the state to propose legislation directly. OK ?

29. (2) The initiative process is a state election vote with no effect on federal (as opposed to state) laws. OK ?

30. (5) Section (b) states that 8% of the number of voters in the last gubernatorial election (election of a governor) are needed for an amendment of the State Constitution. OK ?

31. (3) This is the language of a psychologist. OK ?

32. (3) Choices (1), (2), (4), and (5) are biological factors, determined by heredity. Religion is external, chosen by the individual. `OK` `?`

33. (4) The claim is that almost everyone has already joined the speaker's side, the *band wagon* technique. `OK` `?`

34. (3) The speaker identifies himself as a representative of the most acceptable values and views, the *plain folks* approach. `OK` `?`

35. (2) The speech depends on the *jargon* and abbreviations of finance. `OK` `?`

36. (5) The speech combines fact and fiction, and allows no real choice (*card stacking*). `OK` `?`

37. (4) The birth in the United States assures U.S. citizenship; he is also a citizen of Florida, the state where he lives. `OK` `?`

38. (2) Pluto has been the outermost planet of the Solar System for a very long time, but it was not until 1930 that telescopes were powerful enough to discover the planet. `OK` `?`

39. (1) The fox is often seen as the most sly of the animals in oral literature. `OK` `?`

40. (5) Many fairy tales were originally transmitted by being told rather than by being printed and read. The four wrong answers are printed, not oral, compositions. `OK` `?`

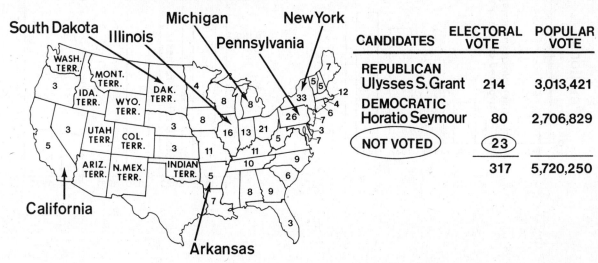

ELECTION OF 1868

CANDIDATES	ELECTORAL VOTE	POPULAR VOTE
REPUBLICAN Ulysses S. Grant	214	3,013,421
DEMOCRATIC Horatio Seymour	80	2,706,829
NOT VOTED	23	
	317	5,720,250

41. (2) Arkansas is to the right of the Indian Territory and is shown with 5 electoral votes. Since it is shown as having electoral votes, it was a state in 1868. `OK` `?`

42. (3) New York had 33 electoral votes; Pennsylvania had 26; Illinois had 16; Michigan had 8; and California had 5. `OK` `?`

43. (5) The map reports 23 electoral votes were not voted. None of the other statements is true according to the map. `OK` `?`

44. (1) South Dakota is still a territory on this map.

45. (3) The prevention of South African companies from selling in the United States is enacted to force a change in South Africa's racial policy (*apartheid*).

46. (5) A state tax would be internal, a local matter. Economic sanctions are normally international in character.

47. (4) Agriculture is the cultivation of plants for food, a *food producing* activity.

48. (3) The term would not apply to all large corporations (choice 1), nor to church groups (choice 2). Choice (3) is a forceful and immediate action in an area (the army) mentioned in the definition.

49. (5) Both increasing the food supply and decreasing the birth rate will help, and the faster, the better.

50. (4) The author insists that increasing the food supply is not enough. Only choice (4) deals with the birth rate rather than the food supply.

51. (5) No "reasonable cause" is given here, only the fact that the police "suspect" criminal activity.

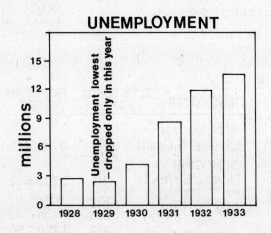

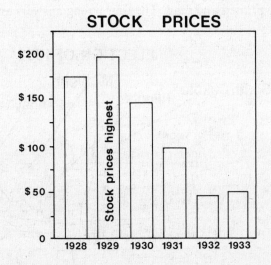

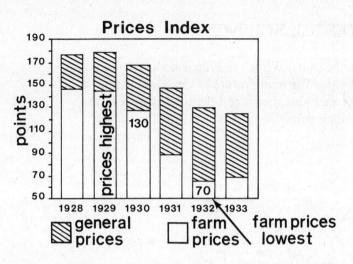

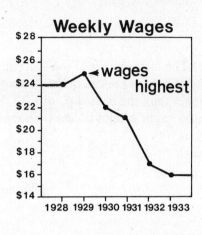

52. (2) In 1929, unemployment is lower and prices, stock prices, and wages are higher than in the other years. OK ?

53. (4) Farm prices are recorded in the lower part of the columns in the third graph. They are lowest in 1932. OK ?

54. (5) In 1930 farm prices were at 130; in 1932 they had fallen 60 points to 70. OK ?

55. (1) The first graph shows that unemployment dropped only in 1929. OK ?

56. (3) The paragraph suggests the compromise was reached between states with large and small populations concerned about their representation in the federal government. OK ?

57. (4) The United States originally had thirteen states (with 26 Senators). There are now fifty states (with 100 Senators). OK ?

58. (4) Speakers D and E wish to change the existing system by some form of action. Speaker B plans to retire from political responsibility. OK ?

59. (2) Speakers A and C are the most indifferent of the choices here. Neither seems to care about what is happening politically. OK ?

60. (3) Speaker C is concerned only with what affects him or her directly. OK ?

61. (5) Speaker E is a zealous antisocialist, confident that he or she knows what is truly American, an attitude usually connected with the right wing. OK ?

62. (1) The athlete would be able to include arguments for the other side easily, would appear to be a credible source, and would be closer in age to the target audience. OK ?

63. (2) By including some argument for the other side, a propagandist will increase his or her credibility by anticipating objections. Choices (3) and (5) are not true of a propagandist. OK ?

64. (5) We may be surprised to learn that to seek a large change of opinion is more likely to be effective than to seek a small one. OK ?

TEST 3: SCIENCE

1. (3) The temperature of the soup stays the same. While the soup is boiling, both liquid and vapor are present in the covered kettle. The temperature of the liquid cannot be higher than the boiling point (212 degrees Fahrenheit), and the temperature of the water vapor cannot be less than the boiling point. So the soup stays at the boiling point.

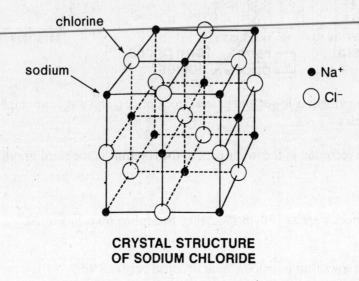

chlorine

sodium

● Na⁺

○ Cl⁻

**CRYSTAL STRUCTURE
OF SODIUM CHLORIDE**

The diagram above shows the crystal structure of sodium chloride, ordinary table salt, with the atoms greatly magnified to show their arrangement. Table **salt is made up of equal numbers of sodium and chlorine atoms.** This solid keeps its shape because the bonding holds the atoms in a rigid, stable arrangement.

2. (2) If you look closely at the diagram, you can see that the closest atoms are sodium (+) and chlorine (−), and that is because unlike charges attract each other. The pattern of alternating sodium and chlorine atoms could be continued in any direction, so salt crystals could be any size. Choice (C) is not correct because the faces are squares.

3. (1) When the salt crystals are dissolved in water, the sodium and chlorine *atoms* separate with different electric charges; the sodium has a +1 charge and the chlorine has a −1 charge. The information states that "salt is made up of equal numbers of sodium and chlorine *atoms*."

4. (1) The fox is a mammal that lives on the Earth's surface. Just like human beings, a fox breathes with lungs.

5. (5) Since the oxygen passes into blood vessels, choices (2) and (4) must be wrong. The question states that the oxygen goes through the body wall, which is the "thin membrane" of Method E. A membrane is simply a sheet or layer.

6. (3) Since the trout gets its oxygen from water, choice (1) must be wrong. You should know that fishes have gills to take oxygen from the water. Method C is the only choice that mentions gills.

7. (2) The question describes the respiration of beetles and never mentions any blood vessels, so choices (1), (3), and (5) are wrong. The "network of tiny tubes" in the question must be the same as the "system of air ducts" mentioned in Method B.

[OK] [?]

8. (4) This question also does not mention any blood vessels, so the answer is not (1), (3), or (5). You must choose between Method B, which mentions "a system of air ducts" and Method D, which mentions "diffusion through a moist surface." Since the internal parasites are moistened by the body fluids of the host, choice (4) is best.

[OK] [?]

9. (4) Probably the easiest way to solve this question is to think of some *large* animals and avoid answers that have to do with their methods of respiration. A human being breathes with lungs (Method A), so you know that answer choices (1) and (2) are wrong. A large fish uses gills (Method C), so answer choices (2), (3), and (5) are wrong. Only choice (4) is left.

[OK] [?]

10. (3) The moss and the fern are the two most simple plants—they do not reproduce by seeds, so these should be the earliest plants to appear. The only choices that list the moss and fern first are choices (1) and (3). Of the two plants with seeds—the pine and the rose—the one with flowers is most advanced. The rose is listed last in choices (3) and (4). So, choice (3) must be right.

[OK] [?]

BOYLE'S LAW   **CHARLES' LAW**

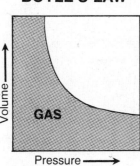 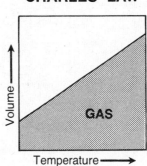

11. (1) The diagram shows that volume increases as temperature increases. This is called a direct relationship.

[OK] [?]

12. (4) The diagram shows that where the pressure is greatest the volume is the least.

[OK] [?]

13. (5) The size, or volume, of the tire will increase because the friction between the tire and the road will cause the temperature to increase. And, according to Charles' Law, an increase in temperature will increase the volume of air inside the tire.

[OK] [?]

14. (4) When you look at any object in a mirror, the light rays from the object have been reflected off the mirror toward your eyes. Of the five processes, reflection best explains an image seen in a mirror.

[OK] [?]

15. (5) Weak tea is a very clear liquid, so you are able to see the spoon inside the cup. As light rays leave the air and enter the tea, they bend and travel at an angle to their original direction. This change in direction of light (refraction) causes the spoon to seem bent as it enters the tea.

[OK] [?]

16. (3) Shadows appear because light obeys the law of linear propagation. As light passes an object, it continues in a straight line and doesn't bend behind the object. The dark zone where the light is blocked by the object is the shadow. Of course, shadows are dark only if there is a strong light coming from one source, like the sun.

17. (2) The heat from the wood burning in the fireplace enters the metal poker and puts energy into its atoms. That added energy escapes from the metal atoms by the process called emission. The light energy is emitted in only some colors. In our example, the hot poker gives off only red light.

18. (1) Sunlight is white light, being a mixture of all the simple colors of the spectrum: red, orange, yellow, green, blue, and violet. When sunlight falls on the apple, all the colors except red are absorbed by the skin of the fruit. The remaining red light can be reflected toward the eye of a person. OK ?

THE CIRCULATORY SYSTEM

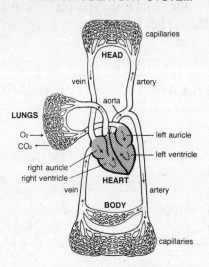

19. (5) The circulatory system is a double loop, and any blood must travel both loops before returning to its starting point. Let's start at the lungs, where the blood picks up fresh oxygen. The blood goes to the left side of the heart, which pumps it out the arteries to the body tissues. The blood returns by the veins to the right side of the heart, which pumps the blood to the lungs, where we started.

20. (2) The long molecules of rubber are kinked and twisted. When the band is pulled, the molecules straighten out. They return to their original shape upon release of the force. This property of returning to the original shape is called *elasticity*.

21. (3) The information classifies animals by their movement and their independence. A hawk moves freely, so it is *mobile*. And a hawk can live by itself, so it is *solitary*. Notice that choice (2) doesn't make sense because the two words, *mobile* and *sessile,* are opposites.

22. (4) A reef coral is fixed in one place on the reef, so the animal is *sessile*. A reef is made of thousands or millions of individual corals, so the animal is *colonial*. Each animal leaves a hard deposit when it dies, and so the reef slowly becomes larger.

23. (1) A hive-dwelling worker honey bee flys some distance searching for food, so it is *mobile*. However, it is usually found in large swarms, or groups, and depends on others for reproduction and new locations for food, so it is *colonial*.

24. (4) The earth gets hotter as you go downward from the surface, so marble formed deep within the earth where the high temperatures could change limestone. Those deep rocks have been exposed at the surface by erosion over a long time. Usually such an area was slowly uplifted by Earth forces at the same time as the erosion was taking place.

	Horse	Cow	Sheep	Pig	Rabbit	Mouse
Horse	0	18	18	17	25	23
Cow	18	0	13	17	26	20
Sheep	18	13	0	18	29	24
Pig	17	17	18	0	26	24
Rabbit	25	26	29	26	0	28
Mouse	23	20	24	24	28	0

25. (2) Since the numbers in the chart are the number of *differences* between the hemoglobin of two animals, the most similar animals will have the *smallest* number on the chart. The zeros don't count because they are where a row and a column are the same animal. The smallest number for two animals is 13, the cow and the sheep.

REFLECTION AND REFRACTION

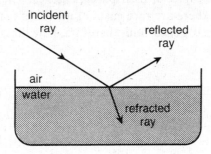

26. (4) Diamonds, water and alcohol are all transparent and, like glass, would allow light to pass through them and bend (refract).

27. (4) Light always bends, or refracts, when it slows down or speeds up. Light is slowed by the molecules in air, glass, or any transparent material.

28. (1) Newton's classic experiment changed our understanding of light. Now we know it is made up of various colors which can be separated by a prism into a spectrum. Choice B is Einstein's famous equation. Choice C is not true. The information beneath the figure says that prisms "bend [refract] light."

29. (4) Mount Saint Helens in Washington exploded because its lava was rich in gas. It is rather like shaking a bottle of soda pop before opening it; the gases escape dramatically. On the other hand, the gas-poor lava of Hawaii simply oozes out of the volcano. Choices (1), (2), and (3) do not refer to the *composition* of the lava.

SOLAR ECLIPSE

30. (5) During an eclipse of the sun, the moon comes between the Earth and the sun and, for those on Earth watching from the site of the eclipse, appears to cover the sun for several minutes. Since the sun is shining, these solar eclipses occur during the daytime and the sky turns temporarily dark. You can see from the diagram that this type of eclipse is seen from only a small area.

31. (5) If the gene for blue eyes were recessive, then each of the parents could have had both brown and blue genes despite their brown eyes. In that case, the baby could have received the blue gene from each parent. Another explanation is that a brown gene had mutated (changed) to a dominant blue gene.

32. (4) The acid or alkaline strength of a solution is measured on the pH scale, where 7 is neutral. A pH less than 7 is acidic, while a pH greater than 7 is alkaline.

33. (4) Vinegar is a weak acid and would cause litmus paper to turn red. Drain opener contains lye and is strongly alkaline, so it would make litmus turn a dark blue color.

34. (4) The unusual fly appeared due to mutation. Most of the flies looked like their parents because their genes were copies of their parents' genes. The genetic copying occurs during reproduction, and there are rare cases of mistakes made during the copying. Such mistakes lead to new genes, and, therefore, new flies. That change is called a *mutation*.

Metal Element	Melting Point in °C	Boiling Point in °C
cesium	29	670
lithium	186	1336
potassium	62	760
rubidium	39	700
sodium	98	880

35. (1) Below the melting point, only a solid metal could exist. The lowest melting point on the list is cesium at 29° C. So in a warm room, cesium occurs as a metallic liquid.

36. (2) The temperature range as a liquid is the difference between boiling point and melting point. You must subtract the melting point of each element from its boiling point. The largest temperature range in the list is for lithium: $1336 - 186 = 1150$.

37. (1) Since we are seeking the *largest* atoms, we must find the *weakest* bonds. The first sentence tells us that gases have weak bonds. Of the five elements, the one with the lowest boiling point (cesium) is the easiest to change into a gas. So cesium has the largest atoms, and lithium has the smallest atoms.

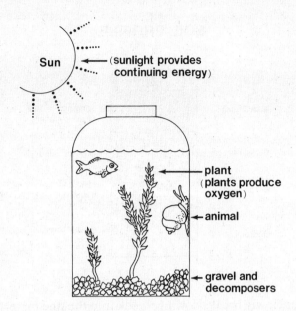

38. (3) Plants have produced most of the free oxygen in our atmosphere. Oxygen is a product of photosynthesis and is a critical need of animals. Plants produce very little carbon dioxide.

   OK   ?

39. (5) Sunlight is the source of the continuing energy needed by this system to survive. Sunlight plays the same role in the larger closed system, the Earth. Without this energy input the plants and then the animals would die. Choices (1), (2), and (4) do provide a small but fairly unimportant energy source.

   OK   ?

40. (2) Since almost all life on the Earth gets its energy directly or indirectly from the sun, only choices (2) and (4) are possible answers. Energy is absorbed and converted to food and oxygen through photosynthesis at the bottom of the food chain (plants). Animals take this food from the plants and use it to live and reproduce. In return the animals give carbon dioxide and minerals (through decomposition) to the plants.

   OK   ?

41. (5) In the container all of the parts are needed to maintain a balanced life cycle. If any part is removed, the system will break down.

   OK   ?

42. (2) The three substances will occur in order of density, with the lightest at the top and the heaviest at the bottom. Natural gas is lighter than the two liquids, so it would be at the top where the drill hole would find it first. Oil floats on top of water (think of salad dressing), so the drill would meet oil second and water third.

   OK   ?

43. (3) A cold-blooded animal cannot control its internal body temperature, so it takes on the temperature of the surrounding air or water. In cold areas the blood of such an animal will be cold, but in hot areas its blood will be hot.

   OK   ?

44. (1) Biotechnology is sometimes described as genetic engineering because it deals with the basic information in the genes. Biotechnology can be used for any problem concerning *life*. But the first choice does not concern life, since Portland cement is an inorganic material produced by burning two rocks, limestone and shale.

   OK   ?

SOIL PROFILE

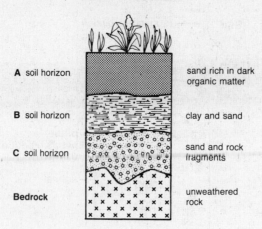

A soil horizon   sand rich in dark organic matter

B soil horizon   clay and sand

C soil horizon   sand and rock fragments

Bedrock   unweathered rock

45. (2) The action of weather slowly breaks down bedrock into the fine material called soil.   `OK` `?`

46. (4) The scale on the thermometer has marks that are evenly spaced. Such a simple scale is possible only because liquid mercury expands in a regular manner when heated. If the expansion were irregular, a simple thermometer would not work. Upon heating, all the mercury expands, including that in the bulb, but the only free direction for the liquid to swell is upward.   `OK` `?`

47. (3) Children are somewhat like their parents because all their genes come from their mother and father. The genes govern the development of the child. The chemical compound that stores that genetic information is deoxyribonucleic acid, commonly abbreviated as DNA. Only choice (3) mentions "genetic information."   `OK` `?`

48. (1) The three compounds are all carbohydrates, because they are sugars. The mention of "sugar beets" is probably the best clue, since sugar beets obviously contain sugar. The ending *ose* is used for all sugars.   `OK` `?`

49. (2) The walls of the blood vessels and other tubes are mainly built from lipids. If you look at the definition of the lipids, you will notice that it says they are needed "for tissues and membranes." Every cell in the body is inside a "skin" of lipids.   `OK` `?`

50. (4) The first sentence of the question mentions three functions of Molecule X, and all three involve the release of energy. Molecule X is therefore a phosphate because those compounds are used to supply energy. The chemical name for this important molecule is adenosine triphosphate, commonly abbreviated as ATP.   `OK` `?`

51. (5) *Polypeptide* is simply another name for *protein*. Its name means that many (*poly*) basic units called *peptide* are linked to form a long molecule. The 20 standard building blocks of proteins are the amino acids. The body breaks down any food protein into the amino acids, then uses those parts to build the specific proteins it needs.   `OK` `?`

52. (3) The average diet gets about one-third of the calories from carbohydrates, one-third from lipids (fats), and one-third from protein. The right answer is choice (3). Food is poor in nucleic acids and phosphates, so the body must make those compounds.   `OK` `?`

53. (5) The animal must pass on its superior features to some offspring, or the new features will merely die out. So the animal must mate and reproduce itself. The phrase "survival of the fittest" means that the animal must survive all threats until it can reproduce.

THE CELL

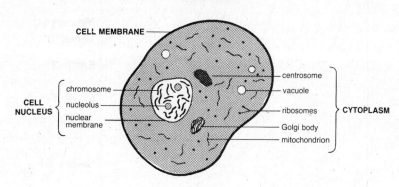

54. (1) The membrane is the outer wall of the cell. It acts as a filter which lets nutrients (including oxygen) enter and lets wastes (including carbon dioxide) leave. The membrane also serves to hold all the cell contents together.

55. (2) The chromosomes contain the genetic material. Inside each chromosome is a long DNA molecule that has a coded message with inherited instructions.

56. (1) The cytoplasm in either plant or animal cells varies in consistency from fluid to semi-solid. You can see that some of the material in the drawing appears to be more solid than other material. And you can eliminate choices (2), (3), and (4) because the diagram shows these are not true. The information in the question tells you that cytoplasm is in "any" cell, so choice (5) is not true.

57. (2) Each type of animal or plant will probably have its own requirements on where to live and what to eat. The slightly different requirements for the different species mean there will be little competition between different species (1), but there is always severe competition between individuals of each separate species.

58. (2) The second conclusion could not come directly from the study of processes now happening because there are no living dinosaurs to study. The other four conclusions are based on what is happening today. Geologists can study today's stream valleys, evaporation ponds, shell beds, and glacial deposits.

59. (3) The molecules in any liquid are continually moving in all directions. If such a molecule hits a small particle, the particle is forced to move. The irregular movement of small particles reveals the invisible motion of molecules. The higher the temperature is, the faster the molecules move.

60. (3) Without enzymes, many of the chemical reactions in the body would not occur fast enough. The reactions are speeded up by enzymes. In the question, the word *catalyst* means a substance which speeds up a reaction. (1) is wrong because an enzyme is not a hormone.

61. (1) The last four choices agree with the idea that such bodies of ore formed from hot water solutions seeping along underground cracks. Choice (1) is true, but magnetism is simply not connected to the formation of the deposits and has nothing to do with water.

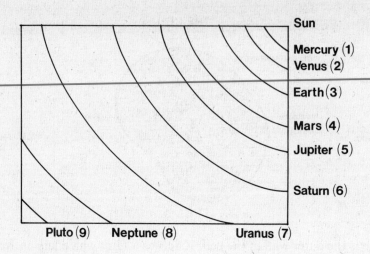

Sun
Mercury (1)
Venus (2)
Earth (3)
Mars (4)
Jupiter (5)
Saturn (6)

Pluto (9)   Neptune (8)   Uranus (7)

	Average Density in Grams per Cubic Centimeter	Surface Temperature in Degrees Centigrade	Diameter at the Equator in Kilometers
(1)	5.3	345 to −175	5,000
(2)	5.2	500	12,100
(3)	5.6	10	12,800
(4)	4.0	−30 to −90	6,787
(5)	1.34	−150	142,800
(6)	0.70	−180	120,000
(7)	1.3	−190	51,800
(8)	1.7	−215	49,000
(9)	?	−230	6,000

62. (5) Any object with a density of less than 1.0 will float on water. Since Saturn has a density of 0.70 g/cm³, it would float.

63. (4) From the information given, A and B are both accurate general relationships. Density is generally greater closer to the sun and temperatures are lower furthest from the sun.

64. (3) Liquid water would be found only on the Earth. The temperatures of the other planets would either be so hot that water would exist as a gas or so cold that it would be a solid.

65. (2) From the information given, Venus has the highest surface temperature of any of the planets (500° C). The other statements are false.

66. (5) No direct or inverse proportions can be concluded from the information. You can see this as you try to make relationships between the density, temperature, and diameter. There are no consistent relationships.

TEST 4: INTERPRETING LITERATURE AND THE ARTS

1. (1) Adding "s" to the beginning of "'weep" would make it "sweep," which is the cry we would expect from a chimney sweep.
   `OK` `?`

2. (2) Line 22, "And got with our bags and our brushes to work," gives us the idea that bags are used by sweepers as part of their work.
   `OK` `?`

3. (4) The dream begins with boys locked up in coffins, and then they are saved from this scary situation by an Angel and ride happily on the clouds.
   `OK` `?`

4. (1) The fifth verse, lines 17–20, describes the boys having a joyful time riding on the clouds. While they are having a good time, the Angel tells Tom that "if he'd be a good boy," he would "never want joy"; that is, he would continue to feel joyful.
   `OK` `?`

5. (5) In line 21, the poet says, "we rose in the dark," and then mentions that it is "morning" in line 23, so we know that he is waking up with Tom very early in the morning, while it is still dark.
   `OK` `?`

6. (2) Throughout the excerpt, the author writes about ants with terms he might use to describe human soldiers. His comparison with human soldiers is clear when he says in lines 26–27 that "human soldiers never fought so resolutely." Choice (3) contradicts the author's comment that the battle between ants was "the only battle which I have ever witnessed" (lines 18–19).
   `OK` `?`

7. (1) The style of the writing is personal (subjective). Choices (2), (3), (4), and (5) (advertisement, history book, scientific study, and news story) are types of writing that are more formal and objective.
   `OK` `?`

8. (3) This ant is described (lines 48–49) as one who has either won his last fight ("despatched his foe") or "not yet taken part in the battle." In either case, he is uninjured ("he had lost none of his limbs").
   `OK` `?`

9. (4) In this part of the excerpt, the author makes it clear that the ants will not give up, and earlier (line 6) he tells us that "having once got hold they never let go." Also, bulldogs are known for holding firmly. None of the other choices fits the description of the battling ants.
   `OK` `?`

10. (1) The author uses the terms and images of human battle to describe the battle between the ants. None of the other choices is supported by the passage.
    `OK` `?`

11. (5) Though the battle probably did take place and so *factual* is a possible answer, the better choice is *imaginative*. If the author really wished to write a factual account, he would probably leave out all of the comparisons of ants and men.
    `OK` `?`

12. (3) This choice describes what the writer is doing in the excerpt; each of the other choices contradicts the unusual imagination of the author.
    `OK` `?`

13. (1) You can see that the word *duellum* looks like *duel* (which it means in Latin), and the author indicates that *bellum* means *war* by following the Latin word with "a war."
    `OK` `?`

14. (2) Mrs. Dashwood is the mother of Elinor and Marianne. The first sentence tells us Elinor is the "eldest daughter." So, the order from oldest to youngest is Mrs. Dashwood, Elinor, Marianne.   `OK` `?`

15. (4) The passage tells us, in lines 11–12, that Elinor's "feelings were strong, but she knew how to govern them." Marianne has "no moderation" (lines 19–20) in her feelings—that is, she does *not* control them.   `OK` `?`

16. (5) Mrs. Dashwood and Marianne are alike. Neither has "moderation."   `OK` `?`

17. (4) The difference the story makes clear is between self-control and uncontrolled feelings—that is, the difference between good sense and too much sensibility (feeling).   `OK` `?`

18. (1) Notice that the excerpt insists that Elinor does have feelings. Since both Mrs. Dashwood and Marianne cannot control their emotions, neither answer (3) nor (4) can be right.   `OK` `?`

19. (3) We first see Vivie reading, taking notes, and lying with a large pile of books and papers nearby. All of these suggest that she is studious.   `OK` `?`

20. (4) Vivie's handshake is much firmer than Mr. Praed had expected, and we see him, in lines 18–19, "exercising his fingers, which are slightly numbed by her greeting."   `OK` `?`

21. (5) Several details in the scene (Mrs. Warren's unexpected visit and Vivie's comment on this, for example) suggest that mother and daughter do not get along well.   `OK` `?`

22. (2) Unlike Vivie, Mr. Praed has very conventional, polite notions about how a man and a young woman should behave.   `OK` `?`

23. (4) Both A (her handshake) and C (her not wishing to meet her mother) are good examples of Vivie's unconventional behavior (behavior that is not normal or expected) in this scene.   `OK` `?`

24. (3) For the rest of the second paragraph, the writer seems to criticize the changing of old movies for profit, suggesting that the studios and networks do not care (as the writer does) about the "visual integrity" of a movie.   `OK` `?`

25. (1) The sentence which begins the third paragraph (lines 29–30) supports this answer choice. "Some people, especially young people nurtured [brought up] on color TV, like the idea."   `OK` `?`

26. (5) "Art director" is being used in the same way as "paintbrush" here. The author is suggesting that the computerized "paintbrush" is not really a paintbrush and the "art director" is not really an art director. Quotation marks are often used for words that are used in a way that is different from the ordinary or normal way.   `OK` `?`

27. (3) *Red River* is listed as one of those movies that display "shades of pearl and ivory," so the paragraph suggests that it is a black-and-white film. You might think that choice (5) is the right answer, but while the article talks about many old films in black and white, it doesn't suggest that they *all* are.   `OK` `?`

28. (1) This answer choice is supported by Petrik's statement (lines 41–42), "We're trying to make great films better." The "great" films he is talking about are black and white, and the "better" films are colored.

29. (2) Line 19 says that colorization is a computerized process. None of the other choices is suggested by the article.

30. (2) "Golf links" is a synonym for (means the same as) "golf course." Because the sentence uses the verb "lie," "golf cart," or "golf players" would not make sense.

31. (3) In this poem, it is children who are working as laborers in the factory while the men play golf. We expect men to work while children play.

32. (4) We know the children work in a mill while men play golf, so it cannot be the Middle Ages (which were from about the year 500 to about 1500—long before there were such industries as mills). The introduction of laws against child labor late in the nineteenth century (1800s) suggests that (4) is the best answer.

33. (2) The poet is ironic—that is, what is real is not what we would expect to be real. The other choices are not good ones. Although something that is "nostalgic" is about the past, it is about something in the past that is thought to be *good*.

34. (4) The writer begins to describe the "wreckage" as "new branches suddenly turned," (their colors have *turned* from green to fall colors), and emphasizes the "fiery" colors of autumn.

35. (1) In lines 25–26, the writer says, "As the dog bounces our hearts bounce also with a happy overload"; in this way, he tells about the happiness in his heart.

36. (5) The writer's amazement at the beauty of nature throughout this excerpt makes (5) the likely choice.

37. (3) "Anthology" is a word usually used to mean a collection of literature selections. In this case, the author is using the word to mean a collection, but one of a different sort, one of "color, shade, and texture" (lines 50–51).

38. (5) The author refers to sights and colors frequently, especially in the second paragraph.

39. (4) We learn from the first sentence that it is "late September" in "New Hampshire" at "dawn."

40. (3) The statement given is preceded by, "His people are many." This tells us that Chief Seattle is comparing the White people to the prairie grass. This shows that the people are many in number, like the blades of grass.

41. (1) In lines 21–22, Seattle says that the White Chief is "willing to allow us enough [land] to live comfortably." Choice (4) is weakened by Seattle's statement that "the Red Man no longer has rights" (lines 23–24).

42. (4) The passage is composed of complete sentences and formal English. But this does not account for its *unique* style (a style that is different from most other writing). The images from nature, in lines 1–18, help make the style of the passage unique.

OK   ?

43. (1) Seattle says that the White Chief's wish to buy Indian land "appears just, even generous" (lines 22–23); these words show an accepting attitude.

OK   ?

44. (4) At the end of the excerpt, Seattle says that "we too may have been somewhat to blame." However, he also suggests in line 29 that the White people had some part in "hastening" the untimely decay of his people.

OK   ?

45. (2) When Chief Seattle compares his words to stars, he means that his words can be trusted. He says that they "never change" (line 6) and that "the great chief at Washington can rely upon" them with "certainty." (lines 6–7)

OK   ?

TEST 5: MATHEMATICS

1. (4) Since you need to find how many groups of 15 trees there are in 200, divide:

$$
\begin{array}{r}
13^{5}/_{15} = 13^{1}/_{3} \\
15\overline{)200} \\
\underline{15} \\
50 \\
\underline{45} \\
5
\end{array}
$$

2. (4) Since 20% is discounted, the buyer will pay 80% of $10,000:

$$80\% \text{ of } \$10,000 = .80 \times \$10,000 = \$8000.00$$

Reminder: "%" means *out of 100* and "of" means *multiply*.

3. (3) Multiply the number of days Lorene jogs by the hours she jogs each day.

Using fractions:

$$5 \times 1\tfrac{1}{2} = \frac{5}{1} \times \frac{3}{2} = \frac{15}{2} = 7\tfrac{1}{2}$$

Or using decimals:

$$5 \times 1.5 = 7.5$$

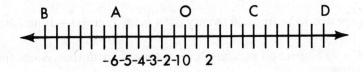

4. (1) 0 is the origin of the number line, with positive numbers to the right and negative numbers to the left. The correct answer is A because it is six units to the left.

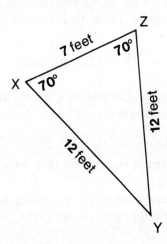

5. (4) Since angle X and angle Z have equal measures, the sides opposite them have equal measures. So ZY = 12 feet. To find the perimeter (distance around the triangle), add the three sides:

$$12 \text{ feet} + 12 \text{ feet} + 7 \text{ feet} = 31 \text{ feet}$$

6. (5) In order to answer this question, you would need to know how many of the scouts collected more than 50 pounds of newspapers. Since this information is not given, this problem cannot be solved.

7. (2) The den is to collect 301 pounds in 14 days. To find how many pounds per day, divide the number of days into the number of pounds:

$$
\begin{array}{r}
21.5 \\
14\overline{)301.0} \\
28 \\
\overline{21} \\
14 \\
\overline{70} \\
70 \\
\overline{0}
\end{array}
$$

8. (4) You want to find how many 25's it takes to make 500, so divide the calls per day (25) into the total calls (500):

$$
\begin{array}{r}
20 \\
25\overline{)500} \\
50 \\
\overline{0} \\
0 \\
\overline{0}
\end{array}
$$

So Jamal would be expected to be finished twenty days from June 1st—June 20th.

9. (4) Add 52% + 23% = 75% spent on purchase payments and insurance. Since the entire graph equals 100%,

$$100\% - 75\% = 25\% \text{ remaining}$$

You can also notice that after purchase payments and insurance are removed, three wedges of the graph remain, state and local fees, maintenance, and fuel. You can add these three to get the answer:

$$4\% + 7\% + 14\% = 25\% \text{ remaining}$$

10. (2) The square root of a number is a number which, when multiplied by itself, produces the number. Example: The square root of 25 is 5 because 5 × 5 = 25.

$$6 \times 6 = \underline{36} \qquad 7 \times 7 = \underline{49}$$

So the square root of 40 must be between 6 and 7 because 40 is between 36 and 49.

11. (5) To answer this question, you would need to know the length of side XY so you could set up a proportion. Since this information is not given, this problem cannot be solved.

12. (3) To find the total number of minutes, add together all the minutes Gary rode:

$$45 + 30 + 40 + 50 = 165 \text{ minutes}$$

To find the total number of calories burned, multiply total minutes by the number of calories burned per minute:

$$165 \times 3.3 = 165(3.3)$$

13. (2) The sum of the three interior angles of any triangle is 180 degrees. To find the measure of the missing angle, first add the two amounts you know:

$$73 \text{ degrees} + 42 \text{ degrees} = 115 \text{ degrees}$$

Now, find how many more degrees are needed for a total of 180:

$$180 \text{ degrees} - 115 \text{ degrees} = 65 \text{ degrees}$$

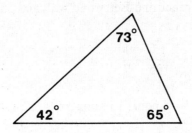

So 65 degrees must be the measure of the third interior angle.

14. (2) To find the volume of a container which stands up straight with its sides perpendicular to its base, find the area of its base:

length × width

Then multiply this by its height:

length × width × height = volume
9 × 6 × 12 = 9(6)(12)

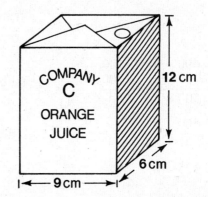

But the package can be filled to only ¾ capacity. So

$$(¾)\ (9)\ (6)\ (12) \text{ is correct}$$

15. (4) You need to find 15% of the total amount spent, so begin by finding the total amount Arnie spent:

$$\$250 + \$380 = \$630$$

Now   15% of $630 = .15 × $630 = $94.50

Reminder: "%" means *out of 100,* and "of" means *multiply.*

16. (3)

$$10^0 = 1 \qquad 10^4 = 10,000$$
$$10^1 = 10 \qquad 10^5 = 100,000$$
$$10^2 = 100 \qquad 10^6 = 1,000,000$$
$$10^3 = 1000$$

So

$$9 \times 10^6 = 9 \times 1,000,000 = 9,000,000 \text{ light years from Earth to Zorbon.}$$

$$3 \times 10^5 = 3 \times 100,000 = 300,000 \text{ light years from Earth to Yeva}$$

And

$$300,000 \times 30 = 9,000,000$$

So Zorbon is 30 times farther than Yeva.

17. (2) At the time of the storm, Lawrence and Betty had watched 15 minutes out of 105 minutes of the movie:

$$\frac{15}{105} = \frac{1}{7}$$

(60 minutes = 1 hour, 30 minutes = ½ hour, 15 minutes = ¼ hour)

18. (2) w = width

$w + 50$ = length (its length is 50 feet more than its width)

Since perimeter means distance around,

perimeter = $w + (w + 50) + w + (w + 50)$

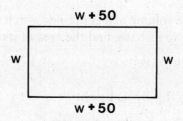

$$600 = 4w + 100$$
$$\underline{-\ 100 \qquad\quad -\ 100}$$
$$500 = 4w$$

(subtract 100 from both sides)

$$\frac{500}{4} = \frac{4w}{4}$$

(divide both sides by 4)

$$125 = w$$

19. (3) To find the mean (average), add all values:

$$186 + 124 + 146 = 456$$

Divide your total by the number of values (in this case, 3):

```
    152
3)456
    3
   15
   15
   06
    6
    0
```

20. (2) Luke's food items (celery, lettuce, chicken) total

$$\$.29 + \$.69 + \$2.68 = \$3.66$$

There is a tax of 6% for nonfood items (dish soap):

$$6\% \text{ of } \$1.50 = .06 \times \$1.50 = \$.09 = \text{tax}$$

So, Luke's total bill is

$$\text{food} + \text{nonfood} + \text{tax} = \$3.66 + \$1.50 + \$.09 = \$5.25$$

21. (1) *Triple* means *multiply by three,* so equation (1) describes this:

$$39 = 3T \qquad 39 \text{ is 3 times Tina's age}$$

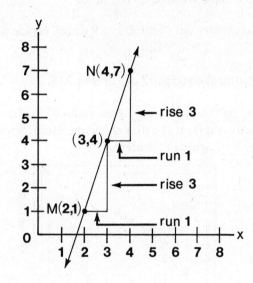

22. (2) Slope = 3

$$3 = \frac{3}{1} = \frac{\text{rise}}{\text{run}}$$

This means that for every unit you "run" to the right, you "rise" 3 units. To "rise" from 1 to 7 (the *y*-coordinates), it will take 2 increments, so you must also have to "run" increments of 1.

23. (3) Substitute 3 for *x* and 4 for *y*:

$$7y + 6x^2 = 7(4) + 6(3)^2 \qquad \text{note: } (3)^2 = 3 \times 3 = 9$$
$$= 7(4) + 6(9)$$
$$= 28 + 54$$
$$= 82$$

Reminder: Do the math in this order (order of operations).

1. parentheses [do the work within them—for example, $6(2 + 1) = 6(3)$] (in the problem above, there is no work within parentheses)
2. powers (for example, $2 + 2^2 = 2 + 4$)
3. multiply and divide—from left to right (for example, $2 + 2 \times 5 = 2 + 10$)
4. add and subtract—from left to right (for example, $2 + 2 - 1 = 3$)

24. (4) *Twice* means *2 times*.

$$y = \text{yellows} \qquad\qquad 2y = \text{reds}$$

Altogether, Dmitri has 120 bulbs (10 dozen = 10 × 12 = 120)

$$\text{yellows} + \text{reds} = 120$$
$$y + 2y = 120$$
$$3y = 120 \qquad \text{(add the } y\text{'s together)}$$
$$\frac{3y}{3} = \frac{120}{3} \qquad \text{(divide both sides by 3)}$$
$$y = 40$$

So, if there are 40 yellow bulbs, there must be 80 red bulbs.   OK   ?

25. (2) There are 2 dozen oatmeal cookies out of a total of 9 dozen cookies:

$$3 + 2 + 4 = 9$$

So the chances of getting an oatmeal cookie is 2 out of 9 or 2/9.   OK   ?

26. (2) The diagonal separates the rectangle into triangles. Each of the triangles is a right triangle (has a 90 degree interior angle) if the diagonals are equal. So, to find the length of the diagonal, use the Pythagorean theorem.

$$a^2 + b^2 = c^2$$
$$12^2 + 16^2 = c^2$$
$$144 + 256 = c^2$$
$$400 = c^2$$
$$20 = c$$

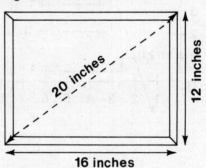

OK   ?

27. (2) *Median* means the *middle value* of a list put in order:

$27,000; $25,000; $25,000; $22,000; $21,000; $20,000; $17,000   OK   ?

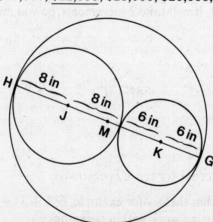

28. (5) Because M is the center of the larger circle, HG is a diameter passing through that center. HG is made up of two 8-inch segments plus two 6-inch segments:

$$2 \times 8 + 2 \times 6 = 16 + 12 = 28$$

OK   ?

29. (3)

$$2 \text{ pounds} \longrightarrow 6 \text{ dozen}$$
$$1 \text{ pound} \longrightarrow 3 \text{ dozen}$$

So, if we multiply both sides of the above by nine:

$$9 \times 1 \text{ pound} \longrightarrow 9 \times 3 \text{ dozen}$$
$$9 \text{ pounds} \longrightarrow 27 \text{ dozen}$$

Or using a proportion:
$$\frac{2}{6} = \frac{x}{27}$$

Reduce to
$$\frac{1}{3} = \frac{x}{27}$$

Now, cross multiply, giving
$$3x = 27$$

Finally, divide by 3:
$$\frac{3x}{3} = \frac{27}{3}$$

$$x = 9$$

30. (1)

$$12 \text{ milk chocolates at } 50¢ \text{ each} = 12(50)$$
$$8 \text{ semisweet chocolates at } 40¢ \text{ each} = 8(40)$$

To total, add: $12(50) + 8(40)$

31. (4) You need to find 8% of $5800:

$$.08 \times \$5800 = \$464$$

Reminder: "%" means *out of 100,* and "of" means *multiply.*

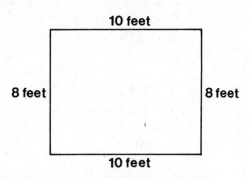

32. (2) Perimeter means distance around, so add all the sides:

$$10 \text{ feet} + 8 \text{ feet} + 10 \text{ feet} + 8 \text{ feet} = 36 \text{ feet}$$

33. (5) How many $5\frac{1}{2}$'s are there in 44?

$$44 \div 5\frac{1}{2} = 44 \div \frac{11}{2} = \frac{\overset{4}{\cancel{44}}}{1} \times \frac{2}{\underset{1}{\cancel{11}}} = 8$$

34. (5) When Al is 21, Chet will be 26 (because Al is 5 years younger than Chet). If Chet is 26, then Tom is 24 (because Chet is 2 years older than Tom). Since Tom and Joe are twins, Joe will also be 24.

35. (2) Let's take a look at Wednesday the 8th through Monday the 20th:

Wed   Thurs   Fri   Sat   Sun   Mon   Tues   Wed   Thurs   Fri   Sat

25 + 25 + 25 + 50 + 75 + 25 + 25 + 25 + 25 + 25 + 50

Sun   Mon

+ 75 + 25 = $4.75   OK   ?

36. (5) Since the discount is 15%, Ahmed's parents will pay 85%:

85% of $500 = .85 × $500 = $425   OK   ?

37. (3) 420 ──────→ 2 acres
     ? ──────→ 12 acres

Since 2 × 6 = 12, 6 of those 420 pound amounts will be needed:

6 × 420 = 2520 pounds

Or, using a proportion:

$$\frac{\text{pounds}}{\text{acres}} = \frac{\text{pounds}}{\text{acres}}$$

$$\frac{420}{2} = \frac{x}{12}$$

Cross multiply: $2x = (12)(420)$
                   $2x = 5040$

Divide by 2: $\dfrac{2x}{2} = \dfrac{5040}{2}$

$x = 2520$ OK   ?

38. (1) Substituting 3 for y and 7 for z

$$x = 5(3)(7 - 1)$$
$$= 5 \times 3 \times 6$$
$$= 15 \times 6$$
$$= 90$$

Reminder: Do the math in this order (order of operations):

1. parentheses (do the work inside them—in this case $7 - 1 = 6$)
2. powers (there are no powers to do in this problem)
3. multiply and divide, from left to right (in this problem, there is only multiplication—$5 \times 3 \times 6 = 15 \times 6 = 90$)
4. add and subtract, from left to right (there is no addition or subtraction remaining in this problem)   OK   ?

39. (2) To find the average, first add all four amounts:

$$\$82.96 + \$58.34 + \$70.25 + \$62.49 = \$274.04$$

Then divide by the number of amounts (in this case, 4):

$$
\begin{array}{r}
68.51 \\
4\overline{)274.04} \\
\underline{24} \\
34 \\
\underline{32} \\
20 \\
\underline{20} \\
4 \\
\underline{4} \\
0
\end{array}
$$

40. (4) Note that the scale on the left says "hundreds of dollars."

$$1970 = \$125 \quad \text{and} \quad 1985 = \$650$$

The question asks for the *increase,* so

$$\$650 - \$125 = \$525 \text{ increase}$$

41. (2) To solve this problem, you need to add up the lengths of all of the edges:

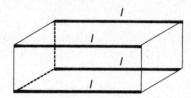 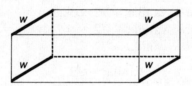 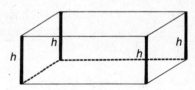

There are

$$
\left.
\begin{array}{l}
4 \text{ edges of length } l \\
4 \text{ edges of length } w \\
4 \text{ edges of length } h
\end{array}
\right\} \quad \text{for a total of } 4l + 4w + 4h
$$

42. (1) When you eat calories, you add them into your body, so add up the total number of calories that Andre ate:

$$250 + 500 + 125 + 275$$

When you burn calories, you take them away from your body, so subtract the number of calories Andre burned:

$$-980$$

So, the net (final) result is

$$250 + 500 + 125 + 275 - 980$$

43. (4) According to the graph, 20% have hazel eyes, while 40% have brown eyes. This means that there are twice as many brown-eyed people as there are hazel-eyed people.

$$62 \text{ people have hazel eyes}$$
$$2 \times 62 \text{ people have brown eyes}$$

So $2 \times 62 = 124$ people who have brown eyes   OK   ?

44. (3) Top Sirloin: 8 pounds + 1 pound =
$$(4 \times \$5.00) + \$2.99 = \quad\quad \text{(Note: 2 pounds for \$5.00)}$$
$$\$20.00 + \$2.99 =$$
$$\$22.99$$

Filet Mignon: 8 pounds =
$$8 \times \$4.00 =$$
$$\$32.00$$

London Broil: 6 pounds + 1 pound =
$$(2 \times \$5.00) + \$1.79 = \quad\quad \text{(Note: 3 pounds for \$5.00)}$$
$$\$10.00 + \$1.79 =$$
$$\$11.79$$

Add to find the total:
$$\$22.99 + \$32.00 + \$11.79 = \$66.78$$ OK   ?

45. (4) There are 12 cookies per dozen, so there are $6 \times 12 = 72$ cookies in the assortment. There are twice as many chocolate as vanilla, so

$$\text{chocolate} + \text{vanilla} = 72 \text{ cookies}$$
$$2 \times \text{vanilla} + \text{vanilla} = 72$$
$$3 \times \text{vanilla} = 72$$

Divide each side by 3: $\dfrac{3 \times \text{vanilla}}{3} = \dfrac{72}{3}$

$$\text{vanilla} = 24$$

So, if there are 24 vanilla cookies, there must be

$$72 - 24 = 48 \text{ chocolate cookies}$$ OK   ?

46. (2) 10% of $\$321 = .10 \times \$321 = \$32.10$

Subtracting: $\$321.00 - \$32.10 = \$288.90$
$$\$288.90 \simeq \text{(approximately equals) } \$290$$

Or, Jason loses 10% of his pay but will get 90% of his pay:

90% of $\$321 = .90 \times \$321 = \$288.90$ OK   ?

47. (5) Chuck has already eaten

2 slices of bread	= 2 × 70	= 140
1 bowl of soup		= 90
2 glasses of milk	= 2 × 120	= 240
2 cookies	= 2 × 95	= 190
1 orange		= 50
TOTAL		= 710

Since Chuck has already eaten food with 710 calories, he can have 490 calories or less and still stay within his 1200 calorie limit.

$$1200 - 710 = 490$$

Combination (5) totals

$$200 \text{ (meat)} + 80 \text{ (potato)} + 75 \text{ (vegetables)} + 120 \text{ (milk)} = 475$$

The other combinations all have too many calories.

48. (3) The sum of the two angles must equal 180 degrees, since they form a straight line.

$$Z + Y = 180$$
$$5Y + Y = 180 \qquad \text{(Z is 5 times Y)}$$
$$6Y = 180 \qquad \text{(combining like terms)}$$
$$\frac{6Y}{6} = \frac{180}{6} \qquad \text{(dividing both sides by 6)}$$
$$Y = 30$$

Since $Z + Y = 180$, and $Y = 30$, Z must equal 150 degrees:

$$180 - 30 = 150$$

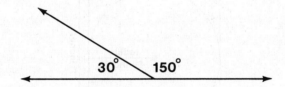

Here is another way to think about it: Since Z is 5 times Y, and $Y = 30$,

$$Z = 5 \times 30 = 150 \text{ degrees}$$

49. (5) $\qquad\qquad 2j \geq 9$

$$\frac{2j}{2} \geq \frac{9}{2} \qquad \text{(dividing both sides by 2)}$$

$$j \geq 4\frac{1}{2}$$

5 is the only amount greater than or equal to $4\frac{1}{2}$. To check:

$$2j \geq 9$$
$$2(5) \geq 9$$
$$10 \geq 9 \qquad \text{TRUE}$$

Reminder: $<$ means *less than*
$\qquad\qquad > $ means *greater than*
$\qquad\qquad \leq$ means *less than or equal to*
$\qquad\qquad \geq$ means *greater than or equal to*
$\qquad\qquad =$ means *equal to*
$\qquad\qquad \neq$ means *not equal to*

50. (4) To find the third side of this right triangle, use the Pythagorean theorem:

$$a^2 + b^2 = c^2$$
$$8^2 + 6^2 = c^2$$
$$64 + 36 = c^2$$
$$100 = c^2$$
$$10 = c \quad \text{(because } 10 \times 10 = 100\text{)}$$

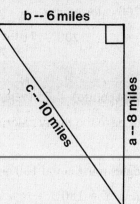

OK   ?

51. (4) Without going off the paper, the *diameter* of the largest circle would be 8½ inches. Since the radius is half the diameter,

$$\frac{1}{2} \text{ of } 8\tfrac{1}{2} = \frac{1}{2} \times 8\tfrac{1}{2} = \frac{1}{2} \times \frac{17}{2} = \frac{17}{4} = 4\tfrac{1}{2}$$

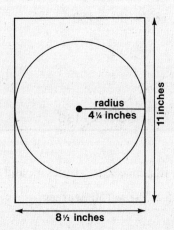

OK   ?

52. (3) To solve this problem, concentrate on the right triangle with legs 3 feet and 4 feet:

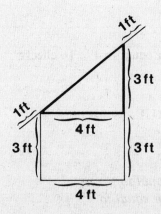

To find the hypotenuse (the middle section of the roof), use the Pythagorean theorem:

$a^2 + b^2 = c^2$
$3^2 + 4^2 = c^2$
$9 + 16 = c^2$
$25 = c^2$
$5 = c$

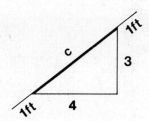 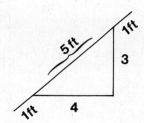

When you add 1 foot to the front and 1 foot to the back for the overhangs, the result is

$$1 + 5 + 1 = 7 \text{ feet}$$

[OK] [?]

53. (1)

$10^0 = 1$	$10^4 = 10,000$
$10^1 = 10$	$10^5 = 100,000$
$10^2 = 100$	$10^6 = 1,000,000$
$10^3 = 1000$	

So

$$2.69753 \times 10^5 = 2.69753 \times 100,000 = 269,753$$

[OK] [?]

54. (3) To calculate Hal's raise, find 18% of $14,000:

$$18\% \text{ of } \$14,000 = .18(\$14,000)$$

Now add this amount to his old salary:

$$\$14,000 + .18(\$14,000)$$

Reminder: "%" means *out of 100,* and "of" means *multiply.*

[OK] [?]

55. (3) The first angle has a measure of one increment, the second has a measure of two increments, and the third has a measure of three increments.

$$1 + 2 + 3 = 6 \text{ increments}$$

The sum of the three interior angles of any triangle is 180 degrees:

6 increments = 180

$$\frac{6 \text{ increments}}{6} = \frac{180}{6} \qquad \text{(dividing by 6)}$$

1 increment = 30

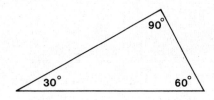

So, the three angles are

30° (1 increment), 60° (2 increments), and 90° (3 increments)

But the easiest and fastest way to find this answer is to look at the answer choices to see which one adds up to 180°. In this case, only answer (3) does, so you know that's the right one, since the three interior angles of a triangle *must* add up to 180°.

[OK] [?]

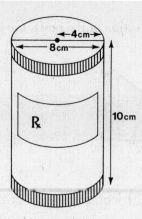

56. (2) To find the volume of a container standing straight with its sides perpendicular to its base,

　1. Find the area of its base (in this case, a circle):

　　area of circle $= \pi r^2 = \pi(4)^2$ (because the diameter is 8, the radius is 4)

　2. Multiply the area of the base (circle) by the height to find the volume:

　area of circle $\times$ height $= \pi(4)^2(10)$

ARE YOU READY?

 1. Make sure that you know where you are taking the test. Be familiar with the test location. Know how to get there and where to park.

 2. Spend the week before the test on a general review of important concepts, test-taking strategies, and techniques.

 3. Don't cram the night before the exam. It's a waste of time!

 4. If you usually eat breakfast, eat a nourishing one before the exam.

 5. Arrive in plenty of time at the testing center.

 6. Remember to bring the proper materials: identification, admission ticket, three or four sharpened Number 2 pencils, an eraser, and a watch.

 7. Dress comfortably. Wear layers of clothing so that you can adjust to the temperature of the room (taking off a sweater if it's too hot or putting one on if it's too cold).

 8. Start off with confidence and with a plan. Answer the questions you know first, and then go back and try to answer the others.

 9. Try to eliminate one or more answer choices before you guess, but make sure that you fill in an answer for each question. There is no penalty for guessing.

 10. Make sure that you are answering "what is being asked."

 11. Remember that working from the answers by eliminating choices is very helpful.

12. Use a Positive Approach, the key to getting the questions right that you should get right and the key to success on the GED!

GED STATISTICAL REPORT

Minimum Score Requirements for Issuing
High School Equivalency Credentials

UNITED   STATES

Jurisdiction	Minimum Scores[1]	Jurisdiction	Minimum Scores[1]
Alabama	35 and 45	Montana	35 and 45
Alaska	35 and 45	Nebraska	40 or 45
Arizona	35 and 45	Nevada	35 and 45
Arkansas	40 and 45	New Hampshire	35 and 45
California	40 and 45	New Jersey	[2] and 45
Colorado	35 and 45	New Mexico	40 or 50
Connecticut	35 and 45	New York	40 and 45
Delaware	40 and 45	North Carolina	35 and 45
District of Columbia	35 and 45	North Dakota	40 or 50
Florida	40 and 45	Ohio	35 and 45
Georgia	35 and 45	Oklahoma	40 and 45
Hawaii	35 and 45	Oregon	40 each test
Idaho	35 and 45	Pennsylvania	35 and 45
Illinois	35 and 45	Rhode Island	35 and 45
Indiana	35 and 45	South Carolina	45 Average
Iowa	35 and 45	South Dakota	40 and 45
Kansas	35 and 45	Tennessee	35 and 45
Kentucky	35 and 45	Texas	40 or 45
Louisiana	40 or 45	Utah	40 and 45
Maine	35 and 45	Vermont	35 and 45
Maryland	40 and 45	Virginia	35 and 45
Massachusetts	35 and 45	Washington	35 and 45
Michigan	35 and 45	West Virginia	40 and 45
Minnesota	35 and 45	Wisconsin	40 and 50
Mississippi	40 or 45	Wyoming	35 and 45
Missouri	35 and 45		

---

[1] Minimum scores of 35 and 45 mean that each test score must be at least 35 and an average of 45 on the battery is required. Minimum scores of 35 or 45 means either that each test score must be at least 35 or an average of 45 on the battery is required.

[2] N.J. = 40 on tests 1 - 3, 44 on test 4 and 43 on test 5.

Minimum Score Requirements for Issuing High School Equivalency Credentials

U.S. TERRITORIES

Jurisdiction	Minimum Scores[1]
American Samoa	40 each test
Commonwealth of the Northern Mariana Is.	40 or 45
Guam	35 and 45
Kwajalein Island	35 and 45
Panama Canal Area	40 and 45
Puerto Rico	40 and 45
Republic of the Marshall Islands	40 or 45
Republic of Palau	40 and 45
Virgin Islands	35 and 45

CANADA

Jurisdiction	Minimum Scores[1]
Alberta	45 each test
British Columbia	45 each test
Manitoba	45 each test
New Brunswick(English)	45 each test
New Brunswick(French)	35 and 45
Newfoundland	40 and 45
Northwest Territories	45 each test
Nova Scotia	45 each test
Prince Edward Island	45 each test
Saskatchewan	45 each test
Yukon Territory	45 each test

Percentage of U.S. High School Seniors Meeting These Requirements

Minimum 40 or Mean 45	73%
Minimum 40 or Mean 50	70%
Mean 45	70%
Minimum 35 and Mean 45	69%
Minimum 40	69%
Minimum 40 and Mean 45	67%
Minimum 40 and Mean 50	51%

---

[1] Minimum scores of 35 and 45 mean that each test score must be at least 35 and an average of 45 on the battery is required. Minimum scores of 35 or 45 means either that each test score must be at least 35 or an average of 45 is is required.